Lecture Notes in Computer Science   2893

Edited by G. Goos, J. Hartmanis, and J. van Leeuwen

T0226191

Springer
Berlin
Heidelberg
New York
Hong Kong
London
Milan
Paris
Tokyo

Jean-Bernard Stefani   Isabelle Demeure
Daniel Hagimont (Eds.)

Distributed Applications and Interoperable Systems

4th IFIP WG 6.1 International Conference, DAIS 2003
Paris, France, November 17-21, 2003
Proceedings

Springer

Series Editors

Gerhard Goos, Karlsruhe University, Germany
Juris Hartmanis, Cornell University, NY, USA
Jan van Leeuwen, Utrecht University, The Netherlands

Volume Editors

Jean-Bernard Stefani
Daniel Hagimont
INRIA Rhône-Alpes
655, avenue de l'Europe, Montbonnot, 38334 St Ismier Cedex, France
E-mail: {Jean-Bernard.Stefani,Daniel.Hagimont}@inrialpes.fr

Isabelle Demeure
Ecole Nationale Supérieure de Télécommunications
46, rue Barrault, 75634 Paris Cedex 13, France
E-mail: isabelle.demeure@enst.fr

Cataloging-in-Publication Data applied for

A catalog record for this book is available from the Library of Congress.

Bibliographic information published by Die Deutsche Bibliothek
Die Deutsche Bibliothek lists this publication in the Deutsche Nationalbibliografie;
detailed bibliographic data is available in the Internet at <http://dnb.ddb.de>.

CR Subject Classification (1998): D.2, C.2.4, I.2.11, D.4, H.4

ISSN 0302-9743
ISBN 3-540-20529-2 Springer-Verlag Berlin Heidelberg New York

Springer-Verlag is a part of Springer Science+Business Media

springeronline.com

© 2003 IFIP International Federation for Information Processing, Hofstraße 3, 2361 Laxenburg, Austria

Typesetting: Camera-ready by author, data conversion by Olgun Computergrafik
Printed on acid-free paper   SPIN: 10968130   06/3142   5 4 3 2 1 0

Preface

This volume contains the proceedings of DAIS 2003, the 4th IFIP WG 6.1 International Conference on Distributed Applications and Interoperable Systems. The conference was held in Paris on November 17–21, 2003. The event was the fourth meeting of this conference series, which is held roughly every two years. Previous editions were held in 1997 in Cottbus (Germany), in 1999 in Helsinki (Finland), and in 2001 in Krakow (Poland).

Following the evolution of the field, DAIS 2003 focused on models, technologies and platforms for reconfigurable, scalable and adaptable distributed applications. In keeping with this focus, the call for papers especially encouraged original unpublished papers addressing the following topics:

- new/extended software architectures and frameworks for reconfiguration and adaptation including component-based approaches (e.g., CORBA Components, EJB, .NET),
- modelling, specifying, monitoring and management of context-aware and adaptive applications,
- support for reconfiguration, self-organization and autonomic behavior in new/existing distributed platforms (e.g., CORBA, J2EE, .NET, WebServices),
- integration of multi-agent distributed decision-making,
- application environments that exploit characteristics of specific technologies (e.g., grid computing, mobile and wireless),
- issues in enterprise-wide and large-scale application reconfiguration,
- semantic interoperability and semantic web services.

We organized a program committee composed of 31 experts of the field. The program committee agreed on a call for papers and reviewed 88 submitted papers, 76 long papers (12 pages) and 12 short papers (5 pages). The program committee selected 21 long papers and 2 short papers; 4 long papers were accepted as short papers. Overall, the acceptance rate was less than 1 in 3.

The DAIS 2003 technical program covered many aspects that reflect the evolution of the field. Among the selected papers, we identified the following topics, each of which corresponded to a session of the conference technical program:

- adaptation, separation of concerns,
- deployment,
- security and transactions,
- replication,
- networking and routing,
- discovery, context-awareness and ontologies,
- asynchronous messaging.

We would like to express our deepest appreciation to the authors of all submitted papers and to the program committee members and external reviewers who did an outstanding job in selecting the best papers for presentation. For the first time, the DAIS conference was held as a joint event in federation with the 6th IFIP WG 6.1 International Conference on Formal Methods for Open Object-based Distributed Systems (FMOODS 2003). The co-location of the 2003 vintages of the FMOODS and DAIS conferences provided an excellent opportunity to the participants for a wide and comprehensive exchange of ideas within the domain of distributed systems and applications. Both FMOODS and DAIS address this domain, the former with its emphasis on formal approaches, the latter on practical solutions. Their combination in a single event meant that both theoretical foundations and practical issues were presented and discussed. Also due to the federation of the two conferences, the topics of reconfigurability and component-based design were particularly emphasized this year, along with the many open issues related to openness and the interoperability of distributed systems and applications. To further the interaction between the two communities, participants at the federated event were offered a single registration procedure and were entitled to choose freely between DAIS and FMOODS sessions. Also several invited speakers were explicitly scheduled in joint sessions. As another novelty, this year's conference included a two-day tutorial and workshop session, the latter again explicitly held as a joint event.

We would like to thank the members of the executive committee, with special thanks to Fabrice Kordon and Laurent Pautet for help with running the electronic submission system.

We are grateful to Bertrand Meyer, Andrew Herbert, Bart Jacobs, Alan Cameron Wills and David Chambliss for agreeing to present invited talks at the conference.

We would also like to thank the DAIS steering committee (Kurt Geihs, Guy Leduc, Hartmut Koenig and Kerry Raymond) for their advice, and the sponsors for their contribution.

November 2003   Jean-Bernard Stefani, General Chair
                        Isabelle Demeure and Daniel Hagimont, Program Chairs
                                                              DAIS 2003

Organization

DAIS 2003 was organized by ENST (École Nationale Supérieure des Télécommunications), Paris. DAIS 2003 was held in conjunction with FMOODS 2003.

Executive Committee

General Chair	Jean-Bernard Stefani (INRIA, France)
Program Chairs	Isabelle Demeure (ENST, France)
	Daniel Hagimont (INRIA, France)
Publicity Chair	Kurt Geihs (Technical University of Berlin)
Workshops Chair	Lynne Blair (University of Lancaster)
Tutorial Chair	Sylvie Vignes (ENST)
Local Organization Chair	Laurent Pautet (ENST)

Sponsoring Institutions

At the time of writing, we had received sponsorship from CNRS-ARP, GET, EDF, ENST, and INRIA. Other contributors were also expected. We extend our thanks to all of them.

Program Committee

M. Ahamed (Georgia Tech, USA)
N. Alonistioti (University of Athens, Greece)
S. Baker (IONA, Ireland)
Y. Berbers (Katholieke Universiteit Leuven, Belgium)
A. Beugnard (ENST Brittany, France)
V. Cahill (Trinity College Dublin, Ireland)
R. Campbell (UIUC, USA)
N. Davies (Lancaster University, UK and University of Arizona, USA)
F. Eliassen (University of Oslo, Norway)
K. Geihs (Technical University of Berlin, Germany)
P. Honeyman (CITI, University of Michigan, USA)
J. Indulska (University of Queensland, Australia)
E. Jul (DIKU, Denmark)
H. Koenig (BTU Cottbus, Germany)
F. Kordon (LIP6, France)
S. Krakowiak (University of Grenoble, France)
H. Krumm (University of Dortmund, Germany)
L. Kutvonen (University of Helsinki, Finland)
W. Lamersdorf (University of Hamburg, Germany)
D. Lea (SUNY Oswego, USA)
P. Linington (University of Kent, UK)
C. Linnhoff-Popien (University of Munich, Germany)
P. Merle (INRIA, France)
G. Muller (École des Mines de Nantes, France)
E. Najm (ENST, France)
L. Pautet (ENST, France)
K. Raymond (DSTC, Australia)
A. Schill (Technical University of Dresden, Germany)
D. Schmidt (University of California, Irvine, USA)
S. Shrivastava (University of Newcastle, UK)
J.-J. Vandewalle (GemPlus, France)

External Reviewers

S. Amundsen
T. Baier
P. Barron
G. Biegel
P. Boddupalli
L. Braubach
T. Buchholz
Z. Choukair
P. Cointe
M. Covington
R. Cunningham
F. Dagnat
V. Danciu
J. Dowling
A. Hanemann
K. Henricksen
K. Herrmann
I. Hochstatter

B. Hughes
C. Efstratiou
M. Jaeger
S. Jun
R. Kalckloesch
C. Kunze
K. Li
T. McFadden
R. Meier
J.-M. Menaud
G. Morgan
G. Muehl
A. Nedos
A. Opitz
S. Parastatidis
A. Pokahr
V. Reynolds
R. Robinson

G. Rojec-Goldmann
E. Saint-James
M. Schiffers
D. Schmitz
S. Schulz
L. Seinturier
R. Staehli
O. Storz
T. Strang
A. Tanner
A. Ulbrich
R. Vishwanath
V. Vold Eide
T. Weis
S. Wheater
C. Zirpins

Table of Contents

Session IV: Replication

Session V: Networking and Routing

Session VI: Discovery – Context-Awareness – Ontology

Session VII: Asynchronous Messaging

Towards a Framework for Self-adaptive Component-Based Applications[*]

Pierre-Charles David and Thomas Ledoux

OBASCO Group, EMN/INRIA
École des Mines de Nantes – Dépt. Informatique
4, rue Alfred Kastler – BP 20722
F-44307 Nantes Cedex 3, France
{pcdavid,ledoux}@emn.fr

Abstract. Nowadays, applications must work in highly dynamic environments, where resources availability, among other factors, can evolve at runtime. To deal with this situation, applications must be *self-adaptive*, that is adapt themselves to their environment and its evolutions. Our goal is to enable systematic development of self-adaptive component-based applications using the Separation of Concerns principle: we consider *adaptation to a specific execution context and its evolutions* as a concern which should be treated separately from the rest of an application. In this paper, we first present the general approach we propose and the corresponding development framework and tools we are developing to support it. Then, in order to validate this approach, we use it on a small component-based application to show how it can be made self-adaptive.

1   Introduction

Given today's fast pace of technological evolutions and diversity of computing platforms (both hardware and software), building applications which can work in such a wide range of systems is becoming more and more challenging. Moreover, even on a specific platform, the execution context and available resources tend to vary a lot at runtime. This is particularly the case with distributed applications, as those have to deal with the heterogeneity of different hosts and rely on network communication, which are often highly variable (especially with newer technologies like wireless networking).

The result of this situation is that applications should be *adaptable* (i.e. able to be adapted), or even better *self-adaptive* (i.e. adapting themselves) to their environment [1]. Adaptation in itself is nothing new, but it is generally done in an ad hoc way, which involves trying to predict future execution conditions at development time and embedding the adaptation decisions in the application code itself. This creates several problems: increased complexity (business logic polluted with non-functional concerns) and poor reuse of components caused

---

[*] This research is supported by the RNTL project ARCAD (http://arcad.essi.fr/)

J.-B. Stefani, I. Demeure, and D. Hagimont (Eds.): DAIS 2003, LNCS 2893, pp. 1–14, 2003.

by a strong coupling with a specific environment. We believe that some kinds of adaptations, most notably those related to resource usage, can be decoupled from pure functional concerns, and that doing so does not have the same drawbacks as the ad hoc approach.

The long term goal of our work is to enable a more systematic (as opposed to ad hoc) way to develop self-adaptive component-based applications. Our approach is based on the Separation of Concerns [2] principle: we consider *adaptation to a specific execution context and its evolutions* as a concern which should be treated separately from the rest of an application. Ideally, application developers should be able to concentrate on pure business logic, and write their code without worrying about the characteristics and resource limitations of the platform(s) it will be deployed on. Then, the *adaptation logic* [1], which deals specifically with the adaptation concern, is added to this non-adaptive code, resulting in a self-adaptive application able to reconfigure its architecture and parameters to always fit its evolving environment.

In this paper, we first present the general approach we propose and the corresponding development framework and tools we are developing to support it. This framework is based on the Fractal component model [3], chosen for its flexibility and dynamicity. To supplement this model, we propose a *context-awareness* service to provide information about the execution context. This information is used by *adaptation policies*, which constitute the third part of our framework and capture the adaptation concern. Then, in order to validate this approach, we present how a small component-based application can be made self-adaptive using it. In this example, we show how different kinds of performance-related adaptations can be applied non-invasively to the original application depending on its dynamic execution context.

This paper is divided in two main parts: in the first one (Sec. 2), we describe our approach in more details and present the three main parts of our framework (Sec. 2.1, 2.2, 2.3); in the second one (Sec. 3), we present a very simple application developed using our approach. Finally, we compare our approach to some other related work (Sec. 4) before concluding (Sec. 5).

2   General Approach

The general idea of our approach is to consider adaptability as a concern [2] which can be separated from the core concerns (i.e. business logic) of an application. We think that regardless of the specific domain of an application, adaptability concerns can often be expressed in the same way. Our goal is thus to identify a general form of these concerns and to capture it in a framework and accompanying tools. In practice, we do not pretend we have found the one and only mean to express adaptability concerns, but we believe that the approach we propose is general enough to be used in a wide range of adaptations.

More concretely, the development model we envision is as follows:

1. First, the application programmers create the core of the application (pure business logic), without worrying about the characteristics of the environment(s) it will/may be deployed in.

2. Then, once the deployer or administrator knows more precisely both the execution context(s) the application will be deployed in and its non-functional requirements , he can specify (using the tools we provide) how the application must be made to adapt itself to this context.

What we need as the output of the first phase is an *adaptable application*: an application which exhibits enough flexibility so that it *can* be reconfigured to fit different execution conditions. In the second phase, we take this adaptable application and make it *self-adaptive* by incorporating the additional logic required to drive these reconfigurations appropriately in response to the evolutions of the execution context. This integration of the adaptation logic can be done by source code transformation of the application, but although it enables adaptations to *happen* at run-time, this approach can not deal with *unanticipated adaptations* [4,5] which will only be known during the execution. The solution we adopted is to host the adaptable application inside a suitable execution platform which is responsible for interpreting the adaptation logic and reconfigure the application when required. This way, not only do the adaptations happen at run-time, but the adaptation logic itself can be modified during the execution, without stopping and restarting the application.

The kind and extent of flexibility the adaptable application provides determine the nature of the adaptations that will be possible. In our case, we deal with component-based applications which are explicitly structured through their *architecture*. The first kind of reconfigurations we support is thus *structural*: modifications of the connections between components and of their containment relationships. This allows for example to disconnect a component and replace it with another one, compatible with it but better suited to a specific usage context. As we will see, the component model we chose, Fractal [3], also supports the notion of component configuration through parameters. The second kind of reconfiguration we provide is thus *parameterization* (for example, changing the colors of GUI components if we know the user is color-blind). These two kinds of reconfiguration already enable powerful adaptations, but they both have the same drawback: they must be anticipated, at least partially, at development time. It is the application programmer (or assembler) who defines the architecture and which component parameters will be reconfigurable. In order to support unanticipated adaptations [5] at run-time, we needed a mechanism to transparently modify the behavior of components. As the Fractal component model did not support this natively, we had to extend it. The extension we added uses reflection to provide a meta-programming [6] interface to Fractal components (see Sec. 2.1 for details).

Having an *adaptable* application with the required level of flexibility and a set of reconfiguration operations is only the first step. In order to make this application *self-adaptive*, we need to add adaptation logic [1] whose role is to determine *when* to apply *which* specific reconfigurations. In our approach, this adaptation logic takes the form of *adaptation policies* which can be attached to or detached from individual components during the execution. An adaptation policy is a set of rules modeled after the Event – Condition – Action rules from active databases [7]: when the event described in the first part of a rule occur, the condition is evaluated, and if it holds, the action is then applied. This allows to react to changes in the execution context by reconfiguring the application.

To summarize the global picture of our approach, the development and execution of a component-based self-adaptive application can be decomposed in two phases:

1. Development of an adaptable application by application programmers and assemblers using an appropriate component model, but without worrying about the details of the execution context it will be deployed in.
2. Definition of adaptation policies and binding of these policies to the components of the application by the deployer. This binding is dynamic and happens at run-time so adaptation policies can be defined and attached to components when the real execution conditions are better known.

The resulting application is executed in an appropriate software platform which interprets the adaptation policies and ensures that all the adaptations are applied correctly (no disruption in the execution of the application, no conflicts between policies...).

2.1   Using Fractal to Build Adaptable Applications

In this section we present the Fractal component model that we have chosen as a base for our framework and show how it supports our requirements for adaptable applications.

Fractal [3] is a general (i.e. not domain-specific) component model for Java part of the ObjectWeb consortium[1]. It supports the definition of primitive and composite components, bindings between the interfaces provided or required by these components, and hierarchic composition (including sharing). Unlike other Java-based component models, like Jiazzy [8] or ArchJava [9], Fractal is not a language extension, but a run-time library which enables the specification and manipulation of components and architectures.

What makes Fractal particularly suited in our case is that because of its nature as a run-time library, it is highly dynamic and reflective. In practice, Fractal is presented as an API which can be used to create and manipulate complex architectures using plain Java classes as building blocks. Its programmatic approach makes it an ideal base to build tools on top of it.

Fractal distinguishes two kinds of components: primitives which contain the actual code, and composites which are only used as a mechanism to deal with a group of components as a whole, while potentially hiding some of the features of the subcomponents. Primitives are actually simple, standard Java classes conforming to some coding conventions. Fractal does not impose any limit on the levels of composition, hence its name. Each Fractal component is made of two parts: a controller which exposes the component's interfaces, and a content which can be either a user class in the case of a primitive or other components in the

---

[1] http://www.objectweb.org/

case of a composite. All interactions between components passes through their controller.

The model thus provides two mechanisms to define the architecture of an application: bindings between interfaces of components, and encapsulation of a group of components into a composite. Because Fractal is fully dynamic and reflective (in the sense that components and interfaces are first-class entities), applications built using it inherently support structural reconfiguration. Fractal also supports component parameterization: if a component can be configured using parameters, it should expose this feature as a Fractal interface identified by a reserved name so that it is available in a standard way. This gives us the second kind of adaptations we want to support.

In order to support adaptations not anticipated at development time [4,5], we needed a mechanism to modify transparently the behavior of Fractal components. Fractal does not provide this kind of mechanism by default. However its reference implementation is very extensible and it was possible to add the required feature, which can be thought of as a simple "Meta Object Protocol" [6] for Fractal. As every interaction between components passes through the controller part, we extended the default Fractal controller so that it can reify all the messages it receives (see Fig. 1). Instead of being sent to its original target, the reified message is sent to a subcomponent which implements a meta-level message invocation interface. The component can then process the message in a generic way, doing pre- or post-processing, or even completely replacing the original behavior. If this meta-level component is a composite, it is then relatively easy to support dynamic addition and removal of multiple generic behavior modifications (though the correct composition of meta-level behaviors is an open problem [10] which we do not address).

2.2 Context-Awareness Service

The role of the context-awareness service is to provide the rest of the framework precise and up-to-date information about the execution context of the application [11]. This information is required to decide when it becomes necessary to trigger an adaptation. We can distinguish three parts in context-awareness:

1. *Acquisition* of raw data from outside the application into a form that can be further manipulated.
2. *Representation* or *structuring* of these informations using an ontology.
3. *Reasoning* on the resulting knowledge to detect interesting situations which ask for a reaction/adaptation.

The remaining of this section describes how these functions are realized in our framework.

Acquisition. In our framework, acquisition is delegated to libraries of probes. A probe is simply a Java object which, when invoked, return an object regrouping named samples (values with a time-stamp indicating the moment it was

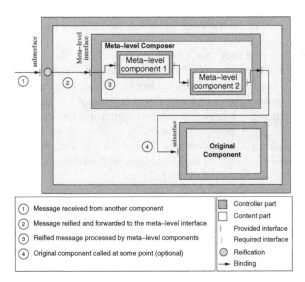

Fig. 1. MOP-like extension for Fractal.

acquired). The system maintains a set of instantiated probes, each with a particular sampling rate. A scheduler running in its own thread invokes each probe in turn, according to its sampling rate, and collects the results of the measures, to be consumed by the other parts of the framework. Libraries of probes to observe different kinds of context can be developed independently of an application, although some would probably depend on the underlying platform (OS, hardware). For example, our current implementation uses Linux's `/proc` pseudo file-system to gather information about the CPU load, available memory, and usage of the network connection.

Representation. The raw data collected by the probes is just a set of unrelated measures, not in a form appropriate to support any kind of sophisticated reasoning. The second step towards context-awareness is to structure this information into a model of the environment using an appropriate ontology. Because our framework is domain-independent, we chose a rather simple and generic meta-model to structure these informations. The context is represented as a tree of *resources* identified by a name. Resources can represent actual elements of the context (like a disk if the domain is hardware resources, or a room if the domain deals with physical informations) or a logical group of other resources (for example, a category named `storage` to regroup disk, memory...). Each resource is described by a set of named attributes, whose value change over time.

The structure of the resource tree is defined by a configuration file read at startup, which also indicates the mapping between the informations gathered by probes and the resources attributes. The current design assumes that the hierarchical structure of resources is fixed at startup time and that neither resources nor attributes can appear or disappear. Future versions will remove these limitations to reflect more accurately the dynamic nature of real execution contexts.

The system supports multiple parallel resource trees, identified by a name. Each such tree is called a *context-domain* and models one particular aspect of the application context. Examples of possible context-domains inlude hardware and software resources (CPU, memory, disk, libraries...), network topology and performance, physical environment (geographic position, temperature...) and user preferences (should applications use sound or stay quiet...). Given the appropriate library of probes and ontology to structure them, all these domains can be treated in a uniform way by our framework.

Reasoning. Even structured, information gathered by the probes are generally very low level and not appropriate for deciding when an adaptation is required. Indeed, which particular information is available to probes can vary from system to system.

In addition to primitive attributes containing raw data collected by probes, it is also possible to define *synthetic attributes*. These attributes are defined by an expression over the whole context domain the attribute belongs to. This feature allows to define more abstract attributes derived from the low level data collected by probes. For example, if probes can get from the underlying OS the number of bytes sent and received by a network interface, these values can be used to compute synthetic attributes representing incoming and outgoing traffic in MB/s. Combining this with the expected maximum throughput of the network card (available thanks to another probe), another attribute could be defined to represent the percentage of the current bandwidth usage.

The system uses the data regularly collected by the scheduler to update the values of all the synthetic variables, automatically taking care of dependencies. This way, an up-to-date model of the execution context of the application is always available to the rest of the system. However, what we have described until now gives us only snapshots (albeit regularly updated) of the state of the context. More sophisticated reasoning requires not only awareness of the immediate state of the context, but also of how it evolves over time. This is supported by the possibility to define composite event in the rules of adaptation policies (see Sec. 2.3).

The context-awareness service is available to the rest of the system through two interfaces: a simple query interface and an asynchronous notification interface. To use the query interface, a client object simply sends a request in the form of an expression, similar to those used to define synthetic variables. The system immediately evaluates the expression relative to the current state of its knowledge and returns the current value of the expression. To use the notification interface, an object also sends the expression it is interested in, but this is used to register the client as a listener to the expression. From this moment, until the client unregisters itself, the context-awareness service will notify the client each time the value of the expression changes. These expressions are actually managed almost exactly like normal synthetic variables, except that they are not associated to a resource but to a client object.

2.3   Adaptation Policies

The role of adaptation policies is twofold: first, to detect significant changes in the execution context of the application using the information made available by the context-awareness service, and then to decide which reconfigurations must be applied to the application when these changes occur.

To do this, an adaptation policy consists in a set of rules, each of the form Event – Condition – Action (modeled after the ECA paradigm used for example in active databases [7]):

- the *event* part describes the circumstances in which a rule must be triggered, using primitive events which can be combined to reason on the evolution of the context over time (see below);
- *conditions* are simple guards, evaluated when a rule is triggered to determine if the action should be applied;
- *action* is a (sequence of) reconfiguration operation(s) among those presented in Sec. 2.1 which are applied to the system when the rule is activated.

Each Fractal component in the application can have one or more adaptation policy dynamically attached to (or detached from) it. The policies are actually contained inside the controller part of the component, and are accessible through a specific Fractal interface automatically added to every self-adaptive component.

We distinguish two kinds of *primitive events* depending on their source (external or internal). The first kind corresponds to changes in the execution context, and more precisely to any change in the value of an expression over a context-domain. The second kind of events corresponds to things happening in the application itself, like messages sent between component, creation of new components or architectural reconfigurations triggered by the application itself (and not by an adaptation policy).

Both kinds of events can be combined to form *composite events* using a set of operators to detect sequences, alternatives or conjunctions of events. Using these mechanisms, it is possible to define adaptation policies which can react not only to the immediate state of the application or of its context, but also to its evolutions.

Conditions are simple boolean expressions defined in the same language as for synthetic variables, used as guards.

Actions consist in a sequence of concrete reconfiguration actions among the set already presented: structural reconfigurations, parameterization, addition or removal of a generic service using the MOP-like extension. Possible actions are limited to those directly implying the component an adaptation policy is attached to.

Although the adaptation policies are currently coded in plain Java, our goal is to define a DSL (Domain Specific Language [12]) to write these. This would enable verifications on the validity of the policies (to be defined more precisely) and to detect possible conflicts between policies, for example when two policies react differently to the same situation, or when their interaction would create unstable behaviors.

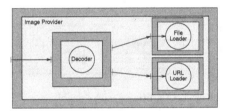

Fig. 2. Initial architecture of the example application.

3   Example Application of Our Approach

This section describes through a small example how the approach we propose can be used to transparently make a component-based application self-adaptive. First, we describe the example application and the problems it can have under certain circumstances. Then, we show how to apply three different (but cumulative) adaptations of this application using our approach, illustrating the three different types of reconfigurations we support. These adaptations overcome the original limitations of the application without breaking the encapsulation of the original components.

The application is an image viewer/browser. At its core is an image decoder component whose role is to interpret the content of an image file (JPEG, PNG...) into a bitmap which can be printed on a screen. It uses another component to load the content of the image files from a source location (local or remote). Figure 2 shows the corresponding part of the initial architecture of the application, coded using Fractal.

3.1   First Adaptation: Conditional Enabling of a Cache

The components in the application have been written to be simple and reusable, implementing one and only one thing. In particular, none of the loaders cache the files it loads. However, adding a cache would improve performance a lot in some circumstances. The first adaptation we will implement is thus the conditional enabling of a transparent caching service. The best place to put a cache is on the decoder (the front end component): this way, we will not only cache the cost of fetching the content of the files but also the cost of decoding the images. Using the meta-programming extension we added to Fractal, it is not very difficult to add a generic caching service to our component: because it works at a meta-level, handling reified messages and responses, the cache doesn't have to be implemented specifically for our example but can be reused from a library of generic services. Figure 3 shows the internal structure of the decoding component once the cache is enabled. Thanks to the dynamicity of Fractal, going from the original decoder to this configuration can be done (and undone) at runtime and completely transparently.

The adaptation policy required to implement this behaviour is very simple, consisting in only one rule:

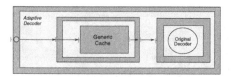

Fig. 3. Conditional cache enabling.

1. **When** the average execution time of a request (to load and decode an image) to the image provider goes above a given threshold, **then** instantiate a new generic cache component and attach it to the image provider.

This way, when the system detects that images take a long time to get, it will automatically adapt the image provider component by adding a cache service to increase performance when the same images are loaded several times. The average execution time of a request is computed by the adaptation policy attached to the component using the time-stamps of method receptions and method returns, two kinds of events available for writing the *Event* part of an adaptation rule.

3.2   Second Adaptation: Automatic Resizing of the Cache

The second adaptation we describe concerns the size of the cache, which we did not precise in the previous section. This can have a high impact on the performance of the system: on the one hand, if the cache is too small we will not use all of its potential; on the other hand, if it is too big compared to the memory available in the system, we risk to pay an even higher price from the use of swap space. The goal of this second adaptation is thus to adapt the size of the cache to the amount of free memory available on the system, which of course changes dynamically.

One originality of our approach which allows us to do this is that the generic cache we added to the application in the previous step is itself a Fractal component. This means we can use the same techniques as for the application component to adapt the cache service itself. To be able to do this, we assume that the cache component exposes its size as a reconfigurable parameter in the standard Fractal way. We can then use on the cache a second kind of reconfiguration: parameterization. The size of the cache will be determined according to the amount of free RAM available in the system. This amount is tracked by the context-awareness service and is available as `res:/storage/memory.free` (to be read as: the `free` attribute of the resource named `memory` in the `storage` category of the `res` context-domain). The adaptation policy to control the size of the cache has three rules (`free` is used as a shorthand for `res:/storage/memory.free`):

1. **When** the value of `free` changes, **if** it is less than *low*, **then** set the cache size to 0.
2. **When** the value of `free` changes, **if** it is greater than *high*, **then** set the cache size to *max*.

3. **When** the value of `free` changes, **then** set the cache size to $(\text{free} - low) \times \frac{max}{high - low}$.

These rules state that when the amount of free memory is below the *low* watermark, the cache is effectively disabled by setting its size to 0 (Rule 1). Otherwise, the size of the cache grows linearly with the amount of free memory (Rule 3) until it reaches a maximum value of *max* when the amount of free memory is more than *high* (Rule 2). By dynamically attaching such a policy to the cache, its size will always be adapted to the available resources.

3.3   Third Adaptation: Replacement Policy Selection

When a cache is full, it uses a replacement policy to decide which of the elements it contains must be removed. The most classical replacement policy is LRU (Least Recently Used), which chooses to drop the element in the cache which was not accessed for the longest time. This works well for random access patterns but can lead to trashing when the data is accessed sequentially [13]. Glass [13] presents a more sophisticated replacement policy called SEQ which behaves like LRU by default, but switches to MRU (Most Recently Used) behaviour when it detects the beginning of a sequential access. Although Glass implemented his SEQ algorithm in an ad hoc and much more sophisticated way, its general idea fits very well in our model of adaptation policies. We can easily implement a simplified version of SEQ in our application to illustrate the last kind of adaptation we support: structural reconfiguration. We suppose that the component implementing the core cache logic uses another component to implement the replacement policy, using a well-defined interface. An adaptation policy attached to the cache which can detect the start and end of sequential accesses to data can then use the structural reconfiguration facilities offered by Fractal to switch between a component which implement LRU and one which implement MRU[2].

Such an adaptation policy could look like this:

1. **When** returning from the invocation of the cached method, **if** the last N requests were consecutive, **then** unbind the LRU component and replace it with the MRU component.
2. **When** returning from the invocation of the cached method, **if** the last N requests were *not* consecutive, **then** unbind the MRU component and replace it with the LRU component.

3.4   Conclusion & Evaluation

In this section, we have shown how our approach to building self-adaptive applications makes it possible to take a simple component-based application written with only business concerns in mind and make it self-adaptive transparently, adding the required adaptation logic well encapsulated in adaptation policies.

---

[2] The state transfer between the two replacement policy components is currently handled in an ad hoc way, but we are investigating more generic solutions.

Although these adaptation policies are currently written in pure Java, we have already achieved complete separation between the core, business concern of the application and its adaptation to the limits and evolution of its execution context.

4   Related Work

Apart from Fractal, several component models have been developed to extend the Java language. Some of them like Jiazzy [8] and Java Layers [14] are purely static (compile-time), and hence can not support dynamic reconfiguration. Arch-Java [9], on the other hand, is a Java extension which supports dynamic reconfigurations, but is not reflective and thus supports only reconfigurations which have been written explicitly at development time. As for the EJBs, the model does not really support the notion of architecture, and a previous experiment [15] showed us than the model was too rigid and restrictive to support the kind of reconfigurations we want. The CORBA Component Model supports all the features we need, but is much more complicated than the others. Although our approach could be ported to this model, its complexity makes it difficult to use as an experimentation platform.

In [11], Capra describes a middleware architecture which uses reflection and context-awareness to support adaptation to changing context. As in our approach, this architecture encapsulates adaptation decisions in XML-based *user profile* (similar in intent to our adaptation policies), and relies on a hierarchical model of the context to take decisions. However, these decisions can be based only according to the immediate state of the context, whereas our approach allows the definition of composite events to reason on the evolution of the context over time. Also, reconfiguration actions are delegated to user code through call-backs, which makes them arbitrary and impossible to analyze.

The QuO (Quality Object) middleware platform [16] uses an approach similar to ours to adapt distributed applications. It uses a sophisticated context-awareness subsystem based on performance models for the application components to compute the expected QoS. The resulting system is very powerful, but heavily biased towards performance-related adaptations, whereas our approach tries to be more generic.

Bergmans et al. present in [17] a middleware architecture inspired by control theory to deal with QoS issues in the platform itself. In this architecture, QoS contracts are attached to bindings between components. Sensors are then used to observe the performance of components. The system compares this measured QoS to what is allowed by the contract, and if it detects a difference, reconfigures the system using actuators. The general idea is close to ours, but the system only deals with the quality of communications between components (contracts are attached to bindings).

5   Conclusion: Current Status & Future Work

In this paper, we have presented our approach to enable systematic development of self-adaptive component-based applications. The approach follows the

Separation of Concerns principle, where the adaptation logic of an application is developed separately from the rest of it. It relies on the use of an appropriate component model (in our case, Fractal) to develop an application that is *adaptable*. This adaptable application is then supplemented by *adaptation policies* which capture the adaptation logic in an appropriate formalism (Event – Condition – Action rules). The application is executed inside a software platform which interprets these policies at run-time, using a generic *context-awareness* service to detect changes in the environment, and dynamically reconfigures the application when appropriate. We have also shown, using an example application, how this approach can be used in practice to adapt transparently an application.

Currently, we have a working implementation of the extension we designed for Fractal, and we are implementing the context-awareness service. Next, we plan to do more experiments to guide the design of the DSL we want to provide to define adaptation policies. Once we have a formal definition of this language, we will use it to ensure that the reconfigurations do not break the application, and to detect conflicts between policies leading (incompatible actions triggered by the same events, rules interactions creating unstable behavior...).

References

1. Dowling, J., Cahill, V.: The K-Component architecture meta-model for self-adaptive software. In Yonezawa, A., Matsuoka, S., eds.: Proceedings of Reflection 2001, The Third Int. Conference on Metalevel Architectures and Separation of Crosscutting Concerns, Kyoto, Japan. LNCS 2192, Springer-Verlag (2001) 81–88
2. Hürsch, W., Lopes, C.V.: Separation of concerns. Technical Report NU-CCS-95-03, Northeastern University, Boston, Massachusetts (1995)
3. Coupaye, T., Éric Bruneton, Stéfani, J.B.: The fractal composition framework. Technical report, The ObjectWeb Group (2002)
4. Redmond, B., Cahill, V.: Supporting unanticipated dynamic adaptation of application behaviour. In: Proceedings of ECOOP 2002. Volume 2374 of LNCS., Malaga, Spain, Springer-Verlag (2002) 205–230
5. The First International Workshop on Unanticipated Software Evolution. In: ECOOP 2002, Malaga, Spain (2002) http://www.joint.org/use2002.
6. Kiczales, G., des Rivières, J., Bobrow, D.G.: The art of the Meta-Object Protocol. MIT Press (1991)
7. Dittrich, K.R., Gatziu, S., Geppert, A.: The active database management system manifesto: A rulebase of a ADBMS features. In: Proceedings of the 2nd Int. Workshop on Rules in Database Systems. Volume 985., Springer (1995) 3–20
8. McDirmid, S., Flatt, M., Hsieh, W.C.: Jiazzi: New-age components for old-fashioned Java. In Northrop, L., ed.: OOPSLA'01 Conference Proceedings, Tampa Bay, Florida, USA, ACM Press (2001) 211–222
9. Aldrich, J., Chambers, C., Notkin, D.: ArchJava: Connecting software architecture to implementation. In: International Conference on Software Engineering, ICSE 2002, Orlando, Florida, USA (2002)
10. Mulet, P., Malenfant, J., Cointe, P.: Towards a methodology for explicit composition of metaobjects. In: Proceedings of OOPSLA'95. Volume 30 of ACM SIGPLAN Notices., austin, Texas, USA (1995) 316–330

11. Capra, L., Emmerich, W., Mascolo, C.: Reflective middleware solutions for context-aware applications. In Yonezawa, A., Matsuoka, S., eds.: Proceedings of Reflection 2001, The Third International Conference on Metalevel Architectures and Separation of Crosscutting Concerns, Kyoto, Japan. LNCS 2192, Springer-Verlag (2001) 126–133

12. Consel, C., Marlet, R.: Architecturing software using a methodology for language development. In: Proceedings of the 10th Int. Symposium on Programming Languages, Implementations, Logics and Programs PLILP/ALP'98, Pisa, Italy (1998)

13. Glass, G., Cao, P.: Adaptive page replacement based on memory reference behavior. In: Proceedings of ACM SIGMETRICS 1997. (1997) 115–126

14. Cardone, R., Batory, D., Lin, C.: Java layers: Extending java to support component-based programming. Technical Report CS-TR-00-11, Computer Sciences Department, University of Texas (2000)

15. Jarir, Z., David, P.C., Ledoux, T.: Dynamic adaptability of services in enterprise JavaBeans architecture. In: Seventh International Workshop on Component-Oriented Programming (WCOP'02) at ECOOP 2002, Malaga, Spain (2002)

16. Zinky, J., Loyall, J., Shapiro, R.: Runtime performance modeling and measurement of adaptive distributed object applications. In Meersam, R., et al, Z.T., eds.: On the Move to Meaningful Internet Systems 2002: CoopIS, DOA, ODBASE 2002. Volume 2519 of LNCS., Irvine, California, USA, Springer-Verlag (2002) 755–772

17. Bergmans, L., van Halteren, A., Pires, L.F., van Sinderen, M., Aksit, M.: A QoS-control architecture for object middleware. In: IDMS'2000 Conference Proceedings. Volume 1905 of LNCS., Springer Verlag (2001) 117–131

A Scheme for the Introduction
of 3rd Party, Application-Specific Adaptation Features in Mobile Service Provision

Nikos Houssos, Nancy Alonistioti, and Lazaros Merakos

Communication Networks Laboratory, Department of Informatics & Telecommunications,
University of Athens, 15784, Athens, Greece
{nhoussos,nancy,merakos}@di.uoa.gr

Abstract. The long term vision of beyond 3G wireless communications describes an evolution towards beyond 3G systems. The ultimate goal of this evolution is a dynamic environment that enables the delivery of situation-aware, personalised multimedia services over heterogeneous, ubiquitous infrastructures. Under this perspective, the need is emerging for applying, in a systematic way, adaptability and reconfigurability concepts for service delivery in largely diverse contexts. Moreover, it is widely recognised that services will be increasingly developed by independent third parties. The present contribution complements previous work by the authors, related to mediating service provision platforms and advanced adaptability and profile management frameworks, by introducing mechanisms that allow third parties to dynamically enhance the service delivery and adaptation middleware in order to achieve application-specific customisations in various aspects of the mobile service provision process.

1 Introduction

The evolution of mobile networks and systems to 3rd generation and beyond is expected to bring about substantial changes to telecommunication service provision. In the envisioned beyond 3G era, a plethora of functionality-rich, profit-creating value-added services (VAS)[1] should be delivered to mobile users [1] over an unprecedented variety of infrastructures and contexts, which could not be predicted or catered for during service design and development. These extensively demanding requirements indicate the need for adaptability of applications as well as service provision and delivery procedures to highly diverse environments. Adaptability, an inherently challenging task, is further complicated by the fact that adaptation intelligence should be generic, portable and interoperable so that it can be flexibly applied to a diversity of entities in different circumstances.

---

[1] In the present paper the terms *service*, *value-added service (VAS)* and *application* are used interchangeably to refer to an information technology product which is directly accessible and perceptible to the end user and whose value resides mostly in functionality and content, rather than transport or connectivity.

J.-B. Stefani, I. Demeure, and D. Hagimont (Eds.): DAIS 2003, LNCS 2893, pp. 15–28, 2003.

In previous research efforts, the authors have developed schemes for addressing the above issue and incorporated them in a middleware platform for service provision [2]. In this paper, we complement this work by providing detailed mechanisms for enabling adaptation logic to be run-time injected into the service provision middleware by 3rd parties. This feature is important, since different services may require different algorithms for matching service requirements with context parameters. As a simple example one could consider a context parameter that is expressed in terms of dimension (e.g., terminal screen resolution). Two services could have the same value in their profile as a dimension requirement, but the algorithm for matching it with the corresponding context value could differ (e.g., one algorithm would require the currently supported screen resolution of the terminal to be just greater than or equal to the value in the service profile, while another one could additionally require that the width/height ratio would be equal to a specific quotient). Implementing such an algorithm is something trivial for the service developer; however, the lack of frameworks that would enable the dynamic loading of suitable service-specific algorithms does not currently allow this type of adaptation flexibility. In this contribution we demonstrate that this can be achieved through a procedure that does not incur significant overhead to the service creator and mainly involves specifying adaptation metadata in RDF/XML [3] and developing the algorithms according to certain simple, non-restrictive guidelines.

The rest of this document is organised as follows: At first, we present the environment where the proposed adaptation mechanism was integrated and applied, namely a software platform for provision of services over 3G mobile networks. We then discuss the platform support for 3rd party adaptation logic introduction. This discussion includes the features offered by the platform, a detailed view of the overall procedure from a third-party perspective and the supporting mechanisms that we have developed. The last sections of this paper are dedicated to summary, conclusions and acknowledgements.

2 Service Provision Platform

The present section introduces a distributed software platform for the flexible provision and management of advanced services in next generation mobile networks. The platform incorporates intelligent adaptation and reconfiguration mechanisms as well as advanced support for 3rd party adaptable service deployment and management. Before elaborating on the internal platform architecture, we provide a brief discussion of the business and service provision models supported by the platform.

Note that the detailed architecture and functionality of the platform, as well as details about the corresponding business models, has been presented by the authors in previous work [5] and is thus beyond the scope of the present paper. Only the basic aspects that are useful for presenting the 3rd party support mechanisms are included herein.

2.1 Business and Service Provision Model

The proposed framework is designed to support flexible, advanced business models that encourage among market players the establishment of strategic partnerships, which ultimately benefit end users by significantly enhancing service provision. The main business entities involved in such models are the following:

Mobile User: The mobile user is the actual consumer of services.

Mobile operator: This is the entity that operates the network infrastructure for mobile user access to services and will typically also provide third-party access to its network through a standardised API (e.g., OSA/Parlay [6], JAIN).

Platform operator: This is the entity that owns and administers the software platform for service provision.

Value-Added Service Provider (VASP): This is the provider (and typically also the developer) of the end-user application.

The platform operator acts as a single point of contact ("one-stop-shop") for:

- *VASPs* that are able to register their services with the platform and this way to have them delivered to a large number of mobile users over multiple networks.
- *Mobile users* that are given the ability to discover, select, download and execute registered value-added services in a flexible, adaptable and personalised manner.

To accomplish these tasks, the platform operator is engaged into business relationships with users, mobile operators and VASPs. A prior subscription with the VASP for using an application is not required for the user, since a dynamic service discovery, download and execution model is applied.

It is worth noting that it is possible for one single entity to undertake several of the roles described above and vice versa. For instance, a mobile or platform operator may also develop its own services and act as a VASP.

The service provision model supported by the RCSPP can be summarised as follows: Before a service becomes available to end-users, it is automatically deployed based on VASP-provided detailed service metadata. This procedure may include sophisticated actions like reconfiguration of the underlying networking infrastructure. From then on, the user is able to dynamically discover, download and execute the service, without the need for a prior subscription with the VASP.

2.2   Overview of Platform Architecture and Functionality

In this section we briefly present a distributed middleware platform that supports adaptability in mobile service provision. The functionality of the platform, which is called Reconfiguration Control and Service Provision Platform (RCSPP), comprises automated procedures for service deployment that include appropriate reconfiguration of the underlying network for optimal service delivery. In addition to that, an intelligent context-aware mobile portal is offered to the end-user, where procedures like service discovesry, downloading and adaptation are fully tailored to terminal capabilities, user preferences and network characteristics.

The architecture of the platform is depicted in Fig. 1. The main components of this architecture are the following:

- The *Reconfiguration Control and Service Provision Manager (RCSPM)* is the central platform component in that it co-ordinates the entire service provision and management process.
- The *Charging, Accounting and Billing (CAB)* system [8] is responsible for producing a single user bill for service access and apportioning the resulting revenue between the involved business players.

- The *End User Terminal Platform (EUT)* [9] resides in the mobile terminal (it is not depicted in Fig. 1) and includes functionality such as service downloading management, GUI clients for service discovery and selection, capturing of event notifications as well as service execution management.
- The *VASP* (or VASP Service Platform Client) component of the platform is located in the VASP domain (e.g., enterprise servers) and handles secure terminal access to a repository of application clients, while also providing web interfaces to RCSPM functionality, through which VASPs can carry out sophisticated service management operations (e.g., service deployment).

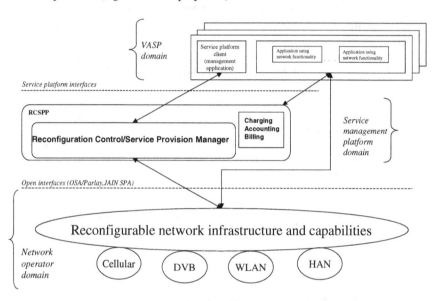

Fig. 1. Architecture for flexible service provision in 3G and beyond networks.

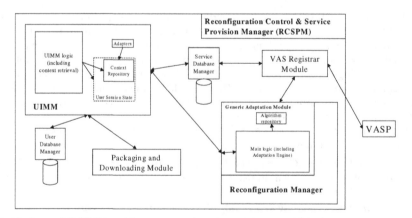

Fig. 2. Internal RCSPM architecture (not complete; only adaptability-relevant modules are depicted).

Adaptability management and 3rd party support in the RCSPP is based on the architectural components depicted in Fig. 2 and presented in the following:

- The VASP component of the platform, as described above.
- A subset of the components and interfaces of the RCSPM, which are described below:

The *User Interaction Management Module (UIMM)* is responsible for providing the user with a highly personalisable, context-aware mobile portal. It manages user sessions with the RCSPP, maintains relevant contextual information and co-ordinates user-related operations like service discovery, selection, adaptation and downloading as well as user profile management.

The *VAS Registrar Module (VASREGM)* is responsible for interacting with 3rd party service providers. Through the VASREGM the platform operator provides VASPs with a way to automatically deploy their services. The VASP compiles an formally specified profile of service attributes. Based on these attributes, the VASREGM co-ordinates service deployment, including various actions like reconfiguration of the underlying infrastructure and uploading of service components to the RCSPM. The service provider is able to manage (add/delete/update) its services via a convenient web interface.

The *Reconfiguration Manager (RCM)* undertakes network, platform and service reconfigurability. The RCM is responsible for executing the appropriate reconfiguration actions on the underlying network during VAS management procedures (registration/de-registration/update), triggered by the VASP. The RCM also comprises a generic adaptation module [2] that is used for supporting adaptation through functions like intelligent profile matching. The adaptation module is able to dynamically load adaptation algorithms from a local repository or remote network locations. These algorithms can be developed by VASPs and inserted to the repository during the service registration operation with the mechanisms described in Section 3.

The *Packaging and Downloading Module (PDM)* [7] is addressing an aspect of adaptable service delivery by being responsible for dynamically creating a single bundle that contains all the software components and other supporting resources (e.g., images, etc.) required for executing a service and for making it available for download to the mobile client. The single archive produced is dynamically tailored to the context of the particular VAS selection request.

The RCSPM also includes database managers that provide interoperable access to the persistent service, user and network profile repositories hosted by the platform.

3 3rd Party Support for Adaptable Service Provision

The current section presents in more detail the 3rd party support features of the RCSPP. At first, we describe the data and mechanisms that the platform provider makes available to VASPs for deploying their applications. Next, we present the detailed sequence of actions that are required from a VASP for the flexible and adaptive provision of a VAS and outline the general structure of the service management operations offered by the RCSPP. Subsequently, we elaborate on the implementation of certain mechanisms that are crucial for 3rd party adaptation support, namely the specification of service profiles, with a particular focus on metadata about adaptation algorithms, as well as the development and loading of the actual adaptation logic.

3.1 What Does the RCSPP Provide?

To offer third parties the capability of developing their own customised adaptation intelligence and injecting it into the system, the platform provider carries out the following actions:

- Supplies service developers with the VASP platform component that enables remote service deployment and data management, normally through an easy to use graphical user interface, typically implemented as a simple web HTML page (as is our demonstrator) or a Java application/applet.
- Publishes the formal specification of the service profile structure. The latter should be defined using a data representation approach that promotes interoperability and extensibility, such as XML or RDF. These approaches include constructs that are employed for describing profile structures, like XML Document Type Definition (DTD) and XML Schema for XML and RDF Schema for RDF. In our prototype, we have used XML and XML DTD for service profile representation and structure specification, respectively. This particular choice was made because it is characterised by simplicity, ease of implementation, although it is extensible and able to represent arbitrarily complex profiles.
- Provides a way for the VASP to bind service requirements in terms of the values of particular context parameters with the algorithms that shall undertake the matching/adapting task regarding these parameters. In our prototype we have devised ways to achieve that in RDF and XML, as described in Section 3.3.1.
- Provides all the necessary information that is required for a third party to develop a custom algorithm. This includes the detailed description of the platform-internal profile representation format and typical guidelines for code extension (e.g., which interfaces can be extended). Moreover, the platform enables the automatic loading of the algorithms into the adaptation module repository during the service registration operation. Notably in our prototype, custom algorithm development is supported only in Java, a language well-suited for extensibility.
- Makes public the type of context profile elements for which there is a default algorithm, as well as the algorithms themselves (including their implementation). The default algorithm is used for adaptation decision-making regarding a specific profile element in the case that the VASP has not explicitly identified an algorithm for this particular element.

3.2 What Does the VASP Have to Do?

Before making use of the platform, a third-party application provider should obtain the corresponding authorisation. This procedure, a part of which is performed through off-line business interaction between platform operator and VASP, is completed when the latter becomes the information (e.g., an SPKI certificate) that enables its authentication by the platform.

The deployment of an application and its delivery to end-users is performed with the support of the platform and requires the following actions from the side of registered VASPs:

1. Development of the service logic. Various versions and implementations may exist for a single service. No particular constraints in terms of programming languages, methodologies and tools is imposed by the platform on the service creator. However, in case a component-based development approach is followed, the on-demand composition of the optimal service configuration is possible, as described in Section 2.1.

2. Specification of service requirements in terms of context parameters. Environmental parameters are bound to all elements (e.g., service client, version, component, implementation) that model the downloadable part of a service offering. Contextual requirements have different "scope", depending on the type of element with which they are associated. That is, the service client software context requirements concern all versions and, therefore, if these requirements are not compatible with a user's current service provision environment no version of the application can be provided to this particular user. Likewise, the version requirements pertain to all components (core and optional) and the component requirements relate to all implementations.

3. Development of custom adaptation/matching algorithms for certain context parameters. This is necessary in case the platform does not provide a default algorithm for these parameters or the provided default algorithm is not appropriate for the application in question. The development of the algorithm should follow the relevant guidelines publicly announced by the platform operator. In general, a VASP is required to implement custom algorithms only for a small number of parameters that are particularly significant for the optimal provision of the service and for which special requirements exist.

4. Identifying and expressing the necessary metadata for service registration in the appropriate format. This metadata constitutes the service profile, which includes a variety of information, as elaborated in Section 3.3.1. A crucial part of the service profile relates to the contextual requirements of the application, for example terminal capabilities, network characteristics and user preferences and status, together with the identification of custom-made algorithms associated with individual parameters, if any. The service descriptor in our prototype is defined in XML and should be compatible with a particular XML DTD. However, parts of the profile, like the requirements and their associated algorithms can be specified in RDF/XML (see Section 3.3.1).

5. Performing the service registration operation through the platform's VASP component.

The platform makes available to VASPs service registration and the relevant service data management operations (service update and deletion), which all have the form of distributed transactions. Typical sub-tasks of these transactions are the following:

- Validation checks, applied on the VASP-originated service profile. The latter should comply (e.g., in terms of billing/pricing data) with the (prior) business agreement between VASP and platform operator. This task is performed by the VASREGM.

- Insertion/update/removal of information stored in the services database. This task is handled by the VASREGM, which makes use of the Service Database Manager interface.

- Insertion/update/removal of algorithm implementations that are stored in the corresponding repository, maintained by the adaptation module of the RCM. This task, which mainly comprises the uploading to the repository of the appropriate binary files/archives, is handled by the VASREGM and involves interactions with the RCM.
- Reconfiguration actions on the underlying infrastructure. The execution of these actions, which are determined by suitable interpretation of service metadata and context information (e.g., network capabilities/load), is co-ordinated by the RCM that receives high-level events (e.g., an update of the pricing policy and/or traffic flow information regarding service "X") and maps them to appropriate signaling (based on standardised or proprietary APIs/protocols) with network/system components/devices (e.g., routers, billing systems).

The co-ordination of the above mentioned transaction is handled by the VASREGM. For example, if during VAS update the reconfiguration of underlying network routers fails, any changes to the service database and algorithm repository should not be committed.

3.3 Supporting Mechanisms

3.3.1 Specification of Service Metadata
The service provision functions of the RCSPP are largely dependent on the availability of accurate metadata regarding the service, which is referred to as the *service profile*. The service profile is formulated by the VASP and communicated to the RCSPM during the service registration operation. The RCSPM maintains this information in an appropriate service database, whose data can be updated at any time by authorised third parties. The current section first describes the contents of the service profile, then elaborates on our choice of the format of its representation and finally presents how adaptation algorithm metadata can be included in service metadata, with the support of RDF.
The application profile encompasses a variety of information, such as:

- General data about the service, like name, version, description and VASP information.
- Data describing the service software architecture, including any optional components.
- Requirements from terminals.
- Requirements from network infrastructure. These include pure technical characteristics like network type (e.g., GSM/GPRS, UMTS, WLAN) and available bandwidth as well as requirements of a hybrid business/technical nature such as revenue sharing policy of network operator and availability of open interfaces (e.g., OSA/Parlay) to network functionality.
- User preferences that are supported by the application (e.g., available languages).
- VAS-specific information about tariffing/billing as well as revenue sharing between VASP and platform provider.
- Security data.

Since service metadata is subject to processing and exchange in different administrative domains, it should be represented in a storage-independent format that promotes interoperability. Two current recommendations of the World-Wide-Web Consortium, XML [11] and RDF [12] can be thus considered as prime candidates for this task. XML is a ubiquitous, widely adopted by industry meta-language, which enables the representation of hierarchical data structures and incorporates capabilities for the definition of new vocabularies and schemata. RDF is a more complex framework that can be used for the encoding of arbitrarily complex information in the form of directed labeled graphs. Notably, XML is the most common format for serialising RDF data.

In general, XML is easier to use and manipulate, while RDF has greater capabilities for expressing semantically rich information. RDF results in more clarity, since there is an explicit format interpretation of any RDF-encoded data, based on the RDF Model Theory [13]. Consequently, a certain piece of information can be represented in RDF in exactly one, unique way, while in XML many different encodings with the same meaning are possible [16]. This advantage of RDF, however, comes at the cost of being more verbose and significantly more complex. The latter characteristic makes it less attractive for the majority of users and developers [14].

```
<!--DTD for VAS descriptor-->
<!--Author: Nikos Houssos, UoA-CNL-->
<!ELEMENT VAS (VASGEN, VASP,  SOFTWAREARCH, SECURITY)>
<!ELEMENT VASGEN (VASName, VASID?, VASVersion, VASDescription, SubscriptionType, Category, Keywords, Availability,
UpdateDescription?, OSA_Parlay_InfoGen?)>

<!ELEMENT VASP (VASPName, VASPType, VASPPublicKey, VASPReference)>

<!ELEMENT SOFTWAREARCH (ServerPart, ClientPart)>

<!ELEMENT ClientPart (ServiceClientVersion+, ContextReq)>
<!ELEMENT ContextReq (TermReq?, NetworkReq?, UserPref?, UserStatus?, OtherReq?)>
<!ELEMENT TermReq (#PCDATA)>
<!ELEMENT NetworkReq (#PCDATA)>
<!ELEMENT UserPref (#PCDATA)>
<!ELEMENT UserStatus (#PCDATA)>
<!ELEMENT OtherReq (#PCDATA)>
<!ELEMENT ServiceClientVersion (CorePart, OptionalPart?, ContextReq, PricingModel, TariffClass, CostDescription, FlowMonitoring,
QoSIndicator)>

<!ELEMENT CorePart (Component+)>
<!ELEMENT OptionalPart (Component+)>
<!ELEMENT Component (Description, Implementation+, ContextReq?, OptionalPart?)>

<!ELEMENT Implementation (Codebase, ContextReq?)>

<!ELEMENT SECURITY (IPRProtection, Confidentiality, VASConditionsOfUse, SecurityDomain, SPKICertificate)>
```

Fig. 3. XML DTD for service profile (Note: only part of it and simplified for readability)

In our approach, the service profile is encoded in XML; an XML Document Type Definition (DTD) is employed for defining the application metadata vocabulary. However, there is the possibility for the incorporation of RDF models as values of certain XML elements, as XML CDATA sections [15]. This has been considered necessary for certain elements, like contextual requirements, which can include information that is not a priori predictable and thus is not possible to include in an XML DTD or XML Schema that is universally adopted by all VASPs. This way, VASPs are allowed to insert in the service profile context requirements, while still producing XML documents that are valid and compatible with the service metadata DTD. The inherent greater extensibility capabilities of RDF [17] have been the main reason for this choice, although some researchers claim that they create challenging validation problems and can potentially create the risk for storing of incorrect data [18].

The above are exemplified by the corresponding DTD displayed in Fig. 3.

An important issue relates to how the VASP can specify custom algorithms that should be used for adaptation/matching of service profiles according to the current service provision context. We have identified a solution for this issue, based on the assumption that the context requirements metadata is encoded in RDF. We have defined a specific RDF property called *ComparatorAlgorithm²*, whose subject can be any RDF resource and whose value is of type *ComparatorDescriptor*. The latter is a class of RDF resources, which represents adaptation/matching algorithms. *ComparatorDescriptor* is a sub-class of the more general *AlgorithmDescriptor* class. A *ComparatorDescriptor* object can have various properties, which provide data adequate for locating and loading the algorithm implementation (e.g., *FullyQualifiedName*, *ImplementationLocation*) or are used for providing general information about the algorithm (e.g., *AlgorithmDescription*, *DeveloperDescriptor*). The corresponding declarations are included in an RDF Schema that we have defined and made publicly available. The schema is shown in Fig. 4.

To illustrate the above, we provide in the following some examples, in which we use certain terminal capability attributes (as specified in the OpenMobileAlliance UAProf specification [19]) as cases of context parameters and assume an RDF/XML serialisation of RDF data.

If the value of the RDF property (context parameter) is compound, it is augmented with an `ComparatorAlgorithm` property element. For instance, the following definition for the `JVMVersion` property:

```
<prf:JVMVersion>
        <rdf:Bag><rdf:li>SunJRE/1.2</rdf:li></rdf:Bag>
</prf:JVMVersion>
```

becomes:

```
<prf:JVMVersion>
        <rdf:Bag><rdf:li>SunJRE/1.2</rdf:li></rdf:Bag>
        <alg:ComparatorAlgorithm>
                <alg:ComparatorType>Matcher</alg:ComparatorType>
        <alg:FullyQualifiedName>gr.uoa.di.cnl.adaptation.VersionMatcher<
/alg:FullyQualifiedName>
        <alg:ImplementationCodebase>http://www.cnl.di.uoa.gr/People/nhou
ssos/Impl/classes/</alg:ImplementationCodebase>
        </alg:ComparatorAlgorithm>
</prf:JVMVersion>
```

Lest the value of the RDF property (context parameter) is atomic (RDF Literal), we use the standard RDF technique for representing higher arity relations using binary relations [17]. Thus, the principal value of the property is included as an rdf:value property and a `ComparatorAlgorithm` property element is also added. Thus, the following definition for a `ScreenSize` property:

```
<prf:ScreenSize>1024x768</prf:ScreenSize>
```

becomes:

```
<prf:ScreenSize>
    <rdf:value>1024x768</rdf:value>
```

---

² In the reference to RDF resources in this paper we present them as "local" resources; we omit the globally qualified name for the sake of readability and simplicity of the text. Thus, for example, we write "ComparatorDescriptor" instead of
"http://www.cnl.di.uoa.gr/People/nhoussos/Schemata/AlgorithmSchema-20030622#ComparatorDescriptor" or "alg:ComparatorDescriptor"

```
    <alg:ComparatorAlgorithm>
<alg:ComparatorType>Matcher</alg:ComparatorType>
<alg:FullyQualifiedName>gr.uoa.di.cnl.adaptation.ScreenSizeMatcher</alg:
FullyQualifiedName>
        <alg:ImplementationCodebase>http://www.cnl.di.uoa.gr/People/nhou
ssos/Impl/classes/</alg:ImplementationCodebase>
        </alg:ComparatorAlgorithm>
</prf:ScreenSize>
```

```
<?xml version="1.0" encoding="UTF-8"?>
<rdf:RDF xmlns:rdf="http://www.w3.org/1999/02/22-rdf-syntax-ns#" xmlns:rdfs="http://www.w3.org/2000/01/rdf-
schema#" xml:base="http://www.cnl.di.uoa.gr/People/nhoussos/Schemata/AlgorithmSchema-20030622">
    <!-- Algorithm Descriptor Definition -->
    <rdf:Description rdf:ID="AlgorithmDescriptor">
        <rdf:type rdf:resource="http://www.w3.org/2000/01/rdf-schema#Class"/>
        <rdfs:comment> The base class for resource classes that represent algorithms.  </rdfs:comment>
    </rdf:Description>
    <!-- Comparator Descriptor Definition -->
    <rdf:Description rdf:ID="ComparatorDescriptor">
        <rdf:type rdf:resource="http://www.w3.org/2000/01/rdf-schema#Class"/>
        <rdfs:subClassOf rdf:resource="#AlgorithmDescriptor"/>
        <rdfs:comment>
        A resource that represents an algorithm used for adaptation/matching.
        </rdfs:comment>
    </rdf:Description>
    <!-- Properties common for all AlgorithmDescriptor resources. -->
    <rdf:Description rdf:ID="FullyQualifiedName">
        <rdf:type rdf:resource="http://www.w3.org/2000/01/rdf-schema#Property"/>
        <rdfs:domain rdf:resource="#AlgorithmDescriptor"/>
        <rdfs:comment>
    Provides the fully qualified name of the algorithm.
    Example: "gr.uoa.di.cnl.adaptation.LocationMatcher"
        </rdfs:comment>
    </rdf:Description>
    <rdf:Description rdf:ID="AlgorithmDescription">
        <rdf:type rdf:resource="http://www.w3.org/2000/01/rdf-schema#Property"/>
        <rdfs:domain rdf:resource="#AlgorithmDescriptor"/>
        <rdfs:comment>Provides a textual description of the algorithm.</rdfs:comment>
    </rdf:Description>
    <rdf:Description rdf:ID="DeveloperDescriptor">
        <rdf:type rdf:resource="http://www.w3.org/2000/01/rdf-schema#Property"/>
        <rdfs:domain rdf:resource="#AlgorithmDescriptor"/>
        <rdfs:comment>Provides a textual description of the entity that has developed the algorithm.</rdfs:comment>
    </rdf:Description>
    <rdf:Description rdf:ID="ImplementationLocation">
        <rdf:type rdf:resource="http://www.w3.org/2000/01/rdf-schema#Property"/>
        <rdfs:domain rdf:resource="#AlgorithmDescriptor"/>
        <rdfs:comment>
    Indicates the network location (codebase) from where the algorithm implementation may be retrieved.
    Example: "http://www.cnl.di.uoa.gr/People/nhoussos/Algorithms/"
        </rdfs:comment>
    </rdf:Description>
    <rdf:Description rdf:ID="TargetResourceInstance">
        <rdf:type rdf:resource="http://www.w3.org/2000/01/rdf-schema#Property"/>
        <rdfs:domain rdf:resource="#AlgorithmDescriptor"/>
        <rdfs:range rdf:resource="http://www.w3.org/2000/01/rdf-schema#Resource"/>
        <rdfs:comment> Indicates the resource instance on which the algorithm will be applied. This property has
meaning only when the algorithm metadata is specified separately from the context requirements metadata.
</rdfs:comment>
    </rdf:Description>
    <!-- Properties specific to ComparatorDescriptor resources. -->
    <rdf:Description rdf:ID="ComparatorType">
        <rdf:type rdf:resource="http://www.w3.org/2000/01/rdf-schema#Property"/>
        <rdfs:domain rdf:resource="#ComparatorDescriptor"/>
        <rdfs:comment>Indicates the type of the Comparator algorithm (Adaptor or Matcher)</rdfs:comment>
    </rdf:Description>
</rdf:RDF>
```

Fig. 4. Algorithm Description RDF Schema

Note that in the above, the alg: prefix refers to the publicly accessible Internet location http://www.cnl.di.uoa.gr/People/nhoussos/Schemata/AlgorithmSchema-20030622#.

As is obvious from the above, the additional property element increases the size of the service profile. However, this additional size should not be a problem, mainly for two reasons:

- Typically a VASP would provide customised algorithms only for a small set of context parameters. The default algorithms (see Section 3.3.2) should suffice for the large majority of cases.
- Service registration as well as the other procedures utilising the service profile are management plane procedures that are not time-critical and do not involve communication over the costly and resource-constrained wireless link to the mobile terminal. Thus, lack of resources is not a principal issue in this case.

3.3.2 Development and Loading of Adaptation Algorithms

Adaptation algorithms, as stated in previous sections, can be developed by VASPs. In this section we elaborate on the framework that enables the easy development and dynamic loading of these algorithms.

Every adaptation procedure includes a phase during which crucial decisions are being made regarding what is the optimal adaptation action that should take place [2]. This procedure is performed based on the comparison of current context parameters and the contextual requirements of the adaptable entity. In the RCSPP this procedure is accomplished by a generic adaptation decision engine [2] that accepts as input two profiles, called the *adaptor* (representing context information) and the *adaptee* (representing the adaptable entity).

All types of profiles in our implementation are represented in a common, internal, object-oriented format, depicted in Fig. 5 [2]. Notably, the adaptee and adaptor profiles are instances of the same class (Profile). Profiles are instances of profile elements and consist of single profile attributes and sub-profiles (this is an application of the Composite design pattern [10]).

The adaptation algorithm is typically encapsulated in an object that implements the Adapter or Matcher interface, is aggregated in a ProfileElement instance and is dynamically loaded. This way, new adaptation algorithms for specific attributes can be introduced without the need to reprogram the code of the ProfileElement classes that represent those attributes (this is an application of the Strategy design pattern [10]).

The RCSPM is able to construct profiles according to the above representation, containing the service information stored in the application database after service registration. Based on the RDF-based algorithm metadata that has been provided by the VASP with the mechanism explained in the previous section, the constructed service profile hierarchies aggregate the appropriate algorithms specified by the VASP. Notably, the adaptation module has a default algorithm per each context parameter, which is used when no customised version is introduced by the VASP.

The implementation of an algorithm in Java (this is the only language supported in our prototype), is quite straightforward. The developer creates a class that implements one of the *Adapter* or *Matcher* interfaces. The algorithm logic typically retrieves the value of certain situational parameters from the context (adaptor) profile and, based on them, reaches a decision according to service-specific criteria. An example of a very simple algorithm regarding matching screen sizes is depicted in Fig. 6.

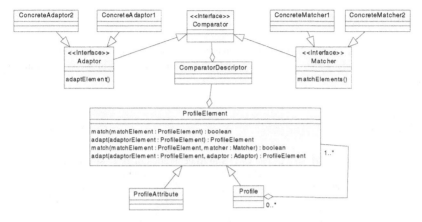

Fig. 5. Generic profile representation.

```
public class ScreenSizeMatcher implements Matcher         {
           public boolean matchElements( ProfileElement element1, ProfileElement element2 )         {
                      boolean returnValue = false;
                      int w1, w2, h1, h2;
                      double ratio1, ratio2;
                      if ( ( element1.getType().equals( "gr.uoa.di.cnl.ScreenSize" ) )
                                  && ( element2.getType().equals( "gr.uoa.di.cnl.ScreenSize" ))   {
                                  w1 = ((Integer) ((ProfileAttribute) element1).getValueAt( 0 )).intValue();
                                  w2 = ((Integer) ((ProfileAttribute) element2).getValueAt( 0 )).intValue();
                                  h1 = ((Integer) ((ProfileAttribute) element1).getValueAt( 1 )).intValue();
                                  h2 = ((Integer) ((ProfileAttribute) element2).getValueAt( 1 )).intValue();
                                  ratio1 = w1/h1;
                                  ratio2 = w2/h2;
                                  if ( ( ratio1 == ratio2  ) && ( w2 < 1.2*w1 ) && ( w2 > 0.8*w1 )
                                                            && ( h2 < 1.2*h1 ) && ( h2 > 0.8*h1 ) )
                                                return true;
                      }
                      return returnValue;
           }
}
```

Fig. 6. Example Matcher implementation.

4 Summary – Conclusions

The significance of adaptation in next generation mobile systems and services is widely recognised. Adaptation capabilities form a principal enabler of ubiquitous, seamless service provision over highly diverse underlying infrastructures. Moreover, third-party VASPs are expected to play an increasingly significant role in the development and delivery of mobile services. The present paper has introduced a scheme for offering third parties advanced capabilities for performing their own adaptations and customisations to the process of the provision of their applications. The proposed scheme exploits knowledge representation and object-orientation techniques to achieve this goal without incurring excessive additional overhead to VASPs.

Acknowledgements

Part of the work included in this paper has been performed in the framework of the project "ANWIRE" (www.anwire.org), which is funded by the European Community under the contract IST-2001-38835.

References

1. UMTS Forum Report No. 9, "The UMTS third generation market - structuring the service revenues opportunities", available from http://www.umts-forum.org/.
2. Houssos, N. et al.: Advanced adaptability and profile management framework for the support of flexible mobile service provision. IEEE Wireless Communication Magazine, Vol. 10, No. 4, August 2003, pp. 52-61.
3. World Wide Web Consortium: RDF/XML Syntax Specification, available from http://www.w3c.org/TR/rdf-syntax-grammar/.
4. Dillinger M., Alonistioti N., Madani K., (Eds.): Software Defined Radio: Architectures, Systems and Functions. John Wiley & Sons, June 2003.
5. Alonistioti N., Houssos N., "The need for network reconfigurability", in [4].
6. Moerdijk A. J., Klostermann L.:Opening the Networks with Parlay/OSA: Standards and Aspects Behind the APIs. IEEE Network, May 2003.
7. Houssos N., Gazis V., Alonistioti A.: Application-Transparent Adaptation in Wireless Systems Beyond 3G. M-Business 2003, Vienna, Austria, 23-24 June 2003.
8. Koutsopoulou M., Kaloxylos A., Alonistioti A.: Charging, Accounting and Billing as a Sophisticated and Reconfigurable Discrete Service for next Generation Mobile Networks. Fall VTC2002, Vancouver, Canada, September 2002.
9. Fouial O., Fadel K. A., Demeure I.: Adaptive Service Provision in Mobile Computing Environments. IEEE MWCN 2002, Stockholm, Sweden, 9-11 September 2002.
10. Gamma E., Helm R., Johnson R., Vlissides J.: Design Patterns: Elements of Reusable Object Oriented Software. Addison Wesley Longman, Inc., 1994.
11. XML: Extensible Markup Language home page, http://www.w3.org/XML/.
12. RDF: Resource Description Framework home page, http://www.w3.org/RDF/.
13. RDF Semantics, http://www.w3.org/TR/rdf-mt/.
14. Butler M., "Barriers to the real world adoption of Semantic Web technologies", HP Technical Report, HPL-2002-333.
15. Extensible Markup Language (XML) 1.0, W3C Recommendation, 6 October 2000.
16. Decker S., et al., "The Semantic Web: the roles of XML and RDF", IEEE Internet Computing, September-October 2000.
17. RDF Model and Syntax Specification, W3C Recommendation, 22 February 1999.
18. Smith C., Butler M., "Validating CC/PP and UAProf Profiles", HP Technical Report, HPL-2002-268.
19. Open Mobile Alliance (OMA): User Agent Profile (UAProf) specification, available from http://www.openmobilealliance.org.

Brenda: Towards a Composition Framework for Non-orthogonal Non-functional Properties

Mikaël Beauvois

France Télécom R&D
Distributed Systems Architecture Department
28 Chemin du Vieux Chêne, BP 98 38243 Meylan, France
mikael.beauvois@rd.francetelecom.com

Abstract. Software infrastructures have to manage distributed and heterogenous entities making them more and more complex. To abstract complexity, the concept of technical services has been introduced, also called non functional properties (functional properties are related to business level) to implement functions related to security, mobility, transactional behaviour, etc. The main challenge is the composition of non functional properties to build these infrastructures.
Our goal is to identify the right abstractions which enable the composition of non functional properties when they are non orthogonal.
In this paper, we analyse how this issue is tackled in AOP (Aspect Oriented Programming) where composition of non functional properties is a composition of aspects. Then, we study a new approach where compositions of non functional properties are compositions of components and automata and show how we have implemented these concepts in a composition framework.

1 Introduction

Composition of non orthogonal non functional properties appears when two or more computations are activated at the same moment and some execution orders between these computations have to be respected.

In this paper, we try to show that the composition of non orthogonal non functional properties must have some formal basis to be resolved [9][4]. Our contribution is an identification of some composition concepts and their implementation in a Java composition framework.

This issue can be found both in industry like execution supports used in application servers (EJB containers [15]), and academic research like Separation of Concerns techniques (e.g. AOP (Aspect Oriented Programming) [10], Composition Filters [5], etc) where non functional properties are defined as *concerns* (*aspects* in AOP, etc). The building process of execution supports used in application servers (such as EJB servers) is a manual composition of technical services, where all these services are statically mixed. The AOP paradigm captures non functional properties as concerns at the design and weaves them in business applications.

J.-B. Stefani, I. Demeure, and D. Hagimont (Eds.): DAIS 2003, LNCS 2893, pp. 29–40, 2003.

We first describe how this issue is tackled in the AOP research domain (section 3). We then present a new approach to resolve the composition of non orthogonal non functional properties (section 4). This approach is based on components architecture enhanced with behavioural composition. It introduces a behaviour model and a component model, both detailed in sections 5 and 6. Finally, we describe the framework, called Brenda, that implements these models. Our approach is illustrated and motivated throughout the paper by an example defined in the next section.

2   Example

In our example, we consider the following non functional properties, that have to be composed:

1. *persistence* is implemented by a *storage manager* which loads compressed data of components and decompresses them before assigning values to business component,
2. *security* is implemented by a *security manager* which checks if authenticated users can execute a business method and logs all operations, and an *encryption manager* which encrypts business component data before sending them over the network.

The above managers are separate components that can be designed and run independently. For example, (1) the storage manager can load data without checking the user-permissions; it doesn't encrypt loaded data; (2) the security manager doesn't load or encrypt any data; (3) the encryption manager encrypts all data of business components without knowing which data are stored. The above managers are structurally independent. This example will be used in what follows.

3   Non-orthogonal Aspects in AOP Paradigm

The non orthogonal composition of non functional properties is addressed in the AOP (Aspect Oriented Programming) paradigm as a composition of non orthogonal aspects when several aspects are defined and activated on the same joinpoint. An execution order between those aspects has to be defined. A joinpoint is the realization of the crosscut on an application target.

The AOP paradigm focused on how to define aspects to apply them in applications, and how to compose them especially when they are not orthogonal. AOP implementations such as AspectJ [2], AspectIX [1], Jac [12], etc are more focused on how to define aspects to apply them in applications than investigating how aspects interact with each other during composition. Some derived concepts like events in EAOP [8] are only introduced to express more sophisticated crosscuts.

3.1   Example in AOP

In the AOP approach, the focus is on the activation of concerns implemented by storage, security and encryption managers: *when* (business method call, field access, etc) and *what* (available manager functions) we have to use. In the example, these concerns are used on all public business methods calls (more precisely before method invocation) of class BusinessObject: they are non orthogonal due to activation on the same joinpoints when they are weaved together. Using the AspectJ tool [2], implementations are:

```
aspect StorageAspect {
    pointcut businessmethodcalls(BusinessObject bo) :
        target(bo) && call(public * * (..));
    before(BusinessObject bo) : businessmethodcalls(bo) {
        if (!bo.isLoaded) load(bo);
    }
...}

aspect SecurityAspect {
    before(BusinessObject bo) : businessmethodcalls(bo) {
        checkPermissions(bo);}
    private void checkPermissions (BusinessObject bo)
        throws SecurityException {
        ...
        log.notify(''Access to object owned by ''
            +bo.getOwner());
    }
...}

aspect EncryptionAspect {
    before(BusinessObject bo) : businessmethodcalls(bo) {
        cryptAndSend(bo);}
...}
```

The weaving process composes these three aspects (StorageAspect, SecurityAspect, EncryptionAspect): a conflict is raised because these three aspects are activated on the same joinpoint. Their executions have to be ordered.

3.2   Drawbacks

The following drawbacks focus on the AOP approach and not on specific implementation details (dynamic addition of aspects, event based AOP, etc).

In the AOP approach, the ordering of aspects on a joinpoint introduced in [2][12] is an interesting idea when very little well-known well-defined aspects are considered, but cannot be generalized. Our work is focused on aspect granularity which is coarse in the AOP approach. In the example, when the security aspect checks execution permissions, it logs the operation made by the business component with some business component data. Thus the data have to be loaded and decompressed before logging and after checking permissions. It appears these aspects cannot be composed together using AOP even if an execution order is defined. This example shows aspects composition is related to the *interweaving of execution sequences*. Defining aspects as crosscut definitions sets limits to the composition capabilities.

Implementing concerns in aspects is not well defined and raises several questions: should a concern be captured by in one or more aspects? Should aspects be implemented first and joinpoints defined afterwards or the converse?, etc. It seems too difficult to implement a complex concern in a single aspect: the aspect implementation is related to aspect crosscut definition.

Aspects are seen at the same level: if a concern is addressed by several aspects, we think all aspects of a same concern have the same importance in the weaving. This leads to a composition like an ordered list of aspects which is a particular case of composition.

In the rest of the paper, we propose solutions to resolve these drawbacks. This work has two main objectives: the first is to give a formal description of the issue of composing non orthogonal aspects in the AOP paradigm, and implement this in a component framework approach. The second is to orientate the AOP research domain towards the composition of aspects, and, more generally, of technical services.

4   Description of Proposal

The goal is to resolve the composition of non orthogonal non functional properties. This issue appears in several domains from techniques of "Separation of Concerns" (AOP, composition filters, etc) to building execution support for application servers such as EJB servers. The solution has to be independent of the many concepts introduced in these domains, but should be generic enough to be integrated in any domain.

Composing concerns is related to interweaving execution sequences. Our solution gives a support to define composition constraints applied to the interweaving of execution sequences when composing non orthogonal concerns. Some computations of concerns are conflictual: in the example, the **log** operation is conflictual with the **decompress** operation, because **log** has to be executed after **decompress**. An operation of a concern is an elementary specification of a computation (a method call like **log** or **decompress**). Our approach focuses on interactions between concerns when they are non orthogonal. These interactions are introduced according to the temporal order relations between conflictual operations.

The result of the composition of concerns is a set of interweavings of the execution sequences of the concerns. Concerns are non orthogonal if there exists one or more execution sequences where the execution order of their conflictual operations is not respected. Composition of non orthogonal concerns consists in defining a set of their execution sequences where the temporal order relations between conflictual operations are respected. The definition of this set cannot be statically processed because of a combinatorial explosion of solutions. Thus, we choose a dynamical processing, i.e., the generation of a scheduler from a scheduling policy (the composition of temporal order relations between conflictual operations).

We deal with execution sequences, so in order to model the behaviour of the concerns, a behavioural description model based on automata is introduced. A component-based approach was chosen because of its aim to define and apply semantics to compose together entities called components. These semantics can be expressed in our approach by scheduling constraints that the conflictual operations have to follow. Concerns, defined as technical services in industrial infrastructures or as aspects in the AOP approach, are defined as *reactive components* in our approach. Thus a concern is a set of reactive components. The temporal order relations are expressed by scheduling constraints that we call composition constraints. They have a particular behavioural semantics expressed using an automaton-based model. Scheduling constraint automata can only react to events coming from changes of the component automata that are impacted by the scheduling constraint. In this model, scheduling constraints are also reactive components, so to apply them to a composition of reactive components represented by a composite, they are added into composite components like any another reactive component.

Non orthogonal concerns are structure independent, but behaviour dependent: they interact according signals initiated by scheduling constraints that define temporal order relations. To sum up, weaving non orthogonal aspects in the AOP approach is, in our approach, a composition process of behaviours of reactive components, including technical components and scheduling constraints. The composition leads to an interweaving of the execution sequences of concerns that respect temporal order relations between conflictual operations.

Our approach resolves AOP drawbacks:

- Granularity: we focus on fine-grained operations and not on coarse-grained concerns;
- Concern implementation is directed by a component approach that comprises abstractions such as composites and explicit bindings that helps designing concerns;
- Concern level: scheduling constraints can be applied to any component: they can be defined either on the root level, or in a composite component.

5   Models

To implement the approach described above, several models must be defined. One must be able to express the behaviour of component, i.e., their possible execution sequences. A model is therefore defined to describe the behaviour of components. The proposed model is an extension of hierarchical FSM (finite state machines).

5.1   Reactive Component Model

At the behavioural level, components are seen as reactive components. These components are reactive because when they receive signals on their interfaces, their automata react to these signals. It means that method calls on a server interface are transformed into two signals: the first is received by the automata describing the component behaviour (method call); the second is emitted by one automaton (method call return).

In the example, the StorageAspect concern which manages compressed data is implemented in our model as two reactive components called StorageComponent which loads data on persistent support and CompressComponent which

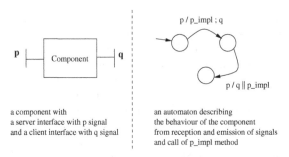

a component with
a server interface with p signal
and a client interface with q signal

an automaton describing
the behaviour of the component
from reception and emission of signals
and call of p_impl method

Fig. 1. A component and its automaton.

compresses or decompresses data. The load signal is defined on the server re-active interface of StorageComponent. The SecurityAspect concern which checks execution permissions is implemented as two reactive components called SecurityComponent, and LogComponent which logs permissions checks.

A scheduling constraint is manipulated like a reactive component. It receives signals that indicate activities on the other automata. It can be added in a composite component (i.e. it is activated), removed (i.e. it is desactivated), composed with another constraint (conjunction, disjunction, negation). In conclusion, in our approach, technical components and scheduling constraints are reactive components.

In the example, two scheduling constraints are introduced: (1) between decompress and log operations defined respectively on automata of StorageComponent and SecurityComponent: log cannot be executed until decompress is done, (2) between checkPermissions and load operations: load cannot be executed until checkPermissions is done.

5.2   Behaviour Description Model

Component. The component behaviour can be described by one or several automata (figure 1). Components communicate with each other using their interfaces. The behaviour of a component is described by the signals that constitute component reactive interfaces and by the component implementation. The elements of the automaton model are states and transitions as illustrated in the following figure; a transition is defined by a signal like p or q (provided by interfaces), a guard (defined from boolean methods of component implementation), and an action (a method call on the component implementation like p_impl, a signal emitted on a client interface like q, a sequence action or a parallel action). A parallel action means there is no execution order between two actions.The automaton model is hierarchical: automata can be defined inside an automaton state.

The more the automaton is detailed, the more the composition can be refined. Composition power is related to the automaton description level. Any reactive component can be described with at least a minimal automaton: with one signal on the single reactive server interface, the component automaton is constitued of one state, one transition with as event the signal defined on its reactive interface and no action.

In the example, the automaton of the StorageComponent component reacts to the load signal and executes in sequence the load operation defined on the implementation, and emits the decompress signal towards the DecompressComponent component through its reactive client interface. The automaton of the SecurityComponent component reacts to the checkPermissions signal and executes in sequence the checkPermissions operation defined on the implementation, and emits the log signal to LogComponent component through its reactive client interface.

Scheduling Constraint. Experiments in defining scheduling constraints in the execution model show us that the constraints can be represented like any another component behaviour. One can thus define them in the same execution language that the one for the component behaviours. The scheduling constraint behaviour model derives from the component behaviour model. In our case, the semantics is based on that of the automaton model.

To schedule the execution of conflictual operations, we are interested in the execution of the actions defined in automaton transitions. The elements are the execution begin and end of the action. The beginning and the end of state are also elements used to express the scheduling of conflictual operations. Those elements are called *automaton element events*. In the automaton, a difference is made between an occurence of an action and a set of actions having the same type.

In the example, the first scheduling constraint (figure 2) between the decompress and log operations can be represented by an automaton with three states and two transitions. The initial state means the decompress operation can be executed. Scheduling constraint automaton moves from initial state to second state when the decompress operation is done (it reacts to the end decompress operation event defined on the transition between initial and second state). The second state means the log operation can be executed. The scheduling constraint automaton moves from second to third state when the log operation is done (it reacts to the end log operation event defined on the transition between second state and third state). The second scheduling constraint follows the same pattern.

end decompress   end log

Fig. 2. First scheduling constraint.

Some conditions can be added into a scheduling constraint. A scheduling constraint can be applied only in certain cases (operations are conflictual in

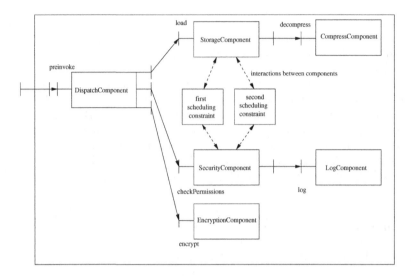

Fig. 3. This figure is the assembly of reactive components introduced in our example. It shows reactive components composition is based on structural composition and results in parallel composition of automata.

some cases only), expressed by a condition. These conditions are expressed either from automaton elements impacted by the scheduling constraint or from boolean methods implemented in scheduling constraint implementation if they cannot be expressed from automaton elements.

6   Composition

This section details the composition process. In our approach, concerns are implemented as reactive components. Thus the concerns composition process is a composition of reactive components. Reactive components behaviours are described by automata. Thus the reactive components composition process is also a composition of automata. We call the composition process the behavioural composition of components. It is based on structural composition of components, i.e., all concepts introduced in structural composition of components (bindings, etc) are present in behavioural composition (figure 3). The automata composition is the parallel composition of the automata describing the behaviours of the components representing the concerns and the scheduling constraints. The interactions between automata are emission and reception of signals defined on the reactive interfaces of components, and events used for synchronization.

At the behaviour level, we believe that adaptability is reached by the capability to modify the behavioural composition process. Composition of concerns is an example of behavioural composition. Adaptability is needed to apply scheduling constraints to the components behaviour.

7 Implementation

This section details the implementation of our proposal: a framework, called Brenda, that implements the concepts introduced in behavioural composition. This framework provides elements to describe components behaviours, to define reactive components, to compose and execute them. The framework design is the best way to introduce and to implement models of our approach. The Brenda framework is an extension of the Fractal framework. The Fractal framework provides a minimal core for components composition. It provides extension mechanisms for any composition type (structural, behavioural, functional) [13].

The behaviour description of a reactive component is given when designing the template of this component. Behavioural composition is based on structural composition as defined in Fractal, so the Brenda framework applies concepts introduced in the Fractal framework (binding, template, composite component, hierarchical model, etc) on behaviour concepts to reach behavioural composition of reactive components.

The Brenda framework architecture is decomposed into two layers: the behaviour layer and an extension of the Fractal specification and of the Julia implementation [7] [3].

Behaviour layer. This layer is dedicated to component behaviour. There is the implementation of automata-based model. Several processes are identified:

1. description: to build automata with automaton elements (state, transitions, actions, etc),
2. generation: to load the behaviour description of a reactive component,
3. composition: to add subcomponents into composite components,
4. binding: to bind signals defined on the interfaces,
5. synchronization: to apply synchronization points on automata impacted by scheduling constraints
6. instantiation: to generate the result of the composition of reactive components.

Each process constructs entities that are elements of behavioural composition: the description process constructs representations of automata, the generation process loads automata, the binding process constructs bindings (signal interactions) between automata, the synchronization process creates and inserts synchronization points which will be used to apply temporal order relations between conflictual operations, the instantiation process constructs the scheduler that is the result of the composition of components and scheduling constraints. The *factory* design pattern is used in each process.

Flexibility points. The framework design provides several *flexibility points*: (1) Factories implementations of the behaviour layer can be changed. For example, new optimized algorithms can be implemented for instantiation process. (2) The behaviour description model can be changed. (3) The execution model can be changed. It has to respect the automata semantics.

8   Instantiation Process and Execution Model

The selected execution model is a reactive synchronous model [14]. The reactive execution model is used for automata reactions when they receive signals. The synchronous execution model allows us to apply synchronization points directly on automata.

Several languages (Esterel [6], Lustre [11], etc) are available, but our instantiation process uses the Esterel language because we focus on runtime performance. Compilation techniques of Esterel language generate a reactive machine that reacts to signals emitted by the environment. The Esterel language provides the parallel operator (parallel composition of automata and parallel action in an automaton transition). The automata composition applied in this model is a synchronous composition of the Esterel automata that result from the conversion of automata of reactive components. This synchronous composition is an automata product. Using the Esterel language restricts framework concepts: no dynamical reconfiguration is available, so no unbinding, no scheduling constraint removal, no reactive component removal (structural reconfiguration implies behavioural reconfiguration), no behavioural reconfiguration can be performed after instantiation. Those restrictions are compromises between runtime performances and dynamical reconfiguration. Scheduling (determining a valid interweaving of execution sequences of concerns) is dynamically processed but the composition is performed statically (i.e., no structural reconfiguration, no behavioural reconfiguration).

The execution model is introduced in the instantiation process. From the behaviour description of components of the composite, this process generates the result of the automata composition which is a global automaton. In a reactive approach, this automaton is implemented inside a reactive machine which reacts to signals defined on reactive interfaces. The instantiation process generates dynamically the code of the reactive component that delimits the synchronous bubble (it emits a signal towards the reactive machine when a method is called, it calls methods defined in the reactive components implementations, etc).

The framework design provides extension mechanisms to apply an instantiation process for any selected execution model.

9   Results

This section presents how composite component composition of concerns can be plugged in an application, and shows execution with interactions between reactive components implementing concerns and scheduling constraints. The framework focuses on component composition. The integration process aims at composing the result of the composition of non orthogonal concerns with the application. The integration process is independent from the composition process. Several ways can be considered for integration process:

- AOP approach : there is a single aspect that is the result of the composition. For example, an aspect can be defined for concerns composition:

```
aspect CompositionAspect {
    private CompositeItf getConcernsCompositionComposite() {...}
    pointcut businessmethodcalls(BusinessObject bo) : target(bo) && call(public * * (..));
    before(BusinessObject bo) : businessmethodcalls(bo) { composite.preInvoke(bo); }
...}
```

The getConcernsCompositionComposite method builds the result of composition
of concerns with scheduling constraints and returns the composite component.

  – Interceptor component: the application is a components configuration. An
    interceptor is a component that reifies the method calls on a business com-
    ponent which it decorates. The interfaces of the interceptor are bound to the
    interfaces of the business component and the interfaces of technical compo-
    nent that is the result of the composition of non orthogonal components.

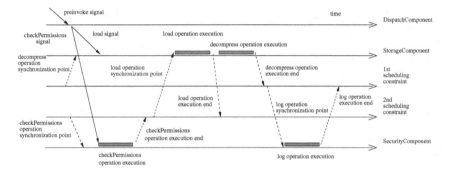

Fig. 4. Interactions between reactive components.

Execution and interactions between reactive components. The figure 4 shows
interactions between reactive components implementing concerns and scheduling constraints. DispatchComponent component emits checkPermissions and load
signals in parallel. The second scheduling constraint automaton emits a synchronization point signal to the automaton of SecurityComponent component
to be able to execute checkPermissions operation. StorageComponent component
automaton is waiting for a synchronization point signal from the second scheduling constraint before executing the load operation. At the end of the execution
of checkPermissions operation, the automaton of SecurityComponent component
emits an event to the second scheduling constraint automaton that moves in a
state where the automaton of StorageComponent component can execute load operation (so it emits a synchronization point signal). The same pattern is applied
with the first scheduling constraint.

10   Conclusion

This paper presents an approach for composing non orthogonal non functional
properties and its Java implementation in the Brenda framework. After detailing the issue of composing non orthogonal concerns, it defines models (behaviour

description and reactive component) and implements them in a framework seen as an increment of Fractal framework. The framework has been implemented and is functional. Our approach provides a way to resolve the composition of non orthogonal concerns by expressing scheduling constraints on component behaviours. The framework generates automatically the results of compositions of non orthogonal concerns, while the AOP approach requires to implement specific weavers for each scheduling constraint.

This work is a combination of several research domains (AOP paradigm, reactive synchronous programming, components architecture and behaviour description modelling). It tries to tackle the well-known but still largely unexplored composition of non orthogonal properties. However, we think progress on those research domains can be directly used to improve our proposal.

We describe an architectural way to express the design of compositions of non orthogonal concerns. We plan to apply these concepts to execution supports in application servers.

Acknowledgements

We'd like to thank Marc Lacoste, Romain Lenglet and Jacques Pulou.

References

1. The AspectIX Project. See http://www.aspectix.org.
2. The AspectJ Project. See http://www.aspectj.org.
3. The Fractal Project. See http://fractal.objectweb.org.
4. J. Andrews. Process-Algebraic Foundations of Aspect-Oriented Programming. In *Proc. REFLECTION'01, LNCS 2192*.
5. L. Bergmans and M. Aksit. Composing Crosscutting Concerns Using Composition Filters. *CACM 44(10)*, 2001.
6. G. Berry and G. Gonthier. The Esterel Synchronous Programming Language: Design, Semantics, Implementation. *Science of Computer Programming*, 19(2):87–152, 1992.
7. E. Bruneton, T. Coupaye, and J.-B. Stefani. Recursive and Dynamic Software Composition Sharing. In *Proc. WCOP'02*.
8. R. Douence, P. Fradet, and M. Südholt. A Framework for the Detection and Resolution of Aspect Interactions. In *Proc.GPCE'02*.
9. R. Douence, P. Fradet, and M. Südholt. Detection and Resolution of Aspect Interactions. Technical report, INRIA, 2002.
10. G. Kiczales et al. Aspect-Oriented Programming. In *Proc. ECOOP'97, LNCS 1241*.
11. P. Caspi et al. LUSTRE: A Declarative Language for Programming Synchronous Systems. In *Proc. POPL'87*.
12. R. Pawlak et al. JAC: A Flexible and Efficient Framework for AOP in Java. In *Proc. REFLECTION'01*.
13. T. Coupaye et al. Composants et composition dans l'architecture des systèmes répartis. *Journées Composants 2001 Besançon*, 2001.
14. N. Halbwachs. Synchronous Programming of Reactive Systems. In *Computer Aided Verification*, pages 1–16, 1998.
15. Sun Microsystems. *Enterprise JavaBeans Specification version 2.1*. 2003.

Meta-programming Middleware
for Distributed Object Computing

Peter Breitling

Technische Universität München, Fakultät für Informatik,
Boltzmannstr. 3, D–85748 Garching, Germany
Peter.Breitling@in.tum.de
http://www11.in.tum.de

Abstract. A multitude of different middleware technologies exist for
distributed object computing (doc). However well-known doc–middleware has practically not established itself in the context of wide–area distributed computing. Prominent examples like CORBA, COM+ or Java/
RMI use quite similar distributed object models, that can be mapped
pairwise with bridges. But they differ in their meta–programming functionality including methods for object generation, distribution, location,
reflection and life–cycle management. A more high–level, abstract model
that encapsulates this functionality and that allows the integration with
existing doc–middleware and web systems can be a central prerequi-
site for emerging a web of objects. This paper introduces the design of a
meta–programming middleware and its mapping to and application with
existing doc– and web–technologies respectively.

1   Introduction

According to [1] meta–programming relates to "programming, where the data
represent programs". Wang et al. [3] examined meta–programming mechanisms
in the CORBA distributed object computing (doc) middleware. This paper
states the term meta–programming in the context of doc as the "adaptability
of distributed applications by allowing their behaviour to be modified without
changing their existing software designs and implementations significantly". The
adaptability of applications has a strong importance for the increasing number
of open systems that are composed of complementary technologies.

In contrast to examining meta–programming mechanisms in existing doc–
middleware we propose an independent middleware layer specifically for meta–
programming. The layer shall provide all means for object– (as data) management and object reconfiguration and adaptation. Common meta–programming
techniques can be defined in this layer and this layer can be built upon different
doc–middleware and web–technologies.

The focus of the independent meta–programming middleware layer for doc
is on the extensible and dynamic object management including:

- *Object life–cycle management:* Common methods for the dynamic creation
  (compiling), registration, deregistration and destruction of distributed objects.

J.-B. Stefani, I. Demeure, and D. Hagimont (Eds.): DAIS 2003, LNCS 2893, pp. 41–48, 2003.

- *Object distribution management:* Object migration and replication between different middleware technologies or platforms.
- *Management events and handlers:* Programmable handlers for observing and reacting onto object life–cycle and distribution management events.
- *Object Reflection:* Reflection mechanisms for object properties including object–type, object–state (e.g. if registered), and –class information dependent of the type (e.g. the object interface) and further extensible meta–data.
- *Object Adaption:* Methods to dynamically create proxy objects for changing an object functionality or for replacing individual objects.
- *Object Reconfiguration:* Manage object references with the ability to reconfigure and dynamically map them to other target objects.

Different doc-middleware technologies in general provide a subset of the described methods and focus on characteristic object distribution and management methodologies[1]. And they apply different methods and semantics for using this functionality. We incorporate the complete life–cycle management into this middleware layer. The layer is capable of generalizing the whole object generation process from the object–source, over the –implementation, up to the distributed instance (service) of the object that can be mapped to different doc–middleware technologies. Thus one result of this work is to provide a common semantic for meta–programming, that can be used independent of the underlying doc–middleware.

Furthermore this middleware proposes a complete isolation of objects that are managed by this middleware. The context of an object includes proprietary access to the underlying doc–middleware, operating system and the network. A complete reconfiguration control over an object requires the ability to intercept every access out of the object to the context. A common example is a simple file access outside an object, which is a common source of problems that prevents the successful reconfiguration and adaptation of an application without changing its implementation. Instead of application specific configuration mechanisms, we propose to fundamentally isolate objects with this middleware layer and introduce the concept of an environment as a single point of access for every type of object. The environment performs the concrete mappings between abstract objects and concrete physical entities on a platform.

To enable these functionalities, especially the life–cycle management and object isolation, the object model itself is refined. We introduce resources that model basic types of objects that can represent programs as data plus the classic object model entities (interface, implementation, instances). The "isolating" environments manage those resources equally. The environments actually provide the meta–programming functionality.

---

[1] These include specific features like object persistency, transactions, caching, etc. but which are not in the part of the meta–programming layer.

2   The Meta-programming Middleware

The independent meta–programming layer provides functions for the reconfiguration and adaptation of objects. A common definition for an object in doc–
middleware "is an identifiable, encapsulated entity that provides one or more services that can be requested by a client" [4]. The question for meta–programming
that treats programs as data and converts data to objects and vice–versa arises:
Is it all about (service) objects? To effectively reconfigure interobject and data
dependencies we raise data and software objects onto the same management
level.

2.1   An Abstract Resource-Layer for Meta-programming

We identified five fundamental resource–classes for the meta–programming layer:
binaries, documents, interfaces, implementations and instances. For these classes
we define common properties that are useful for the management of and meta–
programming on these resources. Figure 1 gives an overview of the properties.

class :	binary	document	interface	implementation	instance
type :	mime-type	doc-type	doc-type	interface	interface
state :	a subset of [serializable | registered | persistent]				
name :	if registered , an identifying name that is unique in the registry for the same type				
attributes :	type specific [life-] attributes which are managed by value to the resource.				

Fig. 1. Resources and their properties

For every resource class we use a specific type system[2]. Every resource has
a state, which expresses the capabilities with respect to management of an object. If a resource is registered it can have a name, which acts as an identifier
local to the registry. Further attributes can be assigned to a resource as simple
name / value pairs to store informating along with the object[3].

The binary resource encapsulates any unstructured block of data. In general
it is mapped to files or binary streams. For the content–type and subtype information on binary resources we use the MIME media type system. Any other
meta–information on the type of a binary resource could be used here, however
this system is well–known and established in the context of wide–area internet
computing. In this system binary resources can always be serialized and the

---

[2] We decided to use well–known type systems that are established in the wide–area
internet computing.

[3] The attributes remain persistent during the objects life–time. Some attributes can be
live–attributes, which are read–only and managed by the system (e.g. the content–
length of a resource).

result of a resource serialization from any other resource class results in this (unregistered) binary resource class.

The document meta–object represents structured data. The eXtensible Markup Language (XML) as the state–of–the–art representation for structured documents is applied in the prototype. But any other syntax for structured data could be applied here. XML provides an analogous classification for documents like interfaces for objects. A document meta–object can have a reference to a document–type definition (in form of a DTD or XML–Schema). In this system a document can always be serialized

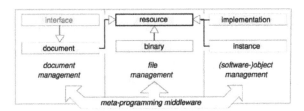

Fig. 2. Resource classes and relations

The interface of an object is a central entity in doc. In this meta–programming middleware it is important for the management and adaptation of objects and for providing reflection mechanisms.

Common RPC systems, such as the Distributed Computing Environment (DCE), and in distributed object environments, such as CORBA define an interface definition languages (IDL) as a standard set of primitive types, method signatures and object interfaces that are mapped to existing languages. We apply the same approach for interfaces in this middleware. However in the extended object model we model interfaces as document resources. In fact interfaces can be managed like documents with structured data containing meta–data for objects. Accordingly the interface resource is subclassed of the document resource. Given the importance of interfaces it is listed among the fundamental resource classes here and presented as a fundamental object. However interfaces are managed and can be accessed as documents in this middleware.

The extended model refines an object into two distinct resource classes, the object implementation and the object instance. The implementation resource is mapped to specific implementations in the underlying doc–middleware. In Java this is represented by the class object, which can be distributed seperately. CORBA in contrast does not allow the explicit distribution management of implementations[4]. The classification for implementations are references to an interface resource which defines the interface for the object–implementation. Dependent of the doc–middleware and platform implementation resources can be

---

[4] this matches the "object as service" view in CORBA.

serialized. This is required for implementation replication, which can be modelled with the serialization and distribution of implementation resources here.

The instance resource class represents an instantiated object. E.g. CORBA distributed objects are mapped to instance objects. The term object is commonly used for instances. We avoid the term "objects" to refer to resources of class instance here to avoid a confusion with that generic name. An Instance resource in general is represented directly by language objects. In this framework it the base class for deriving reconfigurable application objects. An instance object has a reference to the implementation object. Dependent of the doc–middleware and platform implementation resources can be serialized. This is required for object migration, which can be modelled with the serialization and distribution of instance resources here. Figure 2 gives an overview of all resource classes and their relations.

2.2   The Meta-programming Environment

While the resources are mapped to existing entities and provide a common concept across different technologies, the meta–programming environment is the functional part that has to be implemented for every doc–middleware. The environment is the middle–tier between the resources and physical entities. The connector can be viewed from three functional perspectives:

- *Provide a framework for meta–programming:* Map the abstract resources to the platform and language. Subclassing the resources can create new distributed objects. It implements the meta–programming interfaces.
- *Allow arbitrary configuration of the resource mapping:* The mapping of references to resources and physical entities is transparent to the objects. Dependent of the configuration the mapping could be performed locally or be delegated to other environments. The environment can provide a specific user interface for its configuration.
- *Be connected to other environments / services:* Environments can be interconnected or map the access for specific resource classes to other web–systems. Inter–environment connection architectures can range from hierarchical to peer–to–peer approaches. Existing web–services can be mapped into the environment for specific resources (like a web–server as a binary registry or a XML–database as a document registry and access backend).

The mapping of resources and the interconnection to other environments and services are dependent of the concrete implementation of the environment. These parts are transparent to an object, which requests other resources with the framework. The meta–programming framework itself is specified homogeneously across platforms: The abstract resources act as base classes for extending with application specific, adaptable and reconfigurable objects and the application programming interface (API) provides standards functions for meta–programming.

The meta–programming API consists of six interfaces that are be mapped and implemented on top of the underlying doc–middleware and the platform. In the following sections we describe the functionality and task of each interface.

resource–registry: An environment provides a registry where resources in the environment can be registered. Every doc–middleware has a kind of a registry where objects can be dynamically inserted. In COM+ components are registered in the Windows–Registry, while in CORBA objects are registered in the implementation repository. In this abstract middleware we register and deregister resources to and from the resource registry of the environment. Resources are registered with an arbitrary name and their class. The name must be unique in the registry for that resource class. The registry can be mapped to different technologies for each resource class. E.g. the interface or implementation registry can be mapped to the CORBA interface or implementation repository respectively. Or the binary and document registry can be simply mapped to a local file system or a Web–server. Document resources could be ideally mapped to XML databases. With this approach we can map different technologies into the same semantic concepts. The prototype description will show some concrete examples.

reference–resolve: any registered resources can be located with the resource–resolver. The resolver function takes a class, a name and optionally a type and returns a resolved reference if it can locate a corresponding resource. The reference itself is a placeholder for a resource. A reference can have one of three states: unresolved, resolved and mapped. The programmer in general only works with resolved references and maps it to resources. However a reference could be constructed manually. The namespace of a reference is not specified. An Uniform Resource Locator (URL) could be an example representation for a reference that is unresolved. This is dependent of the resolver implementation.

reference–map: The mapping of a reference results in an accessible resource. It is completely transparent to the program if the resource is actually on a remote platform or was migrated or replicated into the local environment.

resource–cast: The casting functionality is the foundation for a complete life–cycle control including the generation of objects starting with code compilation. A binary resource can then be casted to documents, implementations or instances. The serialization operation is the inverse–function to the cast–operation. It results into a binary resource.

registry–events: The registration and deregistration of resources in the registry is observed with an event handler. Every resource class can be individually monitored[5].

resource–factory: Beside of resolving existing resources, new resources can be created with this interface. A typical metaprogramming task would be to create a binary or document resource source code (e.g. a script), cast it to an implementation resource and register it in the environment.

---

[5] modern file systems offer the concept of file system–events to monitor a path for file creation or deletion. This can be well matched with the event–handler for a binary resource registry.

3   MetaDOC: The Java Prototype

An implementation of this middleware requires solutions for each of the three main functional parts of the environment: Provide a meta–programming framework API for the programming language, offer configuration mechanisms for the resource mapping and provide an interconnection layer to other environments or web–systems.

MetaDOC [2] is a first implementation of this meta–programming middleware. For the prototype we chose Java. The language provides reflection capabilities, it can dynamically create and load objects and the CORBA technology is an integral part of the Java 2 platform. It contains an ORB–implementation and API's for the RMI and IDL programming model respectively. Figure 3 gives an overview of the supported protocols (and technologies) in the prototype.

	binary	document	implementation	instance
IN (as server)	WebDAV	IIOP (Xindice)	WebDAV	IIOP / RMI
OUT (as client)	HTTP	HTTP	HTTP	IIOP / RMI
INTERNAL REG.	Filesystem	Xindice	Filesystem	JNDI

Fig. 3. MetaDOC–prototype: Supported resource access protocols

The MetaDOC prototype can be used with existing or new Java applications as:

- *a reconfigurable an integrated data and object access layer:* Binary and Documents can be accessed without committing to a protocol or technology (except this middleware) in an application object. This also applies to remotely accessing distributed objects. Abstract names can be chosen to identify resources. These names can be centrally configured with the environment to concrete resources that reside local or in the web or to dedicated ORB and RMI servers in case of remote object access.
- *a remote Java/CORBA object access layer:* As an alternative to directly programming RMI or CORBA IDL files you can use the framework and inherit dedicated objects from the instance base class. These objects can be registered in the environment. No commitment to one of these technologies is needed.
- *a high–level meta–programming:* In Java all meta–programming and reflection mechanisms that are described could be realized proprietarily by the application itself (in fact the prototype is built purely in Java). With this middleware however an application can access this functionality with high–level functions. Specific Java issues regarding the compiler, the classloader and reflection functions are hidden. Secondly we can meta–program remote objects (that exist on another platform) transparently with the same mechanisms.

4   Conclusions and Outlook

To our knowledge, the design of a flexible model that integrates the file–, document– and object–management in one layer for meta–programming is a new approach. The focus of the system is to provide a homogenous concept for meta–programming using the abstract resource–layer and common operations on that model. The middleware is related to and influenced by a multitude of technologies from different research areas including reflective middleware, system management, web–systems and common meta–programming mechanisms in existing doc–middleware.

This is an open system – it can be built on a number of languages and integrate different technologies. The system specifies only the environment framework API and the basic resource model. All other parts including environment implementation details, configuration methods, resolve strategies, supported protocols and environment interconnections are not fixed. This is in the sense of meta–programming. All those parts remain adaptable and reconfigurable.

Wang et al. [3] evaluated three meta–programming approaches in CORBA: pluggable protocols, smart proxies and interceptors. Here we can extend the list by pluggable technologies (with the open system approach), reconfigurable resource resolving (resource–resolve and –map) and methods for the object generation and life–cycle control (resource–casting).

The netscape cofounder Marc Andreesen stated in the year 1996, that the "HTTP protocol will be replaced by the IIOP protocol in just a few years". Behind that statement is the vision of a worldwide web of objects where applications can be dynamically composed of existing, reusable components.

No single doc–middleware will probably ever replace all existing and forthcoming (problem oriented) protocols with a new universal protocol. In this middleware we don't specify new protocols or doc–capabilities. We just provide one semantic umbrella where various web– and doc–technologies can be assembled. This can be a small step towards a more interoperable and visible web–of–objects.

References

1. J. Barklund. Metaprogramming in logic. In A. Kent and J. Williams, Encyclopedia of Computer Science and Technology., 1994.
2. P. Breitling. Metadoc homepage. http://www.metadoc.org/.
3. D. Schmidt N. Wang, K. Parameswaran and O. Othman. Evaluating metaprogramming mechanisms for orb middleware. In *IEEE Communication Magazine, special issue on Evolving Communications Software*, volume 39, 2001.
4. OMG. The comon object request broker: Architecture and specification. Technical Report PTC/96-03-04, Object Management Group, 1996. Version 2.0.

Middleware Support
for Resource-Constrained Software Deployment

Nicolas Le Sommer and Frédéric Guidec

VALORIA laboratory
University of South Brittany, France
{Nicolas.Le-Sommer,Frederic.Guidec}@univ-ubs.fr

Abstract. The JAMUS platform is dedicated to providing a safe runtime environment for untrusted Java application programs, while offering each of these programs access to the resources it needs to use at runtime. To achieve this goal, JAMUS implements a contractual approach of resource utilisation and control, together with a reservation-based resource management scheme, and a monitoring model. When getting deployed on the platform, a candidate program must first subscribe a contract with the resource manager of the platform. This contract describes the resources the program requires to be able to access at runtime, and how it plans to behave when accessing these resources. Based on this information, the platform can monitor programs at runtime, so that any violation of the contracts they subscribed can be detected and sanctioned. Moreover, since the specific needs of a program are liable to change (or to be refined) dynamically while this program is running, any program hosted by the platform can ask that its contract be re-negotiated at any time.

1 Introduction

The growing popularity of mobile and network-dependent Java application programs leads to an increased demand for deployment platforms that permit to launch and run potentially dangerous Java application programs (such as programs downloaded from untrusted remote Internet sites) in a restrained environment.

Sun Microsystem's platform *Java Web Start* was designed in order to meet this demand. Yet, because this platform relies on the security model of the standard *Java Runtime Environment* (JRE) platform, it shows a number of limitations. For example, security in *Java Web Start* can only be obtained by restraining the access to a strictly pre-defined set of system resource types (namely, network sockets and files). Moreover, security is based solely on access permissions. In our opinion, this approach does not permit sufficient control over the behaviour of application programs.

With JAMUS *(Java Accommodation of Mobile Untrusted Software)* we give some solution to the above-mentioned. Resource access control in JAMUS can be applied to a larger (and easily extensible) variety of resource types (including the CPU and memory), and this control can be performed at a finer grain (for

J.-B. Stefani, I. Demeure, and D. Hagimont (Eds.): DAIS 2003, LNCS 2893, pp. 49–60, 2003.

example, restrictions can be imposed of the amount of CPU time or memory consumed by each Java thread).

JAMUS implements a contractual approach of resource management and access control. Application programs are expected to evaluate and specify their own needs regarding the resources they wish to use at runtime. Based on this information, the platform can decide whether a candidate program should be accepted or rejected. Moreover, when a program has been accepted for running on the platform, its behaviour is monitored, so that any violation of the contract it subscribed with the platform can be readily detected and dealt with.

It is worth mentioning that JAMUS is not exclusively dedicated to enforcing a security policy. It also strives to meet the specific requirements of each of these programs. To achieve this goal the platform implements a resource-reservation scheme. Whenever a program subscribes a contract with the platform, resources are actually reserved for this program from the platform's viewpoint.

The remainder of this paper is organised as follows. Related work is presented in Section 2, which also discusses some of the limitations we observed in other security-oriented projects and middleware platforms. Section 3 presents the general architecture of the JAMUS platform. Section 4 focuses on resource contracting. It shows how contracts can be defined by application programs, and subscribed with the platform. It also shows how the information contained in contracts is used by a resource broker, which implements a reservation scheme in order to satisfy the programs' requirements. Section 5 shows how JAMUS was implemented on top of RAJE *(Resource-Aware Java Environment)*, an object-oriented framework we designed, and which provides many facilities for resource monitoring and control in Java. Section 7 concludes this paper, enumerating some of the topics we plan to address in the near future.

2   Lessons Learned from Related Work

Security in the Java Runtime Environment (JRE) relies on the so-called "sandbox" model. With this model, any program runs in a restrained environment, whose boundaries somehow define the evolution space of this program. In the first versions of the standard JRE (as proposed by *Sun Microsystems*), two alternative configurations were defined. On the one hand, plain Java applications were considered as safe code, and were therefore granted full access to system resources (such as network sockets and files). On the other hand, Java applets (ie code downloaded from remote Internet sites) were considered as potentially malicious pieces of code, and were only granted access to a strictly limited subset of resources [6]. With later releases of the Java platform (up to the current Java 2 platform), this simplistic security model was extended in order to implement the concept of protection domain [7,6]. A protection domain is a runtime environment whose security policy can be specified as a set of permissions.

The security model implemented in the traditional JRE relies on stateless mechanisms. A major limitation of this approach is that access to a specific resource cannot be conditioned by whether the same resource was accessed previously, or by how much of this resource has already been consumed. As a consequence, quantitative restrictions (such as shares of CPU time, or I/O quotas) cannot be set on the resources accessed from protection domains. With this limitation, the security mechanisms implemented in the JRE cannot prevent an over-consumption of resources, such as that observed in denial of service attacks, or with many faulty program codes.

In our opinion, a safe deployment environment for programs of dubious origin should allow that access restrictions be specified in both qualitative and quantitative terms (ie access permissions and access quotas). Environments such as JRes [4], GVM [2] and KaffeOS [1] extend the traditional JRE along this line. They implement mechanisms that make it possible to evaluate how much memory and CPU time is used by an active entity (a thread for JRes, a process for GVM and KaffeOS). With JRes, one can additionally count the number of bytes sent and received through the network.

Although JRes, GVM, and KaffeOS provide advanced facilities for resource consumption accounting, this accounting is only possible at a rather coarse grain. For example, network access accounting in JRes is performed on a per thread basis. Consequently, JRes cannot count the number of bytes exchanged with a given remote host, or with a specific remote port number. Yet, we consider that such fine-grain accounting would be an advantage when deploying untrusted programs, as it would permit the definition and the enforcement of very precise security policies.

Naccio [5] and Ariel [9] are projects that permit such fine-grain resource access accounting. They both define a language for defining a security policy, together with mechanisms for enforcing this policy while an application program is running. Security policy enforcement is carried out statically, by rewriting the application program byte-code, as well as that of the standard Java API. An advantage of this approach is that the cost of the supervision of a program is kept at a minimum since code segments that check the access to a particular kind of resource are inserted in Java API classes only if the selected security policy requires it. However, the generation of an API dedicated to a specific security policy is a quite expensive procedure. The approach proposed in Naccio and Ariel is thus mostly dedicated to the generation of predefined Java APIs that each enforce a generic security policy.

In contrast, our work aims at providing each application program with a runtime environment that fits its needs perfectly. In other words, we wish to launch each program in a sandbox whose boundaries are defined based on information provided by the program itself. Moreover, it must be possible to modify the boundaries of this sandbox dynamically, thus altering the restrictions imposed on the program's behaviour. This condition is motivated by the observation that, in some circumstances, the exact needs of a program can hardly be defined statically (consider for example a program that is meant to read a file whose name will only be discovered at runtime). Another reason is that the needs of a pro-

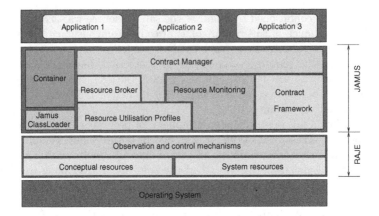

Fig. 1. Architecture of the JAMUS platform.

gram are often liable to change at runtime, especially if this program must run for a long time.

3   Overview of the JAMUS Platform

The architecture of the JAMUS platform is shown in Figure 1. This figure shows many elements, which cannot all be described in details in this paper for the sake of brevity. Indeed, this paper most specifically focuses on those elements of the figure that directly pertain to contract negotiation and contract monitoring. These topics are discussed further in the remainder of this section, and details about their implementation are given in the next sections.

3.1   A Contract-Based Approach of Resource Control

JAMUS implements a contractual approach of resource utilisation and control. Before getting launched on the platform, a candidate program must first subscribe a contract with the contract manager of the platform, thus informing this manager about the resources it plans to use at runtime. The contract manager is responsible for binding contracts with candidate programs, and for the registration of all running contracts. It itself relies on a resource broker, whose role is to keep track of the resources available on the platform at any time, to perform some admission control on behalf of the contract manager (*eg* examining submitted contracts and deciding if they can be accepted), and to reserve resources for admitted programs. The implementation of the contract manager and that of the resource broker are detailed in Section 4, which also gives examples of typical interactions between these elements at runtime.

Since the exact needs of a program are liable to change at runtime, any program running on the platform can ask that its contract be re-negotiated as and when needed. Of course, in such a case the contract manager and resource broker are involved again, as they must decide if the modified contract can still be supported by the platform.

3.2   Security through Contract Monitoring

The contract a program subscribes with the platform effectively defines the boundaries of the sandbox in which this program should be launched and allowed to run. It also implicitly defines how this program should be expected to behave with respect to the resources offered by the platform. The information contained in a program's contract can thus be used at runtime to monitor this program, and to detect any violation of its contract.

Notice that contract monitoring would not be necessary if the programs deployed on the JAMUS platform could all be considered as trustworthy. If that was the case, then any program could reasonably be expected to behave exactly as promised, that is, to access only those resources it required explicitly when subscribing a contract with the platform. However, JAMUS is dedicated to accommodating application programs of dubious origin, such as programs downloaded from untrustable remote Internet sites. Consequently, any application program deployed on the platform must be considered as a potential threat throughout its execution. Once a program has been accepted by the contract manager of the platform, the behaviour of this program must be monitored, so that any violation of its contract can be detected and sanctioned.

Contract monitoring in JAMUS relies on facilities we implemented and assembled in RAJE *(Resource-Aware Java Environment)*, an open and extensible Java-based framework for resource consumption monitoring and control. RAJE is discussed further in Section 5.

4   Resource Contracting

4.1   Specification of Resource Access Conditions

JAMUS implements an object model that makes it possible to reify a program's basic requirements or a platform's restrictions as so-called "resource utilisation profiles". In this model, an instance of class *ResourceUtilisationProfile* is meant to define specific access conditions to a particular resource –or collection of resources– in both qualitative and quantitative terms (eg access permissions and quotas). Basically, a *ResourceUtilisationProfile* object simply aggregates three objects that implement the *ResourcePattern, ResourcePermission,* and *Resource-Quota* interfaces respectively. JAMUS provides specific implementations of these interfaces for each basic resource type (Socket, DatagramSocket, File, Thread, CPU, etc.).

Figure 2 shows how resource utilisation profiles can be defined in Java. By including a given type of *ResourcePattern* in a *ResourceUtilisationProfile,* one indicates that the access conditions defined in this profile are only relevant for

```
int MB = 1024*1024;
ResourceUtilisationProfile P1, P2, P3,;
P1 = new ResourceUtilisationProfile(
             new SocketPattern("http://www.music.com"),
             new SocketPermission(SocketPermission.ALL),
             new SocketQuota(15*MB, 1*MB));
P2 = new ResourceUtilisationProfile(
             new FilePattern("/opt/music"),
             new FilePermission(FilePermission.WRITE_ONLY),
             new FileQuota(0, 40*MB));
P3 = new ResourceUtilisationProfile
             new MemoryPattern(),
             new MemoryPermission(MemoryPermission.ALL),
             new MemoryQuota(2*MB));
```

Fig. 2. Definition of resource utilisation profiles.

those resources whose characteristics match the pattern. For example, the *SocketPattern* in profile *P1* (see Figure 2) indicates that this profile defines conditions for accessing the specified Internet site through a socket-based connection. The *SocketPermission* and *SocketQuota* objects combined in profile *P1* bring additional information: they indicate that once a connection has been established with the remote site, the amounts of bytes sent and received through this connection should remain below the limits specified. The other two profiles similarly specify conditions for accessing a given directory in the filesystem (*P2*), and for consuming memory (*P3*).

By defining profiles such as those shown in Figure 2, an application program can specify its own requirements regarding the resources it plans to use at runtime. For example, by inserting profiles *P1*, *P2* and *P3* in a contract, a program may simultaneously require access to a remote Internet site (with specific access permissions and quotas) and to a given part of the filesystem (again with specific access permissions and quotas), while requiring a certain amount of memory for its sole usage.

Besides serving as a way to describe application programs' requirements, resource utilisation profiles are also used in JAMUS to set limitations on the resources the platform must offer. At startup the resource broker of the platform is given a collection of resource utilisation profiles, that describe which resources should be made available to hosted programs, and in what conditions.

Since JAMUS must be able to negotiate contracts dynamically with Java application programs, we decided that contracts and resource utilisation profiles (which actually serve as contract clauses) should be considered as first-class objects in our model (as suggested in [3]). This is the reason why JAMUS relies on an object model in which contracts and profiles can be defined and managed directly as Java objects. Yet, we also defined an XML dialect for specifying profiles in a more human-readable form, and for storing this kind of information in files. JAMUS implements routines for parsing an XML file, and for instantiating

```
Contract contract1 = new Contract ({P1, P2}, {P3});
Contract contract2 = new Contract ({P1}, {P2, P3});
```

Fig. 3. Definition of two possible contracts that each combine several resource utilisation profiles.

profiles contracts based on the information found in this file. The administrator of a JAMUS platform can thus configure and manage this platform, without ever writing any source code.

4.2   Contract Definition

Any resource utilisation profile defined by a program can be considered as expressing either a *real requirement* of the program (meaning, the program actually requests guarantees about the accessibility of the resource considered in the profile), or as a simple *indication* that the program *may* attempt to access the resource considered at runtime (meaning, the program simply provides information about the boundaries of the sandbox in which it wishes to be launched).

Since the resource broker of the platform implements a reservation scheme, we decided to distinguish between a program's true requirements (those that call for both resource reservation and access monitoring), and simple indications of the program's planned behaviour (that call for monitoring only).

Contracts in JAMUS are thus defined as collections of resource utilisation profiles, but these profiles are assembled in two distinct sets. Profiles in the first set call explicitly for resource reservation, whereas profiles in the second set do not.

Figure 3 shows the definition of two alternative contracts, that each combine several profiles. The first contract in this figure combines profiles *P1, P2* and *P3*, but only the first two profiles should be considered as real requirements (meaning, they call for resource reservation, whereas *P3* does not). The second contract combines profiles *P1, P4,* and *P5*, but only *P1* calls for resource reservation.

A candidate program can thus instantiate one or several alternative *Contract* objects, and submit these contracts to the platform. If one of the contracts is declared admissible by the resource broker, then this contract can be subscribed by the program. If several of the contracts are declared admissible by the resource broker, then the application program can additionally choose which of these contracts it wishes to subscribe.

4.3   Contract Negotiation

Contract negotiation in JAMUS is performed as a two-step process. In the first step, several alternative contracts can be submitted to the platform by the same program. In the second step, one of the contracts the platform has approved (assuming there is at least one) must be selected by the program, and subscribed with the platform. Each contract is examined by the resource broker, whose role it is to decide whether a contract is acceptable or not, and to reserve resources when needed. Resource reservation is only achieved (if and where needed) by the resource broker when a contract is subscribed by a program. By reserving resources (or shares of a resource) a program obtains guarantees that its requirements will be satisfied at runtime.

Figure 4 shows a possible sequence of interactions between a program and the platform's contract manager. It also shows that the resource broker is consulted whenever the contract manager receives a contract submitted by the program. In this example the first contract submitted by the program is rejected by the platform. Such a negative reply might be justified by the detection of a conflict between one of the program's requirement and one (or several) of the platform's restrictions. Notice that whenever a contract is rejected by the resource broker, the candidate program is returned a detailed report that specifies which profiles in the contract could not be accepted by the platform. This kind of information is expected to be useful for candidate programs that are capable of choosing between several behavioural scenarios, or for programs that can adjust their demand about resources based on information returned by the platform.

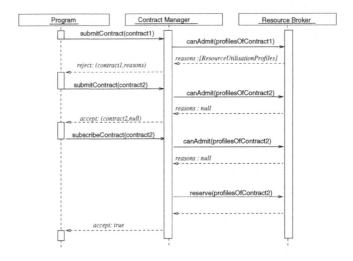

Fig. 4. Sequence of interactions between a candidate program and the platform's contract manager and resource broker.

In Figure 4 the second contract submitted to the platform is accepted by the resource broker. The candidate program can try to subscribe this contract. However, since the platform may be carrying out several negotiations concurrently with as many candidate programs, the status of available resources may change between the time a submitted contract is declared acceptable by the resource broker, and the time this contract is subscribed. Consequently, whenever a program subscribes a contract, the terms of this contract are examined again by the resource broker in order to check whether they are still valid. If so, then the resources required by the candidate program are reserved for this program, as explained in the next section.

The reason why contract submission and contract subscription have been differentiated in the JAMUS platform is that it makes it possible for a candidate program to request that the platform examine several possible contracts (corresponding to different alternative combinations of resource requirements), before the program eventually decides which of these contracts it actually wishes to subscribe with the platform. This approach is meant to foster the development of application programs that can adjust their behaviour (at launch time or dynamically), depending on the resources the platform can offer.

5   Contract Monitoring

5.1   Security through Resource Monitoring

As mentioned in Section 3, any program hosted by the JAMUS platform is considered as not being trustworthy. As a consequence, the platform must monitor all running contracts in order to detect and to sanction any violation of a contract. Since contracts all pertain to the utilisation of resources, monitoring contracts actually comes down to monitoring the way resources are accessed and used by hosted programs.

JAMUS is dedicated to hosting Java programs, which run in a virtual machine. In this context, resource monitoring implies that all resources are reified as objects in the JVM. To achieve this goal, JAMUS relies on the facilities offered by RAJE, an open and extensible framework we designed in order to support the reification and the control of any kind of resource using objects in Java (see Figure 1).

RAJE can be perceived as an extension of the traditional runtime environment of the Java 2 platform. It relies on a modified version of the standard JVM Kaffe (version 1.0.7), which allows the accounting of memory consumption and CPU time consumed by each Java thread. Some classes of the standard Java API (such as *Socket*, *DatagramSocket*, *File*, and *Thread*) were augmented so that any access to the resources they model can be monitored at runtime. New classes were defined in order to model system resources, such as the CPU, system memory, and system swap. Part of the code implemented in RAJE thus consists of native code that permits the extraction of information from the underlying OS, and the interaction with inner parts of the JVM.

More details about the facilities implemented in RAJE (including implementation details) can be found in [8].

By implementing JAMUS on top of RAJE, resource monitoring and control can be performed in JAMUS at a very fine grain. For example any socket or file opened by a Java program can be considered as a specific resource, and any access to such a resource can be accounted for, and restrained if needed. Any Java thread can likewise be considered as a specific resource, and the amounts

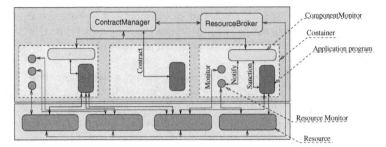

Fig. 5. Monitoring of applications.

of CPU time or memory space consumed by each Java thread can be monitored as well. RAJE also makes it possible to set locks on resources, thus preventing any further utilisation of these resources by application programs.

5.2   Component Monitors and Resource Monitors

Every application program hosted by the JAMUS platform runs under the control of a dedicated component monitor. This monitor uses the resource utilisation profiles contained in the contract subscribed by the program in order to instantiate many resource monitors. Their mission is to monitor the utilisation of the resource –or collection of resources– considered in this profile, and to ensure that this utilisation conforms to the access permissions and quotas defined in the profile.

JAMUS provides a specific implementation of a resource monitor for each basic resource type considered to date in RAJE. Each resource monitor admits a resource utilisation profile as a creation parameter. The role of a resource monitor is to supervise the utilisation of the resource –or collection of resources– considered in this profile, and to ensure that this utilisation conforms to the access permissions and quotas defined in the profile.

The figure 5 shows how the resource monitors, the component monitors, the contract manager and the resource broker interact.

When a resource monitor detects a contract violation, it reports to the component monitor, which in turn applies the sanction defined in the platform's configuration. In the current implementation of the platform, several kinds of sanctions are actually applicable to faulty programs. These sanctions range from a simple warning addressed to a faulty program (using an event based model), up to the immediate termination of this program.

6   Performance Results

When designing a deployment platform such as JAMUS, one can legitimately worry about the overhead imposed by dynamic sandboxing and contract monitoring.

Table 1. Performances observed with an FTP server running either in a standard JVM or in JAMUS (with a varying number of monitors).

JVM	Throughput (Mbps)	
Kaffe (version 1.0.7)	89.5	*(100 %)*
IBM JVM (version 1.4.1)	89.3	*(99.8 %)*
JAMUS (no monitor)	88.9	*(99.3 %)*
JAMUS (2 monitors)	86.3	*(96.4 %)*
JAMUS (3 monitors)	84.6	*(94.5 %)*
JAMUS (5 monitors)	81.9	*(91.5 %)*

In order to evaluate how these mechanisms can impact on the performances of the application programs launched on the platform, we recently initiated an evaluation process. This process consists in running a series of demanding programs (that is, programs that use resources extensively), while measuring their performances in different conditions.

For example we launched an FTP server (written in pure Java code) in JAMUS, and we measured the network throughput observed while downloading large files from this server. This experiment was conducted using two workstations (2.4 GHz Pentium 4 processor, 512 MB RAM) connected by a Fast Ethernet link (100 Mbps, Full Duplex). The throughput observed during file transfers was measured when running the FTP server with two standard JVMs (IBM's and Kaffe), and with JAMUS (which relies on a modified version of Kaffe). Moreover, in the latter case the FTP server was launched with a varying number of requirements, so that at runtime its behaviour was observed by a varying number of resource monitors (typically one monitor for filesystem access, and one or several monitors for network access).

The throughputs we observed are reported in Table 1. In this table the throughput observed with the standard JVM Kaffe is used as a reference value.

We consider that these results are quite satisfactory. Obviously the monitoring infrastructure implemented in JAMUS significantly alters the performances of the application programs launched in this platform. Yet, in our opinion the degradation of performances observed while running the FTP server (which is a quite demanding program as far as filesystem and network resources are concerned) remain acceptable.

Besides, it is worth mentioning that the source code pertaining to resource consumption accounting in RAJE, and to contract monitoring in JAMUS, was primarily developed so as to be readable and flexible. Parts of this code could probably be written differently, though, in order to reduce the overhead imposed on the programs launched on the JAMUS platform.

7   Conclusion

In this paper we have presented the architecture and the implementation of the JAMUS platform, which is dedicated to hosting untrusted Java application programs, provided that these programs can specify their own needs regarding the resources they plan to use at runtime.

JAMUS actually constitutes a demonstrator platform, with which we experiment with the idea of "resource-aware" programs and deployment platforms, that is, programs that can identify and specify their own needs regarding resource utilisation, and platforms that can use this kind of information in order to provide such programs with differentiated services. Although JAMUS is specifically dedicated to hosting non-trustable application programs, it is our conviction that many other application domains and systems (such as agent-based systems, or adaptive systems) could benefit of —or take inspiration from— the models and mechanisms we develop in this particular context.

References

1. Godmar Back, Wilson C. Hsieh, and Jay Lepreau. Processes in KaffeOS: Isolation, Resource Management, and Sharing in Java. In *The 4th Symposium on Operating Systems Design and Implementation*, October 2000.
2. Godmar Back, Patrick Tullmann, Legh Stoller, Wilson C. Hsieh, and Jay Lepreau. Techniques for the Design of Java Operating Systems. In *USENIX Annual Technical Conference*, June 2000.
3. Antoine Beugnard, Jean-Marc Jézéquel, Nol Plouzeau, and Damien Watkins. Making components contract-aware. In IEEE, editor, *Computer*, page 38 44. IEEE, June 1999.
4. Grzegorz Czajkowski and Thorsten von Eicken. JRes: a Resource Accounting Interface for Java. In *ACM OOPSLA Conference*, 1998.
5. David Evans and Andrew Twyman. Flexible Policy-Directed Code Safety. In *IEEE Security and Privacy*, May 1999.
6. Li Gong. Java Security: Present and Near Future. *IEEE Micro*, -:14–19, May 1997.
7. Li Gong and Roland Schemers. Implementing Protection Domains in the Java Development Kit 1.2. In *Internet Society Symposium on Network and Distributed System Scurity*, March 1998.
8. Frédéric Guidec and Nicolas Le Sommer. Towards Resource Consumption Accounting and Control in Java: a Practical Experience. In *ECOOP'2002 (Workshop on Resource Management for Safe Languages)*, June 2002. To be published.
9. Raju Pandey and Brant Hashii. Providing Fine-Grained Access Control for Java Programs. In *The 13th Conference on Object-Oriented Programming, ECOOP'99*. Springer-Verlag, June 1999.

Rational Server Selection for Mobile Agents

Carsten Pils and Stefan Diepolder

Informatik 4 (Communications Systems)
RWTH Aachen, 52056 Aachen, Germany
{pils,diepolder}@informatik.rwth-aachen.de

Abstract. As mobile agents have the ability to operate autonomously and in a disconnected way they are considered to suit mobile computing environments. Mobile users can dispatch agents into the fixed network where the agents operate in the users behalf. Thus, in contrast to client/server interactions agents do not suffer from poor performing wireless access networks. In this paper the performance of mobile agents and client/server interactions are analysed with respect to heterogeneous networks and server resources. It is argued that without a certain knowledge of the available resources agents can hardly decide whether they should migrate or just apply client/server calls to access a remote service. To this end, it is proposed that agents should access server selection systems in order to plan their migration strategy. However, while server selection systems process agent requests the agents are waiting idle. Thus, access to server selection systems comes at a cost and therefore agents must be careful about it. To solve this decision problem an algorithm is proposed which estimates the benefits of accessing server selection systems. Finally, the decision algorithm is evaluated with the help of a simulation model.

1 Introduction

Deployment of wireless access technologies like UMTS and WLAN along with the development of powerful hardware devices are leading to complex mobile applications which are characterised by compelling quality of service requirements. However, network resources are still scarce and therefore applications must efficiently exploit them. In recent years, mobile agents have been considered an attractive approach to cope with these limits and motivated many research studies investigating the benefits of mobile agent deployment in telecommunication systems. In contrast to traditional solutions, a mobile agent can leave the mobile device, migrate to the network location where a service is located, and perform a custom task. While the agent operates in the fixed network it filters information and therefore only the final results are transmitted back to the mobile device. Moreover, the mobile agent can continue its operations even though the mobile device is disconnected. Once the device re-connects, the agent returns its results to the user. Since the agent avoids network transmission of intermediate data and continues even in presence of network disconnections it is expected to complete the overall task much faster than a traditional client/server solution.

J.-B. Stefani, I. Demeure, and D. Hagimont (Eds.): DAIS 2003, LNCS 2893, pp. 61–72, 2003.

Albeit it is apparent that applications operating at the border between fixed and mobile networks have to cope with heterogeneous resources and asymmetric network connections these conditions have not thoroughly investigated in terms of the mobile agent paradigm. However, application developer must understand the performance characteristics of the mobile agent paradigm to develop applications efficiently exploiting resources.

In this paper mobile agent performance in heterogeneous networks is analysed. It is argued that agents need some knowledge about the available resources to plan their migration strategy. To this end, it is proposed that agents should use server selection systems to plan their routes. Section 3 discusses whether the server selection approaches known from literature meet the agent requirements. It is concluded that only slight modifications to the known approaches are required. Since applying server selection comes at a cost a decision algorithm is proposed in section 4 which is analysed with the help of a simulation model described in section 5. Finally, section 6 concludes the paper.

2   Mobile Agent versus Client Server

In contrast to client/server approaches a mobile agent filters information at a remote server and returns the results rather than downloading all data and filtering it locally. Thus, the benefit of mobile agent deployment depends on the quotient of the valuable data size and the total data size to be filtered. Straßer and Schwehm who compared the performance of client/server and mobile agent approaches with the help of analytical models in [1] called this quotient *selectivity*. In their study they analysed the trade-off between the overhead of agent migration and the reduction of the reply size. Ismail and Hagimont investigated a similar scenario in [2] with the help of benchmarks and a network of globally distributed workstations. Pulafito et al analysed the scenario in [3] with stochastic Petri nets and showed that the network bandwidth has a major impact on the agent, i.e. if the network bandwidth is high the computation becomes the bottleneck of the agent interaction. Other studies [4] [5] confirm Puliafito's observation. Yet, none of them analysed the impact of network and server dynamics comprehensively.

2.1   A Simple Performance Model

Apparently, mobile agent and client/server have different resource requirements and therefore dynamics of server and network resource are expected to have a major impact on the performance comparison of the two paradigms. To characterise the impact of resources the performance of a mobile agent MA and its corresponding client/server solution CS is studied with the help of a simple analytic model. The task of both MA and CS is starting at a host A to access a service on a host B and to return the results to A. Furthermore, it is assumed that MA and CS are based on equivalent deterministic algorithms and use the same interfaces to access the service and to interact with the user.

Table 1. Capacities and resource requirements.

Para-meter	Description	Para-meter	Description
r_A	MA's resource requirements at host A	r'_A	CS's resource requirements at host A
$r_{A,B}$	MA's resource requirements on the link between host A and B	$r'_{A,B}$	CS's resource requirements on the link between host A and B
$r_{B,A}$	MA's resource requirements on the link between host B and A	$r'_{B,A}$	CS's resource requirements on the link between host B and A
r_B	MA's resource requirements at host B	r'_B	CS's resource requirements at host B
c_A	Host A's resource capacity	c_B	Host B's resource capacity
$c_{A,B}$	Resource capacity of the server uplink link, i.e. A to B	$c_{B,A}$	Resource capacity of the server downlink, i.e. B to A

DEFINITION 1 (PROCESS DELAY OPERATOR)
Given m the number of resources, a resource requirement $r \in \mathfrak{R}^m_{\geq 0}$ of a process α, and a resource capacity $c \in \mathfrak{R}^m_{\geq 0}$ the process delay operator $\otimes_\alpha : \mathfrak{R}^m_{\geq 0} \times \mathfrak{R}^m_{\geq 0} \mapsto \mathfrak{R}_{\geq 0}$ of a process α maps resource requirement r and the c resource capacity to the process execution time. If a resource capacity c does not meet an application's requirement r the process execution time is $r \otimes_\alpha c = \infty$.

Based on the process delay operator, process execution time T_{ma} of MA and interaction time T_{cs} of CS are given by (see table 1):

$$T_{ma} = r_A \otimes_{ma} c_A + r_{A,B} \otimes_{ma} c_{A,B} + r_B \otimes_{ma} c_B + r_{B,A} \otimes_{ma} c_{B,A}$$
$$T_{cs} = r'_A \otimes_{cs} c_A + r'_{A,B} \otimes_{cs} c_{A,B} + r'_B \otimes_{cs} c_B + r'_{B,A} \otimes_{cs} c_{B,A}$$

Network Resources. While MA must upload its code and data segment CS just sends short request messages. On the downlink however, MA transfers only filtered data while CS filters all data at host A. Thus, if MA's code and data size and CS's request size have minimum representation, CS operation requires only a single interaction, and the relevant link resources are bandwidth and delay the following inequality is satisfied:

$$r_{A,B} \otimes_{ma} c_{A,B} \geq r'_{A,B} \otimes_{cs} c_{A,B}$$

Furthermore, given that $c = c_{A,B} = c_{B,A}$ it is concluded that (selectivity is greater 0):

$$r_{A,B} \otimes_{ma} c + r_{B,A} \otimes_{ma} c \leq r'_{A,B} \otimes_{cs} c + r'_{B,A} \otimes_{cs} c$$
$$\Rightarrow r'_{B,A} \otimes_{cs} c \geq r_{B,A} \otimes_{ma} c$$

Consequently, the uplink is the critical resource of MA while the downlink is critical to CS. In presence of asymmetric connections with considerably poor uplink performance and a well performing downlink, CS outperforms MA even though selectivity is high. On the other hand a poor downlink and well performing uplink support the MA paradigm. If CS requires more than one request/replay pair to reproduce MA functionality, MA benefits from its batch job alike properties (i.e. an agent requires only a single migration and transfer of results). CS, however, suffers from network latency (this effect has been analysed by Puliafito et al who assumed that the number of CS interactions is geometrical distributed).

Processing Resources. Apart from network resources, the benefit of mobile agent deployment depends on the performance of the client and the server machine. Apparently, agent migration, data filtering, and transferring results consume more processing resources than a single agent migration and thus following inequality is satisfied ($c = c_A = c_B$):

$$r_B \otimes_{ma} c \geq r_A \otimes_{ma} c, \forall c \in \mathfrak{R}^m_{\geq 0}$$

Agent management, data retrieval and filtering, and the transfer of results consume more processing resources than data retrieving and forwarding, thus it is concluded that:

$$r_B \otimes_{ma} c_B \geq r'_B \otimes_{cs} c_B, \forall c_B \in \mathfrak{R}^m_{\geq 0}$$

$$r_B \otimes_{ma} c_B \geq r'_A \otimes_{cs} c_A, \ \forall c_B = c_A \in \mathfrak{R}^m_{\geq 0}$$

where $c = c_A = c_B$. Consequently, the load of host B has a major impact on the agent's performance. The benchmark study of Gray et al in [4] shows that even though selectivity is high the client server approach outperforms the mobile agent approach if the server is overloaded and the network bandwidth is high. Johansen showed in [6] that sharing the computational resources between client and server can improve the overall agent performance.

2.2   Agent Migration Strategies

As these rather simple observations show, resource capacities have a strong influence on the optimal (in the sense of smallest response time) agent migration strategy. Particularly, if an agent has the choice between alternative hosts, knowledge of network and host resource becomes crucial for its migration strategy. But, as long as neither network nor hosts provide any quality of service guarantees the resource capacities are hardly known in advance. A solution to this problem are server selection systems. Server selection systems use active resource probing or resource monitoring to route clients to well performing mirror sites or give feedback about server performance. From a client's perspective the benefit of server selection can be expressed by the difference between the average service time $d_\varnothing$ and the service time of the selected server d_{min}.

3   Server Selection for Mobile Agents

Application of server selection to mobile agents is not new. Gray et al proposed in [7] the integration of a server selection system in an agent system. Theilmann and Rothermel studied in [8] so-called dynamic distance maps for mobile agents and claim that agent communication costs are reduced by up to 90%. In [9] Brewington et al propose an agent migration planning support applying a so-called network sensing tool. The way systems measure the network performance has a major impact on their precision. In literature two basic measurement approaches are distinguished: active and passive measurements.

3.1   Active Measurements

By injecting a stimulus into the network and measuring the response active measurement systems estimate the round trip time and the bandwidth. Pathchar [10] and bprobe [11] are prominent examples of active measurement tools. To measure the link speed these tools send successive ICMP ECHO packets and measure the inter-arrival time of the responses. Apparently, active measurement can be used to get information about every connection, however the measurement might take some seconds. Thus, only applications which exchange a large amount of data can benefit from these approaches. Another class of probe based approaches where clients do not suffer from long measurement times are Internet distance maps [12], [13], [14]. Instead of measuring the connections between each client/server pair Internet distance maps probe only the connection performance between dedicated landmarks.

3.2   Passive Measurements

In contrast to active measurement tools, passive tools do not probe the network, but monitor the traffic. Similar to Internet distance maps these tools can instantly provide measurement results, however, there is still a considerable chance that they fail to provide any information. If there has been no traffic between peers of interest passive approaches cannot provide precise information. A representative of such a passive approach is the Shared Passive Network Performance Discovery (SPAND) tool [15] proposed by Seshan et al. A different approach has been proposed by Andrews et al [16] who propose to cluster networks with respect to passive measurements.

3.3   IP-Anycast

None of the server selection approaches discussed so far considers host performance. In [17] Bhattacharjee et al propose an IP-Anycast system where anycast resolvers collect sample data from their care of replica servers and automatically route clients to a well performing one. IP-Anycast is a feature of the IPv6 protocol and is used to address a group of replica servers. A message send to an anycast address will be received by only one server of the group. It is up to the anycast resolver to decide which server is going to receive the message. In the light of agent migration strategies, IP-Anycast has still two disadvantages: Firstly, none of the known anycast approaches provides any performance information to the agent. Secondly, an agent having the choice between different anycast groups can hardly decide. However, the concept of the distributed sample database applied by the anycast resolvers is able to provide the lacking information. Thus, the systems can easily be enhanced to provide the required performance feedback.

3.4   The Server Selection Problem

The benefit of server selection depends on the number of servers to select from and their heterogeneity. The larger the set and the more heterogeneous the servers are the greater the benefit. However, server selection does not come for free as it requires retrieval and processing of sample data. Accordingly, the cost function C_s of server selection is defined as the agent idle time during the selection process and therefore the utility function U is given by: $U = d_\varnothing - d_{min} - C_s$. A consequence of this simple observation is that applying server selection might cause performance loss. In the remainder, this problem is called the *server selection problem*.

4   Rational Server Selection

To analysis the *server selection problem* an omniscient agent is assumed which knows the resource capacity function $c_i(t) : \Re_{\geq 0} \mapsto \Re_{\geq 0}^m$ of each server i. c_i returns the resource capacity vector of server i at time t.

DEFINITION 2 (RESOURCE CONSUMPTION OPERATOR)
The resource consumption operator of a process α $\nabla_\alpha : \Re_{\geq 0}^m \times \Re_{\geq 0}^m \mapsto \Re_m$ maps α's resource requirements to the requirements remaining after consuming a specified resource capacity.

Thus, $r\nabla c = 0$ indicates that the resource requirement r is satisfied if the corresponding process has at least consumed capacity c. Given the agent's resource requirement vector $r \in \Re_{\geq 0}^m$ the service time $d_i(r)$ of server i is:

$$d_i(r) = \min \left\{ x \in \Re_{\geq 0} \middle| r\nabla \int_{t_0}^{t_0+x} c_i(t)dt = 0 \right\}$$

The server selection utility function $U(r)$ is:

$$U(r) = \sum_{i=1}^n \frac{d_i(r)}{n} - \min\left\{d_1(r), \ldots, d_n(r)\right\} - C_s$$

In general, $c(t)$ is even unknown to the server selection system (let alone to the agent). All information a system has is the latest sample data $c_i(t_0)$ which is used to approximate $c(t)$ over an interval $[t_0, t_0 + h]$ by $c(t_0) \cdot h$. Evidently, the absolute approximation error $E_A(h)$ increases with the length of the interval and the instability of the server. Measurements of Internet servers [18] give reason to the assumption that well performing servers are stable. Furthermore, it is expected that well designed server selection algorithms balance the server load and therefore stabilise them. Thus, it is assumed that the gradient of $E_A(h)$ in h is rather small.

4.1   The Estimated Utility Function

The problem in developing a decision algorithm for the *server selection problem* is that the agent does not know the server resource functions $c_i(t)$. However, it is assumed that the agents have a basic knowledge of the system heterogeneity. Let R be the resource capacity distribution describing the probability that a randomly selected server has a resource capacity $X \leq \bar{x}$ ($X, \bar{x} \in \Re_{\geq 0}^m$). With the help of R $d_\varnothing$ can be estimated by:

$$d_\varnothing(\boldsymbol{r}) = \min \left\{ d \in \Re \middle| \boldsymbol{r} \nabla (E[R] \cdot d) = 0 \right\}$$

According to the definition of R its average value $E[R]$ is the resource capacity an agent expects when it selects a server randomly or the number of alternative servers is 1. To estimate d_{min} the random distribution R_n that n randomly selected servers have a resource capacity $X \leq \bar{x}$ is required. Obviously, R_n is an order statistic distribution [19] and thus it is given by:

$$R_n(x) = R_1(x)^n = R(x)^n$$
$$\frac{dR_n(x)}{dx} = n \cdot R(x)^{n-1} \cdot \frac{dR(x)}{dx}$$
$$E[R_n] = \int_0^\infty x \cdot n \cdot R(x)^{n-1} \cdot \frac{dR(x)}{dx}$$

$E[R_n]$ is the average maximum server capacity when a server is selected out of n. Consequently, d_{min} can be estimated by function $d_{min}(\boldsymbol{r}, n)$ as follows:

$$d_{min}(\boldsymbol{r}, n) = \min \left\{ d \in \Re \middle| \boldsymbol{r} \nabla (E[R_n] \cdot d) = 0 \right\}$$

Finally, given the random distribution $Err(x)$ that a server resource has a deviation of $x \leq \bar{x}$ for an interval of length h the estimated utility function is:

$$E[U(\boldsymbol{r}, n)] = \quad d_\varnothing(\boldsymbol{r}) - d_{min}(\boldsymbol{r}, n) - C_s - E[Err(d_\varnothing(\boldsymbol{r}) - d_{min}(\boldsymbol{r}, n))]$$

As for the resource capacities, the waiting time is not known in advance. Particularly, if the server selection system must retrieve sample data from a remote location, the waiting time is hardly known. To this end, the waiting time is assumed to be distributed according to a random distribution F, i.e. C_s is given by F.

4.2   Decision Algorithm

The more time an agent waits the lesser is the benefit of server selection. The agent's situation is similar to the one of a customer waiting for a call centre service. While the customer is waiting for a call centre agent he is weighting the costs of the call (patience or connection costs) against the expected service utility. Since the costs are increasing monotonic in time the customer's question is when he should put down the receiver. The customer's decision problem has gained some attention in literature and is known as the *problem of rational abandonment from invisible queues*. Mandelbaum and Shimkin have analysed the problem in [20]. They proved that there exist an optimal abandonment time T which depends on the monotonic properties of the hazard rate function $H(t) = \frac{dF(t)/dt}{1-F(t)}$. According to the rational server selection problem Mandelbaum and Shimkin define the utility function U_t with respect to the system abandonment time T by:

$$U_t(\boldsymbol{r}, n, T) = E[G(\boldsymbol{r}, n) \cdot I(T \geq V) - \min\{V, T\}]$$

where V is the agent's waiting time, I maps to 1 if the specified condition is true, and $G(\boldsymbol{r}, n)$ is the server selection gain which is given by

$$G(\boldsymbol{r}, n) = d_{\varnothing}(\boldsymbol{r}) - d_{min}(\boldsymbol{r}, n) - E[Err(d_{\varnothing}(\boldsymbol{r}) - d_{min}(\boldsymbol{r}, n))]$$

Considering the waiting time distribution, it is derived:

$$U_t(\boldsymbol{r}, n, T) = \int_0^T \left(G(\boldsymbol{r}, n) - t\right) dF(t) - T \cdot \left(1 - F(T)\right)$$

Preconditioned that $F(T)$ is continuously differentiable for $t > 0$ and that $F(t)dt$ has a right limit at 0 they differentiate F with respect to $T > 0$ and get:

$$\frac{dU_t(\boldsymbol{r}, n, T)}{dT} = \left(G(\boldsymbol{r}, n) - T\right)\frac{dF(T)}{dT} - \frac{(1 - dF(T))}{dT} + T \cdot \frac{dF(T)}{dT}$$

$$= \left(G(\boldsymbol{r}, n)\right) \cdot \left(1 - F(T)\right) \cdot \left(H(T) - \frac{1}{G(\boldsymbol{r}, n)}\right)$$

The first order condition for a local optimum at $T > 0$, namely, $\frac{dU_t(\boldsymbol{r}, n, T)}{dT} = 0$, can be stated as: $H(T) = \frac{1}{G(\boldsymbol{r}, n)}$ Consequently, the local optimum of U_t is the optimal waiting time in terms of the rational selection problem.

4.3   Consequences to the Migration Strategy

To apply the proposed decision algorithm, agents require the average values of the resource distribution and its corresponding n order statistic distributions. Since server selection systems monitor the resources anyway, the systems can calculate the average values and provide them to the agents. According to the decision algorithm, agents can only benefit from server selection if they have the choice between different destination hosts. But even though there is only a single destination host, an agent can still benefit from server selection: Firstly, agents can use the average value of the resource distribution to decide whether agent migration or client/server interaction is statistically optimal for operating an information retrieval task. Secondly, the more agents use server selection the more balanced the resources are.

5 Evaluation of the Rational Server Selection Approach

In this section the system dynamics and their implications to the resource distribution R are studied in case that the fraction of agents which use server selection increases. To this end, let R^x, $x \in [0,1]$ a series of random distributions and x be the fraction of agents applying server selection.

The study is subdivided into two parts: Firstly, some simple general observations are made. In the second part a simulation study is presented.

5.1 General Observations

Since server selection balances the load of the resources it is assumed that the standard deviations $\sigma(R^x)$ satisfy the inequality below given that the agent arrival rate is constant:

$$\sigma(R^x) \leq \sigma(R^y), x \geq y$$

Preconditioned that the investigated system resources can be modelled by $G/G/1$ queuing models and that the server resources are shared, the average values $E[R^x]$ satisfy the inequality:

$$E[R^x] \leq E[R^y], x \geq y$$

This stems from the fact, that the agent average waiting time decreases with the standard deviation of the resources. Consequently, the average number of agents in the system decreases as well. According to the lower and upper bounds of n order statistics found by Morigurti [21] and Huang [22] $E[R_n^x]$ satisfies the inequalities:

$$-\sigma(R^x) \cdot \sqrt{\int_0^1 [\underline{\varphi}_{1,n}(t)]^2 dt - 1} \leq E[R_n^x] - E[R^x] \leq \sigma(R^x) \cdot \sqrt{\int_0^1 [\underline{\varphi}_{n,n}(t)]^2 dt - 1}$$

where $\underline{\varphi}_{1,n}$ and $\underline{\varphi}_{n,n}$ are the greatest convex minorants of the first and second order statistic of the standard uniform distribution. Thus, as expected $E[R_n^x]$ decreases in x as well.

5.2 Simulation Study

The decision algorithm has been evaluated with the help of a simple simulation model. The model comprises a set of 16 servers which have service capacities of $2000ops/sec$, $4000ops/sec$, $8000ops/sec$, and $16000ops/sec$. Each of them serves incoming customers in a round robin fashion. Arrival rate and customer's resource requirements are exponential distributed with mean $1\frac{arrival}{ms}$ and $10ops$ respectively. The waiting time distribution F has been considered to be deterministic with value $10ms$, i.e. $C_s = 10ms$. Based on this model the following three scenarios have been evaluated:

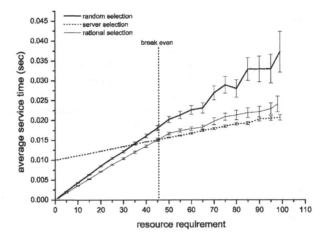

Fig. 1. Service latencies versus resource requirement.

1. **Random selection:** The customers select the destination server randomly.
2. **Native Server selection:** The customers use server selection to select one server out of a random set of three alternatives.
3. **Rational selection:** Like **native server selection** customers select the destination out of a random set. However, in contrast to **native server selection** the customers use the decision algorithm proposed in the previous section. Thus, only those customers having a significant resource requirement apply server selection.

The average service latencies with respect to the service requirements are shown in figure 1. Apparently, the server selection approaches outperform random selection if a customer's resource requirement exceeds the breakeven point. However, those customers which use server selection even though their resource requirements are less than the breakeven point perform poor. Comparison of rational and native server selection shows: If rational selection is used customer's having less resource requirements perform well at the costs of those customers having significant requirements. But if native server selection is used, customer's having considerable requirements perform well at the costs of those having small.

6   Conclusions

Evidently, mobile agent and client/server based applications have different resource requirements. With the help of a simple analytic model the impact of resources on the performance of the two paradigms has been discussed. As a consequence of this study it has been argued that agents require some knowledge about the system resources when planning a migration strategy. However, as long as neither network nor server resources provide any quality of service guarantees information about resource capacity are hardly obtained. In recent years, server selection systems have been proposed to estimate resource capacities of best-effort systems. Selection approaches which are known from literature have been investigated with respect to the agent migration planning problem. It has been concluded that only slight modifications to the known approaches are required to meet agent requirements. But unfortunately, server selection is not for free and thus agents must be careful about accessing these systems. To this end, a decision algorithm has been proposed which helps agents to decide whether there is any advantage in applying server selection. Apparently, this decision algorithm applies to any network application and is not restricted to agent technology. Finally, the decision algorithm has been studied with the help of a simple simulation model. In the simulation model the customers are competing for just a single resource type. The simulation shows that the decision algorithm outperform random selection. Since native selection (i.e. the agents do not use the decision algorithm) perfectly balances the load, it outperforms rational server selection if the agent resource requirements are significant.

References

1. M. Straßer and M. Schwehm, "A performance model for mobile agent systems", in *Proc. of the International Conference on Parallel and Distributed Processing Techniques and Applications*, Las Vegas, July 1997, pp. 1132–1140.
2. L. Ismail and D. Hagimont, "A performance evaluation of the mobile agent paradigm", in *ACM SIGPLAN Notices*, October 1999, vol. 34, pp. 306–313.
3. A. Puliafito, S. Riccobene, and M. Scarpa, "An analytical comparison of the client-server, remote evaluation, and mobile agents paradigms", in *First International Symposium on Agent Systems and Applications/Third International Symposium on Mobile Agents*, Palm Springs, USA, October 1999, pp. 278–92, IEEE Comput. Soc.
4. Robert S. Gray, David Kotz, Ronald A. Peterson, Peter Gerken, Martin Hofmann, Daria Chacon, Greg Hill, and Niranjan Suri, "Mobile-Agent versus Client/Server Performance: Scalability in an Information-Retrieval Task", in *Lecture Notes in Computer Science (LNCS). Mobile Agents. 5th International Conference*, G.P. Picco, Ed., Hanover, NH, December 2001, vol. 2240, pp. 229–243, Springer-Verlag, Berlin.
5. D. Kotz, G. Cybenko, R.S. Gray, Jiang Guofei, R.A. Peterson, M. Hofmann, D.A. Chacon, and K.R. Whitebread, "Performance analysis of mobile agents for filtering data streams on wireless networks", *Mobile Networks and Applications*, vol. 7, no. 2, pp. 163–174, 2002.
6. D. Johansen, "Mobile agent applicability", in *Proceedings of the 2nd Workshop on Mobile Agents (MA'98)*, K Rothermel and F. Hohl, Eds. 1998, vol. 1477 of *Lecture Notes in Computer Science (LNCS)*, pp. 80–98, Springer-Verlag, Germany.
7. Robert S. Gray, David Kotz, Saurab Nog, Daniela Rus, and George Cybenko, "Mobile agents for mobile computing", Tech. Rep. PCS-TR96-285, Dartmouth College, Computer Science, Hanover, NH, May 1996.
8. W. Theilmann and K. Rothermel, "Efficient dissemination of mobile agents", in *Proceedings. 19th IEEE International Conference on Distributed Computing Systems. Workshops on Electronic Commerce and Web-based Applications*, Austin, TX, USA, May 1999, pp. 9–14, IEEE Comput. Soc.

9. B. Brewington, R. Gray, K. Moizumi, D. Kotz, G. Cybenko, and D. Rus, "Mobile agents in distributed information retrieval", in *Intelligent Information Agents*, M. Klusch, Ed., chapter 15, pp. 355–395. Springer-Verlag, Germany, 1999.

10. V. Jacobson, "Pathchar", `ftp://ftp.ee.lbl.gov`, 1997.

11. Robert L. Carter and Mark E. Crovella, "Measuring bottleneck link speed in packet-switched networks", *Perform. Eval. (Netherlands)*, vol. 27-28, pp. 297–318, October 1996.

12. W. Theilmann and K. Rothermel, "Dynamic distance maps of the internet", in *Proceedings IEEE INFOCOM 2000*, Tel Aviv, Israel, March 2000, vol. 1, pp. 275–84, IEEE Comp. Soc.

13. K. M. Hanna, N. Natarajan, and B.N. Levine, "Evaluation of a novel two-step server selection metric", in *Proceedings Ninth International Conference on Network Protocols. ICNP 2001*, Riverside, CA, USA, November 2001, pp. 290–300, IEEE Comput. Soc.

14. S. Ratnasamy, M. Handley, R. Karp, and S. Shenker, "Topologically-aware overlay construction and server selection", in *Proceedings IEEE INFOCOM 2002 Conference on Computer Communications*, New York, NY, USA, June 2002, vol. 3, pp. 1190–1199, IEEE Comp. Soc.

15. S. Seshan, M. Stemm, and R.H. Katz, "Spand: Shared passive network performance discovers", in *USENIX Symposion on Internet Technologies and Systems*. 1997, pp. 135–146, USENIX Association.

16. M. Andrews, B. Shepherd, A. Srinivasan, and F. Winkler, P.and Zane, "Clustering and server selection using passive monitoring", in *Proceedings IEEE INFOCOM 2002 Conference on Computer Communications*, New York, NY, USA, June 2002, vol. 3, pp. 1717–1725, IEEE Comp. Soc.

17. Samrat Bhattacharjee, Mostafa H. Ammar, Ellen W. Zegura, Viren Shah, and Zongming Fei, "Application-layer anycast", in *IEEE INFOCOM '97*, Kobe, Japan, April 1997, vol. 3, pp. 1388–96, IEEE Comput. Soc. Press.

18. A. Myers, P. Dinda, and H. Zhang, "Performance characteristics of mirror servers on the internet", in *Proceedings of IEEE INFOCOM'99*, New York, NY, USA, March 1999, vol. 1, pp. 304–312, IEEE Comp. Soc.

19. Junjiro Ogawa, "Distribution and moments of order statistics", in *Contributions to order statistics*, Ahmed E. Sarhan and Bernhard G. Greenberg, Eds., Wiley publications in statistics, pp. 11–19. John Wiley and Sons, Inc., 1962.

20. Avishai Mandelbaum and Nahum Shimkin, "A model for rational abandonments from invisible queues", *Queueing Systems*, vol. 36, no. 1-3, pp. 141–173, 2000.

21. S. Morigurti, "A modification of schwarz's inequality with application to distributions", *Annual Math. Statist.*, vol. 24, pp. 107–113, 1953.

22. J. S. Huang, "Sharp bounds for the expected value of order statistics", *Statistics and Probability Letters*, vol. 33, pp. 105–107, 1997.

Facilitating the Portability
of User Applications in Grid Environments

Paul Z. Kolano

NASA Advanced Supercomputing Division
NASA Ames Research Center
M/S 258-6, Moffett Field, CA 94035, USA
kolano@nas.nasa.gov

Abstract. Grid computing promises the ability to connect geographically and organizationally distributed resources to increase effective computational power, resource utilization, and resource accessibility. For grid computing to be successful, users must be able to easily execute the same application on different resources. Different resources, however, may be administered by different organizations with different software installed, different file system structures, and different default environment settings. Even within the same organization, the set of software installed on a given resource is in constant flux with additions, upgrades, and removals. Users cannot be expected to understand all of the idiosyncrasies of each resource they may wish to execute jobs on, thus must be provided with automated assistance. This paper describes a new OGSI-compliant grid service (the *Naturalization Service*) that has been implemented as part of NASA's Information Power Grid (IPG) project to automatically establish the execution environment for user applications.

1 Introduction

Grid computing [6] promises the ability to connect geographically and organizationally distributed resources to increase effective computational power, resource utilization, and resource accessibility. Real world experiences with grids [1,11], however, have had mixed results. While gains in computational power were eventually achieved, they were only made a reality after significant efforts to get user applications running on each suitable resource. Differences across resources in installed software, file system structures, and default environment settings required manually transferring dependent software and setting environment variables. This problem is common even in non-grid environments. Users frequently encounter missing or incompatible shared libraries (.so files) on Unix systems or missing dynamic link libraries (.DLL files) on Windows systems when attempting to execute binaries that have been transferred from a similar system. Even in a language that is designed for portability, such as Java, this same problem exists. That is, a Java application can only be executed on a system that has all of the classes installed on which it depends. If all dependent software is present, an application still may not be able to execute if the environment variables are

J.-B. Stefani, I. Demeure, and D. Hagimont (Eds.): DAIS 2003, LNCS 2893, pp. 73–85, 2003.

not set such that it can find that software. In grid environments, this problem is only amplified. For grid computing to be successful, users must be able to easily execute the same application on different resources without being expected to understand or compensate for all of the idiosyncrasies of each resource.

In general, the ability of an application to migrate from one system to another depends on a number of issues. A given application may have dependencies over which an ordinary user has no control such as processor architecture, operating system type, operating system version and features, system architecture, and system configuration. These dependencies limit the set of resources on which the application can execute. An application may also have other dependencies such as software availability, software locations, software versions and features, and environment variable settings. Although the set of resources can also be limited based on these dependencies, this is undesirable as it may eliminate the best resources from consideration even though the user can satisfy these dependencies by copying files and setting path variables appropriately.

The typical approach used for dealing with software dependencies is to rely on statically linked executables or custom packages containing all required software. The drawbacks of statically linked executables are well known including overly large executables, inefficient use of memory, and hard-coding library bugs into code. Building custom software packages correctly and writing an associated setup script may require expert knowledge of dependency analysis techniques, differences in operating systems, and environments required by different software types. Every minute spent by a user constructing a software package or transferring an unnecessarily large file is another minute of the user's time or resource allocations that could be better spent on their real work.

Naturalization is defined[1] as the process of "adapting or acclimating (a plant or animal) to a new environment; introducing and establishing as if native". This paper describes a new grid service (the *Naturalization Service*) developed as part of NASA's Information Power Grid (IPG) project to automatically naturalize user applications to grid resources. The functions of this service include (1) automatically identifying the dependencies of user applications with support for executables, shared libraries, Java classes, and Perl and Python programs, (2) establishing a suitable environment by transferring dependent software and setting key environment variables necessary for each application to run, and (3) managing a flexible software catalog, which is used to locate software dependencies based on both centrally managed and user controlled mappings.

Section 2 presents related work. Section 3 gives a brief overview of the NASA IPG. Section 4 describes the steps involved in establishing the execution environment for an application. Section 5 gives the implementation details of the Naturalization Service. Finally, section 6 presents conclusions and future work.

2   Related Work

There are several projects that address issues similar to those addressed by this work. The Globus Executable Management (GEM) [2] system was implemented

---

[1] American Heritage Dictionary at http://www.bartleby.com/61/6/N0030600.html.

to allow different versions of an executable to be staged to a machine based on its processor architecture type and operating system version. Executables are retrieved from a network-based executable repository. This system only supports executables, however, and has no support for shared libraries, Java classes, or Perl or Python programs, nor does it support automated dependency analysis.

The Uniform Interface to Computing Resources (UNICORE) [4] allows jobs to be built from platform-independent abstract job operations, which are translated into concrete operations that can be executed on an actual system. The translation relies on a static configuration file located on each resource describing the software installed there. For example, an abstract job executing "ls" would be mapped using the configuration file to a concrete job executing "/bin/ls". This approach requires extra administration every time software is added to, removed from, or updated on a system, it only supports executables, and it only allows software to run on systems that already have all required software installed.

The Automatic Configuration Service [10] automatically manages the installation and removal of software for component-based applications according to user-specified dependency information. This service has goals similar to those of the Naturalization Service, but is implemented as a CORBA service as opposed to an OGSI-compliant service. A limitation of this service is that the user must fully specify all dependencies manually. There is also no discussion of managing environment variables, which are required for an application to find installed software and which differ according to software type. In addition, this service uses a centralized repository, thus cannot take advantage of software individually deployed by users.

Installers, package managers, and application management systems [3] are typically used to manage the software installed on standalone systems and systems on the same network. While these approaches greatly increase the ability of system administrators to provide a consistent and stable set of software across an organization's resources, they are only of use when the administrator knows what software will be needed. Since grids enable users from different organizations with different software requirements to share resources, these mechanisms do not provide the necessary level of support.

Replica management systems such as Reptor [8] provide high-level mechanisms for managing the replication, selection, consistency, and security of data to provide users with transparent access to geographically distributed data sets. Much of this functionality is also suitable for managing software across grid resources and is, in fact, the basis of part of the Naturalization Service. Replica management systems do not address software specific issues, however, such as automatic dependency analysis and environment variable settings.

3   NASA Information Power Grid

NASA's Information Power Grid (IPG) [9] is a computational and data grid spanning a number of NASA centers that consists of various high performance supercomputers, storage systems, and data gathering instruments scattered across the United States. The goal of the IPG is to increase the utilization and accessibility of existing resources, ultimately resulting in an increase in productivity at each NASA center.

Although a grid provides access to additional resources, as the number of resources increases, it becomes more and more difficult to use those resources. A user must know the name of each resource, which resources they have accounts on, how many allocations they have on each resource, which resources are least loaded, what software is installed on each system, etc. This becomes a daunting task even when the number of resources is small. For this reason, the IPG project is also developing a set of grid services to facilitate the use of the grid [13]. Three prototype services have been implemented including a Resource Broker for selecting resources meeting specified constraints, a Job Manager for reliable job execution, and the Naturalization Service, which is the subject of this paper.

In the current job model of the IPG, jobs consist of a sequence of file and execution operations, each of which may have an associated cleanup sequence. File operations consist of operations on files and directories including copying, moving, and removing files and creating and removing directories. Execution operations describe an application to execute on a given resource. For the purposes of this paper, an execution operation will consist of a host to run on, the path of the application on that host, and an environment mapping from variable names to variable values. An actual IPG Job Manager job consists of a number of other fields that are not relevant to the discussion of the Naturalization Service including a queue name, a project name, a working directory, stdin, stdout, and stderr redirection, a number of processors, and memory requirements.

Within the current IPG architecture, a job to execute and a set of resource constraints are submitted to the Resource Broker component from a client application. The resource constraints consist of restrictions on resource characteristics (e.g. number of processors, operating system type, processor type, etc.) that must be satisfied for the application to properly execute. The Resource Broker selects a set of resources satisfying those constraints and incorporates those selections into the job and passes it on to the Naturalization Service. The Naturalization Service then transforms the job as necessary to establish the execution environment for each application, which is passed on to the Job Manager for execution. These services are based on the Globus Toolkit [5], which provides grid security through the Grid Security Infrastructure (GSI), low-level job management through the Globus Resource Allocation Manager (GRAM), data transfer through the Grid File Transfer Protocol (GridFTP), and resource/service information through the Monitoring and Discovery Service (MDS).

4   Establishing Execution Environments

The execution environment for an application on a given resource consists of the software existing on that resource and the settings of the environment variables when the application runs. For each execution operation in a given job, the function of the Naturalization Service is to:

1. Determine the software that the execution operation application requires
2. Provide a location for that software on the execution operation host by:
   (a) Determining if the software exists on the execution operation host
   (b) Finding a source for any missing software
   (c) Copying missing software to the execution operation host
3. Set environment variables based on provided software locations

A list of dependencies is associated with each execution operation. A dependency consists of basic requirements including a type, a name, a version range, and a feature list as well as information gathered during processing including a source host and path, a target path, and an "analyzed flag" to indicate its analysis status. The Naturalization Service currently supports five software types: executables, shared libraries, Java classes, and Perl and Python programs. The dependency name holds the canonical name for the software depending on its type (e.g. ls, libc, java.util.List, File::Basename, xml.sax.xmlreader, etc.). The version range consists of a minimum and/or maximum version required. The feature list contains features that the dependency must support. For example, the application might require the w3m browser compiled with SSL support. Currently, versions are only supported for shared libraries and features are not yet supported as a way to derive these automatically has not yet been determined.

The source host and path, target path, and analyzed flag are used to store information as processing proceeds. Stages are only executed if the information they provide has not already been gathered. Thus, a job for which the execution environment has already been fully established can be sent through the Naturalization Service without effect. This allows the user to have complete control of job processing. A user can execute stages individually, can specify dependencies manually, can turn analysis off, can specify an exact source for software, can specify a location where software already exists, or any combination thereof. The Naturalization Service will fill in any gaps in the environment left by the user or return the job unchanged if no modifications are necessary.

Although the Naturalization Service makes its best attempt to establish the execution environment for a job, it is not possible to guarantee that the resulting environment will always be suitable. There are three scenarios for which such a guarantee cannot be made:

1. Application depends on A, but A cannot be located anywhere
2. Application depends on A, which depends on B, but analysis techniques used on A are inadequate to determine B is a dependency
3. Application does not depend on A, but analysis reports A is a dependency

Since executing a job for which the execution environment has not been fully established leads to wasted CPU cycles, it is desirable to notify the user prior to job execution. For the last two scenarios, nothing can be done besides documenting the limitations of the analysis techniques. The first scenario, however, can be identified by searching the resulting job for empty target paths and false analyzed flags. The Naturalization Service provides convenience methods for finding unresolved dependencies to determine if a job should be executed as is.

A pedagogical example job will be used to illustrate the functionality of the Naturalization Service. This job consists of running a Python program "addall.py", which uses a module "Adder.py" as shown in Figure 1. Figure 3 shows the original job and the actual modifications made to that job as it passes through the five stages of the Naturalization Service discussed in the following sections.

4.1   Dependency Analysis

In order to establish the environment for a particular application, it is first necessary to analyze exactly what software the application needs. In general, this problem is undecidable as applications can dynamically load or execute a file derived from an arbitrarily complex computation at any point during execution (e.g. char *lib = complex_func(); dlopen(lib)). Although this type of analysis is infeasible for the general case, the large majority of cases are much simpler and can be handled by appropriate static analysis techniques.

The Naturalization Service first collects the complete set of host/file pairs that need to be analyzed for the given job, which includes the execution operation applications and any manually-specified dependencies with a source location. File operations in the job are traversed to find the original location of each file. A single job is then executed on each collected host in parallel. This job runs a self-contained analysis shell script on the list of files located on that host. The output of this job is a list of dependencies for each file, which are added as dependencies to the appropriate execution operations.

Analyzing software on the system it originates on is advantageous since that system is likely to be the one that the user has tested it on. Thus, it is likely to have all dependencies present, even if they are in non-standard locations such as the user's home directory. This facilitates complete analysis and provides a source for files to be transferred to the target system. The main concern is execution time, since it is undesirable for these jobs to wait in a heavily loaded FIFO queue for execution. Since analysis only requires access to files, however, it is not necessary for the analysis jobs to run on the main compute node of a resource. Instead, they can simply run on the file server for that node, either as GRAM jobs or GSI-enabled ssh jobs, which will execute almost immediately.

Currently, the Naturalization Service analyzes executables, shared libraries, Java classes (both class and jar files), and Perl and Python programs. Executable and shared library analysis is the most straightforward as the Executable and Linking Format (ELF) [15] standard used by Unix systems requires that an executable contain the names of the shared object dependencies necessary for it to execute. This information can be obtained using the "ldd" or "elfdump" commands. Like the ELF format, the Java class file format [14] also contains dependency information. Namely, it contains the list of classes that the given class requires to execute. The analysis code uses a slightly modified version of the com.sun.jini.tool.ClassDep utility of the Jini Software Kit[2].

---

[2]   Available at `http://www.sun.com/software/jini`.

```
# addall.py (add #'s from stdin)
import sys
import string
import Adder
adder = Adder.Adder()
for line in sys.stdin.readlines():
    n = string.atoi(line)
    adder.add(n)
print adder.sum()

# Adder.py (maintain sum)
class Adder:
    def __init__(self):
        self.value = 0
    def add(self, n):
        self.value += n
    def sum(self):
        return self.value
```

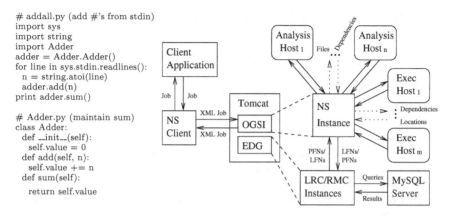

Fig. 1. Example job.   **Fig. 2.** Naturalization Service implementation.

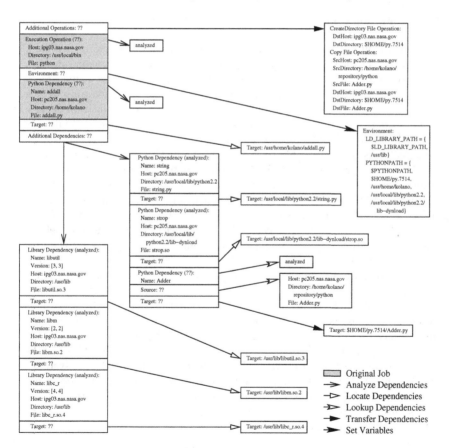

Fig. 3. Stages of job transformation.

Unlike ELF executables and libraries and Java class files, Perl and Python programs do not contain explicit dependency information. These types of programs must either be textually searched for relevant module usage (e.g. "use" or "require" in Perl and "import" in Python) or must be partially evaluated using features of their corresponding compilers such as introspection. The Naturalization Service analysis code is based on the Perl Module:: ScanDeps[3] module, which uses the former approach, and the Python modulefinder module[4], which uses the latter.

After this stage, Figure 3 shows that three Python dependencies have been added to the example job based on the analysis of "addall.py" as well as three library dependencies from the analysis of the "python" executable. The execution operation and all of its dependencies have been marked as "analyzed" with the exception of the Adder Python dependency, whose source could not be found, thus could not be analyzed.

4.2 Dependency Location

Even though different resources may have different sets of software installed, there is a good chance that they also share a significant base of common software. Every piece of software that does not have to be transferred equates to a decrease in the time an application must wait to execute. Thus, after determining the software on which a particular application depends, the Naturalization Service next determines if the software already exists on the target system. While this problem is not undecidable as the number of files on a system is finite, it is impractical to search every file on a system. Thus, the search space must be limited by path variables. Since there is no guarantee these paths are complete or that software is stored in standard locations, there is no guarantee that this procedure will find a particular file even if it actually exists on the system. This problem is amplified through the use of the Globus GRAM as jobs executed by the GRAM job manager do not necessarily run under the user's default shell, so do not incorporate the user's default environment. In this case, even if the user has the path variables set up appropriately, the job still might not be able to find all existing software. In some cases, the user may not have a permanent account on a system, thus may not have the environment set up properly to begin with. Also, the default shell might not be the shell that the user actually uses. This is common on systems where the user cannot control the default shell or where more advanced shells such as bash are not allowed as login shells.

To compensate for this problem, two strategies are employed. First, paths are added according to the Filesystem Hierarchy Standard [12] for Unix systems. This guarantees that most common software will be located as all major Unix distributions conform to this standard. Next, the locator gathers user-defined and system-default environment variable settings from standard shells including bash, csh, ksh, sh, tcsh, and zsh. A variable "var" can be read from a shell

---

[3] Available at `http://search.cpan.org/perldoc?Module::ScanDeps`.

[4] Available as part of the Python 2.3 base distribution at `http://www.python.org`.

"<sh>" using "<sh> -c 'echo $var'". Variables gathered include LD_LIBRARY_ PATH and variants, PATH, CLASSPATH, JAVA_HOME, PERLLIB and variants, PYTHONHOME, and PYTHONPATH. Once the paths are set, files are located by type, using "ls" for executables and libraries and the corresponding interpreter for Java, Perl, and Python dependencies. It is assumed that if the interpreter is not available, then no dependencies of that type exist on the system.

After this stage, Figure 3 shows that all dependencies of the example job have been located on the target system except for the Adder Python dependency.

4.3 Dependency Lookup

Ideally, after the analysis and location stages, every dependency has either been located on the target system or a source for it has been found during analysis. Since this cannot be guaranteed, however, a final attempt is made to find any unresolved dependencies in a software catalog. This catalog utilizes the Local Replica Catalog (LRC) and Replica Metadata Catalog (RMC) of the European DataGrid (EDG) project [8]. The LRC stores one-to-many mappings from logical file names (LFNs) constructed from software type, name, supported operating system, and version to Globally Unique Identifiers (GUIDs). The RMC stores many-to-one mappings from these GUIDs to physical file names (PFNs) where the associated software actually resides. Note that the roles traditionally taken by these components have been reversed to accommodate the uniqueness constraints imposed on both sides of LRC/RMC mappings by the EDG implementation.

Since dependency analysis has already been performed by this stage, the software catalog also stores the pre-identified dependencies of each PFN, which are recursively added as dependencies and looked up as necessary. In this case, the LRC maps each PFN to a set of GUIDs, each of which is mapped by the RMC to an LFN identifying a specific dependency.

Using a catalog instead of a repository allows for a flexible approach to software management. As long as a resource is accessible to the file transfer mechanisms of the IPG Job Manager, the software on that resource can be utilized by the Naturalization Service. If an organization desires a permanent repository, it can dedicate a set of resources to the task with an appropriate repertoire of software and map LFNs into the file systems of those resources. Otherwise, the LFNs can simply point to the locations of software on existing systems. The design also allows users to manage personal software repositories. The Naturalization Service provides a user interface to add and remove mappings from LFNs in a personal namespace based on their grid identity to the PFNs of choice. Thus, users can maintain a collection of software that they frequently use on their personally selected resources, which will be utilized by the Naturalization Service as a source for the software required by their jobs. For a given LFN, the current implementation first selects the user's PFN, if it exists, or if not, selects the first matching PFN from the main catalog. Future versions of the Naturalization Service will perform more intelligent selection based on locality, reliability, etc.

After this stage, Figure 3 shows that the one dependency without a source or target location, the Adder Python dependency, now has a source. In addition, it has been marked as "analyzed" based on its dependency information in the software catalog, which indicated that no additional software was required.

4.4   Dependency Transfer

Transferring the dependencies to the target system is relatively straightforward. One issue, however, is making sure that an appropriate directory hierarchy is created for Java, Perl, and Python dependencies. For example, Java expects non-jar'd class files to be located in a directory structure based on the class name. Thus, to copy the class file "FooBar.class" associated with a class named "foo.bar.FooBar" to a directory "/basedir" in CLASSPATH, it must actually be copied to "/basedir/foo/bar/FooBar.class". Otherwise, Java will not be able to find the class. The Perl and Python cases are similar.

Another issue at this stage is dependency reuse. A job may contain a sequence of execution operations on the same machine. The dependencies of different execution operations may overlap, thus should only be transferred once before the first operation that requires them. The Naturalization Service keeps track of which files need to be transferred and copies them at the appropriate stage.

After this stage, Figure 3 shows that two file operations have been added to the example job to create a directory for and to copy the one dependency without a target location, the Adder Python dependency, to the target system.

4.5   Variable Setup

The final step in establishing the execution environment for a job is setting the environment variables of each execution operation so that all its dependencies can be located during execution. At this stage, as many dependencies as possible either have a location where they currently reside on the target system or a location where they will reside after a transfer from elsewhere. Thus, the Naturalization Service simply adds each dependency's location to the path variable appropriate for that dependency's type. As in the previous stage, care must be taken when handling Java, Perl, and Python dependencies. For the example in the previous section, if a Java class named "foo.bar.FooBar" has a future location of "/basedir/foo/bar/FooBar.class", the CLASSPATH variable must contain "/basedir" and not "/basedir/foo/bar" for Java to properly find the class. For these cases, the Naturalization Service traverses the location back the appropriate number of directories based on the name. Again, this also applies to Perl and Python modules, but not to Java jar files.

After this stage, Figure 3 shows the execution operation of the example job now has environment settings based on the existing and created locations of its dependencies. At this point, the example job has been fully transformed.

5   Implementation

An initial prototype of the Naturalization Service has been implemented in Java with the dependency analysis and location modules written as Bourne shell scripts. The Naturalization Service runs as an Open Grid Services Infrastructure (OGSI) compliant service within the Open Grid Services Architecture (OGSA) framework [7]. In the OGSA model, all grid functionality is provided by named *grid services* that are created dynamically upon request. The newest version of Globus, version 3.0 (GT3), is the reference implementation of OGSI and provides all of the functionality of GT2 as grid services.

Figure 2 shows the current implementation of the Naturalization Service. In this figure, a client application uses the Naturalization Service client API to request the establishment of the execution environment for a given job. The Naturalization Service client converts the Java job object into XML for transmission to an Apache Tomcat server running an OGSI container. The OGSI container creates an instance of the Naturalization Service and invokes its "establishEnvironment" method with the given job. The Naturalization Service uses the OGSI GRAM service to execute the analysis script on each host with files requiring analysis in parallel. All jobs are executed using the grid credentials of the client application user, thus users are not given any additional privileges beyond what they normally have. After all dependencies have been gathered, the location script is then executed in parallel on each execution operation host with unresolved dependencies. For any dependencies that could not be located or for which no source could be found, instances of the EDG LRC and RMC are queried in an attempt to find a source. At this point, the Naturalization Service sets up the return job to copy dependencies as necessary and sets the environment variables appropriately. The job is returned in XML to the Naturalization Service client, which converts the job back into a Java object for the client application.

The Naturalization Service has been fully tested on FreeBSD systems and the analysis and location scripts have been tested on IRIX, SunOS, and FreeBSD. It has not yet been deployed in the NASA IPG as GT3 is not mature enough for production IPG usage. The Naturalization Service also has not yet been integrated with the IPG Resource Broker or Job Manager, which are built on top of GT2, but will be integrated with the next versions of these services, which are currently being implemented and will be OGSI-compliant.

6   Conclusions and Future Work

This paper has described the IPG Naturalization Service, which is an OGSI-compliant grid service that has been implemented to automatically establish the execution environment for user applications. The Naturalization Service analyzes applications to determine their software dependencies, locates the software on the target system, if possible, or elsewhere, if not, arranges the transfer of software as necessary, and sets the environment variables to allow each application to find its required software. The Naturalization Service has a flexible design that gives the user considerable control over job processing including choosing which steps to perform and managing the source for frequently used software in a personal software catalog. The Naturalization Service allows users to execute jobs on resources that may have been previously unsuitable due to missing software dependencies with no or minimal user intervention. The end result is an increase in user productivity by significantly reducing setup time and hassles and increasing the pool of available resources, allowing for faster turnaround times.

There are a number of directions for future research. One inefficiency of the current design is that if two different jobs require the same dependency on the same resource, the Naturalization Service will copy the dependency twice. One solution for this would be to cache software on resources for use by later jobs. More study is necessary to determine how and when this can be done while preventing malicious or accidental modifications to cached software.

Another area for further study is providing additional dependency types and analysis capabilities. Additional types include shell scripts, makefiles, and data dependencies. Additional capabilities include determining "cross-type dependencies" such as executables invoked from Perl scripts. While the general case is undecidable, this analysis may be possible for simple invocation styles that occur frequently in practice (e.g. system("/bin/ls", @args)).

Implementation issues to be addressed in future versions include full IPG deployment, advanced software installation including packages and compilation in addition to basic file transfer, and full dependency version and feature support.

References

1. Allen, G.: Experiences From the SC'02 Demos. Global Grid Forum 7, Mar. 2003. Available at `http://www.zib.de/ggf/apps/meetings/gab-allen.pdf`.
2. Argonne National Laboratory: Extending the ACTS Toolkit for Wide Area Execution: Supporting DOE Applications on Computational Grids, Distributed Systems Laboratory, 1999. Available at `http://www.mcs.anl.gov/dsl/preport.htm`.
3. Carzaniga, A., Fuggetta, A., Hall, R.S., Heimbigner, D., van der Hoek, A., Wolf, A.L.: A Characterization Framework for Software Deployment Technologies. Technical Report CU-CS-857-98, Dept. of Computer Science, Univ. of Colorado, 1998.
4. Erwin, D.W., Snelling, D.F.: UNICORE: A Grid Computing Environment. 7th Intl. Euro-Par Conf., Aug. 2001.
5. Foster, I., Kesselman, C.: Globus: A Metacomputing Infrastructure Toolkit. Intl. J. Supercomputer Applications. 11(2) (1997) 115-128.
6. Foster, I., Kesselman, C. (eds.): The GRID: Blueprint for a New Computing Infrastructure. Morgan-Kaufmann, San Francisco, CA (1999).
7. Foster, I., Kesselman, C., Nick, J., Tuecke, S.: The Physiology of the Grid: An Open Grid Services Architecture for Distributed Systems Integration. Open Grid Service Infrastructure WG, Global Grid Forum, June 2002.
8. Guy, L., Kunszt, P., Laure, E., Stockinger, H., Stockinger, K.: Replica Management in Data Grids. Global Grid Forum Informational Document, GGF5, July 2002.
9. Johnston, W.E., Gannon, D., Nitzberg, B.: Grids as Production Computing Environments: The Engineering Aspects of NASA's Information Power Grid. 8th IEEE Intl. Symp. on High Performance Distributed Computing, Aug. 1999.
10. Kon, F., Yamane, T., Hess, C., Campbell, R., Mickunas, D.: Dynamic Resource Management and Automatic Configuration of Distributed Component Systems. 6th USENIX Conf. on Object-Oriented Technologies and Systems, Jan. 2001.
11. Rogers, S., Tejnil, E., Aftosmis, M.J., Ahmad, J., Pandya, S., Chaderjian, N.: Automated CFD Parameter Studies on Distributed Parallel

Computers. Information Power Grid Wkshp., Feb. 2003. Available at http://www.ipg.nasa.gov/workshops/workshop2003/rogers.ppt.

12. Russell, R., Quinlan, D. (eds.): Filesystem Hierarchy Standard – Version 2.2 Final. May 2001. Available at http://www.pathname.com/fhs.

13. Smith, W., Lisotta, A.: IPG Services. Information Power Grid Wkshp., Feb. 2003. Available at http://www.ipg.nasa.gov/workshops/workshop2003/smith.ppt.

14. Sun Microsystems: The Java Virtual Machine Specification. 2nd edn. (1999). Available at http://java.sun.com/docs/books/vmspec/2nd-edition/html/VMSpecTOC.doc.html.

15. Unix System Laboratories: System V Application Binary Interface. 3rd edn. Prentice Hall, Englewood Cliffs, NJ (1993)

Negotiation as a Generic Component Coordination Primitive

Jean Marc Andreoli and Stefania Castellani

Xerox Research Centre Europe
Grenoble, France
`Firstname.Lastname@xrce.xerox.com`

Abstract. In this paper, we claim that negotiation is a powerful abstract notion for the coordination of distributed autonomous components, and is therefore a suitable candidate for the definition of a generic coordination middleware tool, at the same level as transactions or messaging. Although specific negotiation mechanisms have been proposed in various application contexts, there is still a need to define a truely generic concept of negotiation, suitable for a middleware layer. This paper provides some elements towards the definition of such a concept. A salient feature of our proposal is that it introduces a rich representation of the state of a negotiation, inspired by proof-nets in Linear Logic and their game semantics, well beyond the traditional state-transition graphs. Furthermore, this representation is entirely decoupled from the dynamics of the negotiation processes that may use it, and hence avoids to rely on any specific "rule of the game" as to how a negotiation should proceed. It can thus adapt to any such rule, the definition of which is delegated to the negotiating components themselves.

Keywords: Negotiation, components, coordination, middleware, protocols

1 Introduction

Negotiation is a pervasive aspect of everyday life and it is not surprising that various approaches have been proposed to use computer software to support some forms of negotiation processes in various applications. In particular, the literature on multi-agent systems is rich with proposals to support negotiations in meeting scheduling, electronic trading, service matching and many other collaborative applications. More generic forms of negotiation also exist in service discovery mechanisms, advanced transaction models, quality of service selection etc. While most of these proposals make sense in the context of the applications for which they have been designed, they are hardly transportable across applications, and across architectural layers within an application. In other words, there is no satisfactory *generic* model of negotiation which could provide the basis of a middleware tool that any distributed application could rely on at multiple levels.

Middleware infrastructures, such as Corba [1], Jini [2], but also the more recent WebServices [3], are gaining momentum, following the success of the Internet and private networks, trying to address recurrent needs of distributed

J.-B. Stefani, I. Demeure, and D. Hagimont (Eds.): DAIS 2003, LNCS 2893, pp. 86–97, 2003.

application development, esp. in the domain of e-commerce [4] and trading [5].
From "glue" between various components of a distributed program, middleware
is evolving towards the role of "integration tool" coordinating users and applications. Existing middleware products provide some form of support for network communication, coordination, reliability, scalability, and heterogeneity [6].
In the present paper, we propose negotiation as a new concept to enrich the
set of traditional coordination facilities offered by middleware systems, such as
transactions, messaging, discovery. The challenge here is to devise a notion of
negotiation which, on the one hand, goes beyond simple arbitrary interaction,
and on the other hand, avoids adopting a specific rule of the game (like Contract
Nets or any of the multitude of variants of Auctions studied in the literature)
that would only make sense in specific contexts. This is achieved through a game
theoretic approach, where the negotiation behaviour of a component is understood in terms of moves in an abstract game "component vs rest-of-the-world".

In order to illustrate our model, called **Xplore**, we make use of a sample
case in the domain of collaborative commerce, namely an alliance of printshops
in which each partner has the ability to negotiate the outsourcing of print jobs,
possibly split into multiple slots, to the other partners in the alliance. This
application scenario has been detailed in [7]. Of course, the scope of the proposed
model and methods goes well beyond this specific example, and aims at applying
to any form of negotiation (commercial or not) in any application involving
software objects capable of making autonomous decisions.

Section 2 introduces the basic building blocks of our negotiation model: components, services and data-items. The model itself, based on the notion of negotiation graphs and their partial mirroring, is presented in Section 3 together
with an algorithm exploiting this model to implement a fully generic negotiation process. Section 4 provides a detailed example of use of our model in the
e-commerce application mentioned above. Sections 5 and 6 conclude the paper.

2   Negotiation Concepts

2.1   Components, Services, Data-Items

From a generic viewpoint, the goal of a negotiation is to have a set of components,
behaving as autonomous decision makers, reach an agreement as to a set of
actions to be executed by each of them. Once a rule of the game is adopted,
the participants to a negotiation may have assigned roles, differentiating their
possibilities of interaction, but *a priori*, a negotiation process is essentially *peer-
to-peer*. On the other hand, negotiations do not arise out of the blue, and need
to be initiated by some components inviting other components. This invitation
mechanism is, by nature, *client-server*: the client invites the server and the two
roles (host/guest) are essentially distinct. Hence, negotiations offer a perfect
framework in which to resolve the classical antithesis between the client-server
and peer-to-peer component interaction models.

Without committing to any computational model, we assume that a component is an encapsulated piece of software executing on one or more machines,

and publishing to the outside world an interface composed of a list of services. The notion of interface here is similar to that in object-oriented systems, except that the mechanism of invocation of a service in our system (described below) is fundamentally different from that of a method in the interface of a traditional object, be it synchronous (client-server) or asynchronous (peer-to-peer).

A service declaration in the interface simply consists of a name and a list of formal parameters. We are not concerned here with typing issues, so we assume that the parameters are not explicitly typed. Also, parameters have no attached mode (input or output), since that would not make sense in our invocation mechanism. Invoking a service results in some actions being triggered within the component. They may not be visible outside the component but they may be long-lived and may themselves result in other invocations.

Consider, for example, the sample application mentioned in the introduction, supporting the interactions within an alliance of printshops in the process of outsourcing or insourcing some of their print jobs. We may assume that each printshop A is represented by a software agent performing actions related to outsourcing and insourcing of print jobs (possibly under direct human control), realised through the following services:

- `outsrc(job)`: denotes an action by A of outsourcing a print job named `job` (as a whole or in slots); `outsrc` is the service name and `job` is the (here unique) formal parameter.
- `split(job,job1,job2)`: denotes an action by A of splitting a job named `job` into two slots named `job1` and `job2` respectively.
- `insrc(job)`: denotes an action by A of accepting a job named `job`.

Components manage sets of data-items over which negotiations can be engaged. To support heterogeneity and to achieve genericity, the infrastructure makes no assumption whatsoever as to how the components store these data-items and in what format. The only assumption is that each data-item can be described by its properties. Each property is supposed to describe an "aspect" of the item by a "term" (constraint). In our example, a print job is a data-item that can be described by various aspects such as `cost`, `size`, `deadline`, etc., and the term `cost<20` denotes a property that pertains to the aspect `cost`. From the point of view of the negotiation infrastructure, aspects and terms are uninterpreted.

2.2   Bilateral Negotiations

A service invocation is the most basic form of negotiation, between two components with distinguished roles (client and server). It consists of three phases (detailed in Section 3).

- **Invitation:** client $\rightarrow$ server
  The client initiates the negotiation by specifying a service from the interface of the server, together with a mapping between the formal parameters of the service declaration in the server and local names of data-items in the

client. These data-items constitute the objects of the negotiation. For example split(job=J,job1=J1, job2=J2) denotes an invocation of a service split in the server, with formal parameters job,job1,job2 mapped onto data-items named J,J1,J2 in the client. Hence, there are three negotiation objects in that negotiation, and agreement must be reached on all of them.
- **Unwinding:** peer-to-peer
At the time of the invitation, the client may already have established properties about the negotiation objects. Once the invitation is completed, both the client and the server may iteratively refine these properties. During this phase, the roles of client and server are completely blurred, at least from the infra-structural point of view (of course, under a specific rule of the game, the client and the server may take asymmetric roles).
- **Agreement:** client $\leftarrow$ server
Finally, the negotiation ends when the server is satisfied with the properties of the data-items attached to its parameters. The client may then choose to enact or not the proposed agreement.

2.3 Multi-party Negotiations

Service invocations, which are basic bilateral negotiations, can easily be combined to achieve arbitrary multi-party negotiations. The key here is to have a coordinator component launch multiple bilateral negotiation (ie. service invocations) with each participant, and play with each of them as a copycat representative of the others. The inter-dependencies between the bilateral negotiations are simply achieved by *sharing* of the negotiation objects.

For example, consider a multi-party negotiation in which a printshop A_0 wishes to outsource a job split into two slots allocated to, respectively, printshops A_1 and A_2. Here, the participants are A_0, A_1, A_2. We introduce an additional participant C, whose sole role is to coordinate the negotiation in order to achieve the stated result. C just needs to perform the following invocations in parallel (parallelism is denoted by @), lauching corresponding bilateral negotiations:

$$A_0\text{:outsrc(job=J)} @ A_0\text{:split(job=J,job1=J1,job2=J2)} @$$
$$A_1\text{:insrc(job=J1)} @ A_2\text{:insrc(job=J2)}$$

Here, C manipulates three data-items (print jobs), locally named, respectively, J,J1, J2. Interdependence between the bilateral negotiations launched by C is simply achieved by sharing the negotiation objects, picked among these data-items. Thus, the two bilateral negotiations launched by the invocations A_0:split and A_1:insrc, between C and, respectively, A_0 and A_1, are interdependent simply because they share a common negotiation object, named J1 in C and, respectively, job1 and job in the corresponding servers. As far as J1 is concerned, in the negotiation, C plays with A_0:split exactly as A_1:insrc does with C and, vice-versa, C plays with A_1:insrc exactly as A_0:split does with C. This is an instance of the "copycat" strategy, a quite classical concept of game theory. Note however that here: (*i*) the copycat may involve more than two players and (*ii*)

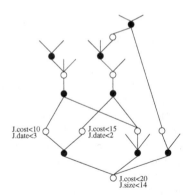

Fig. 1. An example of negotiation graph.

the moves of the players are asynchronous (in fact, the former property is made possible by the latter). Thus, if a data-item named X in C is shared in three bilateral negotiations launched by C as service invocations s_1, s_2, s_3, then, as far as X is concerned, C plays with its partner in s_i as both of its partners play with it in s_j and s_k (where i, j, k is any permutation of $1, 2, 3$).

Note that, although in the example above the set of servers invited by C is statically defined at its initialisation, this need not always be the case. It may very well happen that C starts a bilateral negotiation with a first server, and then, depending on its evolution, C decides to invite other servers. This dynamicity is both conceptually and practically essential. Conceptually, it means there is no boundary to the complexity of the patterns for combining bilateral negotiations. Practically, for example, it is usual to start e-commerce negotiations by selecting a set of potential partners, where the selection process is itself a negotiation, eg. with a yellow-page service such as UDDI [3].

3   Negotiation Model

We focus here on bilateral negotiations obtained by service invocation, since more complex ones can be built from them. In **Xplore**, a component acting as server in a service invocation stores the state of the negotiation as a data structure called a *negotiation graph* which is manipulated via a *negotiation protocol*.

3.1   Negotiation Graphs

It is assumed that a participant to a negotiation, be it client or server, is capable of making decisions, so that: (*i*) during the negotiation, the component may explore several alternatives in a decision, leading to negotiation contexts characterised by different combinations of choices for these alternatives; and (*ii*) each decision by the component, whether it involves alternatives or not, is made on the basis of previous negotiation contexts. Consequently, the overall state of a negotiation for a given component can be captured in a "bi-colored" graph: white nodes represent negotiation contexts and black nodes represent decision points with alternatives. Figure 1 gives an example of such a negotiation graph. The graph must be directed and acyclic, and its edges have the following meaning:

- A white node N has at most one parent node, which must (if any) be black, and represents one alternative in the decision expressed by its parent (black) node. A white node without parent represents a context that does not result of a decision (typically, the initial context of a negotiation).
- A black node N has at least one parent node, which must (all) be white. The context in which the decision represented by N is taken is given by the fusion of all its parent (white) nodes.

To make decisions in an informed way, the participants must have access to the information available at each negotiation context (ie. white node) about the state of the negotiation in that context. Such information consists of pairs composed of a local name of a data-item, and a constraint (term) on that data-item. In our example, such a pair could be $J.cost<20$ (the name and the term constraining its value are on each side of the dot), meaning that the cost of the job J should not exceed a certain threshold 20. Consequently, each white node is decorated with specific information about the negotiation at that node in the form of name-term pairs. By inheritance, the overall information available at a white node is given by the set of such pairs attached to that node and to all its ancestor white nodes.

3.2   The Xplore Protocol

The **Xplore** protocol is a set of primitives allowing a component to express negotiation decisions through manipulations of a negotiation graph.

- **Invitation:** During any negotiation, a component can launch and become client of a new negotiation by invoking a service from another (or the same) component (in server mode). Invitation is a negotiation decision of its own, and hence is attached to a negotiation context (white node).
  - **Connect**(n:*nodeId*, m:*mapping*, c:*component*): invites a component service, specified by c, to join the negotiation from node n onward. This results in the creation of a new graph, initially reduced to the single node n, in the server component. The mapping m specifies the translation table between the formal parameters of server c and the local names of data-items in the client.
- **Unwinding:** At any stage, a component (whether client or server) participating in a negotiation can further refine its graph for that negotiation:
  - **Open**($n, n_1, \ldots, n_p$:*nodeId*): creates a node n (which must not already exist) with parent nodes $n_1, \ldots, n_p$ (which must exist). All the parent nodes $n_1, \ldots, n_p$ (if any) must be of the same colour, and n is then of the opposite colour. If $p = 0$, then n is white (creation of a negotiation root context) and if $p \geq 2$, then n is black, hence $n_1, \ldots, n_p$ must (all) be white (fusion of negotiation contexts). In the latter case, the parent nodes must be pairwise compatible. Two nodes are said to be compatible

when they do not appear on branches of the negotiation graph which diverge at a black node, since that would mean that the two nodes are alternatives and hence cannot be part of any final agreement.

- **Assert**(n:*nodeId*, v:*name*, a:*aspect*, t:*term*): expresses the decision that, in the negotiation context represented by node n in the graph, the value of the data-item named v must have the property expressed by term t pertaining to aspect a. Node n must exist and be white. This is the way to populate context nodes with information about the negotiation state at these nodes, for the other concerned participants to see (and eventually react).
- **Request**(n:*nodeId*, v:*name*, a:*aspect*): expresses that, to proceed with the negotiation, the component is interested in information, obtained through assertions by the other concerned participants, about a particular aspect a of a data-item named v at node n (which must exist and be white).
- **Quit**(n:*nodeId*): expresses that the negotiation will never succeed at node n (which must exist and be white), so the other concerned participants need not elaborate further.

- **Agreement:** A component in server mode in a negotiation may end the negotiation in one branch of the graph
  - **Ready**($n_1, \ldots, n_p$:*nodeId*): expresses that the server is satisfied with the state of the negotiation at nodes $n_1, \ldots, n_p$ (which must exist and be white). In other words, the component has seen enough information and is ready to finalise the negotiation in the state represented by the fusion of these nodes, which must be pairwise compatible.

When a server expresses its readiness, the client must decide whether or not to enact the agreement. This can be obtained by a classical transactional two-phase commit protocol, where the client first **Reserves** the agreement delivered by the server, then **Confirms** or **Cancels** the reservation. This allows real synchronisation of agreements between multiple servers (needed since all the other operations, including the **Ready**, are asynchronous). We do not discuss here further the transactional management of agreements, as this has been widely investigated in the literature. For example, the component coordination infrastructure CLF [8], which had a deep influence on the design of Xplore, proposes a form of light-weight transaction management which is directly applicable here.

3.3 The Xplore Infrastructure

An application in **Xplore** is seen as one big negotiation, with sub-negotiations nested at an arbitrary level by the invitation mechanism (as with nested transactions). Hence, from the negotiation infrastructure point of view, it is possible to represent the state of the application as a tree (also called the invocation network), the vertices of which are labeled by negotiation graphs and the edges of which are the service invocations. The negotiation infrastructure operates on that network, augmented each time the **Connect** primitive is executed. Its main roles are: (*i*) at each edge of the network, to synchronise back and forth the *relevant* decisions taken in the two graphs linked by that edge; and (*ii*) at each vertex of the network, to detect *consensus* at that vertex, ie. agreement decisions at the end vertex of its out-going edges. These two functions form the software core of the **Xplore** infrastructure, which is entirely distributed across the vertices of the invocation network (each vertex lives in a component). The main difficulty arises from the fact that each negotiation operation at a vertex of the network is contextualised by a node in the corresponding negotiation graph, and the topology of the graph must be taken into account to process each operation. For example, the synchronisation algorithm has the following behaviour.

- A call to the **Open** primitive never needs to be mirrored immediately, because it always creates a fresh node with no information attached to it, so it is irrelevant to any neighbour in the invocation network.
- A call of the form **Assert**(n,v,a,t) in one vertex need only be replicated onto those neighbours in the invocation network which have previously made calls of the form **Request**(n',v,a) where nodes n, n' are compatible, ie. do not lie on alternative branches (diverging at a black node). In the replicated call, the local name v must be replaced by its image in the conversion table attached to the concerned neighbour. Furthermore, the replicated call may need to be preceded by calls to the **Open** primitive to make sure that node n is mirrored on the concerned neighbours.
- A call of the form **Request**(n,v,a) in one vertex need only be replicated onto those neighbours in the invocation network which have a local name v' corresponding to v in the conversion table attached to them. The replicated call must specify v' in place of v. As above, the replicated call may require prior node mirroring using **Open**. Furthermore, all the calls of the form **Assert**(n',v,a,t) at any node n' related to n must be replicated on the originator of the **Request** call.

The consensus detection algorithm at a vertex k_o is even more involved as it needs to detect combinations of calls of the form **Ready**(N_k) at a set K of vertices k linked to k_o in the invocation network, ie. at servers invited by k_o as client. Not all the servers invited by k_o need to be included in K, but there must be at least one of them, and if one server k is included in K, then so should all those invited at nodes which are ancestors of the nodes of N_k. Furthermore, all the nodes in $N = \bigcup_{k \in K} N_k$ must be pairwise compatible, ie. not lie on alternative branches (diverging at a black node). In that case, consensus is detected and the primitive **Ready**(N) is called by k_o as server.

An implementation along these lines has been realised, where the components process the calls to the **XPlore** protocol in an asynchronous, actor-like fashion [9].

4   An Example

We now illustrate the negotiation framework presented above on the sample negotiation introduced in Section 2.3:

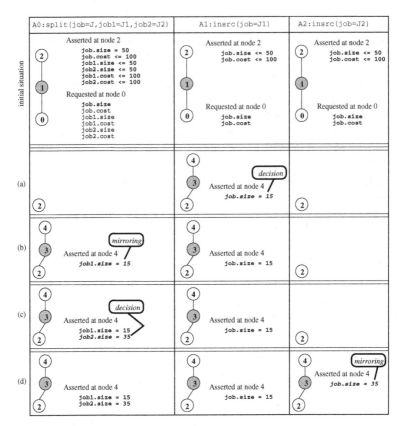

Fig. 2. An example of negotiation graph mirroring.

$$A_0\text{:outsrc(job=J) @ } A_0\text{:split(job=J,job1=J1,job2=J2) @}$$
$$A_1\text{:insrc(job=J1) @ } A_2\text{:insrc(job=J2)}$$

We have here four components: C, A_0, A_1, A_2, where C is a coordinator, and A_0, A_1, A_2 are printshops (their interfaces are described in Section 2.3). At initialisation, the coordinator C creates a graph with a single root node, then, from this graph, invites the participants above in separate bilateral negotiations, using calls to the **Connect** primitives at the root node. In the end, five graphs are created together with four links in the invocation network, between the graph in C and each of the graphs corresponding to the invocations performed by C (ie. two for A_0 and one for each of A_1, A_2). The participants then start to work on their negotiation graphs using the **Xplore** primitives, automatically mirrored in a timely way by the infrastructure. Each path in the graph can be viewed as a dialog between the participants consisting of successive refinements of the terms of the agreement. Having multiple paths in the graph allows several interwoven alternatives to be explored in parallel. For example, the following fragment of a conversation among the three printshops through the coordinator corresponds to a phase of the negotiation where A_1 makes a proposal to A_0 on one slot of a job. Figure 2 shows the negotiation graph mirroring corresponding to this dialog.

- A_1:insrc.{Open(3,2),Open(4,3),Assert(4,job.size=15)}
  A_1:insrc decides to explore one alternative in which the size of the job it would accept is 15. By creating black node 3, it leaves the possibility of exploring other alternatives. At white node 4, A_1 may locally attach resouces which it anticipates will be needed to fulfil its commitment in that alternative, but this need not be made public. These decisions are taken according to its own specific semantics, characterising, here, its strategy in accepting jobs. The resulting situation is depicted in Figure 2(a).
- A_1:insrc$\mapsto$ C.{Open(3,2),Open(4,3),Assert(4,J1.size=15)}
  We assume that C had previously informed A_1:insrc that the size aspect of its job parameter was requested in the negotiation in context 2 (or one of its ancestors). The infrastructure therefore mirrors into C the information it has just asserted on that aspect in context 4. Since C does not know this context yet, the infrastructure mirrors the missing bit of the graph (nodes 3 and 4) into C. Note that the formal parameter name job known by A_1:insrc is converted into the corresponding name J1 known by C.
- $C \mapsto A_0$:split.{Open(3,2),Open(4,3),Assert(4,job1.size=15)}
  The mirroring process continues from C, which now looks for all the participants which had requested information on the size of J1 in the negotiation; here, only A_0:split. The information is therefore passed on to it. Again, node 4 not being heard of yet by A_0:split, the missing bit of the graph is first mirrored. And again, the data-item name J1 is converted into the corresponding parameter name job1. The resulting situation is depicted in Figure 2(b).
- A_0:split.Assert(4,job2.size=35)
  A_0:split had previously been informed that the total size of its job is constrained to be equal to 50 in context 2 (or one of its ancestors). The constraint therefore holds in context 4 since it is a descendent of 2. Furthermore, knowing that in context 4 the size of slot job1 is constrained to be equal to 15, A_0:split infers that the size of the other slot job2 is constrained to be equal to 35 in that context. This constraint propagation, which is here a characteristic of the semantics of service A_0:split, could be performed automatically by a constraint solver. The resulting situation is depicted in Figure 2(c).
- A_0:split$\mapsto$ C.Assert(4,J2.size=35)
  Mirroring is re-activated from A_0:split to C, which had previously requested information on the size of job2. Again, the parameter name job2 is converted into its corresponding name J2 in C.
- $C \mapsto A_2$:insrc.Assert(4,job.size=35)
  The mirroring process continues in C, which passes on the information it has just received on the size of J2 to A_2:insrc which had initially requested it. The name J2 is converted again into the parameter name job. The resulting situation is depicted in Figure 2(d).

5   Discussion

A distinctive feature of distributed applications is that, even when their functionality is simple, they tend to involve a multitude of generic issues such as consistency, awareness, authorisation, etc. Each of these aspects have been studied separately, each leading to a different class of models and solutions. Thus, transactions deal with consistency issues, messaging and discovery with awareness issues, cryptography and security protocols with authorisation issues, etc. Software engineering techniques such as Aspect-Oriented Programming [10] help specify and maintain these aspects separately, but they do not provide a unified model in which these aspects would appear as facets of the same mechanism. We claim here that many aspects, at least those pertaining to component coordination, can be unified into a single model, around a generic notion of *negotiation*.

Negotiation is indeed a proto-typical kind of coordinated process, and the literature on e-negotiation abounds with system descriptions which specify how participants should coordinate in order to achieve certain goals. However, these proposals are often embedded into full-blown applications (eg. [11]), and rely on a plethora of so-called generic mechanisms [12] (Contract-Nets, Auctions, Match-making etc. with many variants) which it is difficult to choose from *a priori*, outside a specific application context. These proposals are therefore not suitable for a generic middleware infrastructure, where the components and the service they offer, hence their negotiation needs, can be widely diverse. Our approach, on the contrary, seeks to abstract away any specific negotiation scheme and to formalise only universal characteristics of negotiation processes: (*i*) the possibility of exploring alternative branches and (*ii*) the incremental refinement of the terms in a negotiation.

The model of negotiation we have presented here draws on ideas coming from constraint programming and constraint propagation [13], in particular distributed constraint satisfaction [14] where constraints are viewed as autonomous agents propagating "no-good" information via their shared variables, and cooperative constraint solving [15]. The other major source of inspiration is proof-theory in formal logic, in particular proof-nets in Linear Logic [16] which offer a totally desequentialised representation of logical inferences as a graph, similar to our negotiation graphs (inferences are here negotiation decisions). The game theoretic interpretation of proofs [17] has also strongly influenced our view of negotiation as games.

6   Conclusion

In this paper, it is claimed that negotiation is an appropriate abstraction for a middleware level service for the coordination of distributed components, on a par with traditional middleware concepts such as transactions, messaging and discovery. Our model provides an abstract representation of the state of a negotiation through a bi-colored graph, and exploits this model to build a fully generic negotiation process, viewed as the partially synchronised construction of such graphs.

References

1. McConnell, S.: Negotiation Facility. Technical report, OMG (1999)
2. Waldo, J.: The Jini Architecture for Network-Centric Computing. Communications of the ACM **42** (1999) 76–82
3. Newcomer, E.: Understanding WebServices: XML, WSDL, SOAP, and UDDI. Addison Wesley Professional (2002)
4. Charles, J.: Middleware Moves to the Forefront. IEEE Computer Magazine **32** (1999) 17–19
5. Marvie, R., Merle, P., Geib, J.M., Leblanc, S.: TORBA: Trading Contracts for CORBA. In: Proc. of COOTS –6th USENIX Conference on Object-Oriented Technologies and Systems, San Antonio, Texas, USA. (2001)
6. Emmerich, W.: Software Engineering and Middleware: A Roadmap. In: Proc. of ICSE 2000, The future of Software Engineering, Munich, Germany (2000)
7. Andreoli, J.M., Castellani, S., Munier, M.: AllianceNet: Information Sharing, Negotiation and Decision-Making for Distributed Organizations. In: Proc. of EcWeb2000, Greenwich, U.K. (2000)
8. Andreoli, J.M., Arregui, D., Pacull, F., Riviere, M., Vion-Dury, J.Y., Willamowski, J.: Clf/mekano: a framework for building virtual-enterprise applications. In: Proc. of EDOC'99, Manheim, Germany (1999)
9. Agha, G., Mason, I., Smith, S., Talcott, C.: A foundation for actor computation. Journal of Functional Programming **7** (1997) 1–72
10. Kiczales, G., Lamping, J., Menhdhekar, A., Maeda, C., Lopes, C., Loingtier, J.M., Irwin, J.: Aspect-oriented programming. In Akşit, M., Matsuoka, S., eds.: Proc. of ECOOP '97, Jyväskylä, Finland, Springer-Verlag (1997)
11. Chavez, A., Maes, P.: Kasbah: An agent marketplace for buying and selling goods. In: Proc. of 1st Conference on Practical Applications of Intelligent Agents and Multi-Agents, London, U.K. (1996) 75–90
12. Dignum, F., Sierra, C., eds.: Agent Mediated Electronic Commerce. LNAI 1991, Springer Verlag (2001)
13. van Hentenryck, P., Saraswat, V.: Strategic directions in constraint programming. ACM Computing Surveys **28** (1996) 701–726
14. Yokoo, M., Hirayama, K.: Algorithms for Distributed Constraint Satisfaction: A Review. Autonomous Agents and Multi-Agent Systems **3** (2000) 185–207
15. Monfroy, E., Castro, C.: Basic operators for solving constraints via collaboration of solvers. In Campbell, J., Roanes-Lozano, E., eds.: Proc. of AISC 2000, Madrid, Spain, Springer-Verlag (2001) 142–156
16. Girard, J.Y.: Linear logic. Theoretical Computer Science **50** (1987) 1–102
17. Laurent, O.: Polarized games. In: Proc. of LICS'02, Copenhagen, Denmark, IEEE Computer Society (2002) 265–275

Jironde: A Flexible Framework
for Making Components Transactional

Marek Prochazka

INRIA Rhône-Alpes
665, avenue de l'Europe, Montbonnot, 38334 Saint Ismier Cedex, France
Marek.Prochazka@inrialpes.fr

Abstract. It is generally agreed that one of the key services of component-based systems are transactions. However, an agreement on how components should be involved in transactions is still missing. In this paper, we discuss some of the key issues of combining components with transactions, and different approaches to achieve an appropriate level of transactional functionality in components. We distinguish between the explicit and implicit component participation approaches that differ by whether a component implements a part of transactional functionality or not. We discuss the influence of both approaches to concurrency control, recovery, and transaction context propagation. Then, we introduce our approach based on the use of several component controllers that manage transactional functionality on behalf of components. For a component, to be transactional, the only requirement is to fulfill a component contract which is specific to different transactional controller implementations. We provide an overview of a prototype implementation of our approach in the Fractal component model. Thanks to the flexibility and reflective nature of Fractal, it is possible to achieve different levels of component transactional functionality by combining different transactional controllers, with only taking their component contracts into account. Our work proves that with an appropriate component framework that supports reflection and flexible component management with clearly defined notions of component composition, lifecycle, and binding, we can make components transactional in an elegant and flexible way.

1 Introduction

During last years, a range of different component models has been proposed in both academia [1, 5, 8, 15, 17] and software industry [9, 10, 13, 24]. It is generally believed that transactions belong to key services of component-based systems. However, there is no agreement on how the transaction service should look like and how components should be involved in transactions. The goal of the paper is twofold:

- We discuss some of the key issues of combining components with transactions, as well as different approaches to achieve transactional components. We distinguish between the *explicit* and *implicit* component participation approaches that differ by whether a component implements a part of transactional functionality or not. We discuss the influence of both approaches to concurrency control, recovery, and transaction context propagation.

J.-B. Stefani, I. Demeure, and D. Hagimont (Eds.): DAIS 2003, LNCS 2893, pp. 98–109, 2003.
© IFIP International Federation for Information Processing 2003

– Then, we introduce Jironde, a flexible framework for making components transactional. Jironde uses several *component controllers* that manage transactional functionality on behalf of a component. We identify several parts of transactional functionality that are implemented by different transactional controllers. For a component, to be transactional, the only requirement is to fulfill a *component contract* which is specific to different transactional controller implementations. We present an overview of the Jironde prototype implemented using the Fractal Composition Framework [15].

The main contribution of Jironde is its flexibility. Combining different transactional controllers makes it possible to achieve different levels of component's transactional functionality, as well as to employ different transactional standards. The only obligation for components is to take component contracts of used transactional controllers into account. We show that with an appropriate component framework that supports reflection as well as flexible component management with well defined notions of component composition, lifecycle, and binding, it is possible to add transactions to components in an elegant and flexible way.

The rest of the paper is organized as follows. In Section 2, we identify several issues and different approaches for combining components and transactions. In Section 3, we introduce our Jironde framework for making components transactional. Section 4 gives details of the Jironde prototype implementation in the Fractal environment. An evaluation and overview of related work is provided in Section 5 and we conclude with Section 6, where we also present our plans for the future.

2 Combining Components and Transactions

The issue of adding transactions to components might seem to be an easy task. At least, there are several standards and architectures that deal with transactional components, e.g. Enterprise JavaBeans (EJB, [24]), CORBA Components (CCM, [13]), and the Component Object Model (COM, [9, 10]) forming together with the Microsoft Transaction Server [6] the COM+ technology. However, most of these standards employ simple ad-hoc solutions without addressing key issues of transactional components. Several research papers have investigated transactional components [2, 3, 21], but their visions of transactional components significantly differ. When speaking about transactional components, we have identified at least the following issues to solve: component participation in a transaction, concurrency control, recovery, and transaction context propagation. Let us discuss each of them separately in the following sections.

2.1 Component Participation in a Transaction

What does it mean that "a component takes part in a transaction" or that "a component is transactional"? Surprisingly, different component systems answer these questions differently. An EJB component, for instance, is transactional thanks to the EJB container that 1) synchronizes the component's persistent state at well defined points in time and 2) associates database connections opened by the component with the current transaction. A CORBA object takes part in transactions if it implements one of the `Resource`, `Synchronization`, or `SubtransactionAwareResource` interfaces in which case it can be registered to a transaction and participate in its two-phase commit. In [18], each component is supervised by a so called spontaneous container, which manages its persistence and participation in transaction in a similar way traditional databases do with ordinary data. In our opinion, all approaches could be divided into two main groups, depending on whether components take part in transactions implicitly or explicitly.

The scenario of involving a component C to a transaction t in the *explicit transaction participation* essentially consists of three steps:

1. C is registered to t. The transaction manager stores a pointer to C. More precisely, to be able to be registered to a transaction, a component has to implement a well defined interface specific to a particular component architecture. For example, in the Java Transaction API (JTA, [25]), objects that implement the XAResource or Synchronization interfaces can be registered to a transaction.
2. The client invokes various operations on C. What makes the explicit transaction participation different from the classical database-like transaction paradigm is that the transaction manager is not aware of these operation executions: it has no scheduler.
3. At the time of t's commit or abort, the transaction manager invokes selected methods of the registered C's interfaces. The order of these invocations reflects a well defined commit protocol. For example, in the CORBA Transaction Service (OTS, [11]), the prepare and commit/abort methods of all registered Resource objects are invoked according to the two-phase commit protocol.

With the explicit transaction participation, scheduling of component operations (that correspond to data operations in database systems) is not driven by the transaction manager. Furthermore, the transaction manager is not aware of transaction effects and therefore is not responsible for their confirmation or cancellation by commit or abort, neither for their recovery in case of a system crash. All this functionality is instead implemented as a part of transactional components. Rather than ensuring ACIDity, standards used in the world of distributed components, such as OTS and JTA, ensure only atomicity of sequences of operations invoked on objects registered to transactions[1].

In the *implicit transaction participation*, all transactional functionality is implemented by the container and its transaction manager themselves. The scenario of involving a component C to a transaction t looks as follows:

1. Any time C is visited by a transaction t, the container keeps all necessary information to manage concurrency control, commit, rollback, and recovery.
2. When a client invokes any operation on C, the container is aware of it. It applies concurrency control protocols and manages C's persistent state. The container behaves for components exactly like a database management system does for traditional data.

---

[1] However, JTA supports ACIDity through the use of XA resources [26]. Concurrency control and recovery is therefore provided at the level of the databases involved. Both the JTA and OTS standards support ACID transactions but they do not provide all means to support all of the ACID properties and some of the properties should be ensured by other system components. For instance, concurrency control in CORBA can be managed through a simple read/write locking as specified in the Concurrency Service [12].

3. At the time of t's commit or abort, the transaction manager commits or rollbacks all effects of t on C (as well as other components it manages). It can eventually take part in two-phase commit of transactions spread on multiple components supervised by different containers.

To summarize what is different between the implicit and explicit transaction participation, the former manages all the transactional functionality itself (therefore it seems to be implicit from the component's point of view), while the latter leaves the implementation of what happens at the time of commit, rollback, or crash recovery on the code of transactional components (transactions are handled by components explicitly).

2.2 Concurrency Control and Recovery

Following the discussion in the previous paragraph, let us discuss what is different between the explicit and implicit transaction participation from the concurrency control point of view. As mentioned before, in the explicit transaction participation, the transaction manager does not support any (implicit) scheduling. For example, EJB use the JTA standard for transactions. However, JTA is not component-aware and only provides an API for managing distributed transactions over XA resources [26] in Java. As for concurrency control, JTA relies on the underlying databases via JDBC connections. To have a locking policy at the component level, EJB add exclusive locking to any visited component. This approach makes it impossible to share any bean instance among transactions even if they are about to invoke read-only methods.

In CORBA, any object visited by a transaction is not locked by default and applications can use the CORBA Concurrency Service (CCS, [12]) or other transaction-aware locking if needed.

To summarize, there is no implicit concurrency control at the level of components if the explicit transaction participation is used. However, components can use an arbitrary transaction-aware concurrency control mechanism, such as CCS-like read/write locking in CORBA or mutual exclusion in EJB.

With the implicit transaction participation, concurrency control is supported by the transaction manager through the container that controls every component invocation. Similarly as in a database system, the container essentially implements the functionality of three entities: the transaction manager, scheduler, and data manager [4]. The transaction manager receives component operations (method invocations) and transaction operations (begin, commit, etc.) and forwards them to the scheduler. The scheduler ensures certain order of component and transaction operations. For each component operation sent by the transaction manager, the scheduler may 1) schedule it immediately by sending it to the data manager, 2) delay it by inserting it into a queue, or 3) reject it and cause the issuing transaction to abort. Various concurrency control policies, ranging from aggressive and optimistic schedulers that avoid delaying operations, to conservative schedulers tending to delay operations and to avoid rejecting them, as well as different implementation techniques, based on e.g. locks, timestamps, or serialization graph testing, can be employed.

As for recovery, the container supporting the implicit transaction participation manages recovery of every deployed component. On the opposite, with the explicit transaction participation, components should manage their recovery themselves, since the container does not have enough information to do that. For example, in CORBA, a reference to a Recovery Coordinator is obtained when registering a resource to a transaction. A recoverable object has to use the Recovery Coordinator to drive the recovery process in certain situations. In EJB, recovery is supported only at the JDBC connection level. In principle, the container is able to continue two-phase commit on all the participating JDBC connections thanks to the XA protocol. There is no recovery protocol at the level of bean instances in EJB.

2.3 Transaction Context Propagation

To allow a component to participate in a client transaction, the transaction context has to be propagated from the client to the component. This implies the support for the transaction context propagation in the communication protocol used (e.g., IIOP or RMI) and the container's ability to determine the transaction context from the client request. Along with the simple transaction propagation, more advanced manipulation of the transaction context can be provided. This includes applying various policies that specify, for example, whether an external transaction has to be present when invoking a particular method, whether a container creates a new (*container-managed*) transaction or the client transaction context is propagated to the component, etc. [21].

Essentially, there is no difference between the implicit and explicit transaction participation, since the propagation policy could be both set implicitly by the container or explicitly by the component author/deployer in both approaches. In EJB, CCM, and COM+, the transaction propagation policy is determined by the value of a single transaction attribute associated with the invoked method. The transaction attribute is defined apart from the business interface specification and the component code as late as in the deployment descriptor of the component. Various frameworks that separate transaction demarcation from the container and allow defining new transaction propagation policies have been proposed [20, 23].

3 Jironde

Jironde is a framework for making components transactional. The architecture of a component enabled to participate in transactions is shown in Fig. 1. The key ideas behind Jironde are as follows:

- To be transactional, a component is extended by several *transactional controllers* that manage transactional functionality on its behalf.
- The functionality implemented by transactional controllers is not fixed or determined by a transactional standard used. Instead, each transactional controller may implement a part of the transactional functionality (e.g., concurrency control) in its own way.
- The set of transactional controllers used by the component is specified during the component deployment. In other words, the way transactions are managed by the component is determined by its deployment configuration.
- The component must fulfill the *component contracts* of all the transactional controllers used in order to manage transactions correctly.

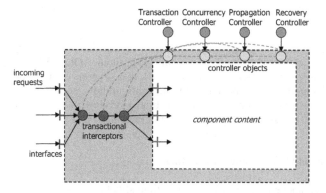

Fig. 1. The architecture of a component enhanced to support transactions. The controller part of the component contains several transactional controllers that manage transaction participation on behalf of the component

We have borrowed our terminology from Fractal, a generic composition framework based on components, which we have also used for a prototype implementation of Jironde (described in Section 4). However, Jironde is not Fractal-specific and can work with any component model that supports reflection, flexible component management through a configurable set of controllers[2], as well as means supporting invocation interception.

With having a configurable set of transactional controllers, we leave the decision whether to follow the explicit or implicit approach (Section 2.1) on particular controller implementations. For example, in our current prototype implementation, we use the explicit transaction participation along with implicit concurrency control and transaction context propagation. Composite components allow us to use transactional controllers at any level of nesting, i.e., a subcomponent of a component can again be deployed with various transactional controllers and therefore can manage transactions in its own way. The component's author does not care about transactional controllers. When deploying a component, it is only necessary to specify which controllers will be present in the target architecture. Obviously, this approach gives component developers/deployers a big portion of flexibility, but the specification of a deployment configuration as well as combining different transactional controllers have to be handled with care.

To participate in transactions correctly, a component has to fulfill requirements of the controllers used – the component contracts. For example, the OTS Transaction Controller in our prototype checks whether the component implements either the `Resource` or `Synchronization` interfaces. If it does, the interfaces are registered to the current OTS transaction. Most of this functionality is done in component interceptors that correspond to related transactional controllers. Each of the interceptors checks whether a transaction is associated with the thread asking for method invocation. Then the code specific to each interceptor is executed.

---

[2] By a *controller* here we mean any runtime entity that provides certain management services for a component. It may have a form of a wrapper, interceptor, adapter, proxy, and others.

4   Implementing Jironde in Fractal

Jironde has been made as a part of the Java Open Transaction Manager (JOTM, [16]), one of the ObjectWeb [14] projects. Fractal [15], another ObjectWeb project, provides a general software composition framework that supports component-based programming, including component definition, configuration, composition, and management. In the next section we provide a brief overview of Fractal, and then we present details of our Jironde implementation in Fractal.

4.1   The Fractal Composition Framework

In Fractal, a component is considered a run-time structure composed of two parts: a *controller part* and a *content part*. The content part (or content) of a component is composed of (a finite number of) other components, which are under control of the controller of the enclosing component. The component model is recursive and allows components to be nested (i.e., to appear in the content of enclosing components) at an arbitrary level. Therefore, we distinguish a *primitive component* with no other component inside, and a *composite component* that contains other components. The notions of subcomponent, parent component, child component, and top-level component are used in the obvious way.

A component interacts with its surrounding environment via its access points called *interfaces*. An interface is a set of *methods* whose invocations reflect component interactions. Visibility of interfaces is managed by the component controller part composed of several *controller objects* (or *controllers* for short). A component may have multiple *server interfaces*, which define the functionality that the component offers to other components, and multiple *client interfaces*, which define the functionality the component requires from the surrounding environment. The controller part of a component embodies the control behavior associated with this component. In particular, a component controller can intercept incoming and outgoing operation invocations and returns targeting or originating from the components in the component content. For example, the Lifecycle Controller manages the component lifecycle and the Binding Controller manages bindings to other components.

4.2   Concurrency Controller

In the Jironde prototype, a component is a unit of concurrency control. The Concurrency Controller works as a database scheduler. It can delay the method execution by temporarily suspending the invoking thread, or reject the method invocation by rolling back the current transaction, or schedule the method invocation.

Our current implementation of the Concurrency Controller uses the JOTM Lock Manager which supports transaction-aware locking with user-defined lock modes and user-defined conflict tables, which may define both non-symmetric and non-transitive conflict relations [16]. Let us have an example component that implements a single `Account` interface with the `balance`, `deposit`, and `withdraw` methods. As `balance` is obviously not modifying the bank account balance, it is not conflicting with the other two methods. Even both `deposit` and `withdraw` modify the account balance, only withdraw is considered conflicting with other operations. The semantics here is that any dirty balance retrieved due to concurrent deposits is considered correct, while multiple withdraw or withdraw combined with non-committed deposit can lead to negative balance of the bank account, which is considered undesirable. The corresponding conflict table is shown in Table 1, where "–" implies no conflict and "+" implies a conflict.

Table 1. The conflict table of the Account component example

	balance	deposit	withdraw
balance	–	–	–
deposit	–	–	+
withdraw	+	+	+

The only thing the author of a component has to do is to define a conflict table of methods of all implemented interfaces in a simple configuration file as follows:

```
1   <lock-controller>
2       <default-conflict value="false" />
3       <lock-mode name="balance">
4           <operation>Account.balance</operation>
5       </lock-mode>
6       <lock-mode name="deposit">
7           <operation>Account.deposit</operation>
8           <conflict held-mode="withdraw" value="true" />
9       </lock-mode>
10      <lock-mode name="withdraw">
11          <operation>Account.withdraw</operation>
12          <conflict held-mode="balance" value="true" />
13          <conflict held-mode="deposit" value="true" />
14          <conflict held-mode="withdraw" value="true" />
15      </lock-mode>
16  </lock-controller>
```

The configuration file is the only component contract of the Concurrency Controller. The lock configuration above reflects the conflict table in Table 1. Inside each lock mode definition (e.g., lines 3-5 for the balance lock mode) is a list of methods associated with the lock mode (the operation element on line 4), together with the definition of conflicts (the conflict elements on lines 8 and 12-14). The default conflict value is false (line 2) and therefore all methods not explicitly listed in the conflict element are considered non-conflicting. An alternative configuration with the traditional read/write lock modes, where balance is associated with the read and both deposit and withdraw are associated with the write lock mode, could be easily defined. The Concurrency Controller works as follows:

- It is initialized during the application instantiation. During the initialization, the configuration file is parsed to detect which interfaces and methods are subjects to locking. There is always a single lock associated with each component. The lock modes are values of lock-mode elements and the conflicts are attribute values of conflict elements in the configuration file. Also, the Concurrency Controller is registered as a transaction participant.
- For each request for method invocation, the Concurrency Interceptor detects whether a transaction is associated with the request.
- If a transaction is associated with the request, the Concurrency Interceptor finds whether the invoked method is a subject for locking. This is true only if the method name was defined in the operation element of one of the lock modes in the configuration file.
- If the method is subject for locking, the JOTM Transaction Lock is acquired in the mode corresponding to the invoked method (the name of the lock mode in whose definition the method was listed in the operation element).
- The lock is released at the time of transaction commit or abort. This is possible thanks to the fact that the Concurrency Controller has been registered as a transaction participant during the initialization phase.

Thanks to the Concurrency Controller based on the JOTM locking with an arbitrary conflict table, the author of a component can exploit method semantics and therefore the component sharing potential is increased comparing to the traditional read/write approach. The controller configuration file is easy to define (a single conflict table per a component type). Our current Concurrency Controller implementation uses the implicit approach (i.e., the component lock is controlled by the controller), but the lock configuration is up to the component's developer/deployer.

4.3 Transaction Controller

The Transaction Controller manages the registration of components to transactions. We have decided to follow the explicit transaction participation approach, especially due to the fact that we do not have any appropriate container being able to manage implicit transaction participation, component persistency, and recovery. We have implemented three Transaction Controllers that are able to register a component to one of the OTS, JTA, and JOTM transactions, respectively. Each Transaction Controller implementation allows to get a transaction object to demarcate transactions, to get the current transaction, and to configure transactions in the component according to the underlying standard.

For every issued method invocation, the interceptor of the corresponding Transaction Controller detects whether a transaction is associated with the request and whether it is the transaction's first visit of the component. If an OTS, JTA, or JOTM transaction is associated with the request, the corresponding Transaction Controller finds whether the component implements the Resource and Synchronization OTS interfaces, the XAResource and Synchronization JTA interfaces, or the EventListener JOTM interface. If yes, the respective interface is registered to the issuing transaction.

The required component contract of the OTS, JTA, and JOTM Transaction Controllers is to implement the corresponding interfaces. To allow components also to register other types of transactional resources, we have also implemented the Generic Transaction Controller. Its component contract states that the component takes the responsibility for the resource registration and implements the `Registration` interface. When intercepting a method invocation, the Generic Transaction Controller finds out if the component implements `Registration` – in this case the `Registration.registerResources` method is invoked. It is up to the component which resources are in this method registered to a transaction that visits the component.

4.4 Propagation Controller

As described in Section 2.3, the Propagation Controller is responsible for the propagation of transaction context to the component. The behavior of the controller is driven according to various transaction propagation policies. When intercepting a method invocation, the Propagation Controller is able to modify the transaction context in which scope the requested component method is invoked. In the current version of our prototype, the Propagation Controller has only a simple policy for transaction propagation: If there is no transaction associated with the client request, the requested component method is not executed in the context of a transaction. If a transaction is associated with the client request, the transaction is propagated to the component. In the future, we expect to have the transaction propagation policy specified in a configuration file similar to the Concurrency Controller one. We plan to employ the Open Transaction Demarcation Framework [23], which has been proposed as a part of JOTM/ObjectWeb.

5 Evaluation

Comparing to the current commercial component architectures, such as EJB, COM+, or CCM, an important feature of Jironde is its flexibility. Combining different transactional controllers makes it possible to achieve different levels of component's transactional functionality as well as to employ different transactional standards. It is, for example, possible to use concurrency control at the level of components if JTA transactions are used or to add EJB-like transaction propagation policies to OTS. The only requirement with respect to the component implementation is to fulfill the component contracts of the employed controllers. In our Fractal prototype implementation of Jironde, for the Transaction Controller it means to implement one of the interfaces that can be registered to a transaction. The Concurrency Controller requires to define the lock modes and the Propagation Controller requires to define propagation policies in a configuration file, but both controllers can also use default values, such as exclusive locking and simple transaction propagation.

Our current implementation does not support dynamic interceptors being able to be added or removed to the interception chain. The authors of [18] use dynamic aspects to extend a component with a transactional functionality at runtime, which is useful especially in mobile environments. Our aim is also to extend our prototype with such a runtime adaptability. We have found our approach very close to the aspect-oriented one. We agree with conclusions in [7] that transactions are hard to aspectize, especially when aspectizing constructs of a programming language. However, it seems to us that aspectizing a well defined architectural and programming framework makes things different. We believe that thanks to the well defined notions of component composition (reflected in Fractal by the Content Controller), component lifecycle (Lifecycle Controller), component binding (Binding Controller), and thanks to the use of reflection, we can address some of the most problematic issues related to aspects (e.g., a composition of multiple aspects).

6 Conclusions

In this paper, we have discussed some of the key issues of combining components with transactions, as well as different approaches to make components transactional. We have introduced Jironde, a flexible framework for making components transactional. The main contribution of Jironde is its flexibility. Thanks to managing transactions in components by a configurable set of transactional controllers, it is possible to achieve different levels of component's transactional functionality, as well as to employ different transactional standards. In the future, we would like to study in more detail the collaboration of transactional controllers with other ones, such as the Binding Controller and Lifecycle Controller. We plan to identify more precisely Jironde requirements on component architectures, as well as limitations of combing transactional controllers with incompatible component contracts. As for the Jironde prototype in Fractal, we plan to implement a Recovery Controller and various Propagation Controllers that will use a controller-managed transaction to form together with a client transaction a parent-child pair in the nested transaction model, or a relation in the split/join transaction model. Another interesting task is to employ dynamic interceptors, which have been recently added to Fractal, to enable transactional controllers to add or remove their interceptors at runtime.

References

1. Allen, R., J., "A Formal Approach to Software Architecture", Ph.D. Thesis (1997)
2. Alonso, G., Fessler, A., Pardon, G., Schek, H.-J., "Correctness in General Configurations of Transactional Components", in Proceedings of the ACM Symposium on Principles of Database Systems (PODS '99), Philadelphia, USA (1999)
3. Andersen, A., Blair, G., Goebel, V., Karlsen, R., Stabell-Kulø, T., Yu, W., "Arctic Beans: Configurable and Reconfigurable Enterprise Component Architectures", IEEE Distributed Systems Online, Vol. 2, No. 7, http://dsonline.computer.org/ (2001)
4. Bernstein, P., A., Hadzilacos, V., Goodman, N., "Concurrency Control and Recovery in Database Systems", Addison Wesley (1987)
5. Giannakopoulou, D., "Model Checking for Concurrent Software Architectures", Doctoral Dissertation, Imperial College, University of London (1999)
6. Gray, S., Lievano, R., Jennings, R., "Microsoft Transaction Server 2.0", Sams Publishing (1997)

7. Kienzle, J., Guerraoui, R., "AOP: Does it Make Sense? The Case of Concurrency and Failures", in Proceedings of the 16ᵗʰ European Conference on Object-Oriented Programming, Malaga, Spain (2002)
8. Luckham, D., C., Kenney, J., J., Augustin, L., M., Vera, J., Bryan, D., Mann, W., "Specification and Analysis of System Architecture Using Rapide", IEEE Transactions on Software Engineering, Vol. 21, No. 4 (1995) 336-355
9. Microsoft Corporation, "Component Object Model (COM) Specification 0.9" (1995)
10. Microsoft Corporation, "Distributed Component Object Model Protocol – DCOM/1.0" (1998)
11. Object Management Group, "Transaction Service", Version 1.2, formal/01-05-02 (2001)
12. Object Management Group, "Concurrency Service", Version 1.0, formal/00-06-14 (2000)
13. Object Management Group, "CORBA Components", Version 3.0, formal/02-06-65 (2002)
14. ObjectWeb, http://www.objectweb.org/
15. ObjectWeb, "The Fractal Composition Framework Specification", Version 1.0, http://www.objectweb.org/fractal/ (2002)
16. ObjectWeb, "The Java Open Transaction Manager", http://jotm.objectweb.org/
17. Plasil, F., Visnovsky, S., "Behavior Protocols for Software Components", IEEE Transactions on Software Engineering, Vol. 28, No. 11 (2002)
18. Popovici, A., Alonso, G., Gross, T., "Spontaneous Container Services", in Proceedings of the 17ᵗʰ European Conference on Object-Oriented Programming, Darmstadt, Germany (2003)
19. Prochazka, M., "Advanced Transactions in Enterprise JavaBeans", in Proceedings of the Engineering Distributed Objects (EDO) Workshop, Davis, USA (2000)
20. Prochazka, M., Plasil, F., "Container-Interposed Transactions", in Proceedings of the Component-Based Software Engineering (CBSE) Special Session of the SNPD '01 Conference, Nagoya, Japan (2001)
21. Prochazka, M., "Advanced Transactions in Component-Based Software Architectures", Ph.D. thesis, Charles University, University of Evry (2002)
22. Prochazka, M., "A Flexible Framework for Adding Transactions to Components", the 8ᵗʰ International Workshop on Component-Oriented Programming (WCOP 2003, in conjunction with ECOOP 2003), Darmstadt, Germany (2003)
23. Rouvoy, R., Merle, P., "Abstraction of Transaction Demarcation in Component-Oriented Platforms", ACM/IFIP/USENIX International Middleware Conference, Rio de Janeiro, Brazil (2003)
24. Sun Microsystems, "Enterprise JavaBeans Specification", Version 2.0, Final Release (2001)
25. Sun Microsystems, "Java Transaction API (JTA)", Version 1.01 (1999)
26. X/Open Distributed Transaction Processing: Reference Model, Version 3 (1996)

A Security Architectural Approach for Risk Assessment Using Multi-agent Systems Engineering

Gustavo A. Santana Torrellas

Instituto Mexicano del Petróleo
Programa de Matemáticas Aplicadas y Computación
Eje Central Lázaro Cárdenas N°152
CP 07730, México, D.F.
gasantan@imp.mx

Abstract. The analysis of incidents resulting in damage to information systems show that most losses were still due to errors or omissions by authorized users, actions of disgruntled employees, and an increase in external penetrations of systems by outsiders. Ideally, information systems security enables management to have confidence that their computational systems will provide the information requested and expected, while denying accessibility to those who have no right to it. Traditional controls are normally inadequate in previous mentioned cases or are focused on the wrong threat, resulting in the exposure of vulnerability. Security is a critical parameter for the expansion and wide usage of agent technology. A threat model is constructed and subsequently the basic techniques to deal effectively with these threats are analyzed. Then this paper presents a dynamic, extensible, configurable and interoperable security architecture for multi-agent systems applied to security assessment services. It is explained how this architecture can be used to tackle a big part of security threats. All the components of the security architecture are analyzed while we also argue for the benefits they offer. . Such information security changes often encourage the creation of new security schemas or security improvements. Accommodating frequent systems information changes requires a network security system be more flexible than currently prevalent systems. Consequently, there has recently been an increasing interest in flexible network security and disaster recovery systems.

1 Introduction

As the complexity of today's distributed computing environments continues to evolve independently, with respect to geographical and technological barriers, the demand for a dynamic, synergistically integrated, and comprehensive information systems security control methodology increases. Unfortunately, the prevalent attitude toward security by management and even some security personnel is that the confidentiality of data is still the primary security issue. That is, physical isolation, access control, audit, and sometimes encryption are the security tools most needed. The primary goal

J.-B. Stefani, I. Demeure, and D. Hagimont (Eds.): DAIS 2003, LNCS 2893, pp. 110–124, 2003.

of any enterprise-wide security program is to support user communities by providing cost-effective protection to information system resources at appropriate levels of integrity, availability, and confidentiality without impacting security, innovation, and creativity in advancing technology within the corporation's overall objectives. Ideally, information systems security enables management to have confidence that their computational systems will provide the information requested and expected, while denying accessibility to those who have no right to it. People dealing with security have a hands-on experience with such issues. A secure system is a system that provides a number of services to a selected group of users and restricts the ways those services can be used. A security service is a software or hardware layer that exports a safe interface out of an unprotected and possibly dangerous primitive service. In order to build a security service we need a security architecture. Having analyzed the security needs of the Mobile Agent (MA) technology we propose in this paper a dynamic, extensible, configurable and interoperable security architecture for mobile agent systems. Software agents [1] are a rapidly multi-directional developing area of research since the early 90s. Mobile Agents shatter the notion of client/server model and eliminate its limitations. Standardization efforts and guidelines that boost the usage of agent technology exist in organizations such as the Object Management Group [11] and the Foundation for Intelligent Physical Agents [12]. Agents are computer and transport independent (they depend only on the execution environment) and therefore promote interoperability among systems and software. Integrity and availability must be addressed as well as ensuring that the total security capability keeps current with technology advancements that make it easier to share geographically distributed computing resources. Security environments have introduced significant opportunity for process reengineering, interdisciplinary synergism, increased security, profitability, and continuous improvement. Enterprise-wide security programs, therefore, must be integrated into a systems integrity engineering discipline carried out at each level of the organization and permeated throughout the organization.

2 Threats in a Distributed Agent Environment:
2 Understanding Distributed Processing Concepts
2 and Corresponding Security-Relevant Issues

There are so many factors influencing security in today's complex computing environments that a structured approach to managing information resources and associated risk(s) is essential. New requirements for using distributed processing capabilities introduces the need to change the way integrity, reliability, and security are applied across diverse, cooperative information systems environments. The formal process for managing security must be linked intrinsically to the existing processes for designing, delivering, operating, and modifying systems to achieve this objective. The operational environment for distributed systems is a combination of multiple separate environments that may individually or collectively store and process information. The controls over each operational environment must be based on a common integrated set of security controls that constitute the foundation for overall information security of the distributed systems. Distributed systems are an organized collection of programs, data, and processes implemented in software, firmware, or hardware that are specifically designed to integrate separate operational systems into a single, logical information system infrastructure.

The foundation of security-relevant requirements for distributed systems is derived from the requirements specified in the following areas:

- Operating systems and support software,
- Information access control,
- Application software development and maintenance,
- Application controls and security,
- Telecommunications,
- Satisfaction of the need for cost-effective security objectives.

Mobile code programming is by its nature a security-critical activity. In an agent based infrastructure the security implications are far more complex than in current static environments. In such an environment author of the MA code, the user, the owner of the hardware, the owner of the execution platform (even the execution place) can be different entities governed by different security policies and possibly competitive interests. In such a heterogeneous environment security becomes an extremely sensitive issue. We identify the threats that exist in an agent-based infrastructure. We can have: misuse of execution environment by mobile agents, misuse of agents by other agents, misuse of agents by the execution environment, misuse by the underlying network infrastructure.

Our approach also provides protection for the two first categories and tries to provide some guarantees to the agent concerning the host code and execution environments.

3 Dealing with Security Risks

Having presented the threat model we will try here to see how we can deal with these problems. Traditionally, when talking about data security usually three security objectives are identified: confidentiality, integrity, and availability. To better suit the needs of electronic security management with all its legal aspects more security objectives have been identified. The most important one is accountability. In such a way the four main security requirements to be satisfied are:

- *Confidentiality.* Describes the state in which data is protected from unauthorized disclosure. A loss of confidentiality occurs when the contents of a communication or a file are disclosed. Private data carried by the agent or used by the platform (such as audit logs) should remain private. Intra- and inter- platform communication should by no mean be revealed to 3rd parties by monitoring or other techniques.
- *Integrity.* Means that the data has not been altered or destroyed which can be done accidentally (e.g. transmission errors) or with malicious intent (e.g. sabotage).Agent code should be protected from unauthorized or accidental modification of code, state and data.

- *Accountability.* If the accountability of a system is guaranteed, the participants of a communication activity can be sure that their communication partner is the one he or she claims to be. So the communication partners can be held accountable for their actions. Agents and platforms should audit their activities and be able to provide detailed info for debugging or security purposes. Every action should be uniquely identified, authenticated and audited.
- *Availability.* Refers to the fact that data and systems can be accessed by authorized persons within an appropriate period of time. Reasons for loss of availability may be attacks or instabilities of the system. Resource management, controlled concurrency, deadlock management, multi-access, detection and recovery from faulty states such as software and hardware failures apply to mostly to platforms.

Several approaches have been developed in order to minimize security risks.

4 The Security Risk Analysis Process

The methodology of security risk analysis also comprises a number of basic steps. These differ between authors, but in general include:

- *Asset Identification.* The asset identification phase should identify the resources that require protection. These will include: hardware, software, data, documentation, and computer services and processes. Financial values can be readily applied to some of these assets, but others are more difficult to price.
- *Vulnerability Analysis.* Having listed the assets of a computer system, the next stage is to determine their vulnerabilities. This stage is more difficult than the first, as it requires a degree of imagination to predict what damage might occur to the assets and from what sources [2]. The general aims of computer security are to ensure data secrecy, data integrity and availability. System vulnerabilities are situations that could cause the loss of any of these qualities. A thorough understanding of the threats to the system is required if all the vulnerabilities are to be identified. Methodical and structured approaches are required if threat identification and vulnerability analysis is to be successful.
- *Likelihood Analysis.* The aim of likelihood analysis is to ascertain how often the system will be exposed to each of the vulnerabilities identified. Likelihood relates to the current security safeguards and the environment in which they are applied. Estimating the probability of exposure to a threat can be difficult. Sources of data for this estimation include: operations logs, local crime statistics and user complaints.
- *Countermeasure Evaluation.* All the analysis so far reflects the current situation. If, from this analysis, it is determined that the projected loss will be unacceptable, new or alternative countermeasures will have to be investigated. New controls will have to be identified, and their effectiveness evaluated.

5 Credentials and Authentication

Because agents are programs, they are intangible and live in a virtual world, we connect the trust model of such an infrastructure with the trust model of real world in order to make security critical decisions. That basically means that since every agent acts on behalf of a user or generally an entity we check to see if we trust that entity and indirectly trust the agent. An agent is signed by one or more entities. Those entities can be either the creator of the code, the user that dispatched the agent (usually this is also the creator), a place of a host and generally any entity that holds a valid certificate. Signing an agent guarantees that i) the creator is the one claimed by the agent, ii) agent's code (at least the signed part) has not been tampered by a 3rd party during transportation. Signing doesn't guarantee that the agent will execute correctly (safety). Furthermore one place can encrypt the agent with the public key of the destination place (only the destination place has the private key to decrypt the agent), protecting in this way the agent while it traverses the net until it reaches the final destination. TLS standard (Transport Layer Security) [5] is also another option. Credentials also touch indirectly the "malicious host" problem. Since each place (or at least each agency) has its own certificate there is proof that this agent is mapped to a legal user who bears responsibility of the behaviour of the agency. Non-changing parts of the agent should be signed for maximum protection.

5.1 Means of Authentication and Authorization

In this section the actual methods or processes that are used to authenticate the identities of users are discussed. The authorisation of the user to gain access to services or resources can be carried out in a system after the user has been authenticated and his identity is resolved through the use of access control lists (ACL), to determine what the particular user is authorised to do. Authorisation is thus at maximum as accurate and correct as the process of authentication. A mechanism like the SPKI could be used, to avoid authentication of the user, but to still provide a reliable authorisation.
Some mechanism for implementing mobile authentication and authorization are:

- **Passwords** – Passwords associated to user names (something that the person knows) are a simple way of authentication. There are several authentication schemes that make use of passwords in combination with some other factor. A simple extension of passwords is one-time passwords.
- **Password with a token** – Passwords can be used in combination with some physical object (something that the person owns). This concept has been extended with the use of integrated circuit cards (ICC) or smart card. A challenge and response method is used in authenticating the user. 'Synchronous one-time passwords' [5] is another similar technique.
- **Biometrics** – Biometrics authentication techniques include fingerprint recognition, retinal scanning, hand geometry scanning and handwriting and voice recognition [5]. These techniques are all based on the physical properties of a person (something he owns / is).
- **Digital Signatures** – When a PKI is put in place, digital signatures can be used to authenticate users. The following sequence of actions has to be carried out in order to authenticate a user by his digital signature:

1. The user requests access to the service or system
2. The system generates some data for the user to encrypt using his private key. Then the data is sent over to the user.
3. The user concatenates the data received from the system and a time stamp and encrypts the whole sequence. (N.B. It is a good practice that e.g. a time stamp is concatenated to the data, so that the data to be encrypted cannot completely be decided by some untrusted party. This is to avoid the possibility of a 'Chosen plain-text attack' as described in [12].) Then the encrypted data (the cipher text) is sent back to the system. Along with the encrypted data a link to the certificate (or the certificate itself) of the user is sent.
4. The system decrypts the received information with the public key of the user, found in the certificate.

The system verifies that the decrypted information is composed of the originally generated data and a valid timestamp. If this seems to be OK, the system has successfully authenticated the user.

5.2 Properties of a Good Authentication and Authorization Mechanism

This section lists the properties that a good identity authentication and authorization mechanism should possess. Some of the features listed are in contradiction of each other, but mostly it should be possible to reach an acceptable Level of compliance with each of the criteria:

- **Correctness** – The results of each individual instance of authentication or authorization carried out should be correct. If it is possible to authenticate the user, the result should always be that either it is found, that the user is who he claims or he is found to be a fraud. Based on this perfectly correct authentication it is further possible to authorize the user to access those services and resources that defined to be accessible for him or to the group or groups he belongs to. In practice it is impossible to get an absolute certainty in authentication. Only a reasonable Level of certainty can be gained.
- **Possibility to anonymity and privacy** – Identity authentication should only be done when absolutely necessary. Whenever authorisation is possible without the user's identity being revealed, it should be done that way.
- **Speed** – The process of authentication should be fast. The user shouldn't have to wait for the result for more than a second does or two.
- **Attack resistance** – The perfect mechanism of authentication should be resistant against any known or unknown types of attacks.
- **Inexpensiveness** – The mechanism shouldn't require extensive investments from either the users or the authenticators.
- **User friendliness** – The mechanism should produce as little overhead to the user as possible. It should also be as easy to use and understand as possible. In the optimum situation the user doesn't have to perform any actions in order to become authenticated. The user shouldn't be forced to carry around any extra equipment, magnetic or smart cards, lists of passwords or other physical objects in order to use the system.

- **Universality** – It should be possible for the user to use the same means or method of authentication in all services and everywhere.

5.3 Access Control Checks

Having successfully identified the agent is only the first step. Trust in the agent's credentials doesn't guarantee that it will behave legitimate nor execute correctly. Thus we monitor and authorize every call it makes to platform's resources. Any access to any resource e.g. network, file, system configuration etc is subject to an access control check. Therefore we need a policy and an enforcement manager to make sure that our policy is enforced. With this second level of check we provide fine-grained control customized per user or group. As users perform various activities not all of them have the same rights. The security is based in protection domains of Java. Those protection domains are defined by the internal agent id (not immutable) and/or by the signer(s) of the agent code (immutable). We can even require a combination of user identities in order to allow an agent to perform a task. A flexible policy scheme guarantees exactly that. Although this second level provides some extra and selective security we understand its limits.

6 The Security Architecture

Secure systems and security applications produce their own special challenges to usability. Since secure systems have been traditionally difficult to use, some people are under the impression that usability and security are innately in conflict. Our model will have to provide a powerful tool for the definition of security policies, but power (that is expressivity) is useless if the user cannot easily figure out how he can employ it. For those reasons, the first requirement of our model is to provide a Graphical User Interface (GUI) that hides the complexity to the user. The GUI should provide the user with:

1   a way to define and modify the security policy
2   a tool to check the policy behaviour
3   a help to "debug" the security policy

Because information technology security planning is primarily a risk management issue, the architecture model, his policy and its associated standards and guidelines focus on the creation of a shared and trusted environment, with particular attention to:

- Common approaches to end-user authentication;
- Consistent and adequate network, server, and data management;
- Appropriate uses of secure network connections;

Approaches that try to incorporate security after the design phase have been proven to fail. The security architecture (Figure 2) for mobile agent systems tries to incorporate all above solutions to the threat model presented before and also to be as open as possible in order to integrate easily future solutions. Furthermore we follow in this approach the MASIF standard for interoperability reasons. The main requirements of the implementation are:

- be secure; for that purpose a general architecture will be defined. Its weak points will have to be detected and protected;
- provide an efficient way to evaluate policies;.

6.1 Places

The agent system (Figure 1) consists of places. A place is a context within an agent system in which an agent is executed. This context can provide services/functions such as access to local resources etc. A place is associated with a location which consists of a place name and the address of the agent system within which the place resides. Places can contain other places. Places are i) dynamically assigned to agents as they enter the agency based on some criteria e.g. all agents coming from a specific user or location or agents belonging to a specific policy scheme etc. or ii) statically (permanently) assigned per entity (e.g. User, enterprise etc). In the latter static resources are given to the place (after agreement with the node provider) and the local resource manager manages them. This offers several advantages e.g. secure communication or paths between organisation-trusted agents etc.

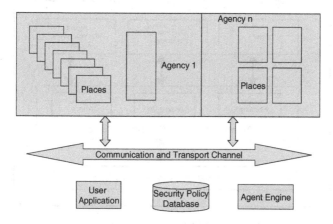

Fig. 1. The Distributed Agent Environment

A policy scheme and a resource access scheme are assigned to each place and the respective policy and resource manager are given the general security guidelines, which can never be bypassed. If an agent has sufficient credentials, then it can fully interact with the components e.g. change the place's policy, ask for more resources, insert elements in the component database etc. Of course advanced security facilities offered by the place can be used to minimize these risks (e.g. a secure communication service via the platform). Furthermore if one wants can use a place as a Test Place (a firewall like approach) and allow suspicious agents to execute there, monitor the results and then determine if it will allow them to execute in the real place. Certainly if you see for instance that an agent changes inappropriately the policy file of the Test Place you forbid it to execute into the desired place. Also agents are somehow isolated since each one has its own class loader. Places beyond having unique IDs, also hold their own public/private keys. An agent can ask to be signed in order to have a proof that it passed via this place. This also helps with the so-called "multi-hop" security problem. If every place signs a specific part of the agent then we can trace back the exact route the agent followed. Based on that info we can take further security decisions.

6.2 Policy Manager

The Policy Manager is responsible for managing the policy schemes stored in the policy database. By separating the policy DB from the enforcement engine we insert a dynamic way of policy modification. The security policy defines the access each piece of code has to resources. Signed code can run with different privileges based on the identity of the person or place who signed it. Thus users can tune their trade-off between security and functionality (of course within limits given by administrator).

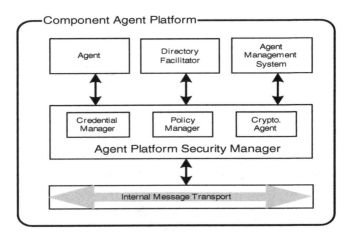

Fig. 2. Secure Agent Platform Architecture

When an agent comes to an agency then he is subjected first to the general agency's policy which is set by the user that initiated the agency (Figure 3) and is considered to be the super-user. Subsequently after passing successfully that control the agent is subjected to the place's specific policy. It is clear that with this sequential check of policies we avoid the problem of granting contradictory access rights for the same action by different policies. One can also simply forbid agents from a specific user/domain for personal. Any attempts to describe the security policy in terms of each individual principal's authority to access each individual object is not scalable and not understandable for those instituting the policy. Making security decisions rather than the individual identities. So we have role-based policy, group policy, clearance labels, domains etc. Furthermore by grouping policies we allow for faster execution times while trying to enforce the policy. In our system all security checks are identity-based in order for an agent to enter a place. After an agent successfully enters a place future security checks become role-based. Thus we don't have each time to verify agent's credentials. We check only to see in which place the agent resides and what the appropriate policy for that place is.

This approach is once more followed in our effort to speed up security checks and improve architecture's performance.

6.2.1 General Security Policy

It is the IT security policy of the policy manager that:

1. Each agency shall operate in a manner consistent with the maintenance of a shared, trusted environment within resource and component manager for the protection of sensitive data and security transactions. Agencies may establish certain autonomous applications, including those hosted by an Applications Service Provider or other third party, outside of the shared, trusted environment, PROVIDED the establishment and operation of such applications follows all guidelines as set forth in this security policy and does not jeopardize the enterprise security environment, specifically:
    - The security protocols (including means of authentication and authorization) relied upon by others; and
    - The integrity, reliability and predictability of the Organisational backbone network.

2. Each agency shall establish its secure state security applications within the guidelines of the Policy Manager and resource manager Network Infrastructure. This requires that all parties interact with agencies through a common security architecture and authentication process. Enforcement Engine shall maintain and operate the shared infrastructure necessary to support applications and data within a trusted environment.

3. Furthermore, each agency that operates its applications and networks within the whole Organisational Network Infrastructure must subscribe to the following principles of shared security:
    - Agencies shall follow security standards established for selecting appropriate assurance levels for specific application or data access and implement the protections and controls specified by the appropriate assurance levels;
    - Agencies shall recognize and support the state's standard means of authenticating external parties needing access to sensitive information and applications;
    - Agencies shall follow security standards established for securing servers and data associated with the secure application; and
    - Agencies shall follow security standards established for creating secure sessions for
    - Application access.

4. Each agency must address the effect of using the Internetworking protocols to conduct transactions for state security with others. Plans for Internet-based transactional applications, including but not limited to e-commerce, must be prepared and incorporated into the agency's portfolio and submitted for security validation.

5. Each agency must review its Information transactions security processes, procedures, and practices at least annually and make appropriate updates after any significant change to its security, computing, or telecommunications environment. Examples of these changes include modifications to physical facility, computer hardware or software, telecommunications hardware or software, telecommunications networks, application systems, organization, or budget. Practices will include appropriate mechanisms for receiving, documenting, and responding to security issues identified by third parties.

6. Each agency must conduct an IT Security Policy and Standards Compliance Audit once as frequently as possible. The audit must be performed by knowledgeable parties independent of the agency's IT organization, such as the General Agent Auditor. The work shall follow audit standards developed and published by the General Agent Auditor. The General Agent Auditor may determine an earlier audit of an agency's IT processing is warranted, in which case they will proceed under their existing authority. The nature and scope of the audit must be commensurate with the extent of the agency's dependence on secure IT to accomplish its critical security functions. Each agency must maintain documentation showing the results of its review or audit and the plan for correcting material deficiencies revealed by the review or audit. To the extent that the audit documentation includes valuable formulate, designs, drawings, computer source codes, object codes or research data, or that disclosure of the audit documentation would be contrary to the public interest and would irreparably damage vital government functions, such audit documentation is exempt from public disclosure.

Credential Manager

Credentials are stored in the credential database. All actions concerning the credentials (including management of the credential database) are handled by the credential manager (CM). The CM checks the validity of the certificates, updates them, maintains the local revocation list etc. The local revocation list acts as a second black list only that this time the user can locally make invalid the agent's certificates and therefore force the system to treat the agent as an anonymous one. While the first list forbids migration to the agency (via SSL authentication) here we have only sandboxing of the agent (treated as possibly malicious). X509v3 Certificates [3] are used as credentials in a heterogeneous environment with a key used as the primary identification of a principal. In our approach we assume that users have certificates and that hosts also have certificates. Places can also have certificates in order to sign results. As the nested-place approach we take is service oriented (place n can belong to a different provider than the sub-place nix), we can ask from the nth place to sign a part of an agent. When checking the validity of certificates the credential manager looks up firstly his local database and his local revocation list. In the local databases a copy of the previous certificates of user's agents that have executed exist.

Component Manager

The Component manager mainly manages all requests concerning components prein-stalled by the administrator as well as user installed components in the component database. The component manager allows first the administrator to install code and selectively via policy make it available to the users. This code can be signed so that agents coming to the agency can verify the originator of the code and decide whether to use it or not. This helps partially with the "Malicious Host" problem. Agents can decide if they trust the code they need in order to perform their goals. Furthermore the agents are able to verify a host before they migrate to it. So if every host n can verify host n+1 then we can make sure that our agent moves in a selected path of hosts. If the host is not trusted then the agent may decide not to execute there. User agents that are given permission can put their own code to this database and make it available to third party agents permanently or for a limited time. This increases the flexibility as well as the security and performance of the platform. The flexibility and performance because each user can have its own implementations of custom code on the node and thus his agents can be more lightweight and less complex. The compo-nent database can be considered a general database of active code, protocols, encryp-tion algorithms, etc. Component database is of great significance to this approach as it ensures the up to date status of various components and also in parallel minimizes security risks for agents and for the platform. Security is by nature overhead in the communication and execution in order to protect the system.

Resource Manager

A resource manager is available in order to handle the resources assigned to the agency or place. We assume that resources are assigned from the administrator (that is the person that creates the place and this can be the agency administrator or one of the previous n-1 place administrators who created the nested place n) to a place n and are managed by the owner of the newly created place. The resources and their man-agement are transparent to place users and to nested places that place n might contain. The place resource manager can handle the resources that are dedicated to a specific place. It can be contacted also directly via the agents that reside in the associated place also in the case that there is a need for more resources. Note that the resources available to a certain place are transparent to the agent and its users. This helps also with the Place Oriented Virtual Private Network (PO-VPN) [13]. In a PO-VPN sce-nario an enterprise can setup places spawned in a network infrastructure and therefore create a VPN of places where its agents can execute according to custom security policies and services.

Cache Manager

The cache (handled by the cache manager) is another essential part of the architecture and its usage is mainly focusing on improvement of the overall performance. Security checks are time and computing consuming processes. In our effort, not to duplicate all the time the necessary security checks, we have a cache. Security checks that have been done via the enforcement engine are stored with a time limit in the cache. If the time limit expires then the security checks are performed again, otherwise the security check is considered valid and is used by the system.

The policy DB can be dynamically updated via the enforcement engine any time. Thus the problem is faced that the cache contains outdated information. We solve this problem by deleting (each time the policy for an entity changes) the cached security checks that are associated with this key/person partially.

Audit Manager

Audit manager handles all audit events. Experience has shown that 100% security is difficult to realize - if not impossible - due to the multiple factors that interfere. Collecting data generated by network activity provides a useful tool in analyzing the existent security and also trace back (if possible) the originators of a security breakout. Having a detailed audit can lead to reconstruction of a sequence of events and better understanding of past security failures. Audit data include any attempt to achieve different security level or change entries in the system's databases etc. Intrusion attempts can also be detected via audit e.g. when we see repetitive failures in an attempt to use a component/service we can adapt our policy so that we prevent any possible intrusions.

7   The Need for Information Security Management Improvement

In a rapidly changing market place with pacing technological developments, pressure to reduce 'time to market' and demands for shorter 'security policies life-cycles' the result is a highly competitive information security environment. Security Policies who succeed in this environment are the ones that take their security schemas to deploying security more efficiently and effectively. Security Management is an activity of security deployment ownership from conception to standardisation. The Security Management function promotes efficiency, effectiveness and information assurance harmony throughout the organisation. In a security environment it is paramount for new security policies to achieve all expectations; successful Security Management is a key success factor in making this happens.

7.1   The Role of the Security Manager

Security Management is the security process that actively manages security policies s throughout their lifecycle. The Security Manager is the owner of the security schema in totality. Security success of the security schema is the ultimate goal of the Security Manager and to this end will require support from the organisation in order to succeed. Cross functional process management and an attitude of "making it happen" are key attributes for the Security Manager.

The Security Management activity should operate within the boundaries laid down in the strategic plan and as such is an integral part of the information technology function. The main objective of a Security Manager is to plan and specify a security policy/security portfolio in line with the long term strategic plan - Security Plans are a fundamental part of this process. Proposed security schemas must provide good synergy within the overall security portfolio i.e. security variants must be planned in accordance to meet security policies needs (Time to deployment) and within the scope and capabilities of the organisation.

8 Summary and Conclusions

Security architecture for agent based systems has been presented. This defensive model of design is focused on designing agent systems to be secure from the scratch. Adding security after the design phase has been shown to be difficult, expensive and inadequate. Security is not an explicitly called service and its treatment as such imposes further security risks in the infrastructure. We have showed that benefits such as simplicity, scalability, flexibility, interoperability, performance and safety have been addressed successfully. The components of the architecture have been analyzed and explained. Per identity/place security and customization as well as the rapid service creation is the main driving force for next generation mobile agent systems. In the future we intent to advance our approach. Our architecture tries to identify and prevent possible malicious agents. For the moment it can't handle collaborative attacks. Taking into account the tools provided (e.g. audit log, encryption tools, etc) one could implement stationary agents (guards) that reside on a place and based on intelligent internal strategy react to environment changes and try to track and eliminate collaborative attacks. Those guards could also work in collaboration thus providing a higher level of security to a number of hosts. As agent technology evolves and becomes more sophisticated a co-operative security infrastructure could be developed and deployed.

References

1. Cetus Links on Mobile Agents : http://www.cetus-links.org/oo_mobile_agents.html
2. F. Hohl, Protecting mobile agents with Blackbox security, Proc. 1997 WS Mobile Agents and security, Univ. of Maryland.
5. IETF Transport Layer Security (TLS) group http://www.consensus.com/ietf-tls/ietf-tls-home.html Protecting Mobile Agents against malicious hosts. Lecture Notes in Computer Science on Mobile Agent Security, November 1997. "Overview of Certification Systems: X.509, CA, PGP and SKIP", Meta-Certificate Group, Novware Softex/Unicamp Brazil.
9. B. Schneier and J. Kelsey, "Cryptographic Support for Secure Logs on Untrusted Machines", The 7th USENIX Security Symposium proceedings, USENIX Press, Jan 1998, pp. 53-62
11. OMG Web Site: http://www.omg.org/
12. FIPA Web Site: http://www.fipa.org/
13. Stamatis Karnouskos, Ingo Busse, Stefan Covaci, "Place-Oriented Virtual Private Networks", HICSS-33, January 4-7 2000, on the island of Maui, Hawaii.

14. Lightweight Directory Access Protocol (LDAP v3), RFC 2251. [15] Unified Modeling Language, Rational Software, URL : http://www.rational.com/uml

16. "Ten Risks of PKI: What You're Not Being Told About Public Key Infrastructure", C. Ellison and B. Schneier, Computer Security Journal, v 16, n 1, 2000, pp. 1-7.

17. Java Security Flaws http://kimera.cs.washington.edu/flaws/

18. MASIF - Mobile Agent System Interoperability Facility, http://www.omg.org/docs/orbos/98-03-09.pdf

Middleware Support
for Non-repudiable Transactional Information
Sharing between Enterprises

Nick Cook[1], Santosh Shrivastava[1], and Stuart Wheater[2]

[1] School of Computing Science
University of Newcastle, UK
{nick.cook,santosh.shrivastava}@ncl.ac.uk
[2] Arjuna Technolgies, Newcastle, UK
stuart.wheater@arjuna.com

Abstract. Enterprises increasingly use the Internet to offer their own services and to utilise the services of others. An extension of this trend is Internet-based collaboration to form virtual enterprises for the delivery of goods or services. Effective formation of a virtual enterprise will require information sharing across organisational boundaries. Despite the requirement to share information, the autonomy and privacy requirements of enterprises must not be compromised. This demands strict policing of inter-enterprise interactions, including non-repudiable access to shared information. For a member of a virtual enterprise, a typical requirement is the ability to inspect/modify shared information together with private information within a single ACID transaction. At the same time, inspection/modification of the shared information should both generate non-repudiation evidence and be consistent with inter-enterprise agreements. The paper describes how information sharing middleware can be enhanced with distributed transaction support to perform regulated transactional information sharing. Design and implementation of a prototype Java middleware is presented.

Keywords: middleware; inter-enterprise interaction; transactions; security

1 Introduction

As noted above, the formation of and continued interaction within a virtual enterprise (VE) demands regulated information sharing. In this context, each party to a multi-party interaction requires: (i) that their own actions on shared information meet locally determined, evaluated and enforced policy, and that their legitimate actions are acknowledged and accepted by the other parties; and (ii) that the actions of the other parties comply with agreed rules and are irrefutably attributable to those parties. These requirements imply the collection, and verification, of non-repudiable evidence of the actions of parties who share and update information. We have implemented distributed object middleware called

J.-B. Stefani, I. Demeure, and D. Hagimont (Eds.): DAIS 2003, LNCS 2893, pp. 125–132, 2003.

B2BObjects [1] that both presents the abstraction of shared state and meets these requirements by regulating, and recording, access and update to shared state. It is assumed that each enterprise has a local set of policies for information sharing that is consistent with an overall information sharing agreement (business contract) between the enterprises. Multi-party coordination protocols ensure that the local policies of an enterprise are not compromised despite failures and/or misbehaviour by other parties; and that, if no party misbehaves, agreed interactions will take place despite a bounded number of temporary network and computer related failures. Each party validates any proposed update to shared information and the update is only accepted if all parties agree to it.

The shared information of a VE does not exist in isolation. There are dependencies between private information held by each member of a VE and the shared information that is held in common. A given enterprise is also likely to be involved in more than one VE, resulting in dependencies between information that is shared in the context of different VEs. To manage these dependencies, support is required to make updates to shared information contingent on successful completion of updates to related private information (and vice versa). From the viewpoint of each member, their Business-To-Business (B2B) application state can be seen as the combination of any private information that is related to the B2B interaction and the information that is shared with the other members. The requirement then is to maintain the integrity and consistency of B2B application state by ensuring that updates to shared information are consistent with updates to private information and that such updates can be completed transactionally (atomically).

The paper presents a novel distributed middleware for updating B2B application state while meeting the above regulatory and consistency requirements. The main contribution of this work is the development of middleware with the ability to manage transactions that span private and shared resources at the same time as observing inter-enterprise agreements that govern update to the shared resources. The middleware is designed to provide local autonomy for each enterprise, within the constraints imposed by the need to share information, and interoperability between and within enterprises. The shared resources participate in transactions using the same mechanism as for private (transactional) resources (such as enterprise databases). Update to shared resources is subject to independent validation by the members of the VE who together own the resources.

Section 2 provides an overview of B2BObjects. Section 3 presents the extension to support distributed transactions over B2B application state. A related technical report [2] provides a more detailed description of the middleware with an example application scenario.

2   Overview of B2BObjects Middleware

This section provides an overview of the B2BObjects middleware, including a brief introduction to the Java API of the experimental implementation. The mid-

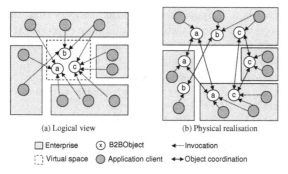

(a) Logical view   (b) Physical realisation

☐ Enterprise   ⊗ B2BObject   ◄···· Invocation
⸢⸣ Virtual space   ◯ Application client ◄─► Object coordination

Fig. 1. B2BObjects-based interaction

dleware addresses the requirement for dependable information sharing between enterprise. The abstraction of shared objects is used to represent the information that enterprises wish to share (or "jointly own"). Coordination protocols provide multi-party agreement on access to and update of object state. As shown in Fig. 1, the logical view of shared objects in a virtual space is realised by the regulated coordination of actions on object replicas held at each enterprise. Application-level invocations on local copies of B2BObjects are intercepted by the middleware and state changes coordinated with remote enterprises. A non-repudiable two-phase commit protocol is used to coordinate object state as follows: the proposer of a new state dispatches a state change proposal, comprising the new state and the proposer's signature on that state, to all other parties for local (application-level) validation. Each recipient produces a response comprising a signed receipt and a signed decision on the (local) validity of the state change. All parties receive the collected responses and a new state is valid if the collective decision represents unanimous agreement to the change. The signing of evidence generated during state validation binds the evidence to the relevant key-holder. The actions of honest parties cannot be misrepresented by dishonest parties and invalid state cannot be imposed on local object replicas. The evidence generated is stored systematically in local non-repudiation logs. Systematic check-pointing of object state provides recovery, in the event of failure, and rollback, in the event of invalidation by one or more parties. Certificate management and non-repudiation services provide: authentication of access to objects; verification of signatures to actions on objects; and logging of evidence of each enterprise's actions.

2.1 B2BObjects API

This brief introduction to the B2BObjects API concentrates on the aspects that provide hooks for transactional update to B2BObjects. The relevant classes of the API are: B2BObject — the augmentation of an application object to ensure access is mediated by the middleware; and B2BObjectController — the local interface to configuration, initiation and control of information sharing. A B2BCoordinator executes the coordination protocols between objects. The

B2BObject interface is a wrapper for application objects that allows the controller to obtain object state, to initiate local validation of proposed state changes and to install newly validated object state following successful state coordination. The relevant part of the controller interface is:

```
public interface B2BObjectController {
    void enter();     // start of scope of access to state
    void examine();   // read in this scope
    void overwrite(); // completely overwrite in this scope
    void update();    // partial update in this scope
    void leave();     // end of scope of access to state
    ...
}
```

Given an application object (appObject) with a typical update operation: setAttribute(SomeType attr), the corresponding B2BObject wrapper code is:

```
setAttribute(SomeType attr) {
    controller.enter();            // start of scope
    controller.overwrite();        // will overwrite object state
    appObject.setAttribute(attr);  // set the appObject attribute
    controller.leave();            // end of scope, trigger coordination
}
```

This code can be auto-generated if the application object's read/write methods are identified. From the application viewpoint, the B2BObject setAttribute method is invoked in the same way as for appObject.

The controller enter and leave operations are used to demarcate the scope of access to object state. These calls may be nested to allow the "rolling-up" of a series of state changes into a single (atomic) coordination event. If overwrite has been called within the current state change scope, then invocation of the final leave triggers execution of the state coordination protocol. If a proposed change is invalidated, the proposer's local object state is rolled-back. A similar process applies to update of a part of object state (indicated by the update operation) as opposed to overwrite of the whole state. The examine operation indicates that object state will be read but not written in the current scope. The controller operations shown provide transactional access to all copies of a single B2BObject and, as described in Section 3.2, are the hooks for transactional update across multiple B2BObjects.

3   Support for Distributed Transactions

Transactions have long been used to ensure the consistency of shared information despite concurrent accesses and system failures — delivering the well-known ACID properties of Atomicity, Consistency, Isolation and Durability. The Java Transaction API (JTA) [3] is a standard interface to Java-based transaction management that includes the XAResource mapping of the XA standard [4] for participation in distributed transactions. In this section we describe a JTA-compliant transaction adapter that presents B2BObjects as transactional resources to a Transaction Manager via an XAResource interface. In this way, distributed transactions can be combined with multi-party coordination of shared state. First we outline the principles of the state transitions that underly B2B-Object support for distributed transactions and then we provide an overview of the Java-based transactional infrastructure.

3.1   Outline of Transactional Support

To support transactions, the notion of B2BObject state, S, is extended to include both the prospective new state of the object (*prospState*) and the retrospective agreed state of the object (*retroState*). That is, for state coordination purposes, B2BObject state is described by the tuple: $S = \langle s_j, s_i \rangle$, where s_j is the prosp-State and s_i is the retroState. Given this description of object state, we can say that: an object is in a **committed state**, if $j = i$ (the prospState is the retroState); and an object is in a **prepared state**, if prospState has been coordinated (and validated) **and** $j \neq i$ (the prospState and retroState are different). The following state transitions are then permitted:

1 *committed* to *committed* : $\langle s_i, s_i \rangle \rightarrow \langle s_{i+1}, s_{i+1} \rangle$
2 *committed* to *prepared* : $\langle s_i, s_i \rangle \rightarrow \langle s_{i+1}, s_i \rangle$
3 *prepared* to *prepared* : $\langle s_{i+1}, s_i \rangle \rightarrow \langle s_{i+2}, s_i \rangle$
4 *prepared* to *committed* : $\langle s_{i+1}, s_i \rangle \rightarrow \langle s_i, s_i \rangle$ (abort)
5 *prepared* to *committed* : $\langle s_{i+1}, s_i \rangle \rightarrow \langle s_{i+1}, s_{i+1} \rangle$ (commit)

Transition 1 describes the behaviour of B2BObjects in [1] — transition from one committed state to the next with no intermediate prepared state. Transitions 2 and 3 to prepared states can be mapped to the prepare phase of a distributed transaction. In both cases, the retroState is unchanged and represents the state to which the object will ultimately return if the prospState is subsequently revoked. A prospState may be revoked because a transaction coordinator requests rollback of resources participating in a transaction or because a subsequent new state proposal is invalidated. Transitions 4 and 5 can be mapped to completion of a transaction: abort (or rollback) to the previously committed state $\langle s_i, s_i \rangle$; and commit of a new committed state $\langle s_{i+1}, s_{i+1} \rangle$, respectively. The difference between a prepared state and a committed state is that the former is revocable. If a prepared state is revoked, the object returns to the most recently committed state (identified by the retroState). If a prepared state is committed, the new retroState is the current prospState.

The following pseudo-code illustrates how the above transitions, demarcated by `enter/leave` blocks, can be combined to perform a distributed transaction across two B2BObjects: `objS` and `objT`. At the start of the transaction the objects are in states $\langle s_i, s_i \rangle$ and $\langle t_j, t_j \rangle$, respectively. The code is annotated with intermediate (prepared) states and the successful commit of final states.

```
// start transaction txId
enter(objS, txId)
enter(objT, txId)
    // perform state changes
```

```
enter(objS)
overwrite(objS) // locally change objS to prospState: s_{i+1}
leave(objS)     // trigger coordination to prepared state: ⟨s_{i+1}, s_i⟩
enter(objT)
overwrite(objT) // locally change objT to prospState: t_{j+1}
leave(objT)     // trigger coordination to prepared state: ⟨t_{j+1}, t_j⟩
...
// Perform further state changes. For each enter/leave block,
// state is coordinated so that, if all changes succeed,
// objS is in state: ⟨s_{i+m}, s_i⟩ and objT is in state: ⟨t_{j+n}, t_j⟩
...
// commit transaction txId
leave(objS, txId, TX_SUCCESS)
              // trigger coordination to committed state: ⟨s_{i+m}, s_{i+m}⟩
leave(objT, txId, TX_SUCCESS);
              // trigger coordination to committed state: ⟨t_{j+n}, t_{j+n}⟩
```

The prepare phase of the transaction corresponds to the following transitions:

$$objS : \langle s_i, s_i \rangle \rightarrow \langle s_{i+1}, s_i \rangle \rightarrow \cdots \rightarrow \langle s_{i+m}, s_i \rangle$$
$$objT : \langle t_j, t_j \rangle \rightarrow \langle t_{j+1}, t_j \rangle \rightarrow \cdots \rightarrow \langle t_{j+n}, t_j \rangle$$

The final transitions to states $\langle s_{i+m}, s_{i+m} \rangle$ and $\langle t_{j+n}, t_{j+n} \rangle$ correspond to the successful commit phase. In contrast, any failure or invalidation of a transition to a prepared state for an individual object would result in transaction abort and the return of each object to the committed states: $\langle s_i, s_i \rangle$ and $\langle t_j, t_j \rangle$.

Any party's agreement to a transition to a prepared state, for example $\langle s_i, s_i \rangle \rightarrow \langle s_{i+1}, s_i \rangle$, implies: (i) application-level validation of prospState s_{i+1} and, therefore, of committed state $\langle s_{i+1}, s_{i+1} \rangle$; and (ii) their commitment to be able to subsequently install either of the related committed states: $\langle s_i, s_i \rangle$ or $\langle s_{i+1}, s_{i+1} \rangle$. That is, to have made persistent the new prospState, s_{i+1}, and to be able to rollback the prospState to s_i. Thus transitions 4 and 5, from prepared to committed states, do not require application-level validation. Nor is it necessary to transfer the physical state of the object being coordinated for these transitions (since each party has already committed to local persistence of the relevant state). The only state that is physically transfered to remote parties is the new prospState for transitions 1, 2 or 3. Unique state transition identifiers are used to reference the retroState for each transition and the prospState for transitions 4 and 5. Coordination from a prepared to a committed state is required to ensure that all parties maintain a consistent view of object state and to generate evidence that the committed state is the currently agreed object state.

3.2   B2BObjects as Transactional Resources

This section describes the infrastructure to facilitate the participation of B2B-Objects as JTA-compliant, transactional resources in distributed transactions. The essential requirements are: (i) that a JTA transaction manager can control

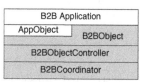

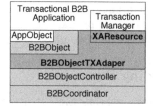

(a) B2BObject-enabled application   (b) Transactional B2BObject-enabled application

Fig. 2. B2BObjects transaction layer

the participation of B2BObjects in transactions through a transaction adapter that exports the XAResource interface; and (ii) that the underlying B2BObject state management and coordination mechanisms can be instrumented to support this participation. The approach is to provide a transactional layer between the underlying layers of the middleware and the transactional application; and to parameterize the B2BObjectController operations described in Section 2.1 to effect the state transitions described above.

Fig. 2(a) shows the B2BObject interface as a wrapper for an application object. The B2B application uses the AppObject interface for operations on the object. The B2BObjects middleware provides the regulated state coordination described in Section 2. Fig. 2(b) shows the insertion of a transaction layer to support transactional applications. The application uses the same AppObject interface to the underlying object. The B2BObjectTXAdapter exports an XAResource interface to a Transaction Manager and instruments the controller to ensure the coordinator executes appropriate state transitions.

The B2BObjectTXAdapter generates a proxy for the application object being coordinated to ensure that, in transactional context, all operations on the object are mediated by the adapter. It maintains the association of the current transaction with the object and propagates this association to the controller. To meet transactional requirements, the adapter maps operations at the XAResource interface to controller operations. The transaction-aware controller guarantees the persistence of B2BObject state to facilitate recovery and rollback; and the persistence of transaction state information.

To ensure that application-level operations on an instance of a B2BObject are mediated by a transaction adapter, a B2BObjectTXAdapterFactory instantiates a single B2BObjectTXAdapter for a given B2BObject. The B2BObjectTXAdapter interface provides operations for the application to obtain an instance of the object proxy and for the Transaction Manager to obtain the adapter's XAResource instance.

To provide transaction-awareness, the B2BObjectController interface shown in Section 2.1 is extended to include parameterised versions of `enter` and `leave` to associate a transaction identifier with these operations. The extension also includes methods for explicit object locking and, for example, to support XAResource operations to manage heuristically completed transactions and recovery of prepared transactions. The XAResource interface provided by the B2BObject-

TXAdapter includes **start** and **end** operations to demarcate work on behalf of a given transaction; and **prepare**, **commit** and **rollback** operations for participation in the transaction two-phase commit protocol.

4   Concluding Remarks

We are not aware of other work that integrates distributed transactions with regulated information sharing between enterprises. The work of Wichert et al [5] is close to our approach to systematic generation of non-repudiation evidence. They provide non-repudiable RPC but do not address validation of state changes for information sharing. The work of Minsky et al on Law Governed Interaction (LGI) [6] supports interaction between organisations governed by global policy. It represents one of the earliest attempts to provide coordination between autonomous organisations. However, support for transactions is not available. Another approach to the automated control of interactions through agreements between enterprises is IBM's tpaML language for B2B integration [7]. Their model of long-running conversations, the state of which is maintained at each party, is similar to our notion of shared interaction state.

Acknowledgements

This work is part-funded by the UK EPSRC under grant GR/N35953/01 on "Information Co-ordination and Sharing in Virtual Environments"; by the EU under project IST-2001-34069: "TAPAS (Trusted and QoS-Aware Provision of Application Services)"; and by the UK e-Science project "GridMist".

References

1. Cook, N., Shrivastava, S., Wheater, S.: Distributed Object Middleware to Support Dependable Information Sharing between Organisations. In: Proc. IEEE Int. Conf. on Dependable Syst. and Networks (DSN), Washington DC (2002)
2. Cook, N., Shrivastava, S., Wheater, S.: Middleware Support for Non-repudiable Transactional Information Sharing between Enterprises. Technical Report 814, School of Computing Science, Univ. Newcastle (2003)
3. Cheung, S., Matena, V.: Java Transaction API (JTA version 1.0.1B). Java Specification (2002)
4. The Open Group: Distributed Transaction Processing: The XA Specification. X/Open CAE Specification XO/CAE/91/300, X/Open Company Ltd. (1991)
5. Wichert, M., Ingham, D., Caughey, S.: Non-repudiation Evidence Generation for CORBA using XML. In: Proc. IEEE Annual Comput. Security Applications Conf., Phoenix, Arizona (1999)
6. Minsky, N., Ungureanu, V.: Law-Governed Interaction: A Coordination and Control Mechanism for Heterogeneous Distributed Systems. ACM Trans. Softw. Eng. and Methodology **9** (2000) 273–305
7. Dan, A., Dias, D., Kearney, R., Lau, T., Nguyen, T., Sachs, M., Shaikh, H.: Business-to-business integration with tpaML and a business-to-business protocol framework. IBM Syst. J. **30** (2001) 68–90

Adaptable Access Control Policies for Medical Information Systems

Tine Verhanneman, Liesbeth Jaco, Bart De Win,
Frank Piessens, and Wouter Joosen

DistriNet, Dept. Computer Science
K.U.Leuven, Celestijnenlaan 200A
3001 Leuven, Belgium
{tine,liesbeth,bartd,frank,wouter}@cs.kuleuven.ac.be

Abstract. IT enforced access control policies in medical information systems have to be fine-grained and dynamic. We justify this observation on the basis of legislation and on the basis of the evolution within the healthcare domain. Consequently, a reconfigurable or at least adaptable implementation of access control facilities has become extremely important. For this purpose, current technology provides insufficient support. We highlight a basic solution to address shortcomings by using interception techniques. In addition, we identify further research that is required to address the challenges of dynamic and fine-grained access control in the long run.

1 Introduction

The healthcare industry spends increasingly more resources on IT, driven by both the need to manage costs and by the changing structure of healthcare organizations. As a side effect, the privacy and security of health care information is a growing concern([2]). Because of these demands, access control in medical IS is a tremendous challenge ([6]). Therefore, the requirements for these systems are characterized in this paper. Moreover, we argue that access control policies are not (and will never be) static and underline the importance of fine-grained IT enforced policies. In an extended version of this paper ([16]) some example policies are described in more detail.

Access control dynamicity is driven by two forces: legislation on the one hand and system changes on the other hand.

There are rules (ethical and legislative rules) that prescribe how medical data should be handled. First of all, since these laws can change, access control policies are by nature not static. Second, the interpretation of the legislation varies. As will be shown in section 2, the applicable law in the USA states that to meet some of the requirements a "reasonable effort" should be done. The concrete interpretation of this term depends on the context, like e.g. the size of the organization and on case law.

Another cause of evolving access control policies are system changes. When for instance not only hospital personnel but also patients and relatives can login

J.-B. Stefani, I. Demeure, and D. Hagimont (Eds.): DAIS 2003, LNCS 2893, pp. 133–140, 2003.

onto the system to access their own clinical information, which can be viewed as an extension in functionality, measures need to be taken. Another example of a system change are adaptations in the IT access control enforcement itself. These are the changes that will be focussed on in this paper, and that will lead us to the conclusion that IT enforced access control policies needs to be *fine grained* and also dependent on information, such as context or application state, as well as subject, object and operation, that are involved in an invocation on the system.

As will be demonstrated, it is essential that the security component in medical information systems includes reconfigurable and/or adaptable access control technology. We now define these terms more precisely. Security policies are said to be *reconfigurable* if the deployer of the application is able to set the security measures without having to dig into the source-code written by the programmer. Access control is set through the interpretation of a configuration file, written in a "non-programming language", such as XML for example. Ideally, the format and language of this configuration file are not too complicated, so that non-programmers are able to draw it up. In the literature, this is often referred to as *declarative security*, which is often opposed to programmatic security, by which is meant that policies are hard-coded in the application.

Adaptability is a weaker requirement than reconfigurability. A system that is highly adaptable requires little effort to be transformed into a system that satisfies new requirements. Hereto all the concerns are to be expressed somehow separately in a modular structure, which doesn't necessarily imply that the access control policy can be changed at deployment time or at run time.

Supporting reconfigurability or adaptability often limits the access control policies that can be implemented, as expressive power is limited, either because the configuration language is limited, or because the access control module does not have access to all information that is required to enable detailed decision making. Expressiveness must be treated with caution, since the more expressive the language the more complex the enforcement mechanism will be.

Having defined these terms, we analyze the requirements for an access control module in a medical IS, first, in section 2, on the basis of the legal and regulatory framework for privacy and security of medical data in the EU and the US and secondly, in section 3, in the perspective of evolution of the healthcare organisation. In section 4, we discuss the impact of our observations when building applications using state-of-the-art platforms such as J2EE and .NET, whoms support for declarative access control proves to be insufficient. The road for future research is laid out in section 5 and a conclusion is formulated in section 6.

2   Access Control Policies in Healthcare

All existing threats against privacy and security of health information are contrary to a concern for patient rights and the well-functioning of health care. In respect to confidentiality this concern is formulated in the Hippocrates oath.

Nowadays, the rules for the use of medical information are extended with the right to dispose of data with guaranteed integrity and availability. Laws are constituted, describing the rights and duties imposed when processing medical data and defining the potential sanctions applied to misuse. On this basis, healthcare institutions formulate policies, containing both organizational and technical security measures. The legislation actually provides for two kinds of rights and duties.

First, the law prescribes the circumstances for medical data to be collected, stored and used, and the authorization rules to access the data. This is input for the access control policy that a healthcare organization should manage.

Second, the law also sets some standards on how well the policy should be *enforced* and it is this kind of legislation that is especially important from the point of view of IT enforcement. Considering the protection of health information in the EU, the Data Protection Law ([8]) augmented with the Recommendation on the Protection of Medical Data ([9]) emphasize on the *appropriateness* according to the faced risks and the *periodical review* of the measures to protect personal data.

The American legislation will be discussed in more detail. The specific law concerning the protection of individually identifiable health information is the Health Insurance Portability and Accountability Act of 1996 (HIPAA). HIPAA is considered as the most significant healthcare legislation passed in years and includes rules on electronic transactions, national identifiers, patient privacy and data security. It obliges healthcare organizations to use information and communication technology to increase efficiency, but it also addresses the problems of deploying these technologies. All healthcare organizations that maintain or transmit electronic health information have to comply, and there are severe civil and criminal penalties for those that do not.

In the context of this paper, two rules of the comprehensive HIPAA regulation are important, namely the Privacy Rule ([12]) and Security Rule ([13]). The former sets forth what uses and disclosures are authorized or required and what rights patients have with respect to their health information while the latter specifies what implementation is obligatory for enforcement of this policy or what reasonable efforts should be done. It describes the necessity for standards at all stages of transmission and storage of electronic health care information to ensure integrity and confidentiality of the records at all phases of the process, before, during and after electronic transmission as well as physical and technical safeguards to protect the confidentiality, integrity and availability of electronic protected health information. Features such as context-based, role-based and user-based access control, were explicitly mentioned in a draft version, but have been deleted and replaced by the requirement that *appropriate* access control should be provided, like in the European legislation. In the following section, it will be illustrated how this requirement leads to the need of IT-enforced dynamic access control policies.

3   IT Enforced Policies Are Dynamic

A security policy can be enforced in many ways: through organizational and through technical measures. In healthcare, there is an old tradition of trusting the care provider. Because of the increased specialization of care providers, and the increased complexity of care procedures, the size of the team of care providers that deals with one patient grows. Teams of ten to fifty are common. Obviously the purely trust-based model does not work. Besides, the increased use of IT makes technical measures to enforce the security policy unavoidable. Many hospitals have already reached the maturity-point where hospital wards are distributed in different, separated buildings. Because each ward has its own administration, data is no longer centralized and communication networks outside the physical boundaries are used to share information. More evolved healthcare organizations offer remote access, which allows doctors or patients to access clinical information from off-site locations.

Many people have increasing (potential) access to personal clinical information of a large number of patients. Therefore IT enforcement becomes essential, organizations rely less on trust ([1]). In this context the term *regular policy* refers to the policy a healthcare organization wishes to impose, independent of the enforcement mechanism. *IT enforced policy* refers to a policy that is actually enforced by IT-based technical measures.

In this paper, the focus is on the IT enforced access control policy. It is unreasonable to suppose that these IT enforced access control policies will remain the same over long periods of time, for the following reasons.

1. *Changes in the regular policy* can be caused by changes in legislation, changes in the interpretation of legislation, or because the hospital management decides that a stricter policy will lead to a competitive advantage as patient awareness about privacy increases.
2. *Appropriate security is necessarily dynamic.* As discussed in section 2, the law states that enforcement of the access control policy should be reviewed regularly.
3. There is a shift of the trust based model towards *more IT enforcement.*
4. *IT enforced policy evolves with system changes.* As system functionality increases, the security rules need to be enforced in more and more situations.

4   Support for Flexible Access Control Policies

4.1   The Need for Expressiveness

Access control rules describe conditions for subjects to access resources. It is obviously not feasible to write a separate rule for any object or subject in the system. Hence, a good policy language should support the grouping of objects with similar access control requirements and the grouping of subjects with similar rights.

Grouping of objects is typically achieved through *policy domains*. Each of the objects in the system belongs to one or maybe several domains. This does not always depend on the class of the object alone, but also on instance properties, the relations the object is involved in, the location where the object instance is deployed, ... A powerful policy language should support fine-grained description of policy domains as well as short, generalizing definitions.

Besides the grouping of objects, some support of grouping *subjects* will be required. An obvious example of this kind of grouping is the notion of a role. A more advanced example is implicit grouping as described in [10], where roles are assigned (dynamically) on the basis of properties of the subject.

A subject may only have limited access to an object. In object-oriented systems, there is a tendency to consider a method as the unit of *privilege*. However, in the majority of the applications in medical IS, it seems that privileges are more naturally expressed in terms of access to and modification of data. This is hard to realize, however, since it cannot always be determined beforehand whether or not a method will access and/or modify a given data-unit.

Last, since the outcome of an access control decision is often influenced by *context information*, such as time, location, etc., a policy language should have access to this kind of context information.

Given all these concerns, it becomes clear that it is in fact the *interaction* in its whole, that must be taken into consideration when describing and executing the access control decision process. An *interaction* is the chain of method invocations that are caused by an invocation of the client on the application server. An interaction is always carried out on behalf of a subject on a set of target-objects in a specific context. This subject can assume one or more roles, which can be activated when and if needed. An interaction can also be tagged with some additional contextual information. Interactions should be identified and grouped into policy domains, in a fine-grained and also flexible manner. Domains then allow for the association of conditions with each individual interaction. This is the ultimate requirement for a policy language.

4.2   An Assessment of J2EE and .NET

Modern application platforms such as J2EE and .NET provide support for activating infrastructural services such as access control in a declarative way. As a consequence, access control policies are reconfigurable at deployment time or even at run time. But the expressiveness of such declarative access control policies is rather limited. For more complex, fine grained policies, access control is enforced in the code, leading to policies that are harder to adapt.

J2EE offers a minimal support for RBAC. Security roles can be defined (in principle by the developer) by grouping users in categories. The mapping of these security roles to security identity is done at deployment time by the application deployer. The permissions assigned to the security roles are based on method-invocations. Each method specification needs to describe the roles that have permission to invoke the method. A J2EE container allows by default all users

("AllUsers") to invoke all methods, so access permissions definitely need to be restricted.

.NET features are comparable with J2EE. A developer can tag methods with the roles that are required to execute the method by using the PrincipalPermissionAttributes. .NET also provides a bridge to the access control support that was present in COM+. The COM+ access control technology allows the deployer to attach required roles to methods that are exposed by the application.

If one uses these declarative security systems, access control is reconfigurable, but fails to offer the expressive power as stated in section 4.1:

- The policy domain is determined by the type (class) of the target object only. This means that it is impossible to enforce access rules that are specific for instances.
- Grouping of subjects is only possible on the basis of roles that have to be assigned statically. Neither role-activation nor the enforcement of dynamic separation of duty is supported. In general, it is the application container that keeps track of the subject on whose behalf the invocation is made. There is no possibility to attach custom-defined data to the invocation.
- Access control rules are set up in terms of method-invocations. If the deployer wants to enforce a data modification access rule, the deployer needs to find out which methods may possibly modify the data.
- Further context information, such as external factors (context, time, . . .) can not be used in the access control decision.

The only way to deal with the above mentioned limitations is by hard coding security into the application. But by using such *programmatic security*, reconfigurability and even adaptability are lost.

4.3   A Solution Based on Extensible Interceptor Chains

A first step toward *interaction*-based access control consists of supporting *extensible interceptor chains*. An interceptor is a construct that intercepts method-invocations and that carries out some extra functionality before passing on, blocking, or redirecting the invocation. Depending on the considered technology, interceptor-instances can be deployed per container, class, object instance and/or context. It is fair to say that both J2EE and .NET provide some preliminary support.

For example, the open source J2EE-compliant JBoss application server tries to disentangle security code and application-logic by the definition of so-called security proxies ([14]). These proxies enforce the security policy outside the bean, but they still have to be coded programmatically.

.NET apparently has configurable interceptor chains built in·already, but this is an undocumented feature rather than a solution. So-called context bound objects in .NET can be decorated with attributes that specify what interceptor should handle all method calls on the object. This interceptor can programmed in any of the .NET languages.

Our team has been experimenting with application architectures that support flexible interceptor chains since about five years, and we have been applying this approach in security frameworks for electronic commerce ([7]). Clearly, if an interceptor is used to implement access control, adaptability can be achieved: the access control logic is encapsulated in the interceptor, and relatively easily replaceable (at least at development time) by another interceptor. This solution has its limitations: reconfigurability is not possible, and access control is certainly not specified at a high level of abstraction. Rules need to be programmed in a general purpose programming language with a reified method call as primary input. Expressiveness however is significantly better, since the interceptor can base its decision on object state, application state and available context information.

5   The Way Forward

Towards reconfigurable, expressive and high level access control.

Extensible interceptor chains as discussed above are only a first step towards achieving the goal of reconfigurable, expressive and high level access control. Some issues still need to be solved.

- Programming interceptors is too low-level: a more developer-friendly programming model is necessary. Most probably, the interceptor should be interpreting a high-level policy language. Therefore, research about policy languages ([5]) is relevant. Then the actual policy can be configured at run time.
- Current application containers do not pass much context information to the objects inside. For instance, context information about the current interaction, such as where the interaction was started (on a remote network or a local network) might influence an access control decision, but this information is not available to an interceptor.

Both issues are (at least in part) addressed by the Aspect Oriented Software Development (AOSD) community ([3]). AOSD has as objective to modularize concerns, such as security, into slices of behavior. This modularization not only consists of the implementation of the required functionality but also the composition of these slices into the overall application and the management of the relations between slices. A variety of techniques are being investigated, varying from the weaving of extra code at compile time (AspectJ [4]) to the (runtime) deployment of wrappers (Lasagne, JAC [11,15]). The main difference between these AOSD systems and the previously described extensible interceptor chains is that there is considerably more support for the creation and composition of these slices of behavior. Often new language primitives are introduced to support the definition of these aspects. This addresses the first issue raised above. In order to support the consistent activation of aspects, and to support client-specific views, Truyen et al. [15] have suggested to attach metadata to interactions to drive the activation. Such techniques can address the second issue raised above: contextual information about the interaction has to travel with the interaction as metadata.

6   Conclusion

This paper has argued, on the basis of legislation and on the basis of the evolution of healthcare, that IT enforced access control policies in medical information systems will be fine-grained and dynamic. As a consequence a reconfigurable or at least adaptable implementation of access control is very important. Current application servers were shown to provide insufficient support for this, and some indications of how these shortcomings could be remedied were given.

References

1. R. J. Anderson, *Patient Confidentiality – At Risk from NHS Wide Networking.* Proceedings of Health Care 96, March 96
2. R. J. Anderson, *A Security Policy Model for Clinical Information Systems.* IEEE Symposium on Security and Privacy, Oakland, CA, pp 30-43, May 1996
3. http://www.aosd.net
4. http://aspectj.org
5. N. Damianou, *A Policy Framework for Management of Distributed Systems*, PhD thesis, Februari 2002
6. I. Denley, S. Weston Smith, *Privacy in Clinical Information Systems in Secondary Care*, British Medical Journal, 318:1328–30, May 1999
7. B. De Win, J. Van den Bergh, F. Matthijs, B. De Decker, and W. Joosen, *A security architecture for electronic commerce applications*, Information Security for Global Information Infrastructures (S. Qing and J. Eloff, eds.), Kluwer Academic Publishers, 2000, pp. 491-500
8. European Parliament and Council of Europe *Directive 95/46/EC, on the protection of individuals with regard to the processing of personal data and on the free movement of such data*, October 24, 1995
9. Council of Europe, *Recommendation R(97)5, On the protection of medical data*, February 12, 1997
10. R. Goodwin, S.F. Foh, F.Y. Wu, *Instance-level access control for business-to-business electronic commerce*, IBM Systems Journal, Volume 41, number 2, Januari 2002
11. R. Pawlak, L. Duchien, G. Florin, L. Seinturier *JAC : a Flexible Solution for Aspect Oriented Programming in Java*, Reflection 2001, Kyoto, Japan, September 2001
12. Secretary of the Department of Health and Human Services, *Final Privacy Rule*, August 14, 2002
13. Secretary of the Department of Health and Human Services, *Final Security Rule*, February 20, 2003
14. L. Taylor *Customized EJB security in JBoss. Separate your security policy from your business logic*, JavaWorld, February 2002
15. E. Truyen, B. Vanhaute, W. Joosen, P. Verbaeten, B. N. Joergensen, *A Dynamic Customization Model for Distributed Component-Based Applications*, accepted for International Workshop on Dynamic and Distributed Multiservice Architectures (DDMA 2001)
16. T. Verhanneman, L. Jaco, B. De Win, F. Piessens, W. Joosen, *Adaptable Access Control Policies for Medical Information Systems: requirements analysis and case studies*, technical report, Katholieke Universiteit Leuven, CW363, August 2003

Client-Side Component Caching

A Flexible Mechanism
for Optimized Component Attribute Caching

Christoph Pohl and Alexander Schill

Technische Universität Dresden
Institut für Systemarchitektur
Lehrstuhl Rechnernetze
D-01062 Dresden, Germany
{pohl,schill}@rn.inf.tu-dresden.de
phone: +49-351-463-38457
fax: +49-351-463-38251

Abstract. Locality of referenced data is an important aspect for distributed computing. Caching is commonly employed to achieve this goal. However, when using current component-oriented middleware client application programmers have to take care of this non-functional aspect by themselves, without direct support from middleware facilities or design tools. The paper at hand describes a novel approach to disburden them from this non-trivial, error-prone task by transparently integrating caching as an orthogonal middleware service using interceptors which are preconfigured at design-time using standard UML extension mechanisms. An advanced mechanism for dynamic adaptation of the caching service to changing access characteristics is introduced in the second part.

Keywords: Caching, distributed component-based middleware, Enterprise JavaBeans, adaptivity, reflection

1 Introduction

Todays middleware platforms, no matter whether procedural, object-, or component-oriented, apparently provide the means for transparent distribution by allowing remote procedure calls or method invocations to be as easily integrated as their local equivalents. However, a closer look reveals the caveats of this approach, at least if it's naively used: Every single remote call results in at least one network round trip which slows the code down by magnitudes.

With platforms like CORBA Components [1] or Enterprise JavaBeans [2], this issue is typically tackled at application level by streamlining remote interfaces, i.e. reducing necessary interactions between remote nodes, or by implementing caching frameworks at the same level. In their pursuit for the best possible locality of reference, distributed programs usually try to collocate data and process. This is either done by patterns like *value object* [3] that transfer bundled object attributes to the client, or by patterns like *session facade* [3]

J.-B. Stefani, I. Demeure, and D. Hagimont (Eds.): DAIS 2003, LNCS 2893, pp. 141–152, 2003.

that place computation-intensive logic at server side. Nevertheless, all of these workarounds violate the principle of transparent distribution, a non-functional aspect that should not bother the application programmer.

Our approach is based on the assumption that most component attributes are more often read than written which makes them suitable for caching. This additional meta-information can already be attached to the application model at design time. Generator tools use this information to preconfigure the caching logic. Integrated into the middleware itself via *interceptors* as reflectional mechanism, it avoids unnecessary network round trips unnoticed by the application programmer, thus forming a transparent proxy layer that completely hides the complexity of attribute storage and retrieval from the client programmer.

Possible use cases include interactive multimedia applications, e.g. eLearning scenarios, where object-oriented "fat client" programs need to communicate frequently with server-side data models. But the concept is also practicable for distributed server-side processing, e.g. web servers or Servlet containers accessing components on application servers. Generally, it's usable wherever component clients and servers are distributed over multiple network nodes.

The first prototype as explained in Sec. 2 relies on explicit, *static* attribute mark-ups at deployment time to enable an augmented container to generate necessary caching functionality. In contrast, our current activities aim at a self-learning concept that relieves the deployer or component assembler from the burden of classifying attributes by *dynamic* run-time adaptation to changing attribute access characteristics. The extensive usage of client-/server-side interceptor pairs also allows for the integration of more sophisticated centralized cache invalidation or update propagation schemes. This approach is introduced in Sec. 3.

2   Static Approach

As mentioned introductorily, our first prototype follows a static approach, i.e. cachability of attributes has to be declared at deployment time. Once considered cachable, an attribute remains in that state. A reference implementation based on Sun's Enterprise JavaBeans (EJB) platform [2] and the open source EJB container JBoss [4] was developed to demonstrate the underlying concepts. One major goal is the explicit, separate handling of the orthogonal non-functional aspect "caching" throughout a component's life cycle.

2.1   Component Design

Considering the standard software development process, developers already get a fair notion about a component's usage scenarios and corresponding data flows at design time, right after thorough analysis. A component's attributes are the most suitable candidates for caching as they contain its actual data. There are basically three categories of attributes[1]:

---

[1] References to other components can be treated in the same way as attributes in respect to caching, although they are technically handled in a different way.

read-only – practically never changes, to be cached upon first access;

cachable – changes rarely[2], to be cached upon first access; appropriate invalidation / update propagation protocol required for consistency;

volatile – non-cachable attributes that are subject to frequent changes or that should only be accessed in a transactional context.

The OMG's Unified Modeling Language [5] provides the means for storing such additional information using so-called stereotypes which imply certain characteristics and roles that can be evaluated by code generators and other tools to deduce applicable algorithms and code segments.

2.2   Component Implementation

As the underlying EJB platform encapsulates component attributes as pairs of `get/setXyz` methods by convention, stereotypes have to be mapped to these representations, accordingly. The Java programming language provides tagged comments, i.e. *JavaDoc*, for storing additional information about language elements that can be evaluated by compiler-independent parsers and tools. Some UML modeling tools already make use of this language feature. Thus, a stereotype $<<$ *cacheable* $>>$ for a component attribute becomes a `/** @stereotype cachable */` comment above the corresponding accessor method, or a component-level constraint *caching.policy=LRUCachePolicy* translates to `/** @invariant caching.policy=LRUCachePolicy */` above the Bean class. We decided to use this feature for our EJB prototype in conjunction with *XDoclet* [6], an open source code generator for EJBs.

Originally intended to bridge the disconnection between bean implementations and interfaces that often tend to get out of sync, XDoclet generates interfaces, deployment descriptors, and auxiliary classes from Bean classes. It allows the construction of arbitrary code segments depending on special JavaDoc comments at class / method level and special template files that actually control the code generation process.

2.3   Code Generation

A special XDoclet Template is used to generate a separate `caching.properties` file conveying this information for client deployment. There is no use to package this information in a XML file along with other deployment descriptors because our static caching approach necessitates no additional processing by the server-side component container. Additionally, the generated `jboss.xml` is adapted to include our `CachingClientInterceptor` in the client-side interceptor chain, as explained below.

2.4   Deployment

To understand the way our caching-enabled components are deployed, a few introductory words about interceptors should be said:

---

[2] The definition of "rarely" is application-specific!

The modular architecture of JBoss features an interceptor framework similar to the OMG's specification [7] but more flexible for caching purposes. Interceptors are a meta-programming facility for distributed middleware platforms. On both client and server side, interceptors can be hooked into the control flow of (remote) operation calls, basically to add parameters and to augment results, but generally to alter virtually any property of a call's context, even its semantics.

The main difference between JBoss interceptors and CORBA Portable Interceptors is the way they are chained and handled: The CORBA specification defines different types of Interceptors and certain access points during request processing when they have to be called. The ORB would typically keep configured interceptors in an array and invoke them sequentially, each interceptor returning control after its task has been accomplished. In contrast to that, JBoss defines a slightly different protocol, described in [8], based on a linked list of interceptors established by the container. Although this imposes on every single interceptor the responsibility to invoke its successor, this allows for greater flexibility, i.e. to cut short the interceptor chain by quickly returning cached results.

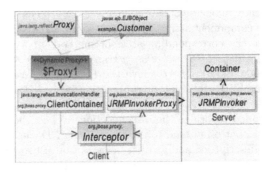

Fig. 1. Interceptors in JBoss Dynamic Proxies.

Client-side integration of these interceptors is shown in Fig. 1: Component proxies are transparently generated and instantiated using Java's Dynamic Reflection API. A `ClientContainer` passes each request through a chain of Interceptors, whose sequential order is determined by the bean provider or application assembler at deployment time. The last interceptor always hands the request to an `InvokerProxy` that finally calls the server. Server-side interceptors are stacked in a similar fashion. When a response returns from the server, it passes through the same interceptor chain in reverse order.

After code generation, the application assembler / deployer is given the opportunity to make certain manual adjustments to given descriptors, e.g. changing cachability of certain attributes, caching policy etc.

When a caching-enabled component is deployed, the interceptor chain is assembled as configured in the component's `jboss.xml` along with a `Proxy` as shown in Fig. 1. This conglomerate is transferred to the client upon its first JNDI lookup of the component. Interceptor instances are then created in the client VM as needed by remote references. The first instance of a CachingClient-Interceptor loads the information about cachable component attributes from the `caching.properties` located in the client class path and initializes the in-memory cache according to configured policies / replacement strategies.

2.5   Runtime

Prototypically, the cache back-end was implemented selectively using JBoss' `LRUCachePolicy` or `TimedCachePolicy` with component identity, method, and parameters as combined keys and results as values, i.e. $(i, m, \{p\}) \rightarrow r$. The basic granularity of cached data is per-attribute but as these are members of identifiable components, collective invalidation of attributes is still possible.

As we already elaborated in [9], *multiple reference handling* is also an important issue for caching services in distributed component middleware. Component references are typically passed around as marshaled objects, i.e. proxies / stubs, which makes it possible for a client to obtain a number of proxy objects for one and the same remote entity. This is counterproductive for memory consumption. `CachingInterceptors` have also been leveraged to support efficient multiple reference handling by checking all returned remote references, i.e. proxies, for duplicates in the local cache, ensuring that at most one reference exists to a given component. The same is done with returned collections of references by querying their elements individually against the cache. Sun's EJB specification [2] explicitly discourages direct equality testing between entities using `equals()`, and `isIdentical()` may result in additional undesired remote calls, so `EJBHandles` are held liable for component equality that is necessary for duplicate checking. Note that JBoss's proxy implementation already transfers handles upon initialization, hence no additional network round-trips are required. Calls to `remove()` methods require the interceptor's special attention because they imply the removal of all cache entries for keys $(i_r, m, \{p\})$ with a given identity i_r.

2.6   Performance and Usability Benefits

Our experiences with the framework showed general feasibility of the concept. The use of client-side interceptors is mandatory with JBoss, so the overhead for invoking yet another interceptor is quite low. Cache lookups turned out to be magnitudes faster than direct component attribute queries. A simple test scenario was set up with both client and server VM running on the same host[3] to eliminate the interfering influence of variable network delays. Preliminary results of cache miss times for queries to a component's *value object* were around $20ms$ per request, compared to $1ms$ and even less for cache hits. Depending on networking infrastructures, several more ms can be added for cache misses in non-local scenarios. More profound data is currently being collected in connection with the results of the following section.

---

[3] AMD Athlon™ XP1600+, 1GB RAM, Linux 2.4.21, Sun J2SE 1.4.1, JBoss 3.0.6.

However, the main advantage of our approach lies in the field of software engineering, formed by the usability benefits of the solution in comparison to traditional pattern-based solutions of the caching challenge.

3   Dynamic Approach

An obvious disadvantage of the above described static approach is necessity for component developers and deployers to precisely describe a component's cachability properties before deployment without any chance of later interference. This drawback gave the motivation for our current endeavors [10] to extend the framework to dynamically adapt cachability status of component attributes at runtime, i.e. whether a certain attribute should be considered for caching or not.

3.1   Server-Side Data Gathering

It has been anticipated in Sec. 2.4 that interceptors are also available at server side in quite a similar fashion. This enables us to centrally collect data about component access characteristics by implementing and chaining `CachingServerInterceptors`. How the gathered information is evaluated and eventually used to dynamically adapt the `ClientCachingInterceptor`'s behavior is shown in Fig. 2.

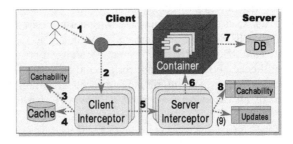

Fig. 2. Adaptive Caching Approach.

1. A container-generated dynamic proxy implementing the desired component's remote interface is called from somewhere within the client application code.
2. The proxy creates an `Invocation` object and passes this through the interceptor chain where a `CachingClientInterceptor` is installed to quickly answer invocations whose results it can anticipate from its cache contents.
3. If the invocation does not refer to an exceptional case like a `create` or `remove` method, the `CachingClientInterceptor` first checks its cachability table, a client-local singleton preconfigured from the `caching.properties` file (optional, if existent) and continuously updated by dynamic adaptation as described below. This table basically contains information about whether to cache certain component attributes based on accessor methods (`getXyz`).

4. Provided the afore mentioned test succeeded, the cache is eventually queried for valid invocation results as already explained in Sec. 2.5. Mutator methods (setXyz) lead to updates of their corresponding attributes before being passed on.
5. If the queried attribute was not found in the cache or is not to be cached for some reason, the invocation will finally be transferred to the server where it will pass another interceptor chain containing the CachingServerInterceptor.
6. At this moment, the interceptor will just hand off the invocation till it gets processed by the component container.
7. Depending on component type and state, the container may also query a database or other back-end information source to retrieve the desired data.
8. On its way back[4], the invocation is logged in a server-side cachability table for counting read / write accesses and deriving a cachability categorization based on the current read / write ratio for a given attribute. The last change time of an attribute's categorization is also logged in this table.
9. Successfully processed mutator methods receive special treatment: They are logged together with their time of occurrence and average time period in between for purposes of update propagation. The average time period is not calculated over all write accesses but rather only over the last five, which seems to be an appropriate heuristic, more economical in respect to memory consumption and more sensitive to rapid changings. These slots are initially set to a configurable default value.

3.2   Update Propagation and Client-Side Cache Adaptation

One Question remains unclear in the above presented procedure: How are clients notified about server-side updates concerning component state and cachability? Earlier experiments with event-based publish-subscribe middleware [11] scaled poorly for increasing numbers of clients due to the tremendous amount of status data and connections the server has to govern when using such an approach. Therefore, the decision was made for a client-driven "pull" strategy that relieves the server from the burden of direct "push" update propagation. The general proceedings of this approach can be described as follows:

– When a cachable attribute is accessed, the CachingServerInterceptor attaches the times of last modification and expiration according to the attribute's current average time span between changes as additional payload to the Invocation object, taken from step (9) above. The JBoss Proxy package uses Invocation objects to encapsulate all data belonging to a remote call. This object is passed through the interceptor chains where interceptors may attach and detach additional context information. The current cachability setting as explained in step (8) is also attached, accordingly.

---

[4] For concision and better readability, the return path has not been explicitly marked in Fig. 2. It basically follows the numbers in reverse order.

- Back on client side, the `CachingClientInterceptor` updates the attribute's cachability categorization if necessary and schedules a `java.util.Timer-Task` with the given expiration time. This TimerTask will enqueue the attribute's identity together with its last modification time in a list of expired objects.
- The next remote call passing a `CachingClientInterceptor` picks up the value pairs from this expiration list and attaches them to the Invocation, thus preventing additional network traffic by this piggy-back strategy.
- Unmarshalled at server side, the expiration list is compared with the last modifications in the cachability and update tables, resulting in the creation of positive list containing a bit mask for changed cachability categorizations and value updates, which is transfered on the call's way back to the client.
- Updated attributes are then discarded from the client-side cache, implicating a normal retrieval upon next access that causes the described procedure to start over again. If an attribute turns out to be not cachable any longer, any of its possibly existing cache entries will also be discarded.

3.3   Performance Considerations

As the described dynamic approach for continuous adaptation of the caching service to changing access characteristics is still partially under development, it naturally contains a number of flaws. At the current status, the considerable overhead for update propagation limits the algorithm's efficiency to scenarios with larger attributes.

A number of optimization is currently being implemented. For instance, the mentioned *value objects* provide a convenient way for grouping attributes with similar access characteristics. Instead of caching individual attributes, single attribute queries can be mapped to cached value objects. Overhead for invalidation decreases as well. The current invalidation scheme could also be enhanced to support update propagation for certain attributes that require fast availability of changes at all replicating nodes, in other words: Instead of transmitting a list of updated attributes, the server-side interceptor could immediately send the changed values, thus saving a network round trip.

4   Related Work

Paradigms for distributed computing can basically be distinguished into distributed shared memory systems (DSM) and systems communicating via message queues or remote procedure calls (RPC). The former ones, typically found in high speed computing environments, share a mutual set of distributed memory pages whose consistency is maintained by the memory subsystem using multicast and similar technologies. Whereas in middleware of the latter category, the application programmer usually has to take care of data distribution and consistency by himself. If caching is used as a special form of partial replication, DSM systems typically rely on page-oriented caching strategies and procedural or message-oriented middleware on object caching algorithms, respectively. As current distributed component middleware platforms like defined by [12] obviously belong to the latter kind, we will concentrate on the corresponding caching issues only.

4.1 Object Caching

A vast multitude of publications exists in the field of object caching, many of them on typical hypertext transfer issues. However, solutions for object-oriented middleware also date back a long way, e.g. to *Arjuna, Shadows* [13], and *Orca* [14], among others. Interesting parallels to "modern" patterns like *value object* [3] can already be found and the issues of invalidation versus update propagation are discussed there.

CASCADE [15], a CORBA caching service for applications in Wide Area Networks offers interesting insights on hierarchical cache management and staggered consistency levels, an aspect also taken up by other publications [16]. *Flex* [17] is a distributed caching system on top of *Fresco* and CORBA that also considers issues about caching object references, like object faulting and access detection, which shows the parallels to object-oriented databases. Although relevant, these publications have a somewhat different focus. Eberhard and Tripathi [18] proposed a transparent caching mechanism for Java RMI with configurable caching strategies and consistency protocols but they did not take changing access characteristics into account.

4.2 Adaptive Caching

The term "adaptive caching" is slightly overloaded, e.g. there are projects trying to combine the virtues of algorithms from page-oriented caching with object-oriented techniques. *ACME* (Adaptive Caching Using Multiple Experts) [19] uses machine-learning algorithms to dynamically weigh cache replacement strategies according to their success, which provides better performance for proxy cascades in web / hyper-media scenarios. *Divergence Caching* [20] illuminates the aspects of static and dynamic caching, i.e. fixed and variable refresh rates. Brügge and Vilsmeier [21] propose a caching strategy for CORBA Calls similar to the one presented in our paper, with focus on prefetching of attribute groups based on statistical evaluations of past invocations. However, no approaches to dynamically determine cachability are known to the authors.

4.3 Meta-programming

Meta-Programming or *reflectional programming* usually refers to coding on the abstract meta-level of a programming language that is used to describe the executed code itself, i.e. in terms of classes, methods etc. The basic mechanisms have not changed greatly since Smith's thesis about reflection [22]: programs or components should have a notion about their current context and (limited) control over their interpretive environment. Interfaces to this meta-level are defined by *meta-object protocols* (MOP) like interceptors as they are used in the context of this paper. Several recent publications [23,24] leverage interceptors for building frameworks that more or less try to partly hide the complexity of metaprogramming or to add a higher abstraction level. As we are using interceptors only as the means for integrating orthogonal functionality, current research on this field is slightly out of this paper's scope. The OMG's CORBA Portable Interceptor specification [7] is an attempt to standardize various research directions in this field, but offers less flexibility than the JBoss interceptor framework [8] used in our approach.

ArchJava [25] recently supports a wide range of connector abstractions for communication between components, including caches, but the focus is more on the ease of use provided by ArchJava's language extensions. In contrast to that, we completely resign the use of such extensions for the sake of transparency. An article of Filman et al. [26] is quite comparable to that but aims more at the shortcomings of Aspect-oriented Programming [27]; caching is also mentioned there as an example application of their approach.

5   Conclusion and Outlook

Our static approach to distributed component attribute caching showed the potential performance benefits and gave a first impression of the transparent integration into a component's life cycle. The proposed UML extension mechanisms are currently being summarized in a special UML profile for caching.

First directions for improvement have already been outlined in Sec. 3.3: *Value objects* provide a potential to decrease overhead by grouping attributes with similar access characteristics. Update propagation can be selectively used as an alternative to invalidation for rapidly changing, *volatile* attributes. The protocol should be easy to adapt in this direction.

Further investigations will include prefetching, i.e. possibilities to transfer data to client-side caches *before* it is queried, which especially suitable if cached components are organized in a hierarchical way. The greatest challenge in this connection will be the automatic detection of such data dependencies. Persistent caching will also be a focus of our future work because it provides an interesting feature for use cases like off-line client applications.

References

1. Object Management Group: CORBA Components. (2001) ptc/01-11-03.
2. DeMichiel, L.G., Yalçinalp, L.Ü., Krishnan, S.: Enterprise JavaBeans Specification Version 2.0. Sun Microsystems. Final release edn. (2001)
3. Sun Microsystems: Design Patterns Catalog. J2EE design patterns edn. (2001) http://java.sun.com/blueprints/patterns/j2ee_patterns/catalog.html.
4. JBoss Group: JBoss. (2003) Project homepage: http://www.jboss.org/.
5. Object Management Group: Unified Modeling Language, v1.4. (2001) formal/01-09-67.

6. Öberg, R., Schaefer, A., Abrahamian, A., Hellesøy, A., Colebatch, D., Harcq, V.: XDoclet. Project homepage: http:// xdoclet.sourceforge.net/ (2003)
7. Object Management Group: CORBA Portable Interceptor Specification. (2001) ptc/01-03-04, formal/02-05-18.
8. Fleury, M., Reverbel, F.: The JBoss extensible server. In Endler, M., Schmidt, D., eds.: International Middleware Conference. Volume 2672 of LNCS., Rio de Janeiro, Brazil, ACM / IFIP / USENIX, Springer (2003) 344–373
9. Pohl, C., Schill, A.: Middleware support for transparent client-side caching. In: European conference on Theory And Practice of Software (ETAPS'02). Volume 65 of Electronic Notes in Theoretical Computer Science., Grenoble, France, Elsevier (2002) Software Composition Workshop.
10. Pohl, C.: Adaptively caching distributed components. In: Middleware2003 Companion, Rio de Janeiro, Brazil, PUC–Rio (2003) 325
11. Neumann, O., Pohl, C., Franze, K.: Caching in Stubs und Events mit Enterprise Java Beans bei Einsatz einer objektorientierten Datenbank. In Cap, C.H., ed.: Java-Informations-Tage JIT'99. Informatik Aktuell, Düsseldorf, Springer (1999) 17–25
12. Szyperski, C.: Component Software: Beyond Object-Oriented Programming. Addison-Wesley (1997)
13. Caughey, S.J., Parrington, G.D., Shrivastava, S.K.: Shadows - a flexible support system for objects in distributed systems. In: 3rd International Workshop on Object Orientation and Operating Systems (IWOODS'93), Asheville, NC (USA) (1993) 73–82
14. Bal, H.E., Kaashoek, M.F., Tanenbaum, A.S., Jansen, J.: Replication techniques for speeding up parallel applications on distributed systems. Concurrency: Practice and Experience 4 (1992) 337–355
15. Chockler, G., Dolev, D., Friedman, R., Vitenberg, R.: Implementing a caching service for distributed CORBA objects. In: Middleware'00, Heidelberg, Germany, Springer (2000) 1–23
16. Krishnaswamy, V., Ganev, I.B., Dharap, J.M., Ahamad, M.: Distributed object implementations for interactive applications. In: Middleware 2000. (2000)
17. Kordale, R., Ahamad, M., Devarakonda, M.V.: Object caching in a CORBA compliant system. Computing Systems 9 (1996) 377–404
18. Eberhard, J., Tripathi, A.: Efficient object caching for distributed Java RMI applications. In Guerraoui, R., ed.: Proceedings of the International Middleware Conference (Middleware 2001). LNCS, Heidelberg, Germany, ACM / IFIP / USENIX, Springer (2001) 15–35
19. Ari, I., Amer, A., Gramacy, R., Miller, E.L., Brandt, S.A., Long, D.D.E.: ACME: Adaptive caching using multiple experts. In: Workshop on Distributed Data and Structures (WDAS 2002), Carleton Scientific (2002)
20. Huang, Y., Sloan, R.H., Wolfson, O.: Divergence caching in client-server architectures. In: Third International Conference on Parallel and Distributed Information Systems (PDIS '94), Austin, TX, IEEE (1994) 131–139
21. Brügge, B., Vilsmeier, C.: Reducing CORBA call latency by caching and prefetching. IEEE Distributed Systems Online (2003)
22. Smith, B.C.: Procedural Reflection in Programming Languages. PhD thesis, Department of Electrical Engineering and Computer Science, MIT, Cambridge, Massachusetts, USA (1982)
23. Blair, G.S., Coulson, G., Robin, P., Papathomas, M.: An architecture for next generation middleware. In: International Conference on Distributed Systems Platforms and Open Distributed Processing, London, IFIP, Springer (1998)

24. Truyen, E., Vanhaute, B., Joosen, W., Verbaeten, P., Jørgensen, B.N.: Dynamic and selective combination of extensions in component-based applications. In: International Conference on Software Engineering, IEEE (2001) 233–242
25. Aldrich, J., Sazawal, V., Chambers, C., Notkin, D.: Language support for connector abstractions. In: ECOOP 2003 Proceedings. Volume 2743 of LNCS., Darmstadt, Germany, AITO / ACM SIGPLAN, Springer (2003)
26. Filman, R.E., Barrett, S., Lee, D.D., Linden, T.: Inserting ilities by controlling communications. Communications of the ACM **45** (2002) 116–122
27. Kiczales, G., Lamping, J., Menhdhekar, A., Maeda, C., Lopes, C., Loingtier, J.M., Irwin, J.: Aspect-oriented programming. In Akşit, M., Matsuoka, S., eds.: European Conference on Object-Oriented Programming (ECOOP'97). Volume 1241., Springer (1997) 220–242

A Variable Cache Consistency Protocol for Mobile Systems Using Time Locks

Abhinav Vora, Zahir Tari, and Peter Bertok

RMIT University
Melbourne, VIC 3001, Australia
{avora,zahirt,pbertok}@cs.rmit.edu.au

Abstract. By locally caching data, mobile hosts can operate while disconnected from the central server, however, consistency of data becomes more difficult to maintain. In this paper we propose a protocol that makes a distinction between two classes of consistency: *weak* and *strict*, and treats them differently. Strict consistency is used for data that needs to be consistent all the time, whereas weak consistency is for cases when stale data can be tolerated in the form of requiring only specific updates. Consistency is maintained by using strict read/write and permissive read/write time locks that enable data sharing for a fixed time period and support concurrency control. A Notification Protocol is also proposed, which enables propagating updates to clients and retrieving data from clients in a consistent manner. Performance tests have demonstrated that switching from strict to weak consistency can reduce the number of aborts (due to no access to a lock or conflicting operations) by almost half, even with high read-write sharing.

1 Introduction

With mobile computing devices becoming smaller and faster and networks supporting higher bandwidth and better reliability, mobile computing is becoming a major player in the computing arena and has a strong impact on how applications are designed. Handheld devices enable users to be active participants in distributed computing while on the move. Constraints and restrictions imposed by the mobile and often wireless environments include intermittent and weak connections, wide variations from high bandwidth, low latency through to low bandwidth, high latency to no connectivity at all [3,6].

Mobile clients can switch between connected and disconnected modes of operation in order to either reduce the cost of connection or overcome availability problems. Clients may also have to deal with weak connections that cannot be improved but still they may need to maintain continuous operation regardless of being connected or disconnected [6,7,10].

Disconnected operations are usually supported by caching information on mobile hosts. Lot of work on caching in mobile environments has been done apart from bearing many analogs in Database and File Systems. The Coda File System [7] differentiates between first-class (server copies) and second-class

J.-B. Stefani, I. Demeure, and D. Hagimont (Eds.): DAIS 2003, LNCS 2893, pp. 153–166, 2003.

(client cache) replicas and uses a optimistic concurrency control scheme (based on the premise of low write-sharing) to manage these replicas. In [4], a log-based approach for updating client caches in a relational database system is presented. Updates are centralised at the server; before accessing its cache, a client has to retrieve, from the server, log-records of updates since the cached copy of the data item was last updated.

Our aim here, is not to discuss all this work, but to briefly describe some of the recent and more advanced caching techniques for mobile environments (e.g. [9][8]).

- Pitoura and Bhargava [9] proposed different operations (e.g. *weak read* and *weak write*) in addition to the standard operations in a mobile database environment. Data located at strongly connected sites are grouped together to form clusters. Mutual consistency is required for copies at the same cluster, while different degrees of consistency are tolerated for copies at different clusters. Weak operations are supported within the same cluster, allowing operations on locally available data. Weak reads access inconsistent copies and weak writes make conditional updates. Strict (normal) read/write operations are also supported for strict consistency. This scheme, even though flexible and satisfies varying consistency requirements, is restrictive due to the strict database environment and transactional ACID properties. Furthermore, strict operations are not permitted while clients are in disconnected mode. Such restrictions are generally not necessary or less stringent in non-database environments.
- Lee et al. [8] proposed maintaining cache consistency by using invalidation/update reports. The server periodically broadcasts update or invalidation messages to clients, who update the content of the cache according to these messages. Update reports reflect the changing state of the database. A drawback of this method is that invalidation messages impose a high processing load on clients. Clients have to listen to all reports, even though there may be no changes to the data they cache or they may not even cache the data for which the report was issued or they are not interested in that specific update. Clients cannot disconnect to reduce the usage of the wireless link either, since they need to be connected and wait for the update reports.

In this paper we describe a flexible cache consistency protocol for mobile distributed systems. First, we propose a notification protocol that caters for various consistency requirements. For cached data, clients can specify consistency requirements at different granularity (e.g. attribute level, object level), time intervals between update propagation and predicates (which trigger the updates) for the data they are interested in. This protocol is responsible for propagating and maintaining client specific information.

Data consistency is maintained through the use of shared time-locks, namely *"strict read/write lock"* and *"permissive read/write lock"*. All these locks have time limits, after which they expire. Strict and permissive read locks are shareable between clients for the same data item, whereas strict write locks and permissive write locks (called ownership server locks) are exclusive write locks (that can only be held by one client). The difference between ownership write locks and strict write locks is the way the propagation of writes is performed. Ownership server locks have writes immediately propagated to the server, effectively implementing write-through caching. Strict write locks have writes applied locally to data and updates are flushed to the server at commit time.

Operation efficiency, or its counterpart inefficiency measured by the number of operations rejected as they would lead to inconsistent data, indicates a noticeably better performance of the weak consistency protocol over the strict consistency protocol in every case. With increasing read-write sharing, the performance improvement is increasingly noticeable, e.g. in case of 3/4th overlapping read-write operations the weak protocol rejects only half as many operations as the strict protocol.

Section 2 describes the Notification Protocol, which defines the semantics of the client-server communication. The notions of strict and weak data consistency are defined along with the respective protocols are presented in Section 3. Section 4 discusses the results before concluding the paper in section 5.

2   Notification Protocol

This protocol has two types of messages: Notification Request and Update Notification message. After a short introduction, the two message types are described in this section.

A server manages data and access to that data on behalf of clients. Clients can cache replicas and work remotely on cached data. Multiple clients can cache the same data, hence the server needs to provide a concurrent access scheme to ensure the consistency of both, the data cached by the client and the data residing on the server. The concurrency control method implemented here is based on time locks that clients need to obtain from the server before they can work on locally cached data. In the proposed approach, different clients can have different consistency requirements for the same data item. At the same time any given client can have different consistency requirements for different data items that are cached locally. In addition to catering for the above consistency requirements with guarantees, the proposed protocol also has the following features.

– Clients can specify the granularity at which they would like to maintain consistency. E.g. a mobile funds transfer system that has cached a customer account object locally would like to maintain consistency at a attribute level (balance attribute) instead of the entire account object.
– Clients can specify the degree of consistency required for the cached data item. E.g. the mobile funds transfer system (from the above example) may wish to maintain strict consistency for the balance attribute whereas it might be happy with weak consistency for the address attribute.
– Clients can specify a predicate, whose false condition would trigger notification update messages. E.g. A client can request that updates be sent if only if the balance attribute of a the account object falls below \$200.

- Clients can propagate updates to the server. E.g. when the mobile funds transfer system completes an operation, it will update the value balance attribute on the server.
- Clients can receive updates (that are relevant to them and they would like to know about) committed by other clients. E.g. if there are more than two clients caching the balance attribute of the same account object and if one of them updates it, then other clients that are holding a cached copy can receive the update that was committed on the server.

The proposed protocol keeps track of each client's requirements and provides the required consistency.

2.1   Notification Request

In case of a cache miss, i.e. when the requested data item is not available locally, the client retrieves the requested data from the server and puts it in the local cache. However, the client cannot start using the data until it acquires an appropriate lock on that data item. After a lock has been granted the client can analyse the data and send a Notification Request message indicating its consistency requirements for that data item to the server.

A Notification Request message can only be sent by a client holding a valid lock. A client can send multiple Notification Request messages over the duration it holds the locks, the last Notification Message received by the server overwrites any previous Notification Request messages. Between acquiring a lock and sending a Notification Message, other clients can modify or read the locked data item, if they have valid locks (e.g. in the case of shared read-write locks). This situation is dealt in the usual way as described in the Consistency protocol.

The Notification Request message is a tuple of the form

$$(X : T, \{a_1, a_2, \ldots, a_n\}, P \vee Q, \xi_T)$$

where, T is a type and X is an object of type T, $a_1, a_2, \ldots, a_n$ are attributes of X, Δ is the set of all possible attributes; that is $a_i \in \Delta \cup \{ANY\}$, Σ_X is the set of all operations over X, where $\{ANY\} \subset \Sigma_X$. P and Q are predicates, they are in the form of $S_1 \wedge S_2 \wedge \ldots \wedge S_n$, where $S_i \in \Sigma_X$ and ξ_T is a time interval specified in seconds.

$X : a_i$ is a pair that uniquely identifies an object and one of its data members. a_i can have the special value of ANY, which represents all data members of object X. P and Q are predicates, which when false would trigger the server to send an Update Notification message. P or Q can have the special value of ANY, which signifies any change to object X. ξ_T represents the maximum delay from the time an update of $X : a_i$ pair is registered until the relevant update notification message is sent. A value of zero signals an immediate update requirement and a value of T indicates that the client can put up with a T second notification delay. In addition to setting the degree of consistency, this field can also be used to improve performance by reducing communication costs, as the server can combine several updates to clients into a single message. E.g. if there is a outstanding message for client C which needs to be delivered in 10 seconds, and another update is processed which requires a message to be delivered immediately, both of these updates can be sent together to C.

Servers maintains large amounts of data on behalf of clients. An client operation typically accesses only a small subset of the data and setting the granularity of concurrency control mechanisms appropriately, i.e. locking only the required part of the data, can avoid unnecessary blocking of other operations (by other clients) that want to access the non-required data. E.g. if a banking application locks all customer accounts at a branch, only one bank clerk can perform an online banking transaction at any time - which is clearly an unacceptable constraint in most cases. The proposed $X : a_i$ field solves this problem by enabling the client to specify the granularity of the object at which it would like to maintain consistency. A typical use is strict consistency for critical data members of an object, whereas for irrelevant or less important data it could choose not to be notified of modifications or have weak consistency.

When a client does not care/wish to be notified about any updates, it can send an appropriate Notification Request message for that *object:attribute* pair, which will result in the client never being notified of updates on that object. For example, a Mobile Electronic Funds Transfer system would not like to be notified of an address change of the account holder, it would only care for the current balance. Alternatively, when the client has weak consistency requirements, it could specify a Notification Request message of the type $(x : Account, value, ANY, 1000)$. E.g. a share price monitoring system would not care about price fluctuations of stocks that the user does not own or does not plan to watch, while during trading hours may need strict consistency for stock that the user owns, and relatively weaker consistency for stocks that the user has on his watch list.

2.2   Update Notification

Once an update is committed on the server, the update is matched against the predicate of all the Notification Request messages for the updated data item. The condition of update messages is met if the predicate condition of the Notification Request message is true. For every client that meets the condition of update messages, an Update Notification message is sent. This message is of the form:

$$(X : T, \{a_1, a_2, \ldots, a_n\}, \{c_1, c_2, \ldots, c_n\}, TS)$$

where T is a type, X is an object of type T, $\{a_1, a_2, \ldots, a_n\}$ is a set of attributes for which updates are sent (along with the old values), and $\{c_1, c_2, \ldots, c_n\}$ is the corresponding set of new values for the above attributes.

TS is the timestamp indicating when the update was accepted at the server. Clients can examine the TS value and check un-committed operations on the cached data to see whether there were any conflicting operations that need to be rolled-back by the client, such as local updates bearing time-stamps larger than the times-tamp of the update received from the server and using earlier values.

Consistency requirements determine the amount of messaging performed by the server, strict consistency requirements, i.e. immediate notification requests representing disproportionally higher load, because weaker consistency requirements allow grouping of several updates into one message, apart from filtering updates. The server can use a Dependency Table [1] for data and clients to determine which clients are affected by an update and who needs to be notified of the changes.

3   Consistency

This section briefly describes the concept of various time-locks along with their corresponding semantics. We then look at the issue of maintaining consistency. We describe the different consistency levels (i.e. strict and weak consistency) and their corresponding protocols.

3.1   Locks

In traditional and database systems [11,2], a *lock* is an operation that, when applied on a data item, ensures and guarantees continous access to the data item. Locks are used to provide concurrent access in a consistent manner to data when there are several clients accessing the same data simultaneously.

Typically, a lock is assigned to a client until it gives it up. All other lock requests for the same data item cannot be granted until the client holding the lock gives it up. This can be counter-productive for concurrency, since a client could get a lock for a data item and hold it indefinitely or the client could go off-line and be unable to give up a lock. This is a serious issue in mobile systems due to the unreliability of the mobile link. Clients face the prospect of frequent disconnection, coupled with the fact that typically mobile devices have limited battery life, a lock could be held indefinitely, thus effecting the concurrency of the system.

The idea or time-locks has been motivated from *leases* as presented in [5]. A lease gives its holder specific rights to perform some operation for a fixed duration of time. We extend a lease to different types (some being shareable) with varied durations. Time-locks are used as a means to force clients to give-up locks within a preassigned time and as a means of concurrent read-write sharing. The notion of locks being valid for a certain time period is important and required in mobile systems, so that, if clients that are holding locks get disconnected for long periods, the locks can be reclaimed after they expire and assigned to other clients. Also, clients would be aware of the validity of a lock at any given time without having to remain connected. They can now invalidate cached data when a lock expires, thus avoiding operation on stale data that might result in a conflicting operation.

Proposed Locks. We briefly describe the proposed locks, which were presented in [13], followed by a description of lock-time durations. The four types of time-locks are:

(A) **Strict Read Locks** (SRLs)

An SRL is a variation of a traditional read lock. Multiple SRLs can exist at any one time for the same data item. Before performing a write operation, the client needs to upgrade the SRL to a strict write lock (SWL). By obtaining an SRL, a client is guaranteed that no other clients will modify the data item.

(B) **Strict Write Locks** (SWL)

SWL is a variation of a traditional write lock. Only one client can hold an SWL on a data item at a time. Once a client gives up an SWL, or when it expires, the server sends an Update Notification (UN) message to all clients who have a cached a copy of the given data item.

(C) **Permissive Read Locks** (PRL)

PRL is a shared read lock that can be held by multiple clients. On gaining a PRL, all clients get concurrent read access to the data item (i.e. they can read from the local cache). Clients are notified of any updates on the data item while it holds a PRL for it.

(D) **Ownership Server Locks** (OSL)

An OSL is a shared write lock. Multiple clients can have a PRL on data item X while a client has a OSL on the same item x. The client having the OSL employs write-through caching by writing any update directly to the server. The server notifies the other clients holding PRLs on x, of the changes made to x.

Locks can be either upgraded or renewed upon the expiry of their validation period. Table 1 summarises the compatibility for the locks. Based on these lock properties we can split the locks into the following two pair-types: strict pair (SRL and SWL), and permissive pair (PRL and OSL).

Based on these lock properties we can split the locks into the following two pair-types: strict pair (**SRL** and **SWL**), and permissive pair (**PRL** and **OSL**).

Table 1. Lock Compatibility Matrix.

Current	PRL	SRL	SWL	OSL
none	Y	Y	Y	Y
PRL	Y	Y	Y	Y
SRL	Y	Y	N	N
SWL	Y	N	N	N
OSL	Y	N	N	N

Lock Periods. The validity of the time-locks introduced in section 3.1 expires after the lapse of the time period they were granted for. Clients can request for a lock to be allocated for a certain period, however, a server cannot always permit a lock to be allocated for the duration requested by a client, since it has to serve other clients and maintain a high level of concurrency. Hence, the server moderates the client requested time period and allocates the lock for a duration it determines to be ideal.

We have developed a simple model for determining lock-time periods, considering that a complete model would be very complex and involve parameters like application requirements, past data usage patterns, time of day and popularity of the data. We propose using previous lock times for a data item in determining the maximum time period a client can attain a lock. The actual lock times (opposed to the time a lock was initially granted) for the last n client requests is stored and used to calculate future lock periods. Using the actual lock times of previous operations in determining the duration of locks can be used reasonably accurately to predict the time periods for future requests. Formally, we calculate the average lock duration for a particular data item by

$$t_d^{average_n} = \frac{\sum_{i=1}^{n} t_d^{actual_i}}{n}$$

where $t_d^{average_n}$ is the average lock-time (for last n client requests) for data item d. $t_d^{actual_i}$ is the actual lock duration for the last i^{th} client request.

To calculate $t_d^{average_n}$ we used a value of 10 for n, i.e. the lock times for future requests for data item d would be the average of the actual lock time for the last 10 operations. The general usage of a system is determined by the time of the day, it would be expected that a system would be relatively idle at off-peak (night) times as compared to peak (day) times. If we were to choose a high value of n, it could result in an average time encompassing the entire day or more (depending on system workload and data contention). Locks can be granted for a longer period of time during off-peak times due to the fact that it would not result in decreased concurrency (due to low number of concurrent users), while the converse is true for peak times. Hence, taking an average that spans different times of the day (i.e. different usage patterns) is not an appropriate policy to determine lock times, rather taking an average time from the last n operations in the same usage pattern would result in a more accurate prediction. The value of n is based on the system usage and the contention for data and it needs to be fine-tuned for accurate times.

3.2   Data Consistency

With the existence of multiple copies of data the task of maintaining consistency amongst them is important. It is critical for replicas to be up-to-date with the primary copy (which resides on the server) as well as with other replicas. Consistency between these replicas can be maintained by using a scheme, where each update sent to the server is propagated by the server to all other replicas. Efficiency is an important consideration with cached data. The amount of messages that needs to be sent is proportional to the number of replicas that exist for a data item at any time. For example in a scenario with a high number of write requests, the Update Notification conditions, i.e. the predicates and time delay parameter, have to be selected carefully, otherwise weak consistency may turn out to be very inefficient, as not all clients would be interested in each update immediately. A few clients might be interested in certain data items only and would like to be notified only if that value changes. Others might want to be notified only if the new value of the data item satisfies a certain predicate (e.g. Notify if x is greater than 10) or might not care about changes in certain data items at all.

The task of maintaining consistency for cached remote data can be split into two tasks: (1) *Maintaining consistency between replicas* and (2) *Moderating concurrent access and managing concurrent updates of data at the server.*

The first task is to ensure that the replicas are consistent with each other and with the primary copy at the server. For example, if an object x is stored at server s and cached at clients c_1, c_2 and c_3 and c_1 was to modify and propagate the updated value of x to s, maintaining consistency would entail s to propagate or inform the other clients, c_2 and c_3 of the new value of $'x'$. The clients c_2 and c_3 could have different consistency requirements and it may or may not be necessary for the server to notify clients with weak consistency requirements immediately. At the same time, clients with strict consistency requirements would need to be notified immediately or have their copy invalidated from the cache.

The second task pertains to managing concurrent updates at the server and ensuring consistency of objects with regards to concurrent operations. It involves ordering the different client operations and determining the final value of the data item. For example, if the server receives an update request for an object x from both c_1 and c_2 at the same time; the server should determine which request is to be satisfied first and whether the second operation should be allowed to proceed or should it be rejected.

The task of maintaining consistency is different for strict consistency requirements and for weak consistency requirements, and we treat them separately. However, the task of moderating concurrent access is the same for both weak and strict consistency requirements, as global consistency of the data needs to be maintained.

If two or more requests for a lock arrive at the server at the same time and only one of the requests can be granted the lock, a decision needs to be made based on which a request came first (First Come First Served – FCFS), how long is the lock period requested, what is the frequency of disconnection of the client, or a combination of these factors. The assignment of locks can lead to deadlocks or clients may starve [2]. A FCFS approach does not guarantee that all clients will be served and it does not stop a client from renewing locks and making other processes starve. Such situations, however, can be dealt with by applying already known techniques mentioned e.g. in [2,11].

Another problem relates to message latency. Let's assume that a request for a lock arrives at the server at time t and the previous write lock was released at time k. If the client server message latency is greater than $(t - k)/2$, the client can have inconsistent data as the Notification Protocol may not have managed to deliver the last Update Message to the client in question. To address this issue, the client request for a write lock needs to include a counter signifying the number of writes seen by the client on the data item. The server compares this counter with the actual number of writes that have been applied to the data on the server. If these values are not the same, the write request has to be rejected and the client needs to send a new request. The new value of the data can be piggy-backed to the client with the reject message; or alternatively we could wait for the Notification Protocol to deliver the new value. If the server's and client's write counters contain the same value, the lock is granted.

Strict Consistency Protocol. Consistency requirements for a particular data item are termed as strict requirements when the client would like to get immediate notification about every update on the data item and would like all updates it makes to be final. Updates committed on the server are immediately propagated to all clients with strict consistency requirements. For example, a financial application making decisions based on the current balance of an account would immediately like to know of any changes in the balance. Similarly, if an application debits a sum against an account, the effect of this operation has to be final that cannot be rolled back.

A client wanting to maintain strict consistency would use strict locks for the purpose. In case of a cache miss (client request for an operation on data that is not in the client cache) the client request is relayed to the server. The server returns a replica of the data item, and the client has to reply by specifying the granularity and type of its consistency requirements via the Notification Protocol.

Strict Locks. A client wishing to read data, requests an SRL for it. Multiple clients can hold SRLs on the same data simultaneously. A client can request the SRL to be upgraded to a SWL when it wishes to make updates to the data. A request for a SWL is granted if there are no other write locks on the data item. All read locks are revoked when a SWL is granted to a client: the Notification Protocol sends an invalidation message to all clients having a read lock on that data item.

This scheme might seem a bit unfair for clients holding a SRL, since their lock is not guaranteed to stay for the duration it was granted. This scheme can be modified such that no SRLs are revoked, instead, requests for new SRLs are rejected and the request for a SWL is queued. Once all current SRLs expire, the request for the strict write lock can be completed, thus not starving clients that are only interested in reading.

To reduce unnecessary data transfer, when a client's SRL is invalidated, the client is not required to clear its cache, i.e. it can still keep the cached copy, but before reading or writing data it needs to obtain an appropriate lock from the server. When a client sends a requests for any lock to the server, the server checks and ensures that the client has valid data in its cache. If the cached data is invalid, the server piggy-backs the new value. A client c holding a SWL on a data item x can disconnect from the server, work with the locally cached copy, reconnect before the lock expires to either, renew the lock or send the updates to the server and release the lock. The protocol guarantees, for the duration of the lock, that no other client would read or update x until the lock expires or c voluntarily releases it. When the SWL is released, the server propagates the updates by sending Update Notification messages to all clients holding a cached copy of x.

Weak Consistency Protocol. Weak consistency is used when a client does not need up-to-date data all the time. Update messages may be delayed or even omitted if the changes are considered to be insignificant; e.g. the client can inform the server that changes below a given threshold need not be communicated.

However, a client using weakly consistent data is susceptible to conflicts arising out of read-write or write-write data sharing, since it may have missed an update and read or worked with stale data. Clients employing weak consistency use the permissive pair of locks as defined above. In the following discussion, the use of permissive locks for the weak consistency protocol is given.

Permissive Locks. The permissive pair of locks allows a client to hold read locks on data items that are locked by other clients for writing. Consistency is maintained by forcing the owner of the write lock to make write-through updates directly to the server. The server then propagates updates to clients that hold a PRL on the data item.

As discussed earlier, permissive locks are time locks and are allocated for a period determined by the server. Clients send a request for a Permissive Read Locks (PRL) from the server when they want to read a data item. Multiple clients can hold a PRL on the same data item at the same time. The server assures clients with a PRL that they would be informed of any changes to the data item for which they hold the lock. The maximum delay (assuming that the client is connected) in propagating updates is the message latency from the server to the client. Before the PRL expires, a client can either renew the PRL or upgrade it to an Ownership Server Lock (OSL) in order for the client to retain the PRL or make updates to it respectively. In the case that the client fails to do so, the lock expires.

Once a PRL is granted to a client, the server guarantees, for the duration of the PRL, that all updates on the locked data will be propagated to the client. The client can relax this by nominating a predicate that need to be satisfied in order to receive an update. The client can also specify the maximum delay (update latency) for the duration of the lock, i.e. updates need not to be sent immediately when they are received by the server. Before the PRL expires, the client can either renew it, upgrade it to an OSL (to make updates) or release it.

The OSL is a write lock that forces the holder to make write-through updates. This allows the server to immediately propagate changes to other clients holding a PRL on the updated item. A client with an OSL cannot make changes to data while disconnected, as consistency guarantees can not be accomplished, including propagating updates to PRL holders and imposing write-through updates.

Clients using the permissive pair of locks need to have good connections and must stay connected for the duration of the lock. If they fail to do so, there is a high probability of having conflicting operations due to missed updates. Clients with less reliable connection or wanting to work offline should use the strict locks.

The two lock-pairs can inter-operate as shown in table 1. For example, two clients could have different consistency requirements for the same data item. One might want strict consistency while the other requires weak consistency. A client with weak read requirements can be easily accommodated with any type of lock (strict or weak), though OSL cannot exist in the presence of any form of strict locks since it would be impossible to provide strict guarantees while there are concurrent weak write locks on the same data item.

This scheme can be seen to give precedence to strict consistency requirements over weak consistency requirements. This can be justified since the chances of a weak operation completing are lower than a strict operation completing. Under such a condition, it would be beneficial (in terms of the system throughput) to aid in the completion and be sure about a commit for a strict operation rather than taking a chance with a weak operation that might have to abort.

4   Discussion

We have simulated the proposed approach and the results were presented in [12]. A comparision of the proposed approaches was made to two-phase locking (2PL) [11] and optimistic concurrency control [2]. The strict and weak protocols were compared to each other and the number of operations completed was measured. The throughput and the scalability of the systems were also simulated.

The proposed approach performs better than 2PL [11] in terms of higher data availability and higher resulting system throughput. 2PL requires that all locks be obtained before any commit, which prevents other clients from getting locks on data items on which locks are already held, even though the clients holding the locks may have finished processing the locked data item. In our approach, the use of permissive locks allows clients to share both read and write locks which results in higher concurrent processing of data. Even though this may lead to aborts if there is a read-write or write-write conflict, effective sharing can be achieved when there are less writers and more readers, since the updates are propagated to clients via the notification protocol.

The performance of the optimistic concurrency control scheme is marginally better than that of the strict consistency protocol. This can be attributed to the fact that a higher number of messages need to be exchanged for the strict consistency protocol.

In terms of the amount of data being transferred between clients and servers, the proposed approach broadcasts less and more relevant data to the clients than the methods that use broadcasting invalidation and update reports [8]. The Notification Protocol provides a method by which clients can elect to be notified only if an event occurs or if a certain class of conditions is true, this dispenses with updates that clients are not interested in. With broadcast reports, the onus of listening to updates is on the clients. This not only limits the clients' ability to work offline, but also results in an increase in the processing load of the client, as it ends up listening to updates it is not interested in, in order not to miss updates that it is interested in. In our approach, this filtering is done on the server side, and hence it can be guaranteed that all the updates sent to the client are those it is interested in.

The weak consistency protocol works well in situations with high data contention. As shown in [12], the weak consistency protocol performs better by a factor or almost two and a half over the strict consistency protocol. However, the weak consistency protocol requires a high amount of message traffic between clients and servers. There is a linear increase in the number of messages that are exchanged for every write operation. This is due to the weak consistency protocol's use of write-through caching, which also allows it to sustain a higher share rate, and eventually higher operation completion rate. The strict consistency protocol requires a stable number of messages regardless of the number of updates that are made, since updates are only propagated to the server at the end. This also means that other clients cannot receive these updates on time and operations may need to be aborted by the server due to conflicting writes.

The weak consistency protocol is ideal for clients with reliable connections that do not intend to work in disconnected mode. The strict consistency protocol is better for disconnected operations, since it guarantees that if a client holds a strict write lock, no other client can modify that data item. Of course this affects concurrency and could result in higher abort rate of operations by other clients. Starvation of clients requests is prevented by the use of time-locks.

5   Conclusion

In this paper we have demonstrated that the weak consistency protocol, with a linear increase in messages over the number of writes, works reasonably well compared to Two-phase locking, optimistic concurrency control and even the strict consistency protocol. The weak consistency protocol has been shown to be appropriate for clients with relatively strong network connection and who wish to work while connected, while the strict consistency protocol is more applicable for operation in disconnected mode.

The notification protocol presented is responsible for propagating updates to clients, and obtaining and maintaining client specific information such as time interval within which updates need to be propagated and predicates that would trigger an update message. This paper clearly demonstrated that it is possible to support disconnected operations with a reasonable degree of concurrency and low message overhead. A loose sharing method for data was shown which performed very well even under high read/read or read/write sharing environments. A real life example, implemented and run successfully, proved the viability of the method and highlighted its advantages. The proposed techniques harness a tremendous sharing potential and proved to be scalable over a large client base.

Acknowledgements

This work was supported by the Australian Research Council (ARC) Linkage-project grant no. LP0218853.

References

1. J. Challenger, A. Iyengar and P. Dantzig, "A Scalable System for Consistently Caching Dynamic Web Data", *Proc. of the 18th Annual Joint Conf. of the IEEE Computer and Communications Societies*, New York, 1999.
2. G. Coulouris, J. Dollimore and T. Kindberg, "Distributed Systems: Concepts and Design. (2nd Ed)", *Addison-Wesley*, 1994.
3. G. H. Forma and J. Zahorjan, "The Challenges of Mobile Computing", *IEEE Computer*, 27(6), 1994, pp. 38-47.
4. A. Delis and N. Roussopoulos, "Performance and Scalability of Client-Server Database Architectures", *In Proc. of the 18th Int. Conf. on Very Large Databases*, August 1992.
5. C. G. Gray and D. R. Cheriton. "Leases: An Efficient Fault-Tolerant Mechanism for Distributed File Cache Consistency", *Proc. of the 12th ACM Symposium on Operating Systems Principles*, 1989.
6. T. Imienlinski and B. R. Badrinath, "Wireless Mobile Computing: Challenges in Data Management", *Communication of the ACM*, 37(10), 1994.
7. J. J. Kistler and M. Satyanarayanan, "Disconnected Operation in the Coda File System", *ACM Transactions Computer Systems*, 10(1), 1992, pp. 213-225.
8. S. Lee, C. Hwang and H. Yu, "Supporting Transactional Cache Consistency in Mobile Database Systems", *Proce. of MobiDE*, Seattle, 1999, pp. 6-13.
9. E. Pitoura, B. Bhargava, "Data Consistency in Intermittently Connected Distributed Systems", *IEEE Transaction on Knowledge and Data Engineering*, 11(6), 1998, pp. 896-915.
10. E. Pitoura and B. Bhargava, "Building Information Systems for Mobile Environments", *Proc. of 3rd Intl. Conf. on Information and Knowledge Management*, 1994, pp. 371-378.
11. R. Ramakrishnan and J. Gehrke, "Database Management Systems. (2nd Ed.)", *McGraw Hill Publication*, 1999.
12. A. Vora, Z. Tari and P. Bertok, "A Flexible Cache Consistency Protocol for Mobile Systems Using Shareable Read/Write Time Locks", Technical Report TR-02-4, RMIT University, July 2002.
13. A. Vora, Z. Tari and P. Bertok, "A Mobile Cache Consistency Protocol using Shareable Read/Write Time Locks", *Proc. of 9th Intl. Conf. on Parallel and Distributed Systems*, Taipei, Taiwan, December 2002.

DataWarp: Building Applications
Which Make Progress in an Inconsistent World

Peter Henderson, Robert John Walters, Stephen Crouch, and Qinglai Ni

Declarative Systems and Software Engineering Group,
Department of Electronics and Computer Science,
University of Southampton,
Southampton, UK. SO17 1BJ
{ph,rjw1,stc,qn}@ecs.soton.ac.uk

Abstract. The usual approach to dealing with imperfections in data is to attempt to eliminate them. However, the nature of modern systems means this is often futile. This paper describes an approach which permits applications to operate notwithstanding inconsistent data. Instead of attempting to extract a single, correct view of the world from its data, a DataWarp application constructs a collection of interpretations. It adopts one of these and continues work. Since it acts on assumptions, the DataWarp application considers its recent work to be provisional, expecting eventually most of these actions will become definitive. Should the application decide to adopt an alternative data view, it may then need to void provisional actions before resuming work. We describe the DataWarp architecture, discuss its implementation and describe an experiment in which a DataWarp application in an environment containing inconsistent data achieves better results than its conventional counterpart.

1 Introduction

With the continued fall in the cost of computer hardware and the adoption of the same technologies for distributed computing on intranets within organisations and the global internet [1-4], we are seeing the creation of an everything connected to everything else information utility [5].

In their origins, even the largest of computer systems were comprised of a single process. This process worked with a collection of data which could be assumed to faithfully reflect the state of the real world. In turn, this permits applications to expect rules which apply to the real world to be reflected in the data. As systems have evolved they have developed into networks of communicating components which are assembled into complete applications. Increasingly these networks are adopting asynchronous architectures using a variety of technologies [6-11]. These components may understand that the data they have is incomplete, but they expect the subset that they have to be faithful to some notion of reality. In other words, they suppose that the data they hold provides them with a window into some complete and accurate data store for the whole system which is free from inconsistency as shown in Fig. 1. Here, A and B each have a partial view of the overall state of the system. By exchanging data, they are able to make their views of the data compatible but their assumption about the data they hold goes further. They both suppose that there exists some definitive value

J.-B. Stefani, I. Demeure, and D. Hagimont (Eds.): DAIS 2003, LNCS 2893, pp. 167–178, 2003.

for the true state of the system and that the data they hold is consistent with it. These ideals are both difficult to establish and maintain.

Distribution and replication of data can impart additional resilience and performance to applications [12, 13]. However, as the accumulated mass of data grows it is becoming ever more difficult to maintain the illusion of universal consistency which underpins much of the reasoning applied by applications [14, 15]. Schemes, such as distributed transactions [16, 17] can guarantee this consistency. Their operation requires co-ordination and co-operation between the various locations at which the data is held. The effort associated with this co-ordination is appropriate for some processes, such as a Bank transfer where it is essential that neither end of the transaction can occur without the other. However they are too restrictive to be applied universally [18, 19], especially in enterprise and inter-enterprise systems.

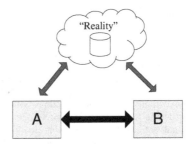

Fig. 1. The view of data of a traditional application

Instead of forcing the data to fit the understanding of our applications, we need to find ways to implement applications in such a way that they can operate in the imperfect data environment in which they necessarily find themselves. If we are to do this, we need to relax the reliance on the assumption of global consistency in data.

This paper introduces DataWarp. A DataWarp application:

- Maintains many *views* of data
- Selects a view based on *assumptions*,
- Is prepared to *alter its assumptions* and take remedial action

2   An Example: MQ Defence

Whilst there are many real enterprise systems which are faced with inconsistent data, these are not ideal subjects for study for two reasons. Firstly, they are so large that describing how they operate is difficult. Secondly, their users and developers have worked hard to prevent, or ameliorate the effects of, what we perceive as interesting behaviour: being tolerant of *inconsistency*. Recognising this, we have constructed an experimental system which uses the asynchronous technologies of enterprise systems (specifically Message Queue) but is not crafted a priori to work around data inconsistency problems.

The system is a defence simulation in which ships move around a two dimensional grid. It is implemented as a collection of applications which communicate using a commercial message passing middleware product (MSMQ, [7, 20]). Each ship has its own message queue which it is required to read promptly.

Any ship in the system is able to perform a number of actions:

- Move. Ships are artificially constrained by the edges of the grid but otherwise are free to move in any direction at any time.
- Sense local information. Each ship has a sensor which it is able to interrogate. A ship's sensor responds with a message containing a list of ships within its range. Information supplied by sensors is similar to that which a real ship at sea might collect using radar.
- Communicate. A ship may establish a communication channel between itself and any other ship it knows, enabling it to interrogate other ships in a similar way to its sensor. The usual response from a ship to such an enquiry is a message detailing its present view of the entire grid. However, unlike sensors, ships may not respond to all enquiries (see below). Channels operate in both directions, so the ship at either end may use a channel. In establishing a channel, a ship gives away its existence, location and identity.

The range of the sensors is limited and the ships move, so no ship can establish and maintain a complete, up to date view of the grid using its sensor alone since at any time there will be areas which are beyond the range of its sensor. However, by communicating ships can assist each other by sharing information, but at the expense of being prepared to resolve inconsistencies. Consider three stationery ships which have established communications when a fourth moves out of the sensor range of one ship into the sensor range of another. In communication, the third ship will receive reports from the two who have seen the moving ship, placing it in two locations (its true position when last observed) leaving the third ship with a decision to make.

This environment is sufficiently simple to enable us to identify and reason about what is happening whilst also sufficiently realistic to present many of the problems of inter-enterprise distributed computing (not least delays and unreliability) [21].

For this experiment, the ships has have a notion of allegiance and are able to attack one another using missiles which usually, but not always, destroy their target. A ship which fires a missile directs it to a location on the grid which it takes time to reach. Thus a ship may survive an attack if it is lucky or moves far enough whilst the missile is in transit. Each ship is allocated to one of two sides and each navy assists their side's effort to dominate the grid by supplying information to their allies and attacking their enemies. Ships don't respond to enquiries from their enemies so a ship which responds to an enquiry is a friend. A ship which doesn't respond is likely to be an enemy, although it could be a friend who has failed to respond, or whose response is delayed or lost in transit. The information supplied by sensors does not include the allegiance of contacts. Fig. 2 shows an example ship's view of the world. It is aware of four ships, itself (One), a friend (Two), an enemy out of range (Three) and a ship of unknown allegiance (Four).

In this scenario, there is a further element to the data inconsistency problem faced by the ships. In addition to needing a strategy to resolve conflicting reports about the location of other ships, they now have the urgent need to decide what to do about unidentified ships which are within reach of their weapons (and so probably close enough to launch an attack if they are an enemy), such as a contact which has been observed for the first time by the local sensor or one for which conflicting data has been received.

For the experiment, we pitched two types of ship against each other; ships following the DataWarp philosophy and standards ship using a more traditional behaviour.

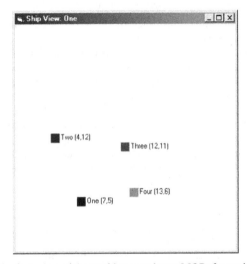

Fig. 2. A view of the world as seen by an MQDefence ship

We use rules as a universal means of describing behaviour at a suitable level of abstraction. Fig. 3 describes a ship *not* using DataWarp. The rules are divided into two sections. The first describes the way the ship reacts to stimuli (the reactive rules), the second describes autonomous behaviour which the ship initiates itself (the proactive rules). This behaviour reflects the usual attitude of applications. For this example, we will concentrate on the issue of the unidentified contact. Faced with a situation such as that shown in Fig. 2, should the unidentified ship Four be within range, the standard ship doesn't know what to do. Before it can proceed it must identify the ship. It cannot do otherwise for fear of attacking a friendly ship. The ship could try asking its ally (named Two in Fig. 2), but it may not know either. The only option certain to give a result is to open a channel. However this is risky: in trying to communicate with an unidentified contact, a ship gives away its own position and allegiance. If the contact is an enemy, it might launch an immediate attack.

```
/* Reactive rules */
Attack any enemy ship within range.
Open a channel to any unidentified ship within range.
A ship which replies on a channel is an ally.
Store data received from sensor.
Store data received along channels.
Respond to enquiries from allies with details of our view.
Reconstruct our view of the grid when the data store changes.

/* Proactive rules */
Move according to algorithm.
Send enquiries on channels.
Read sensor.
```

Fig. 3. Behaviour of a Standard Ship

Fig. 4 outlines the alternative behaviour of a DataWarp ship. This differs from the standard ship in that it resolves problems in its data by constructing a collection of views of the grid and picking one to act upon. In this particular example, the problem is the allegiance of ship Four which must be either an ally or an enemy. This leads to the creation of a set of possible views which can be divided into two subsets: those in which Four is an ally and those in which Four is an enemy. The ship makes its choice by reference to the rules by which it operates. If it elects to assume Four is an enemy, it picks a view from the set in which Four is hostile. The particular view chosen will depend on how this DataWarp ship resolves the positional issues in its data. Should Four come within range, it will be attacked (as an enemy), followed by an attempt at communication. Should Four identify itself as a friend, the DataWarp ship would then know that it chose the wrong view of the gird and abandon it in favour of an alternative in which Four is an ally. In this particular circumstance, the allegiance of Four is now certain so those views in which Four is assumed to be hostile may be discarded. However, in general, views which are presently discounted need to be retained. A side effect of changing its view is that the DataWarp ship will realise that it has launched a missile at an ally and destroy it before it can do any harm. A criticism might be that, should a friendly contact fail to respond in time our ship would destroy an ally. This is indeed a risk. However, the standard ship is worse – if one of its contacts fails to respond, it launches an irretrievable attack.

```
/* Reactive rules */
Attack any ship within range known or assumed to be an enemy.
Where a ship is attacked on the assumption of hostility, open a channel
  to that ship.
Destroy a missile in flight to an ally.
A ship which replies on a channel is an ally.
Store data received from sensor.
Store data received along channels.
Respond to enquiries from allies with a details of our view.
Reconstruct candidate views of the grid when the data store changes.
If data affecting assumptions changes, reselect view of grid.
Send corrections when a change of view changes allegiances of contacts
  advised to allies.

/* Proactive rules */
Move according to algorithm.
Send enquiries on channels.
Read sensor.
Reconsider assumptions.

/* Assumptions */
An unidentified ship is an enemy.
/* Other assumptions and guidelines about resolving positional issues */
```

Fig. 4. Behaviour of a DataWarp Ship

Should Four be an ally, the DataWarp ship will also realise that it may have misinformed other allies with which it has been in communication whilst the assumption was in force. It will attempt to correct any consequences of this by sending corrections. These corrections have the potential to ripple around if they cause ships that receive them to change views too.

In addition to the experiments performed in the MQDefence environment which is actually distributed and uses MSMQ for messages, we have performed further experiments using a less elaborate simulation written in Java.

To run the experiments, we have needed to add some detail to the definitions given above. This has concerned matters such as the size of the grid, the ranges of sensors and missiles, the time a ship waits for a response to a communication before concluding another is an enemy and the time a missile takes to reach its target. The experiments have been run using a 300x300 sector grid. The number of ships in each navy, as well as the range of sensors and missiles, is a balance. More ships on the grid, and longer ranges for the weapons and sensors mean ships find and destroy each other more easily and lead to shorter experiments.

The pro-active rules are implemented using a simple timer which, on expiry, reads the ship's sensor, reads each of its channels and moves the ship a single division of the grid in a random direction which is weighted in favour of continuing in the same direction as the previous move. All ships use the same moving algorithm and have the same sensor and weapon ranges. For most experiments, the range of the sensors has been set slightly in excess of the range of weapons.

Initial experiments were performed on a number of machines in the laboratory with six ships on each side, missile and sensor ranges of 45 and 50 respectively. These were permitted to run until one fleet is eliminated, and show that DataWarp ships win approaching 80% of the battles, though they do use more missiles. Even after adjusting the parameters to favour the standard ships, the DataWarp side still wins convincingly, though in some configurations the number of DataWarp ships attacking their allies is significant. Strictly limiting the number of missiles of each ship means that the DataWarp ships are likely to run out – making them vulnerable to attack and unable to contribute further to the success of their side. However, they still enjoy a significant advantage.

There is a considerable element of chance to where and when ships encounter each other which can affect the outcome. This is clearly a consequence of the moving algorithm, but we retained this algorithm since we wish to avoid the possibility that either type of ship should enjoy an advantage as an accident of the way the ships movement algorithm interacts with the features of the system.

Following on from the initial experiments, we have conducted several extended experiments in which the number of ships on the grid has been maintained by replacing each one which is destroyed with another of the same allegiance at a random location at the edge of the grid. In these experiments there can be no question of either side achieving dominance of the grid by destroying all of their opponents since they are replaced as they are destroyed. However the objective of each of the participants remains unchanged - to assist its side towards that goal by destroying their enemies. Hence the relative number of ships lost by the two sides is a reasonable measure of their relative success. The examples shown are selected from those experiments where the DataWarp ships enjoyed the least advantage. Ironically, even in those experiments the standard ships still didn't manage to sink opponents with much of the improvement in their apparent performance accounted for by DataWarp ships sinking each other. Nevertheless, typically twice as many of the standard ships are destroyed as the DataWarp ships. Table 1 and Table 2 give sample results from some extended runs of the experiment in MQDefence.

Table 1. Sample results, Standard vs. Standard ships

	Experiment 1	Experiment 2
Ships destroyed: side 1	16	27
Ships destroyed: side 2	11	18
Total	27	45

Table 2. Sample results, Standard vs. DataWarp ships

		Experiment 1		Experiment 2
Standard ships destroyed		130		123
DataWarp ships destroyed by standard ships	24		8	
DataWarp ships destroyed by DataWarp ships	28	52	35	43
Total		182		166

3 DataWarp

The traditional approach adopted by applications faced with unreliable data is to subject it to validation procedures to identify and eliminate problematic data. Once past this verification, applications essentially accept data as being absolute and act accordingly. When anomalies arise, the typical action is to report them as exceptions which generally demand external intervention, often from human operators.

DataWarp was initially inspired by TimeWarp [22, 23], which was developed for the implementation of distributed simulation. The processes in a TimeWarp environment do not have a synchronised notion of time. There is no central record of time in the system at all. However, they still manage to operate in such a way that the results of their computations are unaffected. This ability for a system without a consistent notion of time is extended by DataWarp towards data in general.

However, our motivation is different. With TimeWarp, a consistent global notion of the current time is traded for improved performance within a controlled environment. Our applications have no choice about their environment: they operate in the context of the uncontrolled, asynchronous, ever changing and more connected world of enterprise systems. This environment is increasingly polluted with poor data over which no single application exerts control. Accepting that dirty data is inevitable, DataWarp applications adopt local behaviours towards data which are similar in spirit to those of a TimeWarp process towards time.

In place of the usual behaviour, in which an application develops a single view of the world, when faced with inconsistencies in data, a DataWarp application constructs a collection of alternative data views which it regards as candidates for the view of the world it will use. With the passage of time and the arrival of further data, the application maintains this view-set, adding more when additional inconsistency arises and removing views where new data permits them to be discounted.

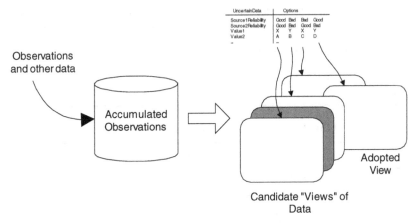

Fig. 5. DataWarp

DataWarp applications act promptly on input as it is received but retain a history of state, input and actions so that when errors come to light, they are able to re-consider and, where necessary undo actions or make compensations. Imposing an obligation onto applications to retain a history of actions may appear onerous, but in fact most commercial applications already record this information in audit trails.

There are real differences between a TimeWarp process and a DataWarp application which concern:

- The environment in which they operate
- The nature of the data which could be subject to amendment
- Identifying the need to rollback
- The actions which may be required to achieve a rollback

TimeWarp is concerned with time - a single valued data item which (in some general sense) always progresses. The processes of a TimeWarp system may be thought of as being distributed along a time-line. The extent to which the processes are distributed along this line will depend on the pattern of communication between them. Since there is no co-ordination of time in the system, so long as the processes operate in isolation their clocks will tend to drift apart. The effect of communication depends on the relationship between the local times in the processes concerned. A side-effect of a message which causes the receiving process to rollback is the near synchronisation of the clocks of the sending and receiving processes. More communication between processes is likely to cause the times on their local clocks to bunch together. Additionally, despite temporary variations, in the long term the collection of processes as a whole progress along this line from the past into the future.

In contrast, DataWarp is concerned with many unordered data items. Its applications might be considered as being distributed about a multi-dimensional space instead of along a line. In common with TimeWarp, it is reasonable to expect that applications which communicate will tend to approach each other in this space, but there is no equivalent of the relentless progress of time from the past to the future so, faced with two incompatible pieces of data there is no simple universal way for a DataWarp application to choose between them. Where a TimeWarp application is able to identify situations where rollbacks are necessary by simple comparisons between the timestamp on a message and the value on its local clock, a DataWarp application has no such a simple test. Instead, it has to identify inconsistencies in the data it has received (and acted upon) using application specific consistency rules. However, where the traditional application resorts to raising an exception demanding some external intervention, the DataWarp application will be able to cope. In the example above the DataWarp ship, on discovering faulty data and having to change its view destroys any missile which it has fired at an ally and sends corrections to the information it has supplied to any of its allies.

The details of when and how DataWarp applications identify which particular data items are at fault, and how far to rollback has to be application specific. During execution, the DataWarp application accumulates a collection of data items about which it has made assumptions. These assumptions may be directed towards using values which are the most likely to be true but according to the circumstances, other strategies are also appropriate. For example, the application may elect to use values which are most easily defended (should that become necessary) or the least likely to cause damage in the event that they have to be changed. When the complexity of the uncertainty being managed warrants it, technologies like belief revision (or truth maintenance) [24, 25] have to be employed.

The fact that a DataWarp application works with many pieces of data does bring one particular advantage: when an error is discovered and a roll-back is required, the application does not need to revert fully to its state before any of the erroneous actions were taken. Instead the application need only address those actions which may have been affected by the data concerned. For example, on discovering an error in its record of a customer's address, there is no need for an online store to rollback all of its actions. It only needs to consider rolling back actions relating to that particular customer. The remainder can be allowed to stand, making the rollback a less onerous task.

There is one further complication which the DataWarp application has to be able to accommodate. TimeWarp processes operate in a controlled environment. This environment is populated with TimeWarp-aware processes, enabling a process which needs to perform a rollback to retract actions and communications since the destination processes will be equipped to accept the retraction (and instigate their own rollback, if required). However, the DataWarp application does not have this luxury. It has to be able to handle the consequences of wishing to retract messages already sent where the receiver may not be prepared to accept message retractions or even understand them. The DataWarp application needing to perform a rollback handles this by examining the actions it needs to retract and dividing them into two categories according to whether any evidence of the action has yet been disclosed to the outside world. Those actions which have been disclosed are described as having hardened. Those actions which have not yet hardened can always be reversed because they affect only state internal to the application. Of the remainder, some aspect of the action has been seen by another application. Where it is known that the other application will accept message retractions, perhaps because the application advertises this facility to potential users, then this is the preferred option. Otherwise, some kind of compensating action will have to be performed. According to the nature of the action, and possibly how long ago the action was initially performed, the application may well have to accept that the effect of the compensating action may fall short of completely eliminating the effects of the original action.

In deciding how to act upon data as it arrives, there is a judgement for the application to make about how quickly to allow its actions to become externally visible and so liable to harden (when a third party sees them) since hardened actions are more difficult to retract. An application applying DataWarp to its processing may gain an advantage over its competitors because, since by processing work optimistically it is able to respond more quickly than its traditional peers. Alternatively, at least for some transactions, it may feel that it is appropriate to conceal the effects of some transactions for a short time in order to increase the probability that, should a rollback be necessary it will not have to deal with hardened actions. Consider the situation faced by an online bookshop receiving an order. In a traditional view of operation, the shop will process the order as a sequence of actions, starting with checking its stock, followed by processing the payment, sending the book and noting the sale to order replacement stock. The DataWarp shop can process this order differently. Instead of carrying out the actions in sequence, it can set all of them in motion as soon as the order arrives: it assumes the book is in stock and the clients payment will be honoured. If, for example, the book is not in stock then the order needs to be rolled back and its processing re-started. In this case, in place of sending the book the shop may send a communication to the client informing them of the situation and requesting confirmation that they still want to buy and cancel the request for payment (or make a refund). The automated re-order action on the sale may not now be appropriate either. It might be replaced as a customer specific order or cancelled completely pending further contact from the client.

4 Conclusion

As computer systems become larger and more widespread, they are collecting huge amounts of data. Many systems already have so much data that they struggle to keep it up to date and consistent. The continuing trend of connecting systems into even larger systems is making this problem more difficult and the situation is unlikely to improve. The situation is further complicated by the mobile systems which only maintain intermittent contact with our connected world and the asynchronous architectures which are being increasingly used. The traditional approach to managing problems arising from inconsistencies in data is to avoid the problem by enforcing consistency using strategies such as distributed transaction processing. However, the volume of data and the complexity of the interconnections between the systems which process is increasing whilst at the same time, the data environments are becoming less controlled and more varied. Together these mean that the task of maintaining consistency is becoming overwhelming. Contemporary systems need to be able to succeed despite having to work with data which they know contains errors and inconsistencies. They need to be *inconsistency tolerant*.

We have performed a collection of experiments both in an experimental environment built using a commercial message passing middleware product and in a simulation environment which shows that an application adopting a DataWarp approach enjoys a considerable advantage when faced with inconsistent data.

In DataWarp, applications proceed provisionally with their work but are prepared to revoke actions in the event that the data which motivated them turns out to be incorrect and re-commence operations with the new, (hopefully) better data. As time passes, these provisional actions become more nearly permanent. Eventually they can be regarded as definitive. In common with the attitude of TimeWarp processes towards time, the DataWarp applications do not concern themselves with maintaining a view of the world which is consistent with others using the same data unless or until they are forced to do so by interaction. When they do acquire additional data they decide whether if they need to adopt a different data view.

In summary, DataWarp is an architecture for building applications which are inconsistency tolerant. A DataWarp application:

- Maintains many *views* of data
- Selects a view based on *assumptions*,
- Is prepared to *alter its assumptions* and take remedial action

References

1. Universal Description Discovery and Integration (UDDI)), Technical White Paper, see http://www.uddi.org (2000)
2. Christensen, E., et al.: Web Services Description Language (WSDL), see http://msdn.microsoft (2000)
3. Hunter, D., et al.: Beginning XML, Wrox Press Inc (2000)
4. Snell, J., D. Tidwell, and P. Kulchenko: Programming Web Services with SOAP. First Edition, O'Reilly & Associates Inc. (2002)
5. Nicolle, L.: John Taylor - The Bulletin Interview, British Computer Society, The Computer Bulletin. (1999)
6. Microsoft: Legacy File Integration Using Microsoft® BizTalk Server 2000, see http://www.microsoft.com/biztalk/techinfo/LegacyFileIntegrationWP.doc, Microsoft (2000)
7. Microsoft: Microsoft Message Queuing Services, see http://www.microsoft.com/ http://www.microsoft.com/ntserver/appservice/techdetails/overview/msmqrevguide.asp, Microsoft (2001)
8. Object Management Group: Common Object Request Broker: Architecture Specification, see http://www.omg.com
9. Sun Microsystems: Enterprise Java Beans, see http://www.sun.com
10. Szyperski, C.: Component Software, Longman (1998)
11. Thomas, A.: Enterprise JavaBeans Technology, Patricia Seybold Group. (1998)
12. Kemme, B. and G. Alonso: A Suite of Database Replication Protocols based on Group Communication Primitives. Proceedings of 18th International Con-ference on Distributed Systems (ICDCS), Amsterdam, The Netherlands (1998)
13. Wiesmann, M., et al.: Database Replication Techniques: a three parameter classification. Proceedings of 19th IEEE Symposium on Reliable Distributed Systems (SRDS2000), Nurenberg, Germany, IEEE Computer Society Press (2000)
14. Sircar, S. and A. Kott: Enterprise Architecture Analysis Using an Architecture Description Language. Proceedings of DARPA Symposium on Advances in Enterprise Control, Minneapolis (2000)
15. Dayal, U., M. Hsu, and R. Ladin: Business Process Coordination: State of the Art, Trends, and Open Issues. The VLDB Journal. Vol. (2001) 3-13.

16. Gray, J.N.: The Transaction Concept: Virtues and Limitations. Proceedings of 7th International Conference on Very Large Data Bases, Cannes, France (1981)
17. Gray, J.N.: Notes on Database Operating Systems, in Operating Systems: An Advanced Course. R. Bayer, R. Graham, and G. Segmuller, Editors, Springer, (1978) 391-481
18. Henderson, P., R.J. Walters, and S. Crouch: Inconsistency Tolerance across Enterprise Solutions. Proceedings of 8th IEEE Workshop in Future Trends of Distributed Computer Systems (FTDCS01), Bologna, Italy (2001)
19. Henderson, P., R.J. Walters, and S. Crouch: RICES: Reasoning about Infor-mation Consistency across Enterprise Solutions, in Systems Engineering for Business Process Change: New Directions, Springer-Verlag London Limited, London, (2002) 367-371
20. IBM: MQSeries Family, see http://www-4.ibm.com/software/ts/mqseries/ (2001)
21. Henderson, P.: Reasoning about Asynchronous Behaviour in Distributed Sys-tems. Proceedings of The 8th IEEE International Conference on Engineering of Complex Computer Systems (ICECCS'02), Greenbelt, Maryland (2002)
22. Jefferson, D.R.: Virtual Time. ACM Transactions on Programming Lan-guages and Systems. Vol. 7(3). (1985) 404-425.
23. Jefferson, D.R.: Virtual Time II: Storage Management in Distributed Simula-tion. Proceedings of 9th Annual ACM Symposium on Principles of Distrib-uted Computing, Quebec City, Quebec, Canada, ACM (1990)
24. Friedman, N. and J.Y. Halpern: Belief Revision: A Critique. Journal of Logic, Language and Information. Vol. 8(4). (1999) 401-420.
25. Shaprio, S.C.: Belief Revision and Truth Maintenance Systems: An Overview and a Proposal, Department of Computer Science and Engineering and Center for Multisource Information Fusion and Center for Cognitive Science, State University of New York at Buffalo, Buffalo (1998)

Hand-Over Video Cache Policy for Mobile Users

Damien Charlet, Pascal Chatonnay, and François Spies

Laboratoire d'Informatique de l'université de Franche-Comté

Abstract. Nowadays, wireless links are shared between clients and the available bandwidth fluctuates, so the video stream must be adaptive in order to optimize the transmitted quality. In this article, we present a tool called MoVie to distribute multimedia streaming on large wireless networks. The two main aspects of MoVie deal with network access and managing systems. The management of video streams is realized using video caches linked to a physical area. This article describes the policy used to take into account the mobility of the clients and the hierarchical aspect of the streams by preparing the neighboring caches to receive roaming clients.

Keywords: Multimedia streaming, mobile devices, distributed video caches

1 Introduction

The delivery of digital multimedia contents over networks has dramatically increased over the last decade. Satellites can broadcast digital video over a wide population and, in the near future, terrestrial wireless digital transmissions will emerge. However powerful these technologies may be, they are still deprived of interactivity and mobility. Video and news on demand are currently well identified services of transmitting video content to one device. But, taking into account mobility, heterogeneity, adaptation and migration is hard to integrate on such services.

The development of the bandwidth of the wireless networks will change the way people consume multimedia contents [1]. Three technologies are emerging: GPRS [2], UMTS [3] and WiFi [4]. Various types of devices can access these networks which induce a large heterogeneity at the end of the connection. The need of adaptability is real in order to make the video transfer possible in such conditions. Only one video quality transmission is not possible to achieve and specific techniques for variable video quality must be used in order to tackle these problems. Few solutions allow variable multimedia quality such as stream switching, scalable streaming or transcoding. This induces new strategies of storing and managing data to avoid redundancy.

The number of clients connected to large wireless networks will be very important. The system delivery must share these accesses between various components in order to avoid bottlenecks. There are currently two ways to realize this partition: replicating a monolithic server many times or developing a distributed

J.-B. Stefani, I. Demeure, and D. Hagimont (Eds.): DAIS 2003, LNCS 2893, pp. 179–186, 2003.
© IFIP International Federation for Information Processing 2003

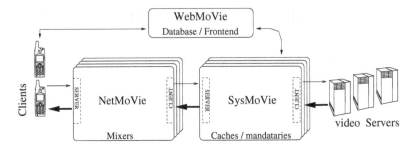

Fig. 1. The MoVie architecture.

system. The solution we retain is a distributed set of caches streaming multimedia sequences using specific management policies adapted to mobile clients.

The first section outlines our solution called MoVie and describes one of its components called SysMoVie, the distributed system layer. The next section introduces and evaluates by simulation one of the admission policies for distributed caches.

2   The MoVie Project

The architecture of the MoVie platform aims at delivering short-time multimedia streams on a large scale wireless network. MoVie must integrate the following characteristics in order to be efficient, fast and functional: being compatible with standard streaming clients (RTP/RTCP and RTSP); taking the mobility of clients and the stream migration into account; integrating a web-like query interface; being distributed and interoperable (ORB); managing the accessible video sequences from a hierarchical point of view.

We have structured this platform into modules in order to cover all the aspects of this new type of service: WebMoVie, NetMoVie and SysMoVie. WebMoVie represents the query interface of our platform. It is the entry point of clients where they are identified and decide which sequence they want to watch. NetMoVie [5] is the network level part. It integrates the RTP/RTCP protocol, receives different video sequence quality and selects the most adapted one depending on the current situation. SysMoVie [6] is the orchestration layer. It gathers ORB components and manages the cooperatives video caches. The strategy of video cache management is specific to the particular temporal data and the various quality levels of the same content. This is the part studied in this article and will therefore be described in more depth thereafter.

2.1   SysMoVie

The first task of the SysMoVie module is to enhance the quality of the transmission by bringing the sequences closer to the clients like web caches do. Thus, we have to deal with completely different type of content, large and continuous. The phone network covering a very wide area and serving many users, a centralized server could neither cope with the huge number of clients nor have decent responsiveness. The application must be distributed. Moreover, the mobile phone network being already divided into cells, the territorial partitioning is simplified.

As SysMoVie is composed of a set of distributed caches, we have to deal with one of the main concerns of this type of architecture: referencing and localizing the contents in the system. Using a centralized database makes the system lose its attractiveness because of bottlenecks, while a distributed database brings greater latencies. Moreover, in a very large system where there may be lots of replicas, we need a fast decision process to get effective targets. In our system, this is achieved by taking advantage of the trading service framework of CORBA [7]. A trader has two complementary roles: it collects the sequences the caches attached to it declare and it answers queries about its content database. The sequences are described by the mean of static or dynamic properties. Traders also have the ability to be linked and therefore cooperate. This mechanism is described more in depth in [8].

Because of the architecture of the 3G frameworks and our choice to only use standards players, the only path between the user and the system during the transmission is the multimedia stream between the video player and the mixer. However we may need to collect more informations to put in place smarter policies, for example to prefetch sequences according to the user habits. We also need real time informations and the history of his localization to cope with mobility. To answer these needs, we have decided to use mobile agents. Each agent is a representative of one client inside the system and has its profile at its disposal. It updates in real time according to the actions of the user and can follow him along its way. It is placed nearest to the client, near the mixers, and can migrate from mixer to mixer. During the diffusion the mandatary performs three main actions: it manages the optimization of the quality streamed to its client, it cooperates with the NetMoVie components to prepare and supervise mixer swapping when the client moves and it moves each part of the streamed sequence closer. The mandatary is an adaptive component which copes with the context to make the system more suited to the current usage. It takes into account geographical information, clients' habits, streaming quality, and the responses of other components to evaluate the adequation between caches and mixers. The simultaneous work of all the mandataries allow the system to compose a matrix which is used to manage most of the operations done by caches.

2.2   The Caches

In continuous media caching, the documents are not as dynamic as web pages are. The contents of a video sequence neither change over time nor may be dynamically modified by the user's interaction. We can safely make the assumption that a document cached in the system will be valid whenever requested. Therefore we do not need to use a strict coherency algorithm for the sequences. However, we will see thereafter that we use a weak coherency algorithm for the pieces of data assigned to the management of prefetching.

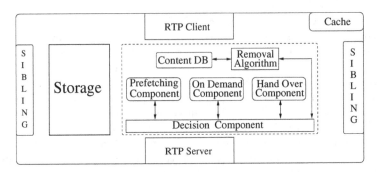

Fig. 2. Cache Architecture.

The video caches we introduce in SysMoVie implement three distinct mechanisms: video streaming, removal and insertion.

Video streaming to the mixer is performed by an RTP module integrated into the cache. Our architecture is a hierarchical client / server scheme. Each level is a server for its lower level, and a client for its superior level. The same server module can be found in the mixer on the user side. Like this, the cache is seen as a server for the mixer, and so is the mixer for the client. In the same way the RTP module has a client side used by the caches and the mixers. The caches can communicate with the exterior servers and they look like usual clients. A complete description of this module may be found in [5].

Cache removal management is a well-known, widely-studied domain in traditional caches. Lots of algorithms try to optimize the renewal of the cache contents, from traditional LRU, LFU or Size to more elaborate ones like GDSP, GDSF or Hybrid [9]. However, continuous media cannot be managed using these traditional techniques because of the huge size of each document and its transmission scheme. The size gives a grain much too large to be efficient, and the multimedia sequences cannot be completely downloaded at once and must be segmented. Tewari et al. [10] proposed the RBC algorithm to take these facts into account. None of these techniques take into account layered video, as used in this project. Even if the grain was refined, none of these techniques would be efficient. Podlipnig et al. [11] proposed a policy which treats the case of layered sequences. Our technique is a refinement, based on matrices of values for temporal and quality data. We also link the different streams representing the same sequence but encoded with a different quality [8].

Cache insertion is processed by three distinct mechanisms. Each of them manages a different level of prediction and differently takes the mobility of clients into account.

On-demand insertion is a traditional technique which treats none of these problems. It is equivalent to the answer given for a cache miss in web caches. In MoVie, users do not directly contact the caches. However a cache miss corresponds to the state where WebMoVie cannot find the document requested inside the system, or if it is present on a cache not usable for the mixer. The document is then fetched from an outside server or a distant cache and is stocked on the cache to ensure an almost on-the-fly streaming.

Prefetching means inserting sequences into the cache which are supposed to be requested later. To accomplish this, our system uses local and distributed usage statistics. If both preceding techniques are time constraints, the latter is totally asynchronous and can be calculated while the system is low on load, and the movies fetched while the network is free.We try to anticipate future requests by processing a set of probable sequences that we insert in the cache. This method is based on a classification made by parsing the requests logs. As we are in a distributed system, we should also take advantage of the sorting made by the peer caches. Taking into account foreign request may lead to inserting sequences which are not locally known yet.

The technique named "hand over" consists in inserting the next part of a sequence being watched by a user in a bordering cell prior to its venue.

The on-demand algorithm looks much like traditional algorithms and therefore will not be described in more depth herein. A detailed description of our prefetching method may be found in [6]. The hand-over method brings interesting points and is described in further detail in the next section.

3   The Hand-Over Policy

The hand-over policy consists in inserting the remaining part of a sequence currently watched by a user in a cache of a bordering zone prior to its request. If the client moves out of its zone, one of the caches of the new zone already possesses the part being streamed. Therefore the system only has to initiate the connection and the user doesn't suffer from too much lag for a hand over, giving a good reactivity.

The mechanism used to perform this insertion is based on two types of information: the probability for a zone to receive a client in the near future and the cache and mixer adequation for the probable streaming zones. From this information we calculate an indicator evaluating the interest of loading the sequence. We use thresholds determining for each cache if we should insert the whole remaining part of the sequence, and which quality to use (i.e. the number of enhancement layers cached). In each case the reactivity is enhanced, in the worst case with a degraded quality for a small amount of time.

The most interesting part of the territory for this task is the set of zones bordering the current one. The probability of presence is processed by another component, the mandatary, which is described in section 2. The set of probabilities of presence $P_{0...z}$ is presented in a vector $\overrightarrow{V_p}$ whose dimension is the number of bordering zones (z) plus one for the current. P_0 is the probability of presence for the current zone. With the knowledge of the list of caches able to accept the client in each new zone and the set of mixers, we rebuild a smaller cache-mixer adequation matrix $\mathcal{M}_{cm}$. We then multiply $\mathcal{M}_{cm}$ and $\overrightarrow{V_p}$ to obtain the evaluation vector V_e giving each cache a score.

$$\mathcal{M}_{cm} \quad \times \quad \vec{V_p} \; = \; \vec{V_e}$$

$$\begin{pmatrix} C_1 M_1 \dots C_1 M_z \\ \vdots \quad \ddots \quad \vdots \\ C_c M_1 \dots C_c M_z \end{pmatrix} \times \begin{vmatrix} P_0 \\ \vdots \\ P_z \end{vmatrix} = \begin{vmatrix} e_1 \\ \vdots \\ e_m \end{vmatrix} \tag{1}$$

Then, we define two values: $T, \alpha \in [0 \dots 1]$. From these two values we build two thresholds $T.P_0$ and $\alpha.T.P_0$ with $\alpha.T.P_0 < T.P_0$ such as if the evaluation of a cache is over $T.P_0$ we fetch the whole remaining part of the sequence, if the evaluation is less than $\alpha.T.P_0$ we do not fetch anything, else if the evaluation is between those two thresholds we only fetch part of the remaining sequence. This ensures that almost wherever the user moves the streaming will go on, in the worst case temporarily with lower quality, without jagging the caches. The caches are just hinted and their admission control and insertion policies could still refuse the new sequence or client.

The main improvement in the near future will consist in optimizing the bandwidth used for the prefetching. As the base layer and several enhancement layers are diffused on to different caches of the neighborhood at the same time, we plan using a hierarchical multicast algorithm [12] where the caches can subscribe to the group where the layers they request are sent.

Case Study

In this case study we show by simulation the impact of the two parameters "Threshold" (T) and the coefficient "α" on the fetching and hit rate for three characteristics distributions of probabilities. Here, we consider seven zones isolated (ie. caches do not interact outside their own zone), each one possessing one cache. We choose these characteristics to emphasize the role of α and T in the optimization of both reactivity and space saving.

In these simulations we consider that the current zone is already fulfilled with the full sequence and that the others do not have any parts of this sequence. We consider the probability of a user to be in each zone according to different situations: staying in place, going north, and a user in a train. These are depicted on the first column of figure 3. We then apply our hand-over policy with two different couples (T, α), extract the types of fetchs which apply and count the number of full hits, partial hits and miss. This is described in the other columns. The values of the couples used in the first figure of each distribution are chosen to optimize the reactivity (ie. full fetch). The values of the couples used in the seconds figures are chosen to save storage with good chance of avoiding misses (ie. partial).

As can be seen on the results of the figure 3, our policy gives at least 8 full hit out of 10 when we maximize the reactivity. This is done by loading only one cache in the first case, two in the second case and three in the third case instead of the whole six. In the second set of results, where we save storage while avoiding miss by fetching partial sequence, we obtain the same number of

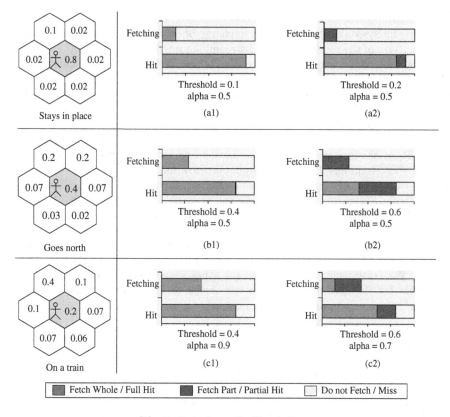

Fig. 3. Data from the Simulation.

miss in each case so we can easily maintain the streaming for eight out of ten zones but eventually with a degraded quality. At the same time, at least 55% of storage space has been saved. This simulation has shown that the hand-over policy gives a good reactivity and that we could tune this reactivity by selecting a couple (T, α) according to the resources we accept to use. By putting in place a mechanism letting the system compute the values for T and α, the system would self adapt according to the amount of resources available and the reactivity it has been asked to maintain.

4   Conclusion

The aim of the MoVie project is to allow the diffusion of video sequences on large wireless networks. The problems consist in increasing the capacity of diffusion, ensuring the extensibility of the system, maintaining a good reactivity and managing the clients' heterogeneity (phone, pda, notebook computers, desktop computers).

We have presented the principles and the architecture of MoVie and particularly of the SysMoVie layer which is in charge of ensuring the extensibility and the reactivity of the video on-demand streaming system. The extensibility is ensured by cooperative and distributed caches. The reactivity is taken in charge by the pre-loading of caches with sequences in the more or less short term. The constraints linked to the heterogeneity of the clients and their mobility are assumed in part by the representatives of the clients inside the system: the mandataries.

We have approached the set of problems release of the storage space in the caches. We have shown how we insert sequences into the caches in real time (on demand), in advance in the short (hand-over) and medium term (prefetching). For the short-term insertion we use probabilities of migration and an adequation matrix from a set of caches to a set of streaming zones. This matrix is built in a distributed, asynchronous way while the system is running. It is built with the caches, the mixers and the mandataries cooperating. It's an auto-adaptive mechanism to regulate the sysMoVie layer.

Several points are still to be studied. Particularly, the optimization at the network level of data insertion into the cache has not been approached in this article. We are working on a mechanism using a peer-to-peer communication paradigm for the exchanges between the caches and the mixers, mixed when possible with layered multicast transmissions.

References

1. B. Girod and N. Färber. *Compressed Video over Networks*, chapter Wireless Video. Signal Processing Series, Marcel Dekker, 2000.
2. Regis J. Bates. *GPRS: General Packet Radio Service*. McGraw-Hill Prof., 2001.
3. A. Samukic. UMTS Universal Mobile Telecommunications System: Development of standards for the third generation. *IEEE VTC*, 47(4):1099–1104, 1998.
4. R. Flickenger. *Building Wireless Community Networks*. O'Reilly edition, 2001.
5. J. et al. Bourgeois. Optimization of multimedia contents delivery towards mobile devices. *Journal of System Architecture, Elsevier Science*, 2003.
6. D. Charlet et al. SysMoVie: Managing interoperability in a video distribution framework for mobile environment. Technical report, LIFC, University of Franche-Comté, 2003. Ref: TR/CDM03-02.
7. Trading object service specifications, omg/00-06-27, June 2000.
8. D. Charlet et al. SysMoVie: Managing interoperability in a video distribution framework for mobile environment. In *Proceedings of PDPTA'02*, 2002.
9. S. Williams et al. Removal policies in network caches for World-Wide Web documents. In *Proceedings of the ACM SIGCOMM '96*, Stanford, CA, 1996.
10. R. Tewari et al. Resource-based caching for Web servers. In *Proceedings of ACM/SPIE MMCN'98*, 1998.
11. S. Podlipnig and L. Boszormenyi. Replacement strategies for quality based video caching. In *IEEE International Conference on Multimedia and Expo*, 2002.
12. D. Rubenstein et al. The impact of multicast layering on network fairness. In *SIGCOMM*, pages 27–38, 1999.

Planning for Network-Aware Paths

Xiaodong Fu and Vijay Karamcheti

New York University
New York, NY 10012, USA
{xiaodong,vijayk}@cs.nyu.edu

Abstract. Communication in distributed applications across a wide area network needs to cope with heterogenous and constantly changing network conditions. A promising approach to address this is to augment the *whole* communication path with *network awareness* by using "bridging" components that are capable of caching, protocol conversion, transcoding, etc. While several such path-based approaches have been proposed, current approaches lack mechanisms for automatically creating effective network paths whose performance is optimized for encountered network conditions.

This paper describes a solution for this problem. Our approach, which is built into an application-level programmable network infrastructure called CANS (Composable Adaptive Network Services), constructs network-aware communication paths that enhance application performance by taking into account both application performance preferences and dynamic resource availability.

Our experiments with typical applications verify that communication paths automatically created with our path creation algorithms do bring applications with considerable performance advantages, and fine tuned, desirable adaptation behaviors, with only minimal input from applications.

1 Introduction

Heterogeneous and dynamically changing network environments are an important cause for unsatisfactory behaviors of distributed applications whose performance is directly related to the quality of the underlying data communication. A promising approach ([2, 4, 8, 9, 11–13, 15]) for addressing this is to make the communication path *network aware* by using application-specific components that handle stream degradation, reconnection, transcoding, caching, and protocol conversion operations, thereby serving to "impedance match" application performance requirements with the underlying network conditions. The more general among these infrastructures [4, 9, 12, 13, 15] propose to realize such network awareness throughout *the whole communication path*. While there have been a large number of proposals, such *path-based* systems have focused primarily on providing system support to allow dynamic insertion and deletion of components, leaving unanswered a key question: how to automatically construct such network aware paths, without user involvement, so that applications can perform better in a dynamic network environment where resource availability changes continually.

In this paper, we propose an automatic strategy for building such network aware paths with optimized performance in accordance with application performance requirements and underlying resource availability. In addition to calculating a whole path, our

J.-B. Stefani, I. Demeure, and D. Hagimont (Eds.): DAIS 2003, LNCS 2893, pp. 187–199, 2003.
© IFIP International Federation for Information Processing 2003

solution can also be used with disjoint segments of an existing path independently while maintaining some overall performance guarantee. Furthermore, the calculation of communication paths can be conducted in a distributed fashion (i.e. from one network domain to another). These properties make our approach applicable in a wide area setting, where multiple network domains are usually involved in setting up and maintaining a communication path.

This strategy is a general solution that can be applied to any path based system. To evaluate it, we have implemented it within a programmable network infrastructure called CANS (Composable Adaptive Network Services) [4], and have conducted a series of experiments, using two representative applications: web access and image streaming in environments with different network and end-device characteristics. The results validate our approach, verifying that (1) automatic path creation is achievable and does in fact yield substantial performance benefits; and that (2) our approach is effective for providing applications that have different performance preferences with fine tuned, desirable adaptation behaviors.

The rest of this paper is organized as follows. Section 2 provides a brief overview of the CANS infrastructure. Section 3 defines the path creation problem and our model. Section 4 describes our automatic path creation algorithm and extensions. Section 5 evaluates these mechanisms using the two applications. Section 6 reviews related work and summarizes the novel aspects of our approach. We conclude in Section 7.

2   Background: Overview of the CANS Architecture

The Composable Adaptive Network Services (CANS) infrastructure [4] views network environments as consisting of client *applications* and *services*, connected by *communication paths*. CANS extends the notion of a communication path, traditionally limited to data transmission, to include dynamically injected application-specific components. Serving as the basic building block for CANS paths, components are standalone *mobile* code modules that can be composed via a standard *data port* interface.

The CANS network is realized by partitioning service and components belonging to data paths onto physical hosts, connected using existing communication mechanisms. Data processing code in a driver is executed in CANS Execution Environments (EE) that run on hosts along the network route. CANS further provides support for dynamic path reconfiguration. A more detailed description of the CANS infrastructure can be found in [4].

3   Modeling the Path Creation Problem

In general, creation of a network aware data path consists of two steps: *route selection* where a graph of nodes and links is selected for deploying the path, and *component selection and mapping* where appropriate components are selected and mapped to the selected route. Route selection is typically driven by external factors (such as connectivity considerations, ISP-level agreements, etc.) and so here we focus only on the problem of component selection and mapping. We call the procedure of constructing such paths as *planning*.

3.1 Components and Network Resources

We first need ways of characterizing the impact of a particular component on the resource utilization along a path as well as a means for associating performance metrics with the overall path.

Types. The functionality of a component in a path is modeled as transforming data from one type to another. For example, a compression component using the zip algorithm can transform a MIME/TXT type to a "zipped" MIME/TXT type. Components can be connected together only if their type information is compatible. Type compatibility is defined in a **type graph** G_t: a vertex in the graph represents a type, and an edge represents a component that can transform data from the source type to the sink type. The primary benefit of such type-based modeling is that it permits description of valid candidate paths without explicit enumeration, simply looking for all type-compatible sequences of components that transform the source type to the required destination type.

The performance of an individual path is determined by resource availability and performance characteristics of components in the path.

Network Resources. Each network resource is modeled in terms of its performance characteristics, i.e. computation capacity for a node, and bandwidth and latency for a network link. For an individual path that passes through a shared network resource, the value used is the corresponding value of the allocated portion.

Furthermore, network resources may also affect the data passing through them in a way that is independent of resource capacities. For example, the effect is different for transmitting sensitive data across a network link with the same bandwidth/latency parameters, depending on whether the link is trusted (no eavesdropper) or not. To model such effects, CANS incorporates a notion of *augmented types* [4], which extend data types with environment properties. Network resources are modeled as entities that can transform the environment properties of augmented types in a type-specific fashion.

Modeling both application data types and resource constraints using a unified framework has the advantage that valid paths (even in the presence of resource constraints) continue to be concisely represented using the notion of type compatibility on the augmented types. Our automatic path creation strategy exploits this fact.

Component Resource Utilization Model. To characterize the resource utilization and performance of a component, each component c is modeled in terms of its *computation load factor* ($\mathrm{load}(c)$), the average per-input byte cost of running the component, and its *bandwidth impact factor* ($\mathrm{bwf}(c)$), the average ratio between input and output data volume. This simple model can be extended to allow components to have multiple configurations.

A path ($D = \{c_1, \ldots, c_n\}$) consists of a sequence of components. A **route** $R = \{n_1, n_2, \ldots, n_p\}$ for a path is a sequence of network resources (nodes and links between them). A **mapping**, $M : D \rightarrow R$, associates components on data path D with nodes in route R. We are only interested in mappings that satisfy the following restriction: $M(c_i) = n_u, M(c_{i+1}) = n_q \Rightarrow u \leq q$: sending data back and forth between nodes in a route usually results in poor performance and resource waste.

3.2 Problem Definition

The path creation problem can be stated as the following: given a route R (with resources allocated to the path), a type graph G_t, a source data type t_s, a destination data type t_d, select a data path D that 1) transforms t_s to t_d and can be mapped to R, and 2) provides optimal performance (e.g. maximum throughput or minimal latency).

4 Algorithm

Our path creation strategy, in addition to satisfying type requirements, respects constraints imposed by node and link capacities and properties and optimizes some overall path metric (e.g., latency or throughput). The heart of our strategy is a dynamic programming algorithm, which simultaneously selects and maps a type-compatible component sequence to optimize some performance metric.

We first describe a base version of the algorithm in which a single performance metric needs to be optimized. We then present an extension for applications that require the value of some performance metric to be in an *acceptable range*. For such applications, only after that range has been met does the application worry about other preferences. For example, most media streaming applications usually demand a suitable data transmission rate (in some range); once the transmission rate is kept in that range, other factors such as data quality become the concern for the application. We use the terms *range metrics* and *performance metrics* to refer to the two types of preferences. Lastly, we describe a distributed implementation of this strategy.

4.1 Base Algorithm

Unfortunately, finding the optimal solution for the path creation problem defined in Section 3.2 is an NP-hard problem. The complexity mainly comes from the large numbers for both components and the possible ways to compose them, as well as different ways to map them to network resources.

However, this problem can be made tractable with a reasonable simplification: we partition the computation capacities of nodes into a fixed number of *discrete* load intervals; i.e., capacity is allocated to components only at interval granularity. This practical assumption allows us to define, for a route R, the notion of an *available computation resource vector*, $A(R) = (r_1, r_2, \ldots, r_p)$, where r_i reflects the available capacity intervals on node n_i (normalized to the interval $[0,1]$).

In the description that follows, we use maximum throughput as the goal of performance optimization (other performance metrics can also be used); we use p to denote the number of hosts in route R (i.e. $p = |R|$); m for the total number of types (i.e. $m = |V(G_t)|$); and n for the total number of components.

Dynamic Programming Strategy. The intuition behind the algorithm is to incrementally construct, for different amounts of route resources, optimal mappings with increasing numbers of components, say $i + 1$, using as input optimal partial solutions involving i or fewer components.

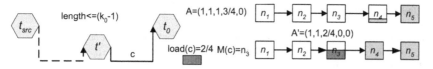

Fig. 1. Map c to n_3 and lookup solution with A'.

To construct a solution with $i + 1$ (or fewer components) for a given destination type t and resource vector A, we consider all possible intermediate types t' that can be transformed to t; i.e., all those types for which an edge (t', t) is present in the type graph. For each such t', we consider all possible mappings of the associated component c on nodes along the route that use no more than A resources. For each such mapping that transforms the available resource vector to A' (after accounting for load(c)), we combine this component with the previously calculated solution for t' with i (or fewer) components with resource vector A. The combined mapping that yields the maximum throughput is deemed the solution at step $i + 1$ for type t.

Because this procedure runs backwards from the destination (i.e. c_{j+1} is mapped before c_j), consequently, only resource vectors of the form $(1, ..., 1, r_j \in [0, 1], 0, ..., 0)$ will be used in the calculation. These set of resource vectors is designated RA. The size of RA is $O(p)$.

Formally, the algorithm fills up a table of partial optimal solutions ($s[t_s, t, A, i]$) in the order $i = 0, 1, 2, ...$. The solution $s[t_s, t, A, i]$ is the data path that yields maximum throughput for transforming the source type t_s to type t, using i or fewer components and requiring no more resources than $A(A \in \text{RA})$. Figure 1 shows the moment in the calculation of $s[t_s, t_0, (1, 1, 1, 3/4, 0), i + 1]$ when the the component c is mapped to node n_3, and appended with partial solution $s[t_s, t', (1, 1, 2/4, 0, 0), i]$. Note that in this example, computation capacity of nodes is partitioned into 4 intervals.

The algorithm terminates at Step $p \times n$, with the solution in $s[t_s, t_d, (1, ..., 1), p \times n]$. This follows from the observation that there is no performance benefit from mapping multiple copies of the same component to a node. The complexity of this algorithm is $O(n^2 \times m \times p^3) = O(n^3 \times p^3)$ [1] as opposed to $O(p^n)$ for an exhaustive enumeration strategy. n, the total number of components, usually is a big number. Even for a simple operation, such as compression, there may exists many different candidates, not to mention that each component may have multiple configurations. Therefore, $O(p^n)$ is infeasible in practice. In most scenarios, p is expected to be a small constant, therefore overall complexity of our path creation algorithm is determined by the number of components. The pseudo code of this algorithm is shown in Figure 2.

4.2 Extension: Planning for Value Ranges

Given that our planning algorithm constructs communication paths by incrementally filling in a solution table of $s[t_s, t, A, i]$, it is natural to extend this to check that retained solutions satisfy two conditions: (1) values of range metrics achieved on the current

---

[1] It is safe to assume that $m < n$.

Algorithm *Plan*
Input: t_s, t_d, G_t, R
Output: The data path that yields maximal throughput from type t_s to t_d on route R
1.   (∗ Step 1: Initialization for partial plans with zero components ∗)
2.   **for all** $t, \mathbf{A} \in$ RA
3.   **do** calculate $s[t_s, t, \mathbf{A}, 0]$
4.   (∗ Step 2: Incrementally building partial solutions ∗)
5.   **for** $i \leftarrow 1$ **to** $p \times n$
6.   **do for all** $t \in V(G_t), \mathbf{A} \in$ RA
7.   **do** $s[t_s, t, \mathbf{A}, i] \leftarrow s[t_s, t, \mathbf{A}, i-1]$
8.   **for all** $c = (t', t) \in E(G_t)$
9.   **do for all** n_j that $\mathbf{A}[n_j] > 0$
10.   **do** $M(c) \leftarrow n_j$
11. $\mathbf{A}' \leftarrow (\mathbf{A}[0], \dots, \mathbf{A}[n_j - 1], \mathbf{A}[n_j] - \mathrm{load}(c), 0, \dots)$
12.   TH $\leftarrow$ throughput(append($s[t_s, t', \mathbf{A}', i-1], c, \mathbf{A}$))
13.   **if** TH $> s[t_s, t, \mathbf{A}, i]$
14.   **then** $s[t_s, t, \mathbf{A}, i] \leftarrow$ TH
15.   **return** $s[t_s, t_d, \mathbf{A} = [1, 1, \dots, 1], p \times n]$

Fig. 2. Base Path Creation Algorithm.

solution will lie within the desired range, and (2) the value of any performance metrics is in fact optimized.

Although this is the basic idea of the extension, for some range metrics, such as path latency, additional work is needed. For such range metrics, even if the current value of the range metrics is not in the range for a partial solution, this does not exclude the possibility that this partial path may actually become a part of the final solution (e.g. appending compression components to a partial path can bring down overall latency). To *estimate* whether the desired range can in fact be achieved by appending additional components, we employ a procedure called *complementary planning*, which just runs the planning algorithm in reverse, providing information about whether or not the range metrics can meet the requirement using residual resources along a path that transforms type t to t_d. Using this information, when calculating $s[t_s, t, \mathbf{A}, i]$, those partial solutions that can not meet the requirement will be discarded in the first place. Heuristic functions are used for choosing among candidate paths that can all meet the required range. Note that complementary planning needs to be run just once. Planning for value ranges can further be extended to calculate plans for a portion of the whole path. Such a local mechanism allows disjointed segments of a data path to change their behaviors independently and concurrently while maintaining some overall performance guarantee. Due to space limitations, we omit the details about the local planning mechanism, which can be found in a technical report [3].

4.3   Distributed (Incremental) Planning

Though our path creation strategy has so far been described in a centralized manner, it can easily be extended to run in a distributed fashion. To do that, each node (n_i) on the

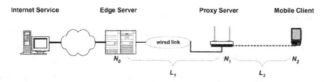

Fig. 3. A typical network path between a mobile client and an internet services.

route just needs to calculate $s[t_s, t, \boldsymbol{A} = \underbrace{(1, ..., 1}_{i}, 0, ..., 0), \sum_{j=0}^{i}(\text{CN}_j)]$ (where CN_j
is the total number of components in node n_j), and send these partial solutions to the
next node. This procedure starts from the server node and continues until it reaches the
client node.

The primary benefit of this distributed version is that there is no need for a centralized planner that has a complete knowledge of components and types for all nodes
in the route. By incrementally calculating a path in such a distributed fashion, only
knowledge for common types that are used across different network domains is necessary. This distributed version, combined with the local mechanisms described earlier,
enables a path-based system to be used in a wide area network, where a communication
path usually spans multiple administration domains.

The traffic incurred for the distributed planning is just messages of partial solutions
between adjacent nodes. It should be noted here that these messages carry only values
of the performance metric, transmission of components is unnecessary.

5   Performance Evaluation

To evaluate the effectiveness of our approach, we have built the automatic path creation
support into the CANS infrastructure, and conducted a series of experiments in the
context of a web access application and an image streaming application.

5.1   Experimental Platform

We consider a typical network path between a mobile client and an Internet server as
shown in Figure 3. This platform models a mobile user using a portable device (N_2)
to access network services in a shared wireless environment. The communication path
from the device to the service typically spans three hops: a wireless link (L_2) connecting
the user's device to an access point, a wired link (L_1) between the wireless access point
and a gateway to the general Internet, and finally a WAN link between the gateway and
the host running the service. We assume that CANS components can be deployed on
three sites: N_0, N_1, and N_2.

The **web access application** is a browser client, which downloads web pages (both
HTML page and images) from a standard web server. For this application, short response time is preferred. The **image streaming application** is a simple JMF application that continuously fetches JPEG frames from an image server and displays them. To
perform appropriately, this application requires a certain frame rate, and prefers high
data quality.

Components used in the automatically generated paths included: `ImageFilter` and `ImageResizer` which are used to degrade image quality or resize JPEG images (to a factor of 0.2) respectively; `Zip` and `Unzip`, which work together to compress/decompress text. The load and bandwidth factor values, which are omitted here for brevity, were profiled using representative data inputs: a web page containing 14 KB text and six 25 KB JPEG images.

5.2   Effectiveness of the Base Path Creation Algorithm

To evaluate the effective of the base path creation strategy, we experimented with the web access application, running under a wide range of network conditions.

In particular, we defined twelve different configurations listed in Table 1. These configurations represent the network bandwidth and node capacity available to a single client, and reflect different loading of shared resources and different mobile connectivity options[2]. These configurations are grouped into three categories, based on whether the mobile link L_2 exhibits cellular, infrared, or wireless LAN-like characteristics. Five of the configurations correspond to real hardware setups (tagged with a *), the remainder were emulated by restricting (via system call interception) CPU and network resources available to the application [1]. The computation power of different nodes is normalized to a 1 GHz Pentium III node.

Table 1 also identifies, for each platform configuration, the automatically generated plan for the web access application. The plans themselves are shown in Table 2, identifying the components that were automatically placed along the image and text paths. For example, plan A, which is used in platform 1 and 2, places a `ImageFilter` and a `ImageResizer` on node N_1 along the image path, and a `Zip` and `Unzip` driver combination on nodes N_0 and N_2 along the text path.

Figure 4 shows the performance advantages of the automatically generated plans when compared to the response times incurred for direct interaction between the browser client and the server (denoted **Direct** in the figure). The bars in Figure 4 are normalized with respect to the best response time achieved on each platform. In all twelve configurations, the generated plans provide the best performance, improving the response time metric by up to a factor of seven. Note that part of the lower response times come at the cost of degraded image quality, but this is to be expected. The point here is that our approach *automates* the decisions of when such degradation is necessary.

Figure 4 also shows that different platforms require a different "optimal" plan, stressing the importance of automating the component selection and mapping procedure. In each case, the plan generated by our path creation strategy is the one that yields the best performance, also improving performance by up to a factor of seven over the worst-performing path. Note that while similar behavior can in principle be obtained by other strategies, such as using hard coded rules to deploy components, unlike our application-neutral approach, such strategies require significant domain knowledge, and usually cannot find the best path for network conditions that change continually.

---

[2] The bandwidth between the internet server and edge server available to a single client is assumed to be 10 Mbps.

Table 1. Twelve configurations representing different loads and mobile network connectivity scenarios, identifying the CANS plan automatically generated in each case.

Platform	Edge Server (N_0)	L_1	Proxy Server (N_1)	L_2	Client (N_2)	Plan
1	Medium	Ethernet	High	19.2 Kbps	Cell Phone	A
2	Medium	Ethernet	High	19.2 Kbps	Pocket PC	A
3*	High	Fast Ethernet	Medium	57.6 Kbps	Laptop	B
4*	High	Fast Ethernet	Medium	115.2 Kbps	Laptop	B
5	Medium	Ethernet	High	384 Kbps	Pocket PC	A
6*	High	Fast Ethernet	Medium	576 Kbps	Laptop	B
7*	Medium	Fast Ethernet	High	1 Mbps	Laptop	C
8	Medium	Ethernet	High	3.84 Mbps	Pocket PC	D
9	Medium	Ethernet	High	3.84 Mbps	Laptop	D
10	Medium	DSL	High	3.84 Mbps	Laptop	B
11	Medium	DSL	Low	3.84 Mbps	Laptop	B
12*	Medium	Fast Ethernet	High	5.5 Mbps	Laptop	E

Relative computation power of different node types (normalized to a 1 GHz Pentium III node):
High = **1.0**, Medium = **0.5**, Laptop = **0.5**, Low = **0.25**, Pocket PC = **0.1**, Cell Phone = **0.05**
Link bandwidths: Fast Ethernet = **100 Mbps**, Ethernet = **10 Mbps**, DSL = **384 Kbps**

Table 2. Component placement for the five automatically generated plans.

Plan	N_0 (Img/Txt)	N_1 (Img/Txt)	N_2 (Img/Txt)
A	-/Zip	(Filter, Resizer)/-	-/Unzip
B	(Filter, Resizer)/Zip	-/-	-/Unzip
C	-/-	Filter/Zip	-/Unzip
D	-/Zip	-/-	-/Unzip
E	-/-	-/Zip	-/Unzip

5.3   Planning for Value Ranges

Unlike the web accessing application, the image streaming application requires throughput of the data path to be in a particular range so that the received data can be appropriately rendered on the client devices. To validate our range planning strategy and further investigate the adaptation behavior achieved using our approach in dynamic environments, we experimented with this application.

The experiment modeled the following scenario: initially a user receives a bandwidth allocation of 150 KBps on the wireless link (L_2), which then goes down to 10 KBps in increments of 10 KBps every 40 seconds (modeling new user arrivals or movement away from the access point) before rising back to 150 KBps at the same rate (modeling user departures or movement towards the access point). The data path is allocated a (fixed) computation capacity of 1.0 (normalized to a 1 GHz Pentium III node) on nodes N_1 and N_2 respectively and a bandwidth of 500 KBps on L_1. N_1, N_2, and L_1 are wired resources and consequently more capable of maintaining a certain minimum allocation (e.g., by employing additional geographically distributed resources) than the wireless link L_2. The experiments were run on a wired network with the wireless link

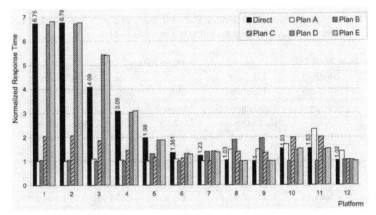

Fig. 4. Response times achieved by different plans for each of the twelve platform configurations compared to that achieved by direct interaction. All times are normalized to the best performing plan for each configuration.

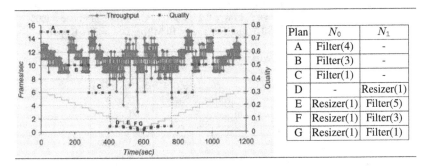

Fig. 5. Performance of the Image Streaming Application.

behavior emulated by controlling available bandwidth of the application via system call interception [1], as in some configurations in the web access experiment. In this experiment, an external module was used to inform the path about resource availability changes[3].

The components used in the image streaming example include the ImageFilter and ImageResizer introduced previously. In addition, we also allowed both components in our image streaming application to support multiple configurations: nine configurations for ImageFilter with quality values ranging from 0.1 to 0.9, four configurations for ImageResizer with scale factors ranging from 0.2 to 0.8. To display incoming images appropriately, incoming throughput (frame rate) is required to be between 8 to 15 frames/sec. Within that range, better image quality is preferred.

---

[3] In practice, due to the unstable nature of shared wireless networks, this module must include filtering mechanisms to determine whether a reconfiguration is in fact required when a change is detected. We defer the construction of appropriate filters to our future work, noting only that other researchers have looked at similar issues [7].

Figure 5 shows the throughput and image quality achieved by the data path over the 20 minute run of the experiment; the plans are shown in the table to the right. The plot needs some explanation. The light-gray staircase pattern near the bottom of the graph shows the bandwidth of link L_2 normalized to the throughput of a 25 KB image transmitted over the link; so, a link bandwidth of 150 KBps corresponds to a throughput of 6 frames/sec. The dashed black line corresponds to the quality achieved by the path. The jagged curve shows the number of frames received every second; because of border effects (a frame may arrive just after the measurement), this number fluctuates around the mean. The plateaus in the quality curve are labelled with the plan that is deployed during the corresponding time interval.

The results in Figure 5 show that the plans automatically created with our range mechanism do provide desirable adaptation behavior. First, the throughput is kept in the required range for the whole duration of the experiment (except for transition points caused by reconfigurations). Second, as a result of our range planning strategy, the image quality is decreased gradually, resulting in smooth variations in path quality. Using optimization solely for throughput will select paths with more compression capability, resulting in unnecessarily high throughput at the expense of worse image quality. The large number of automatically selected plans, which are required for satisfying the application preferences are yet another indication of the benefits of an automatic approach: accomplishing similar behaviors using a hard-coded approach would necessitate detailed domain knowledge and comprehensive involvement of application developers.

6 Related Work

Our work is related to previous work on constructing network aware communication paths.

The Ninja project's Automatic Path Creation (APC) service [5] deploys components at proxy sites (active proxies) to distill/transform data to suitable formats for different types of end devices. The primary focus of Ninja APC is to address the diversity in capacity of end devices and last hop links. Our approach takes a more general view that network resource conditions at each part of the network path can be different, and more importantly, these conditions can change continually. As a result, paths created with Ninja APC are basically function-oriented without further optimization for performance, essentially offering differentiated service access according to a small number of classes. Paths built using our approach are performance-oriented in the sense that they can provide applications with performance optimized for the conditions.

Template-based or reusable plan sets are used in the Scout [9] and Panda projects [10]. Unlike our approach, these approaches require a database of predefined path templates (or reusable plan sets), simply instantiating an appropriate template based on other programmer-provided rules that decide whether or not a component can be created on a resource. As our experimental results show, such template-based approaches would need to rely on a significant amount of domain knowledge that may or may not be appropriate for network resources that can change continually.

Recent work on multimedia content delivery [14] has also proposed an approach to find a safest path (by mapping a sequence of processing operators) on a media service proxy network to minimize the possibility of failing to deliver the content. Though resource availability is considered in this work, such paths do not provide optimized performance. Furthermore, since the approach is designed for multimedia content delivery, the selection of components benefits from more domain knowledge than general application-neutral path-based approaches.

The same path construction problem exists in service composition across a wide area network with QoS requirements. Recent work [6] has proposed the use of heuristic strategies to map a given sequence of service instances for required QoS parameters. Differing from this work that focuses only on the mapping of service instances, our approach solves component selection and mapping as a combined problem. Dividing the component selection and mapping into two separate stages may exclude valid solutions and impair the optimality of the produced path.

7   Conclusions

This paper has presented a model and corresponding algorithms for building network-aware communication paths whose performance is optimized for the underlying network conditions. Though built in the CANS infrastructure, our approach is applicable for all general path-based systems that aim to provide applications with support for adapting to dynamic changes in the network. The experiment results validate our approach, showing that the paths created automatically with our approach not only bring applications considerable performance benefits, but also provides desirable adaptation behaviors, requiring only minimal input from the applications. Furthermore, our algorithm can be applied to disjoint segments of a path independently and can be calculated in a distributed fashion, thus making it suitable for being used in a wide area network.

Acknowledgements

We'd like to thank Weisong Shi for his help with experiments using the web access application. This research was sponsored by DARPA agreements N66001-00-1-8920 and N66001-01-1-8929; by NSF grant CAREER: CCR-9876128 and CCR-9988176; and Microsoft.

References

1. F. Chang, A. Itzkovitz, and V. Karamcheti. User-level Resource-Constrained Sandboxing. In *Proc. of the 4th USENIX Windows Systems Symposium*, August 2000.
2. A. Fox, S. Gribble, Y. Chawathe, and E. A. Brewer. Adapting to Network and Client Variation Using Active Proxies: Lessons and Perspectives. *IEEE Personal Communication*, September 1998.
3. X. Fu and V. Karamcheti. Automatic creation and reconfiguration of network-aware service access paths. Technical Report TR2002-824, New York University, March 2002.
4. X. Fu, W. Shi, A. Akkerman, and V. Karamcheti. CANS:Composable, Adaptive Network Services Infrastructure. In *Proc. of the 3rd USENIX Symposium on Internet Technologies and Systems (USITS)*, March 2001.

5. S. D. Gribble and et al. The Ninja Architecture for Robust Internet-Scale Systems and Services. *Special Issue of IEEE Computer Networks on Pervasive Computing*, 2000.
6. X. Gu, K. Nahrstedt, R. N. Chang, and C. Ward. Qos-assured service composition in managed service overlay networks. In *Proceedings of The 23rd International Conference on Distributed Computing Systems*, May 2003.
7. M. Kim and B. Noble. Mobile network estimation. In *Proceedings of the Seventh ACM Conference on Mobile Computing and Networking*, July 2001.
8. A. Mallet, J. Chung, and J. Smith. Operating System Support for Protocol Boosters. In *Proc. of HIPPARCH Workshop*, June 1997.
9. A. Nakao, L. Peterson, and A. Bavier. Constructing End-to-End Paths for Playing Media Objects. In *Proc. of the OpenArch'2001*, March 2001.
10. P. Reiher, R. Guy, M. Yavis, and A. Rudenko. Automated Planning for Open Architectures. In *Proc. of OpenArch'2000*, March 2000.
11. P. Sudame and B. Badrinath. Transformer Tunnels: A Framework for Providing Route-Specific Adaptations. In *Proc. of the USENIX Technical Conf.*, June 1998.
12. D. Tennenhouse and D. Wetherall. Towards an Active Network Architecture. *Computer Communications Review*, April 1996.
13. D. J. Wethrall, J. V. Guttag, and D. L. Tennenhouse. ANTS: A toolkit for building and dynamically deploying network protocols. In *Proc. of 2nd IEEE OPENARCH*, 1998.
14. D. Xu and K. Nahrstedt. Finding service paths in a media service proxy network. In *Proc. of SPIE/ACM Conf. on Multimedia Computing and Networking (MMCN 2002)*, Jan 2002.
15. M. Yavis, A. Wang, A. Rudenko, P. Reiher, and G. J. Popek. Conductor: Distributed Adaptation for complex Networks. In *Proc. of the Seventh Workshop on Hot Topics in Operating Systems*, March 1999.

Integrating the Unreliable Multicast
Inter-ORB Protocol in MJACO

Alysson Neves Bessani[1], Lau Cheuk Lung[2],
Joni da Silva Fraga[1], and Alcides Calsavara[2]

[1] Laboratório de Controle e Microinformática – DAS
Universidade Federal de Santa Catarina – Florianópolis – SC Brazil
{neves,fraga}@das.ufsc.br
[2] Graduate Program in Applied Computer Science – CCET
Pontifical Catholic University of Paraná – Curitiba – Paraná – Brazil
{lau,alcides}@ppgia.pucpr.br

Abstract. This paper presents our experience in implementing OMG Unreliable Multicast Inter-ORB Protocol specifications into an ORB. An integration model is proposed to allow the coexistence of two different protocol stacks (IIOP/TCP/IP and MIOP/UDP/IP multicast) making possible a large spectrum of middleware support for distributed objects communication. That integration model is discussed in this paper, giving evidence of the compatibility of our approach with the CORBA specifications. In order to evaluate that integration, different tests were made considering interoperability, performance and scalability aspects.

1 Introduction

Nowadays, the CORBA architecture (Common Object Request Broker Architecture) [9] constitutes the most important middleware specification for supporting distributed objects. The main component of this architecture is the ORB (Object Request Broker) which, among other things, implements the communication semantics defined in the architecture. Messages and formats follow the General Inter-ORB Protocol (GIOP) which is a generic protocol used to support remote invocation. GIOP is a protocol that allows communication despite of different ORB implementations and transport technologies. The Internet Inter-ORB Protocol (IIOP) specifies how GIOP messages are exchanged using TCP/IP connections. Although the IIOP and TCP/IP combination provides a reliable solution for point-to-point communications - handling flow control errors, FIFO order, etc. - many other communication paradigms, when implemented over these protocols, may not use some important characteristics of lower levels of the network. This difficulty always reflects in the performance costs of these paradigms.

Some distributed applications depend on abstractions such as group communication to allow a sender to multicast messages to many receivers. These applications (e.g. groupware systems) require a better employment of network services. In 1999, the OMG published a request for proposal defining a set of requirements for an unreliable multicast service based in IP multicast. IP multicast

J.-B. Stefani, I. Demeure, and D. Hagimont (Eds.): DAIS 2003, LNCS 2893, pp. 200–211, 2003.

is an extension of the Internet Protocol (IP) that enables multipoint communications [2]. This protocol is characterized by the absence of guarantees and by it's high performance, particularly in local network. Therefore, in 2001, the OMG published the UMIOP specifications (Unreliable Multicast Inter-ORB Protocol) [10], which specifies a concretization of GIOP over the stack UDP/IP multicast. UMIOP is the key for providing an unreliable multicast into the ORB.

The group paradigm in open systems has been the theme of many research projects [6,4,7] and standardization proposals [3,8,10]. To provide the concept of group to distributed applications, it is necessary a combination of protocols that deal with group management and group communication. Within the OMG, these facilities are being standardized separately. Group management (e.g. fault detection and membership) is defined in the FT-CORBA specifications [8][1]. However, OMG has not yet published a specification for group communication in the CORBA architecture that meets different levels of guarantees and semantics available in the usual group processing models [5]. OMG started to deal with group communication with the publication of the UMIOP specifications, for unreliable multicast - the least restrictive model of group communication.

This paper presents our experiences with the integration of UMIOP into an ORB that complies with OMG specifications. Our integration model is discussed in this text, which shows evidence of the compliance of our approach to the CORBA specifications. For evaluating this implementation, tests were performed concerning interoperability, performance and scalability aspects. We present comparative measures collected with our unreliable multicast mechanism (based on the MIOP[2]/UDP/IP multicast stack), and the use of UDP sockets for IP multicast communication.

In section 2 the paper presents a short description of the IP multicast. Aspects of the specification describing the MIOP and the necessary structures to the ORB for providing unreliable multicast are presented in section 3. In section 4, we propose an integration model aiming to preserve two protocol stacks: one for point-to-point, and the other for multipoint communications. Details of implementation are described in section 5. In section 6, some tests and measures are presented and discussed and, finally, in section 7, the final considerations of this work are presented.

2   IP Multicast

Through IP multicast service, it is possible to send an IP packet to a group of hosts identified by an IP address. When a datagram is sent to a group, an attempt is made to deliver it to each host member of this group. However, as in IP unicast, there is no guarantee of delivery. That is, this service does not provide any guarantees concerning: the delivery of packets to all members of the group, the integrity of the packets and the packet delivery order.

---

[1] Currently the FT-CORBA specification is part of the CORBA specification [9].

[2] UMIOP is the name of the specification, MIOP is the name of the protocol defined in this specification.

Table 1. IP Multicast Management Operations.

Operation	Description
CreateGroup	Create a temporary group with the invoking host as its only member
JoinGroup	Add the invoking host to the specified group (permanent or temporary)
LeaveGroup	Remove the invoking host from the specified group

The IP multicast specifications [3] define two types of groups: permanent groups and temporary groups. Furthermore, there is no membership service. Each host knows what group it belongs to, but does not know about the other members. The management of members of a group is dynamic, so the association of IP addresses with hosts is quite flexible. Thus, at a given instant, a host may belong to one or more groups, or to no group. This dynamic association is carried out through three management operations, provide by the IP module. These operations are shown in table 1. Note that there is no operation for the destruction of groups, which is justified by the fact that permanent groups cannot be destroyed and temporary groups only exist as long as their number of members is more than zero.

Management operations are implemented through the IGMP protocol (Internet Group Management Protocol) [2], which is used in communication among local network hosts and multicast agents. Every network that supports IP multicast must contain at least one active multicast agent, usually implemented in the gateway of the network. The agent is the entity encharged for groups creation and maintenance, and for messages exchange in the Internet. Each multicast agent must know which groups have members in its network.

3   UMIOP Object Model

The current CORBA objects model (stack IIOP/TCP/IP) specifies an Interoperable Object Reference (IOR) which is associated to a single implementation. Furthermore, the CORBA remote method invocation implements an at-most-once semantic based on TCP connections that provides error handling that adds reliability to the point-to-point communication regarding the message delivery and, also, the FIFO ordering that can be defined to wait or do not for a reply.

The delivery of GIOP messages via unreliable multicast service establishes a different communication context from that cited above. The UMIOP specification defines an unreliable multicast mechanism for communications among distributed objects. At distributed object level, these mechanisms are reduced to the mapping of GIOP messages in UDP/IP packets - the MIOP protocol - and some facilities for group management. Information about the group is added in its corresponding reference (group IOR) for the group management. The group management is simplified since reliability is not required in MIOP and a membership service is unnecessary as there is no need to know how many or who are the group members.

Actually, a group of objects in the UMIOP specification consists of information about how to access it through the network. This information is contained in the UIPMC profile, available through the group reference (figure 1). The UIPMC profile differs from the traditional IIOP profile presented in a single object IOR by the following points:

- There is no object key[3];
- The host IP address of the IIOP profile is replaced on the UIPMC by a field that must contain an IP multicast address, or an alias of this address.

Object keys and host addresses absences in the UIPMC profile is pertinent: the unreliable multicast service is defined under the assumption of non-existence of membership. Even so, it is possible to reach group members (an object) from the UIPMC profile, using POAs (Portable Object Adapter[4]) in the hosts that received the multicast message.

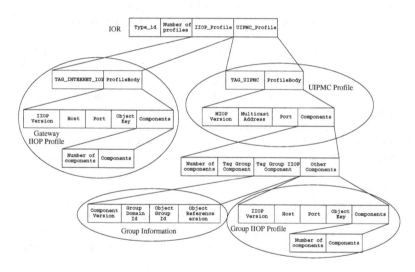

Fig. 1. Group Interoperable Object Reference.

This scenario is much more complex than that of IIOP profiles, which identify only one interface implementation. Besides protocol version, IP multicast address, and port information, the UIPMC profile also provides a set of other components such as: an IIOP profile for requests demanding replies (multicast is used only for oneway requests) and a group information structure which contains group id, domain and version.

---

[3] The object key is the object id into the ORB. It is used, with the IP address and ORB port, to locate an object implementation.

[4] ORB component responsible to activate implementations and also to forward received messages to these.

Besides the UIPMC profile (mandatory), a group IOR can optionally have one or more IIOP gateway profiles to be used by clients that do not support IP multicast. A group IOR is then used, basically, in three types of invocations:

- When the client is unable to execute multicast through its ORB, an IIOP gateway supplies the information needed in this case;
- When client and servers have UMIOP support, implement the same interface and belong to the same group, UIPMC profile is used for multicasting messages among the group members;
- When a group member is on an IIOP server and communicates using two-way operations, IIOP group profile is needed to support it.

Figure 1 presents the complete structure of a group IOR, with the UIPMC profile, group information, IIOP gateway and IIOP group profile of an object group. As mentioned before, the UIPMC profile does not define object keys to access members of a group. Thus, a POA must use the associated group information (id, domain and version) described at the UIPMC profile to identify local members of the group.

Association among groups and local members implementations requires a new internal table in the POA. The Active Groups Map table, using UIPMC group information, makes accessible through its adaptor the corresponding implementation of local group members. In this way, the inclusion of members in a group is always performed locally through calls to the activated POAs. For that, UMIOP specifications provide four new operations on the interface `PortableObject:POA`. These operations make it possible to associate/dissociate registered implementations to the group references; as well as to make lists of the implementations that belong to a given group, offering, a sort of local membership service.

In figure 2, the Java code shows the association of an object implementation to a group reference. Lines 1 - 4, show how ORB and POA references are obtained. Next, in lines 5 - 7, a group IOR is created through a corbaloc[5] URL. This URL defines a UIPMC profile to the group and an IIOP profile for operations with reply.

After getting the group IOR, lines 8 and 9 present the instantiation of the object `member` and its activation by the POA. The line 10 shows the operation `associate_reference_with_id`, an extension of the POA interface, used for associating the activated implementation to the group reference, and finally, at line 11 the ORB is activated, making it ready to receive requests.

When compared to other group supports (e.g., FT-CORBA), group creation and member association showed in figure 2 can be considered very complex, involving low-level structures manipulations. To avoid this problem, the UMIOP specification defines an optional service object called MGM (Multicast Group Manager), which is introduced to offer a high level group management interface. The MGM service supplies less complex operations for creating and destroying

---

[5] Used to represent object references as URLs.

```
1  ORB orb = ORB.init(args,null);
2  Object poaObj = orb.resolve_initial_references("RootPOA");
3  POA poa = POAHelper.narrow(poaObj);
4  poa.the_POAManager().activate();
5  Object group = orb.string_to_object("corbaloc:" +
6    "miop:1.0@1.0-mydomain-1-2/225.1.2.5:7676;" +
7    "iiop:1.1@localhost:1236/MyObjectKey");
8  MyGroupMemberImpl member = new MyGroupMemberImpl();
9  byte[] memberId = poa.activate_object(member);
10 poa.associate_reference_with_id(group,memberId);
```

Fig. 2. Association in POA of a Group IOR with an Implementation Object.

groups. Other operations for managing groups properties (group IIOP components, gateway, multicast address and port) are available too.

At message level, a GIOP message is always encapsulated in a set of MIOP packets. A MIOP packet is composed by a header and a GIOP block of data. The maximum size of a GIOP data block that can be contained in a MIOP packet usually depends on the frame size supported by the network utilized.

4 UMIOP Integration Model

Figure 3 presents our UMIOP integration model, implemented in the MJACO project. MJACO is an extension of JacORB [1], a CORBA compliant ORB. The architecture MJACO is proposed to allow the co-existence IIOP/TCP/IP and MIOP/UDP/IP multicast protocol stacks in the same ORB, contributing in this way, for a better interoperability and portability. In figure 3, we presents a ORB integrating two protocol stacks: one for point-to-point communication based on IIOP mapped on TCP/IP services; and the other one for multipoint communication composed by MIOP, using UDP/IP multicast as a transfer mechanism for its packages. Our integration model presents several elements defined in the specification in its support with the two communication models. Also, extensions and other components not defined in the specifications were added to the support whose purpose is to facilitate the different stacks integration and improve the efficiency of the set.

Our approach proposes a local object service MGM+ which extends the MGM of the UMIOP specifications, by adding functionalities for group management at object level. By creating group references, implemented through ORB calls, MGM+ registers the created group IOR on a CORBA name server, making the group reference automatically available to any other application. Other MGM+ facilities concerning the membership changes (locally) are available through **add_member** and **delete_member** operations. These operations centralize in the MGM+ the interactions for associating groups and implementations of local members through active groups map of the POA (section 3).

Another component, part of our integration model, is the Multicast Adaptor which is responsible for managing the multicast sockets used in the reception of

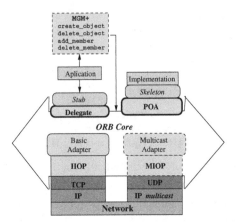

Fig. 3. MJaco Architecture.

MIOP packets and for delivering messages addressed to group members by the active POAs. MIOP module executes tasks described in the UMIOP specification which refers to the translation of the GIOP messages into collections of MIOP packets and vice-versa. POA and Delegate are the main ORB components that were extended. Delegate is altered in some points in order to support the sending of GIOP messages to groups; it is the first internal component of the ORB to be activated when a method call is executed on the stub. In our approach, the delegate decides, based on the corresponding method call, which protocol stacks will be used to send a GIOP message. The POA, besides the addition of the four primitives described in the UMIOP specification, must be altered to search the active groups map in order to obtain implementations of local group members. The local group members receive through the POAs the messages addressed to the group to process the corresponding method requests. POA is also responsible for the activation of the multicast adaptor which executes operations on IP multicast interface for group management. For example, when an `associate_reference_with_id` call is made to register the first member of a group in the ORB, POA activates the multicast adaptor to create a socket and to execute the IP multicast operation *JoinGroup* at the address defined on the UIPMC profile present in the group reference. From then on, the ORB receives messages addressed to this group. The other POA operations related to groups result in the execution of IP multicast management operations.

5   MJaco: Implementing UMIOP on JacORB

For implementing the UMIOP specifications and the model presented in the section 4, the JacORB platform (http://www.jacorb.org) was selected. JacORB is a open source ORB that was chosen because of its recognized quality and performance and our experience with it in other two projects: GroupPac and JaCoWeb (http://www.das.ufsc.br/grouppac).

Figure 4 presents a class diagram in UML describing classes that process requests within the client JacORB. The set of classes shown are activated when a CORBA client makes a method call on the stub. The stub is responsible for the serialization of the method invocation; the message is sent using the `Delegate` class. This class maintains an open TCP connection to the server ORB, where the implementation corresponding to the stub is registered and it implements the operations related to the `CORBA::Object`, the base interface of all defined for CORBA objects.

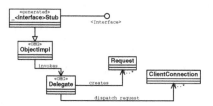

Fig. 4. Request Processing on CORBA Clients.

On the server side, the requests processing is much more complex. Figure 5 presents a class diagram with the main components in the request processing activated by a GIOP message arrival in the socket.

An object of the `Listener` class waits for requests on one TCP connection. When a request is received in this port, the object creates a new instance of the `RequestReceptor` class, which is responsible for interpreting the request and forwarding it to a destination POA[6]. Once the POA is located, the request is placed in a list to be processed by the target implementation (subclass of `Servant`). Note that some classes showed in figure 5 have the stereotype thread; these classes represent the points of JacORB structure that implement their multithreading architecture.

To process MIOP packets, a new structure of classes must be added to the JacORB diagrams (showed in figures 4 and 5) to represent classes that send and receive MIOP packet collections. Figure 6 presents a new diagram with these new classes. In this diagram we identify `Delegate` class, within the ORB, as the point for communication stack selection. In this class, when the IOR of the destination object corresponds to a group reference and the requested operation is oneway, the processing is deviated to the class `MulticastSender`, which encapsulates the GIOP request in a collection of MIOP packets to be sent via IP multicast.

On the server, an object of `MulticastListener` class is created for each group in which the ORB has members registered (one listener for each port and one port for each group) by the multicast adaptor (class `MulticastAdapter`). These listeners receive and store MIOP packets until to complete the corresponding GIOP message. When that message is completed, a thread (instance of class

---

[6] The POA in which the target implementation is registered.

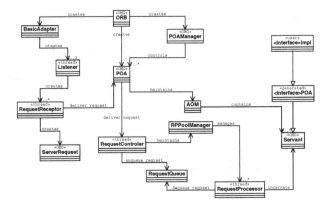

Fig. 5. Request Processing on CORBA Servers.

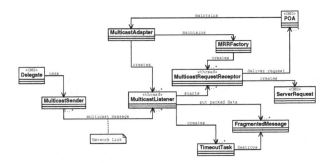

Fig. 6. UMIOP Extensions.

MulticastRequestReceptor) is activated from the thread pool to receive the original GIOP message and pass it to all POAs of the ORB. In each POA, using the active groups map (AGM) and group information contained in the header of the GIOP message, a set of local object identifiers belonging to the target group are located in this POA.

Note that the request is forwarded to all the active POAs, even those that do not register objects implementations of the destination group. This algorithm for delivery was developed with the objective of making the class AGM as simple as possible and of avoiding the processing overhead imposed by the destination POA search. Another factor that justifies this option is the fact that in the majority of the applications, not many POAs are activated at the same time.

6   Obtained Results

This section presents some tests performed with the aim of evaluating the implementation performance of MJACO. The tests were executed on a local network using computers with the same configuration[7], connected to the same hub. Two versions of a distributed program were implemented for measuring round-trip times[8]: the first one using multicast sockets and the other using MJACO.

The first experiment was setup as follows: two instances of the test program were initiated on four machines, thus eight members in the group. One of these members was the sender that sent message of variable size to the group. To configure the round-trip, the sender was kept waiting for all the confirmations from members who received that message. This procedure was repeated 10000 times. The experiment was executed with each of the program versions built, and the results obtained are shown in figure 7.

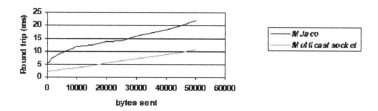

Fig. 7. MJACO Performance.

In figure 7, it can be verified that the use of multicast sockets program results in a performance approximately 60% better (on the average) than the one using MJACO. This was expected, since MJACO places a whole software layer for object and request management, as well as for message serialization (see figure 3); but distributed programs using multicast sockets in some part of the application code might have to perform the same functionalities that our little multicast sockets program does not implement. It is also worth pointing out that the MJACO implementation was realized with the least possible dependence on JacORB, which caused some performance losses that must be minimized since the implementations are evolving.

An important point to be emphasized is that, in this current version of the prototype, starting with 50 Kbyte messages the system begins to lose some messages. That is due to the weak reliability of the UDP/IP communications which does not avoid packet losses.

In the second experiment we evaluated the scalability of MJACO. The tests were executed in following way: on each host an instance of the test program was initiated, specifying how many objects of the group had to be instantiated and registered on the MJACO support. One of the object members created on the system hosts was the sender, the one that multicast the message with 4 Kbytes of data and was responsible for measuring the round-trip times. The

---

[7] Pentium III 900 Mhz with 198 Mb RAM memory over Ethernet 10Mbps.

[8] round-trip time represents the time period between the beginning of the message multicasting to all the group members and finishing with the sender reception of the last confirmation message sent by the receiving members.

number of messages multicast during a round-trip was $4n + 1$ where n is the number of group objects registered in each host (one request message and an acknowledgement for each member object of the group). The round-trip process was repeated for a different number of objects per host and the results of these experiments are shown in figure 8.

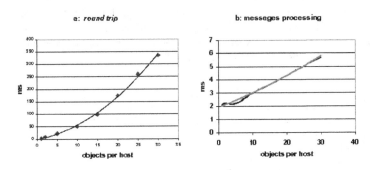

Fig. 8. MJACO Scalability.

Figure 8.a shows a situation in which, when we increase the group members, the round-trip time also increases considerably. This is due to the substantial increasing of the number of messages generated on the network. For instance, with two objects per host (eight members in the group), nine messages are exchanged for one round-trip (one data message and eight acknowledgements). For ten objects per host, 41 messages are exchanged in the network. So, if the round-trip duration is divided by its corresponding message number, an estimative is obtained from average transfer time for one message in the system. Figure 8.b shows these values with respect to the number of group members. In this graph, it is possible to verify that this average time is linear, and increases approximately 0.1 ms for each new object included in each system host. According to the results of this last test, we conclude that the solutions adopted in MJACO prototype presents a good scalability.

7   Conclusions

The Unreliable Multicast Inter-ORB Protocol is the first step towards a complete group communication solution in the CORBA architecture. We are developing studies on multicast protocols and evaluating different ways to adapt them to the CORBA, especially the UMIOP specifications, since the objective of this project is to implement a reliable multicast mechanism over MIOP on MJACO. For this reason, questions involving loss of packets, performance analysis, fault-tolerance, etc, were not discussed here. Our intention, in this paper, is to have an unreliable multicast support available into an ORB.

In this paper our solutions were presented for the integration of IP multicast into a CORBA ORB. The integration model proposed does not jeopardize aspects of interoperability and portability of ORB as a whole. The ORB is capable of making invocations using both IIOP and MIOP. This model can very well be adopted to integrate other communication protocols, since they have an available API. Furthermore, our experiences with MJACO implementation was also presented in this paper. This implementation, which had as a basis the integration model proposed, were built over JacORB, a Java free ORB. These implementations can be obtained on the Web at http://grouppac.sourceforge.net/.

We are now focusing our efforts to integrate MIOP to the FT-CORBA infrastructure. The solutions presented here are part of GROUPPAC project, which uses the Fault-Tolerant CORBA specifications, towards the conception of active replication models [11], inexistent in current OMG specifications.

References

1. Gerald Brose. Jacorb: Implementation and design of a javaorb. In *Proceedings of IFIP WG 6.1 International Working Conference on Distributed Applications and Interoperable Systems*, 1997.
2. S. E. Deering. Host extensions for ip multicasting (rfc 988). IETF Request For Comments, July 1986.
3. S. E. Deering and D. R. Cheriton. Host groups: A multicast extension to the internet protocol (rfc 966). IETF Request For Comments, December 1985.
4. Pascal Felber, Benot Garbinato, and Rachid Guerraoui. The design of a CORBA group communication service. In *Proceedings of the 15th Symposium on Reliable Distributed Systems*, pages 150–159, Niagara-on-the-Lake, Canada, 1996.
5. Vassos Hadzilacos and Sam Toueg. A modular approach to the specification and implementation of fault-tolerant broadcasts. Technical report, Department of Computer Science, Cornell University, New York - USA, May 1994.
6. Silvano Maffeis. Adding group communication and fault-tolerance to CORBA. In *Proceedings of the USENIX Conference on Object Oriented Technologies*, pages 135–146, Monterey, Canada, June 1995.
7. L. Moser, P. Melliar-Smith, P. Narasimhan, R. Koch, and K. Berket. A multicast group communication protocol, engine, and bridge for corba. *Concurrency and Computation Pratice and Experience*, 13(7):579–603, June 2001.
8. Object Management Group. Fault-tolerant corba specification v1.0. OMG Standart, 2000.
9. Object Management Group. The common object request broker architecture: Core specification v3.0. OMG Standart formal/02-12-06, December 2002.
10. OMG. Unreliable multicast inter-orb protocol specification v1.0. OMG Standart ptc/03-01-11, October 2001.
11. Fred B. Schneider. Implementing fault-tolerant service using the state machine aproach: A tutorial. *ACM Computing Surveys*, 22(4):299–319, December 1990.

A-GATE: A System of Relay and Translation Gateways for Communication among Heterogeneous Agents in Ad Hoc Wireless Environments

Leelani Kumari Wickramasinghe[1], Seng Wai Loke[2],
Arkady Zaslavsky[2], and Damminda Alahakoon[1]

[1] School of Business Systems,
Monash University, VIC 3145, Australia
kumari.wickramasinghe@infotech.monash.edu.au
damminda.alahakoon@infotech.monash.edu.au
[2] School of Computer Science and Software Engineering,
Monash University, VIC 3145, Australia
seng.loke@infotech.monash.edu.au
arkady.zaslavsky@csse.monash.edu.au

Abstract. The devices in an ad hoc network are expected to perform network functionalities by themselves due to the absence of proper networking infrastructure. Generally the routing is multi-hop as nodes may not be within the wireless transmission range of each other. This paper describes a system named A-GATE to support the high-level communication needs of agents in such a network. Agents are used to support the interoperability among devices and the system is capable of handling heterogeneity in agent platforms. A-GATE proposes a novel routing mechanism for locating the intended recipient of a message. The system aims to be self-organizing and self-configuring to suit the dynamic nature of ad hoc networks.

1 Introduction

There is a surge of interest in mobile computing mainly due to the continued miniaturization of mobile devices and their ability to enable mobility. At the same time, wireless ad hoc networks are becoming quite popular due to their inherent feature of "the network" at user disposal. People wish to download a roadmap on their way so that they know what is available in close proximity to them or they wish to receive driving suggestions on the global positioning system (GPS) of their car [1].

A mobile ad hoc network is formed by a collection of mobile nodes. There is no established networking infrastructure for the mobile devices to rely on. As a result, all the networking functionalities have to be performed by the nodes themselves. Mobile devices take an active role in creating a network infrastructure and routing of data. Cooperation among nodes is an essential requirement: for example, if two nodes need to communicate, intermediate nodes are expected to forward the messages [1, 2].

When developing an application for ad hoc environments, there are challenges to be addressed [3]. The topology of the ad hoc network is dynamic and nodes join and leave the network spontaneously. There is no central server that knows the nodes'

J.-B. Stefani, I. Demeure, and D. Hagimont (Eds.): DAIS 2003, LNCS 2893, pp. 212–223, 2003.
© IFIP International Federation for Information Processing 2003

current locations and the networks to which the devices shifted. The cost of communication is high as the devices have a limited battery power.

Due to the distributed and dynamic nature of mobile ad hoc networks and the potential need for proactive, spontaneous and intelligent interaction, agent technology has been considered promising for building applications in such ad hoc wireless environments [3]. With the spread of distributed systems, a large number of agent systems has been developed. Each agent system has a different agent platform and it is really difficult to get agents on heterogeneous systems to work together. Most agent systems require homogeneity in agent systems for agents to communicate and migrate. When it comes to agents on ad hoc networks, they should be capable of interacting with agents on any other device no matter what the communication language or agent platform of the other agent.

Agent interactions are handled by standardizing the language of communication. KQML [4] and FIPA [5] are two such specifications. Before communication starts agents should have priori knowledge of where the other agents reside. It is an extra overhead if the communication initiation agent has to locate the target agent. Infrastructure support should be capable of locating the target agent, keeping the source agent away from network level issues.

The aim of this paper is to make it possible for agents running on devices interconnected ad hoc and wirelessly to communicate without concern for underlying network level issues or heterogeneity of agent platforms. The proposed system, A-GATE, will take responsibility for locating the target agent and delivering the message successfully, regardless of the above heterogeneity.

One possible scenario would be the exchange of business cards among the participants in a conference room using agents residing on mobile devices. Another scenario would be an infrastructure-less office environment composed of mobile devices. Communication among devices can be handled by agents residing in each device.

The approach is explained in the following sections: Section 2 describes some existing systems that handle heterogenous agent platforms and applicability of mobile agents for the communication needs of ad hoc networks. The proposed system, A-GATE is described in detail in Section 3. Experiments done to evaluate the applicability of A-GATE as a generic communication system for an ad hoc wireless network are presented in Section 4. Section 5 discusses the conclusion and future work.

2   Related Work

In most agent systems, agents require a homogeneous platform to migrate. In [6] is described an approach where migration of agents in a heterogeneous network is possible by way of a blueprint. The blueprint consists of the agent's functionality and its state. The receiving platform regenerates a mobile agent as it migrates to its new location. In the A-GATE system only agents on heterogeneous systems are needed to communicate. The recreation of agents consumes time and resources whereas communication between agents should be faster and simple.

A model based on middleware or an interface between agents and platforms is proposed in [7]. This layer is visible to an application programmer on one side and on the other side there is a platform dependent layer.

There are guest interfaces of one per platform. According to the platform, the required java classes have to be downloaded. Our approach is quite similar to this one but the required agent platforms are loaded at configuration time as it is much faster with real time communication. Our goal is to provide a fast and secure communication support for agents in mobile devices.

A network protocol called Agent Platform Protocol (APP) is designed for agent interactions among heterogeneous platforms [8]. In this approach, agents are free from the management of network level issues. It uses peer-to-peer communication. But when agents are deployed in a mobile network, direct peer-to-peer communication among any two peers is not possible due to the short range coverage of the underlying wireless protocols. Peers need to forward messages via other peers as A-GATE facilitates.

The advantages of using mobile agents for the communication needs of an ad hoc networks is described in [9]. Mobile agents can function as "wrappers" on messages, which enable the messages to propagate themselves to the intended destinations. But the transmission overhead associated with mobility is high. Mobile devices need interoperability with minimum pay load in scenarios such as exchange of business cards in a conference or infrastructure-less office environments. The system proposed in this paper has a store and forward concept with a minimal transmission overhead.

3   Proposed System

A-GATE is based on the concept of a gateway (gw), as illustrated in Fig. 1, where agents on mobile devices interact with a gateway which is located within the reachable area of the device, to communicate with any other agent. The importance of this concept is that both the gateways and agents reside on mobile devices and gateways come into existence only when they are required, as will be described in Section 3.5.1

The block diagram of a gateway is shown in Fig 2. It consists of 5 components: Message Accepting Relay Agents, Message Extractor, Message Translator, Message Re-builder and Message Dispatching Relay Agents. The gateway application itself spawns

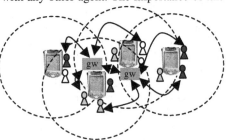

Fig. 1. A-GATE System Architecture

relay agent platforms depending on the number of agent platforms the system needs to support while there is only one generic process known as METR consisting of Message Extractor, Message Translator, and Message Re-builder units.

A gateway provides two main functionalities to the agents on mobile devices: a message translation service and a message relaying service. When an agent sends messages in its own language without considering the language of the target agent, message translation service takes care of the translation to a language understood by the destination agent. The message relaying service consists of Message Accepting Relay Agents and Message Dispatching Relay Agents (see left and right hand corners of Fig 2). The Message Accepting Relay Agent accepts messages from a source agent or an intermediate message routing gateway while the Message Dispatching Relay Agent dispatches the message to the intended recipient.

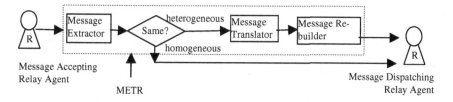

Fig. 2. Block Diagram of the Gateway Application

Each gateway maintains two registers: agent registry and gateway registry. Agent registry maintains information related to the agents reachable from the gateway while the gateway registry maintains information related to other gateways. The agent registry stores reachable agents' identifications, their platforms and communication languages while the gateway registry stores reachable gateways' identifications. The process to identify reachable agents and gateways is described in Section 3.4. The main units of the application are described in Sections 3.1 and 3.2.

3.1 Message Accepting and Dispatching Relay Agents

Generally, agent platforms have an inbuilt messaging system to interact with agents from homogeneous systems. What is needed is a system in which heterogeneous agent systems communicate. To accomplish this task, the Gateway application spawns relay agent platforms to match the agent platforms used by the two communicating mobile devices. Relay agents are there to accept messages or deliver messages to the source and destination agent respectively. The Message Accepting Relay agent accepts the message from the source agent and forwards it to the Message Extractor. Once the message is rebuilt, the Message Dispatching Relay Agent forwards the message to the destination agent. The advantage of having platform specific relay agents is that, when a new agent platform is introduced to the system it is just a matter of deploying an agent of that platform as a relay agent without needing any modifications to the generic gateway application.

3.2 Message Extractor, Translator and Re-builder (METR)

Once a message is accepted by a Message Accepting Relay Agent, it is forwarded to the Message Extractor unit. This unit extracts the message and gets the recipient address. Then it checks whether the recipient is a reachable agent by going through its routing table (information about the routing table can be found in Section 3.4.2). If the recipient is a reachable agent, it checks for the agent platform of the recipient. If the agent platform of the sender is different from that of the receiver, the message is sent to the Translator unit. Otherwise, the message is directly sent to the Dispatching Relay Agent. Message Translator takes the content of the message and translates it to a format understood by the recipient agent considering the agent platform of the recipient. Once this is done, the message is forwarded to the Re-builder unit which attaches the appropriate headers to the message and forwards it to the Message dispatching relay agent. If the recipient is not reachable, the message is forwarded to a gateway which is capable of delivering the message. Identification of such a gateway is done by going through the contents in the routing table. But in this case, before forwarding the message, the Message Extractor unit adds another optional field called "sender's agent platform" to the original message, which is needed by any other gateway to deliver the message in a format understood by the receiving agent. The complete algorithm of METR is listed below:

> extract the sender address
> extract the recipient address
> check for the recipient address in the agent registry
> if an entry found
>> check for the optional field "sender's agent platform"
>> if field found
>>> extract the senders platform (P1)
>> else
>>> check whether sender got any entry in the agent registry
>>> if an entry found
>>>> get the senders platform (P1) from the list entry
>>> else
>>>> drop the message
>> check for the agent platform of the recipient (P2)
>> if (P1 != P2)
>>> translate the message to the P2 platform
>>> dispatch the message to the Message re-builder
>> dispatch the message to the Message Dispatching Relay Agent
> if an entry is not found
>> go through the routing table
>> check for a gateway which can route the message to the recipient
>> if a gateway found
>>> sends the message to that gateway
>> else
>>> drop the message

A somewhat similar algorithm is proposed in [10], where mobile hosts actively modify their trajectories to transmit messages. It involves trajectory modification of each host to approach the immediate host within the transmission range of the host, which is applicable for devices which have automated moving capabilities (for example moving cars and robots).

3.3 Address Schema

A unique way of identifying an agent on a mobile device is required. Each agent on a mobile device is given a unique identity according to the concepts in cellular phones, where each phone is assigned a unique identity referred to as Numeric Assignment Module (NAM) [11]. There can be number of agents acting on a single device. Therefore, an identifier for an agent would be:

Identifier for the mobile device + some identifier for the agent (x)

The ID stored in a digital certificate [12] could be considered as an identifier for the mobile device as security can also be built upon it.

The agent unique identifier could be matched to IP:port relationship in networking. There are well known port addresses [13] such as 80 for web 21 for ftp and so on. Value of x could be based on this well known port address technique in networking. "Well known agents" are required by relating agents to the services they perform such as information retrieval, database accesses and exchanging information: for example, if the mobile user has a digital certificate for his email address user1@company.com and the well known agent for information exchange is 20, then the unique identifier of the information exchanging agent on user1's mobile device would be user1@company.com:20

3.4 Communication Process

Communication is achieved through agents and gateways residing on mobile devices. Agents are originators and consumers, while gateways are intermediate processes to transfer messages from originators to consumers. For the system to function properly, agents should have an understanding about which gateways they can directly communicate, while gateways should know about other reachable gateways. Facilitating this, agents send periodic network broadcasts in a neighbour to neighbour fashion on a pre-identified port address that the gateways and other agents monitor. Similarly, gateways send periodic broadcast messages on another pre-identified port address that only the gateways monitor.

3.4.1 Agent-Gateway Communication.
A broadcast sent by an agent is considered as a notification of the existence of the agent. It consists of agent identification, agent platform and communication language. Once the broadcast is received by the gateways, they reply with their identifications. Agent stores this gateway identification to be used in future communication needs. If the agent receives replies from more than one gateway, it can either store the address of only one gateway or store all the gateway addresses so that, if one gateway goes down or changes its location, it can use the next gateway to accomplish its communication needs. In the latter case, deciding factors would be the basis of service such as First Come First Served (FIFS) or the signal strength of each gateway. Consequently, agents reply to the chosen gateway or gateways so that gateways can insert or update the entries in their agent registries.

3.4.2 Gateway-Gateway Communication.
The broadcasts sent by gateways consist of the gateway identification and information about the reachable agents and gateways. This broadcast is considered to be a technique of exchanging routing tables among gateways. A routing protocol for ad hoc networks based on routing tables is presented in [14]. All the

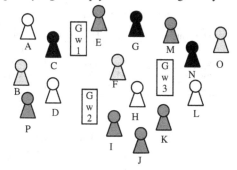

Fig. 3. Agents and Gateways in a Network

gateways which receive this message update their routing tables accordingly, which means each gateway on the ad hoc network has a complete picture of how the agents reside on the network at a given time. Gateways are proactive, meaning when a sender needs to send a message the next hop to the intended recipient is already known by the gateways. Maintaining the complete routing table is a reasonable approach as there are a limited number of devices on the ad hoc network.

Fig. 3 outlines the concept of routing tables. If it is assumed that the agents C and D are reachable by gateways 1 and 2, agent G is reachable by gateways 1 and 3, agent H is reachable by gateways 2 and 3 and agent F is reachable by all three gateways. In addition, gw1 and gw2 are reachable and gw2 and gw3 are reachable by each other.

Routing tables of gateways Gw1, Gw2 and Gw3 are presented in Tables 1, 2 and 3 respectively. As shown in Table 1, Gateway 1 (gw1) is within the reachable area of agents A, C, D, E, F and G, listed under "Direct agents". Gateway gw2 is located within the reachable area of Gw1; therefore it is listed under the "Direct gateways". Agents B, F, I, H, J and P can reach gw2 while agents M, N, O, L and K can reach gw3. They have two separate entries as "Via gw2 agents" and "Via gw3 agents". Gateway gw3 is contactable via gw2; so gw3 is listed in "Via gw2 gateways". The other two routing tables are also based on this concept.

Due to the dynamic nature of the ad hoc network, gateways and agents can appear and disappear with time and they can move to new locations. Gateways exchange their routing tables periodically so that each receiving gateway can update their routing tables to suit the current state of the ad hoc network.

3.4.3 End to End Message Delivery. When an agent needs to send a message, it sends a delivery request message to the gateway it is registered with, or to one of the gateways it got registered with. The message consists of the sender, intended recipient and the content to be delivered. As with any other device in an ad hoc network, gateways may appear and disappear. Therefore, when a gateway receives a delivery request, it sends an acknowledgement back to the sender to indicate it has received the delivery request. But the acknowledgement does not guarantee an end-to-end delivery of the message. The delivery of the message is handled as described in the Sections 3.1 and 3.2.

Table 1. Routing Table of Gw1

Direct agents	A, C, D, E, F, G
Direct gateways	gw2
Via gw2 agents	B, F, I, H, J, P
Via gw3 agents	M, N, O, L, K
Via gw2 gateways	gw3

Table 2. Routing Table of Gw2

Direct agents	B, D, P, C, F, I, H, J
Direct gateways	gw1, gw3
Via gw1 agents	A, E, G
Via gw3 agents	G, M, N, O, L, K

Table 3. Routing Table of Gw3

Direct agents	G, M, N, O, L, K, H, F
Direct gateways	gw2
Via gw1 agents	A, C, E
Via gw2 agents	B, D, P, C, I, J
Via gw2 gateways	gw1

3.5 Gateways

Gateway is the main application which handles the communication process. It resides on the mobile device and come into existence only when needed as described in Section 3.5.1. Once a gateway comes into existence, how to retain it for further communication needs is explained in Section 3.5.2 and deciding factors for a gateway to shut down is explained in Section 3.5.3. Gateways can be used for load balancing as detailed in Section 3.5.4.

3.5.1 Creation of Gateways. When an agent needs to communicate, it usually generates the message and sends it to a gateway it is registered with. But if the agent has not received a reply from any of the gateways for its initial broadcast, it will retry with the same broadcast in random time delays. After three such consecutive attempts, if there is no reply and if there is any mobile device within the reachable area, the device itself can voluntarily become a gateway.

Using an arbitrary node 'X' intending to communicate with the node 'Y', if the node X has not registered with a gateway at time t1, it sends a network broadcast informing it of its existence. Then it waits for some time to receive a reply from the gateway. After waiting for a random time period, if it does not get any reply it will do another broadcast for the second time at time t4. If still no reply, then a third broadcast is done at time t8. If the same condition remains, it will listen to check whether there is any notification of existence messages from other devices in the network. If there are any such devices, X would voluntarily become a gateway and send a network broadcast informing its existence as a gateway.

Also if a node detects there exist two gateways which do not know about each other then that node should become a gateway. This is needed in order to facilitate the communication between the nodes which have got registered with one of the two gateways. To determine whether one gateway knows about other one, the node can try to send a message to one gateway via other one. If the first gateway drops the message, then that means there is no route from that gateway to the second one and vice versa and the node itself can become a gateway.

3.5.2 Retention of Gateways. Once a gateway is formed it is better to retain it for some time as a gateway for the other devices on the network to communicate with. But in an ad hoc network where all the nodes do not belong to the same authority, each node tries to maximise the benefits it receives from the network. Perhaps nodes are not willing to provide gateway functionalities to the other nodes. Nodes might become selfish to save limited resources such as battery power, memory and CPU cycles. But, considering the network as a whole, gateway functionality is essential.

The nuglet counter concept described in [15] can be considered as a technique for retaining gateways. If a device voluntarily becomes a gateway it will earn 3 nuglets. That means it can send 3 of its own messages without acting as a gateway to other agents. As long as the gateway has enough nuglets it can send its own messages. Whenever it sends its own message the nuglet counter gets decreased. But it can earn more nuglets by acting as a gateway to other messages. This would become useful if the device acting as a gateway knew that it may want to send more of its own messages in the near future. In that case, till the time comes, it can collect nuglets by being a gateway to the neighbouring devices.

3.5.3 Shut down of Gateways. Two situations have been identified for shutting down
   a) Isolated gateways: In an ad hoc network, as each device can move, gateways can
get isolated. If a gateway does not receive any notifica-
tion of existence broadcasts it is an indication as to no
neighbouring devices within the reachable area of that
gateway. Once a gateway identifies itself as an isolated
device it can terminate its functionality and shut down.

   b) Redundant gateways: There can be situations
where more than one device is acting as a gateway to
the same set of nodes as shown in Fig 4. As all the
agents are within the reachable area of each gateway, it
is enough to have one gateway rather than two. Gateways themselves can identify this issue by going
through their routing tables. In that case, they can
negotiate with each other and come to a conclusion as to which gateway to shut down.
Metrics to consideration could be the available resources, the processing power and
memory.

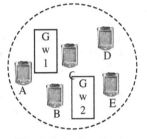

Fig. 4. Redundant Gateways

3.5.4 Load Balancing Using Gateways. If it is assumed that, after the negotiation,
gw2 went down, but later gw1 finds that there is a huge traffic between agents A and
E which is difficult to be handled alone by gw1, it can send a disaster message indicating it is overloaded. In that case gw2 or some other device can come into existence
to balance the load.

4   Experiments

To evaluate A-GATE as a generic agent interaction system, the gateway application
was implemented for the process of exchanging business cards in an ad hoc network.
Heterogeneous agent systems, Grasshopper [16] and Kaariboga [17] were used as the
test agent platforms. Grasshopper is a commercial agent platform while Kaariboga is
an open source agent platform.

4.1   Implementation

The system consists of a Message class which needs to be used by the agent systems
to send messages. This Message class is portable to many programming languages. At
the initial implementation level, message class contains three main attributes: sender,
receiver and content.

   The communication between platform-specific relay agents and gateway application is handled via TCP/IP sockets. The system is implemented on java platform using
java socket programming [18] for communication. Relay agents and gateway application listen on specific ports so that whenever a relay agent receives a message, it can
forward it to METR. Similarly once the address resolution for routing and translations
are done at METR, it can forward the message to the correct platform specific agent
on the receiving side. Fig 5 is a simplified diagram of the Grasshopper and Kaariboga
test system.

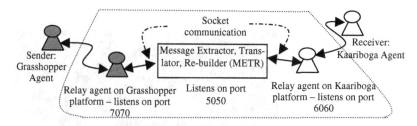

Fig. 5. Test System with Grasshopper and Kaariboga Agents

For testing, a generic message class was imported to both agent platforms. Using the agent creation concepts in Grasshopper platform, a dynamic client agent and a dynamic server agent were created to act as the message sender and the corresponding message accepting relay agent respectively. Changes had to be made to IDynamicServerAgent.java and IDynamicServerAgentP.java to use the generic message class. Similarly a message receiver and message sender agents were created in the Kaariboga platform. KaaribogaMessage.java class was configured to handle the messages of our generic message class. Fig 6 illustrates Gateway application, where a Grasshopper agent on one device sends the business card details to a Kaariboga agent in another device.

4.2 Performance Testing

To evaluate the performance of A-GATE, it was tested with the traditional client server architecture as it can support agent communication. The result was encouraging as both the systems take the same amount of time to send a message from a source agent to destination agents. In addition, the byte overhead of the generic message class is limited to the two address fields: senders and receivers, which is acceptable with any communication system. Currently the system is being tested in a network with around 50 nodes (some of which are mobile) and the performance has to be evaluated as to what happens when the number of gateways is increased. There should be a threshold number of gateways after which the performance of the system would not be significant.

5 Conclusion and Future Work

The A-GATE system, as presented in this paper can be used for the agents on an ad hoc network to communicate without concern for the underlying network level issues or heterogeneity of agent platforms. The technique used for creating, retaining and shutting down gateways provides a novel solution to the infrastructure-less ad hoc networks where the devices on the network have to handle all the required networking functionalities. We believe our work complements existing work on low level ad hoc networking, as our work is at the application or agent level, where more sophisticating reasoning concerning when and how to relay and high level semantics of translations can be considered.

Fig. 6. Screen Output of Gateway Application

The immediate target is to evaluate the performance of the system in a large network of mobile devices connected via short-range wireless networks. The amount of flooding in the network when there is large number of devices in the network needs to be measured.

Future work will include building a Semantic Translator Engine and a Content Translator Engine to the Message Translator unit of the Gateway. Semantic Translator Engine is to handle multilingual messages where both the performative and content need to be translated. Once it is done agents can communicate in their native language, be they English, Chinese or Japanese. Content Translator is to handle the contents of the message, for example to translate the "Prolog facts" in a message to "KIF facts".

References

1. Perkins, C.E., *Ad hoc networking*. 2001, Boston: Addison-Wesley. xii, 370.
2. Corson, S., J. Freebersyser, and A. Sastry, *Mobile Networks and Applications (MONET)*. Special Issue on Mobile Ad Hoc Networking, 1999.
3. "Agents in Ad Hoc Environments", *http://www.fipa.org/docs/input/f-in-00068/ f-in-00068A.htm*

4. Finin, T., Y. Labrou, and J. Mayfield, *KQML as an agent communication language*, in *Software Agents*, J. Bradshaw, Editor. 1997, MIT Press: Cambridge. p. 291-316.

5. "Foundation for Intelligent Physical Agent Specification", *http://www.fipa.org*,

6. Brazier, F.M.T., et al. *Agents, interactions, mobility and systems: Agent factory: generative migration of mobile agents in heterogeneous environments*. in *2002 ACM symposium on Applied computing*. 2002. Madrid, Spain: ACM Press New York, NY, USA.

7. Magnin, L., et al. *Our guest agents are welcome to your agent platforms*. in *2002 ACM symposium on Applied computing*. 2002. Madrid, Spain: ACM Press New York, USA.

8. Takahashi, K.i., G. Zhong, and D. Matsuno. *Interoperability between KODAMA and JADE using Agent Platform Protocol*. in *The First International Joint Conference on Autonomous Agents and Multi agent systems*. 2002. Italy.

9. Kotz, D., et al., *AGENT TCL: targeting the needs of mobile computers*. Internet Computing, IEEE, 1997. **1**(4): p. 58-67.

10. Qun Li and D. Rus. *Message relay in disconnected ad-hoc networks*. in *Mobility and Wireless Access Workshop, 2002. MobiWac 2002. International*. 2002.

11. Bates, R., *Cellular Communications*, in *Wireless networked communications: concepts, technology, and implementation*. 1995. p. 73-95.

12. Feghhi, J., J. Feghhi, and P. Williams, *Digital Certificates:Applied Internet Security*. 1999: Addison-Wesley.

13. "Port Numbers", *http://www.iana.org/assignments/port-numbers*,

14. Basagni, S., et al. *A distance routing effect algorithm for mobility (DREAM)*. in *Fourth Annual ACM/IEEE International Conference in Mobile Computing and Networking (MobiCom)*. 1998. Dellas,TX.

15. Buttyan, L. and J.-P. Hubaux, *Stimulating cooperation in self-organizing mobile ad hoc networks*. MONET Journal of Mobile Networks, 2002.

16. "Grasshopper - The Agent Platform", *http://www.grasshopper.de./*,

17. "Kaariboga Mobile Agents", *http://www.projectory.de/kaariboga/*,

18. Heaton, J., *Programming Spiders, Bots, and Aggregators in Java*. 2002: Richard Mills.

Scalable Location Management for Context-Aware Systems*

Jadwiga Indulska[1], Ted McFadden[2], Matthias Kind[2], and Karen Henricksen[1]

[1] School of Information Technology and Electrical Engineering
The University of Queensland, St Lucia QLD 4072 Australia
{jaga,karen}@itee.uq.edu.au
[2] CRC for Enterprise Distributed Systems Technology (DSTC)
The University of Queensland, St Lucia QLD 4072 Australia
{mcfadden,mkind}@dstc.edu.au

Abstract. Location information is commonly used in context-aware applications and pervasive systems. These applications and systems may require knowledge of the location of users, devices and services. This paper presents a location management system able to gather, process and manage location information from a variety of physical and virtual location sensors. The system scales to the complexity of context-aware applications, to a variety of types and large number of location sensors and clients, and to geographical size of the system. The proposed location management system provides conflict resolution of location information and mechanisms to ensure privacy.

1 Introduction

Pervasive/ubiquitous systems require context awareness to provide both a seamless computing infrastructure and adaptive context-aware applications to mobile users. Computing devices currently take many forms, from traditional mobile devices such as mobile phones and handheld computers, to networked home appliances, wearable computers and "smart items" (objects with embedded storage, computing and communication capabilities [1] which can create communities of smart items and can interact with other entities).

Pervasive systems need to deal with mobility of users, their devices and their applications and also with users who may want to change their computing device whilst running some computing applications. A pervasive computing infrastructure should allow users to move their computational tasks easily from one computing environment to another and should allow them to take advantage of the capabilities and resources of their current environment. As a result, pervasive systems have to be context-aware, i.e., aware of the state of the computing environment and also of the requirements and current state of computing applications. One type of context information is location information (e.g., the

---

* The work reported in this paper has been funded in part by the Co-operative Research Centre Program through the Department of Industry, Science and Tourism of the Commonwealth Government of Australia.

J.-B. Stefani, I. Demeure, and D. Hagimont (Eds.): DAIS 2003, LNCS 2893, pp. 224–235, 2003.

location of users, devices and services) which needs to be gathered from a variety of location sensors. The location information can be physical (e.g., location provided by a GPS device and a variety of other physical sensors), or virtual (e.g., a calendar application, camera reading, or IP address).

There are already many approaches to define location information, to track the location of users and devices, to manage such location information, and to utilize location information to support mobile users. Location management systems which gather and manage location information can be used for a variety of purposes and their complexity depends upon their purpose. Such systems are often used to provide users with information which is specific to user location (e.g. tourist guides [2]) or to support the delivery of personalized and location-sensitive information as in the BlueLocator project [3]. Location information can also be used as one of the elements of complex context information which supports pervasive/ubiquitous systems [4]. As pervasive systems are very complex and can use location information from a variety of sources and for a variety of purposes, gathering and managing location information is a challenging task. There are a variety of issues which need to be addressed in such systems, including: (i) types of location information (many sources and kinds of location information), (ii) location resolution and associated errors, (iii) resolution of conflicting location information, (iv) location information access and privacy (who can access location information and how can it be used), (v) architectures of location management systems, and (vi) integration of location management system with general context management in pervasive systems in a way which ensures scalability of the whole system.

In this paper we present a scalable location management system (LMS) which can deal with location information requests of various complexity from simple location services which deliver a reading from a single user location senor (e.g. GPS in a PDA) to a complex support of infrastructures in pervasive systems. The latter requires location information from a variety of sensors and therefore conflicting location information is possible and privacy issues need to be addressed. We describe the architecture of such a system and present our solution for the difficult issue of conflict resolution. We also show how a Platform For Privacy Preferences (P3P) [5] privacy approach has been integrated into our LMS to provide a manageable solution for defining privacy rules for location information.

The structure of this paper is as follows. Section 2 presents an overview of issues related to processing of location information, describes the architecture of our location management system and discusses the scalability of this system. Section 3 describes our solution for resolution of conflicting location information and compares this solution to the existing IBM approach for aggregation of location information. Section 4 shows the application of P3P for defining privacy rules for location information access and illustrates an extension to provide a user friendly mechanism for defining privacy policies. Section 5 concludes the paper.

2   Challenges in Location Management

2.1   Sources of Location Information

Location sensors can be physical or virtual. Physical location sensors provide information about the position of a physical device. Examples of devices are GPS receivers, mobile phones, passive and active badges, cameras used for face recognistion, magnetic-stripe cards and even simple barcodes. Physical location sensors can provide either position or proximity information. Position sensors attempt to provide the coordinates of a device relative to some coordinate system. Different sensors will have different resolutions and associated errors. Proximity sensors locate an entity or device as being within a region but cannot precisely position the device within that region. Region sizes may range from tens of centimeters (e.g. RFID passive tags) to tens of meters (e.g. Bluetooth and 802.11 cells) to hundreds of meters (e.g. mobile phone cells). Proximity sensors with overlapping detection regions can form the basis of position sensors (via triangulation or trilateration).

Virtual location sensors extract location information from virtual space, i.e. software applications, operating systems and networks. Sensor processes can monitor application events (a networked calendar system, travel booking, etc.), operating system events (monitoring keyboard or mouse use by a logged-in user, file server use, etc.) or network events (IP address, etc). The location readings from virtual sensors usually have to be combined with information from other sources (e.g. a database of the locations of fixed equipment like magnetic card readers or desktop computers) to infer physical location information.

2.2   Processing of Location Information

Sources of location information are heterogenous. Location sensor agents produce fragments of location information which differ in type, spatiotemporal characteristics (location, orientation, motion, time), resolution (i.e. level of accuracy), and data format - to list the most important differences. Sensor agents may have different policies governing when location information is reported.

The location information has to be gathered from sensors and reconciled, i.e., various types of location information about particular entities (e.g. users, devices, applications, and smart items) have to be compared and evaluated in order to compute the location of the entities. Therefore, the location information represented in formats specific for particular sensor types has to be transformed to a common format. Moreover, if the location readings provide conflicting information such conflicts have to be resolved. Conflicts which stem from differences in sensor resolutions are easy to resolve. There are, however, numerous conflicts which go beyond differences between position and proximity location sensors and also differences in resolution. If a user has many devices (e.g. mobile phone, PDA, laptop) which can provide physical location information and in addition the system is able to gather some virtual location information (e.g., from software agents interacting with the user) the location management system may need to deal with conflicting information and has to provide a means for resolution of such conflicts.

When processing location queries another important issue has to be addressed: privacy of location information. The importance of this issue is illustrated by the difficulties that many telecommunication companies currently have with providing location-based services and which now limit the provision of user location information to user's devices only.

2.3   Architecture and Scalability

Location management systems gather location information from many sources and process it to create the final representation available for a variety of clients. The location management systems developed so far for mobile distributed computing and location-based applications usually have a hierarchical architecture with the following layers: Application/Presentation Layer, Fusion Layer, Abstraction Layer, Reception Layer, and Sensor Layer [6]. The hierarchical architecture reflects the complex functionality of location management systems as shown in the following brief description of the functionality of particular layers:

Sensor Layer. The lowest level of the location management architecture is the Sensor Layer which represents the variety of physical and logical location sensor agents producing sensor-specific location information.

Reception Layer. The fragments of location information produced by sensor agents are delivered by the Reception Layer to the Abstraction Layer.

Abstraction Layer. This layer takes sensor-specific location information delivered by the Reception Layer and transforms it into a standard format. This layer needs to capture relationships between locations and their identifying features as it needs to associate attributes (eg. mobile cell identifiers) with physical places (for example, suburbs). The Abstraction Layer has to provide these transformations for both physical and virtual location information and needs to provide mappings between virtual (conceptual) and physical location information.

Fusion Layer. The Fusion Layer aggregates the location information gathered by the abstraction layer for a particular entity to provide a single, coherent location of the entity. If there are conflicts in the location information they should be resolved at this layer.

Application/Presentation Layer. This layer interacts with the variety of clients of the location management system and therefore needs to address several issues including access rights to location information (who can access the information and to what degree of accuracy), privacy of location information (how the location information can be used) and security of interactions between clients and the location management system.

Our location management system in general follows the above hierarchical architecture, however some solutions were introduced at particular layers to achieve our goal which is to provide a scalable location management system able to deal with conflicts of location information and ensure privacy of location information.

The issue of scalability of location management systems is important as these systems have to deal with the following challenges:

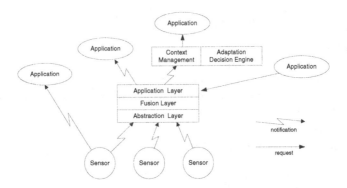

Fig. 1. Location Management Architecture.

1. Various levels of complexity of location applications from simple tourist guide applications using one location sensor (e.g. a PDA with a GPS sensor) where no aggregation of location information is needed, there is no conflict possible and no location information privacy issues are involved, to location information support for infrastructures of pervasive systems which evaluate context changes (including location changes) to make decisions about application and/or system adaptation to the changing context.
2. Potential large number of sensors and a large number of clients of the location management system.
3. Distribution of location management (users moving through domains).
4. Large number of updates of location information for moving objects.

There is a large body of research for the problem described in 4 coming from the database community, therefore we concentrate in this paper on the first three problems.

Various levels of complexity. As shown in the architecture of our LMS (Figure 1) simple applications can directly receive location information from the Sensor Layer, while other applications which require complex processing of location information are served by several layers.

Large number of sensors and clients. In our location management system we use a distributed notification service Elvin [7]. It provides the functionality of the Reception Layer as it forwards notifications between the Sensor Layer and the Abstraction Layer. The same notification system is used for delivering notifications about location changes between the Application Layer and the clients of the location management system unless a synchronous interaction is requested by an application. Elvin provides a scalable solution as it is able to cope with a large number of sensors and clients due to selective forwarding of messages. Different clients (users, applications, infrastructure of the pervasive system) may have different requirements with regard to mode of interaction (pull/push) and granularity of location information. For some clients, the pull mode (client/server) of interactions may be suitable as they need location information only when they request it. However, for other clients (e.g. infrastructure of pervasive systems) the push model (information about location is "pushed" to the client when the location information changes) is more appropriate. Our system allows either pull or push mode to be used for client interactions. As Elvin allows entities to register for notification about location changes and the granularity of this notification, this further increases the scalability of our solution. Figure 1 illustrates both the Reception Layer (Elvin) and the clients' interactions with the system.

In addition, location information is stored in a persistent repository in the Abstraction Layer. In our LMS this repository is a relational database. This allows aggregation of location information (Fusion Layer), including conflict resolution, to be performed on demand, in response to user queries, instead of each time new sensor data is received. There could be a great difference between the frequency of location updates from sensors and the frequency of location information requests from the clients of the location management system. Moreover, once a location is determined at the Fusion Layer it is cached as a complete location description which will be valid until another update pertaining to that entity is received at the Abstraction Layer. As a result, many requests for a single entity's location can be served without significantly increasing the cost of generating the location from individual location fragments if location information updates are not very frequent.

Distribution of LMS. As pervasive systems may be geographically large and have a heterogeneous computing and networking infrastructure, one of the scalability requirements is distribution of location managers in this infrastructure. Our location management system can be easily distributed due to the layered approach and the notification system used. Wide-area coverage can be achieved by deploying a number of managers implementing the Abstraction Layer which gather location information from geographically close sensors. Multiple Abstraction Managers can update a single Fusion Layer manager. The solution allows distribution of not only the Abstraction Layer but also the Fusion Layer and the Application/Presentation Layer. On the other hand, if a tracked entity moves a large distance from its home location management system, provision can be made for the creation of a visitor location profile in the Abstraction, Fusion and Application Managers at the new destination.

3   Conflict Resolution

The conflict resolution of location information has to take into account differences in resolution, time of location readings, confidence in readings, and relevance of readings to a particular entity. There already exists an algorithm [8], developed at IBM, which aggregates location readings from several sensing devices. For n location sensors D_i, $1 \leq i \leq n$, location readings are of the form $R_i = (C_i, T_i, L_i)$, where C_i is the "associative confidence" of device D_i, T_i is the timestamp of the location reading, and L_i is the location reading reported by D_i. The associative confidence is a probability that the device reporting a location is actually at the same location as the user being tracked. The confidence adopted for a given device depends upon whether it is moving or stationary, with the rationale being that a moving device generally has a higher probability of being located with its user than one that has been stationary for a long time. The algorithm sorts readings by timestamps (such that recent readings are viewed as more probable than those with older timestamps), then uses associative confidences to resolve conflicts between readings with similar timestamps.

The algorithm works reasonably well, if (i) all the location readings come from physical (position or proximity) sensors, (ii) sensor readings are frequent, and (iii) the readings are reasonably correct (i.e., the sensing device is actually located with the user). Let's assume that a user left a phone in a taxi (which is driven by somebody else), recently employed a swipe card to enter a room, and is now typing at a computer. There will be three location readings, originating from the swipe card, operating system and phone. Assuming that the timestamps of the readings are close, the associative confidence will be taken into account and the reading from the mobile phone will be erroneously selected.

It can be seen that the algorithm is not general enough to cope with physical and logical sensors and a variety of interaction types these sensors can have with a location management system. We argue that association confidence values should account for more than the mobility of the sensor. The keyboard is stationary but it is active which provides a high confidence in the reading. The phone is moving but it is not active (there were no recent calls), which should provide less confidence. Moreover, sensors like cameras or swipe cards provide location readings with some accuracy but the confidence of such readings is only high at time of the reading. To deal with these problems, our location management system defines different confidences for different types of sensors. The confidences for sensors are based on whether the sensor is (i) mobile and (ii) active (where active has a meaning depending on the sensor type).

Using timestamps as the main deciding factor in conflict resolution is also inappropriate in general location management systems. Some sensors produce notifications when a state changes (e.g. the operating system sends notifications when the user starts or stops using a keyboard), therefore the readings will be valid for a long time. In our approach, timestamps are only used to calculate confidence values for particular sensor readings and are not directly used to resolve the conflicts. A form of history is built into the algorithm, however, as sensors that are found to be producing incorrect readings are assigned a "diminished confidence" value. This implies that less weight is subsequently placed on their readings, until the readings are again found to be correct and the status is removed.

Our conflict resolution algorithm, shown in Figure 2, assumes that all location readings are mapped to a representation consisting of a set of coordinates and a resolution. The algorithm aggregates location readings into non-conflicting subsets, then performs conflict resolution amongst the subsets using confidence values. For each subset, a representative reading is selected; this is chosen as the reading with the smallest resolution, which is always fully contained in all of the other readings in the subset. Its confidence is calculated as the average of the

1. For each reading, compute its confidence as the product of the stationary/ mobile and active/non-active confidences of the corresponding sensor (unless the sensor has the "diminished confidence" value, in which case this value is adopted instead).
2. Compare each pair of location readings; if one reading is fully contained within the other, the readings are merged into a common subset for step 3.
3. For each subset of n consistent readings produced in step 2, compute a representative reading as follows:
   - The coordinates and resolution of the reading possessing the best (smallest) resolution are adopted.
   - The confidence for the representative reading is computed as the average of the confidence values for the group, adjusted according to the cardinality of the group. If the confidence values for the group are $c_1, ..., c_n$, this is:

$$1 - \frac{\sum_{i=1}^{n} 1 - c_i}{n^2}$$

4. The representative readings produced in step 3 are ranked by confidence, and the reading with the highest confidence selected as the result.
5. The "diminished confidence" value is set for sensors that produced readings conflicting with the reading chosen at 4, and is removed (if necessary) for sensors that produced consistent readings.

Fig. 2. Conflict resolution algorithm.

confidences for the set, adjusted to account for cardinality such that larger sets of consistent readings are assigned higher confidences. Finally, the representative readings are ordered by confidence. If there is only one subset, its representative reading is chosen as the correct reading; otherwise, the reading with the highest confidence is selected.

As the conflict resolution algorithm is applied dynamically during location queries, efficiency is crucial. Our algorithm completes in $O(n^2)$ time, where n is the number of location readings that need to be resolved. As only the most recent reading from each sensor is considered, n is bounded by the number of distinct location sensors that can be used to track a given individual, and is therefore small. When evaluated against sample data sets, the algorithm performs efficiently with high accuracy, and we aim to further improve the accuracy by exploiting historical data (past movements of the object being tracked) to resolve readings with similar confidence values.

4   Privacy

Privacy is extremely important to individuals and is reflected in the adoption of very strict privacy laws is many countries [9]. Protection of location information from unauthorized use is paramount to the success of emerging location-based services. The problem of maintaining location privacy will become greater in

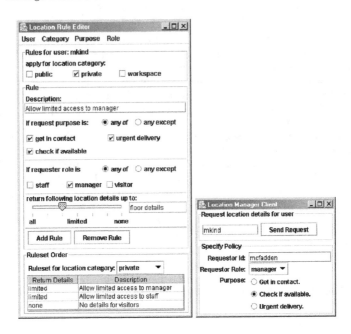

(a) Location Privacy Editor   (b) Query Interface

Fig. 3. User Interfaces.

future pervasive systems as the number of sensors and services that can infer a user's location increases dramatically.

Location management systems are presented with the challenge of incorporating privacy protection at the Application Layer while still allowing users to release location information to trusted service providers in a controlled and accountable fashion. As a precursor to privacy, basic security must be provided. At a minimum, location information exchange must be encrypted and service clients must be authenticated. Key policies that a location manager must address for privacy are:

- *request policy* (which allow a client to define the purposes for which requested location information will be used); and
- *access control policy* (which allow a provider to define under what context access to location information will be granted and what location detail will be provided).

There are no comprehensive solutions for location access control and privacy protection in pervasive systems as yet. The P3P initiative is a promising approach to providing privacy for users accessing web resources. P3P defines an XML based policy language allowing web services to define how potentially sensitive information collected from clients will be used, and a mechanism for user agents to retrieve these policies. The related P3P Preference Exchange Language

```
<RULESET xmlns="http://www.w3.org/2001/02/APPELv1"
         xmlns:p3p="http://www.w3.org/2000/12/P3Pv1">
  <RULE behavior="limited" description="Allow limited access to manager.">
    <p3p:POLICY><p3p:STATEMENT>
      <p3p:RECIPIENT connective="or">
        <p3p:same>manager</p3p:same></p3p:RECIPIENT>
      <p3p:PURPOSE connective="or">
        <p3p:other-purpose>get in contact</p3p:other-purpose>
        <p3p:other-purpose>urgent delivery</p3p:other-purpose>
        <p3p:other-purpose>check if available</p3p:other-purpose>
      </p3p:PURPOSE>
    </p3p:STATEMENT></p3p:POLICY>
  </RULE>
</RULESET>
```

Fig. 4. Generated APPEL Privacy Ruleset.

1.0 (APPEL1.0) [10] defines a policy language which allows users to specify privacy preferences in rule-sets. A browser or other user agent then uses the APPEL rule-sets to evaluate the acceptability of web service P3P policies.

In our location management system we use P3P (and APPEL) to provide mechanisms ensuring privacy of location information. Each location request is accompanied by a P3P policy. This policy may be static or dynamically generated by a client agent. Upon receiving a location query, the location manager evaluates the query and the accompanying P3P policy using the appropriate APPEL preferences based on the user's current context. Based on the APPEL evaluation the request is either satisfied, denied, or partially satisfied (i.e., the returned location information is generalized.) Other systems addressing privacy in the pervasive space are also based on P3P [11,12]. Our early experience with applying P3P to location information yielded mixed results:

- It was possible to use P3P to define location request policy, and APPEL rule-sets for access control.
- However, the use of generic P3P policy / XML editors [13,14] made the generation of location related policies and preferences non-intuitive and dificult for users.

To address usability issues related to the definition of privacy policy (for both request and access control) we developed domain specific user interfaces at the Application Layer that dynamically generate P3P policies and preferences.

Figure 3 (a) illustrates the user location privacy policy editor. The editor allows the definition of context sensitive privacy rules. A user may specify different privacy rules for different location zones. For example, a *public* zone would be an office lobby and a *private* zone, a restroom. For rule definition, the role of the requesting agent is considered (visitor, staff, manager). Finally, the level of location detail returned in a given situation can be adjusted. Figure 4 shows one of the compact APPEL rule-sets automatically generated from the GUI illustrated in Figure 3 (a). In the current implementation, the detail of location

```
<POLICIES xmlns="http://www.w3.org/2002/01/P3Pv1">
  <POLICY discuri="disclaimer.html" opturi="opt-in-out.html">
    <ENTITY>...</ENTITY>
    <ACCESS><nonident/></ACCESS>
    <STATEMENT>
      <PURPOSE><other-purpose>check if available</other-purpose></PURPOSE>
      <RECIPIENT><same>role=manager;user=mcfadden</same></RECIPIENT>
      <RETENTION><no-retention/></RETENTION>
    </STATEMENT>
  </POLICY>
</POLICIES>
```

Fig. 5. Generated Policy.

information returned is determined by the resultant APPEL behavior (block, limited, request) and context sensitive post-processing by the location manager. In the future this will be enhanced by defining location detail categories in the APPEL rule *persona* attribute. This will allow a more granular approach to location detail control using APPEL itself.

An application specific P3P policy generator was also implemented for a simple location client, allowing one user to query the location of another (Figure 3 (b)). The interface is simple, leaves little room for error, and dynamically generates a P3P policy (Figure 5) for each location query.

Our approach transforms a manual and cumbersome preparation of policies and preferences for location information into a dynamic generation of such policies and preferences from simple user GUIs.

5   Conclusions

The proliferation of mobile devices has created a demand for location-based services. There is a large body of research on the basic issues of location-based computing: technologies for location sensors, location determination for mobile devices, location representation formats, and early approaches to aggregation of location information (conflict resolution). In this paper we presented the architecture and functionality of a location management system, which is able to support not only location-aware applications using a limited number of sensors, but can also be used as a part of the infrastructure of large scale pervasive systems. In the latter case, the location management system feeds location information into a more comprehensive context management system. Such location management systems are very complex due to the enormous variety of physical and virtual location sensors, very large scale (in terms of sensors and entities supported by the system), high probability of conflicts in location information and complex location access and privacy rules. The location management system which we have developed and integrated with our infrastructure for pervasive systems allows either asynchronous or synchronous interactions between clients and the location management system, scales to large numbers of sensors and clients, and allows a geographical distribution of the location management system. The algorithm for the resolution of conflicting location information developed for this system has low computational complexity and provides highly accurate results on a variety of sample location data. The system uses P3P and APPEL as mechanisms for supporting privacy of location information and provides a user friendly interface for automatic generation of privacy policies and preferences.

References

1. Beigl, M., Gellersen, H., Schmidt, A.: Mediacups: Experience with design and use of computer-augmented everyday artefacts. Computer Networks,Special Issue on Pervasive Computing **35** (2001) 401–409
2. Cheverest, K., Davies, N., Mitchell, K., Friday, A., Efstratiou, C.: Developing a context-aware electronic tourist guide: some issues and experiences. In: Proceedings of the Conference on Human Factors and Computing Systems. (2000)
3. Chen, Y., X.Chen, Ding, X., Rao, F., Liu, D.: Bluelocator: Enabling enterprise location-based services. In: Proceedings of the Third International Conference on Mobile Data Management, IEEE Computer Society (2002)
4. Henricksen, K., Indulska, J., Rakotonirainy, A.: Modeling context information in pervasive computing systems. In: Proceedings of The First International Conference on Pervasive Computing, Pervasive 2002. Volume 2414 of Lecture Notes in Computer Science., Zurich, Switzerland, Springer (2002) 169–180
5. Cranor, L., Langheinrich, M., Marchiori, M., Reagle, J.: The platform for privacy preferences 1.0 (P3P1.0) specification. http://www.w3.org/TR/P3P/ (2002) W3C Recommendation.
6. Leonhardt, U.: Supporting Location-Awareness in Open Distributed Systems. PhD Thesis, Imperial College, London (1998)
7. Segal, B., Arnold, D., Boot, J., Henderson, M., Phelps, T.: Content based routing with elvin4. In: Proceedings of the AUUG2K Conference. (2000)
8. Myllymaki, J., Edlund, S.: Location aggregation from multiple sources. In: Proceedings of the Third International·Conference on Mobile Data Management, IEEE Computer Society (2002)
9. Beinat, E.: Privacy and location-based services. Geo Informatics (2001) http://www.geoinformatics.com/issueonline/issues/2001/09_2001/pdf_09_20%01/14_17_euro.pdf.
10. Langheinrich, M., Cranor, L., Marchiori, M.: A P3P Preference Exchange Language (APPEL 1.0). http://www.w3.org/TR/P3P-preferences/ (2002) W3C Working Draft.
11. Langheinrich, M.: A privacy awareness system for ubiquitous computing environments. In Borriello, G., Holmquist, L., eds.: 4th International Conference on Ubiquitous Computing (UbiComp2002). Number 2498 in LNCS, Springer-Verlag (2002) 237–245
12. Myles, G., Friday, A., Davies, N.: Preserving privacy in environments with location based applications. IEEE Pervasive Computing **2** (2003) 56–64
13. IBM Corporation: P3P Policy Editor (2002) http://www.alphaworks.ibm.com/tech/p3peditor.
14. Joint Research Center European Commission: JRC P3P APPEL Privacy Preference Editor (2002) http://p3p.jrc.it/downloadP3P.php.

CoOL: A Context Ontology Language to Enable Contextual Interoperability

Thomas Strang[1], Claudia Linnhoff-Popien[2], and Korbinian Frank[2]

[1] German Aerospace Center (DLR), Oberpfaffenhofen, Germany
thomas.strang@dlr.de
[2] Ludwig-Maximilians-University (LMU), Munich, Germany
{linnhoff,frank}@informatik.uni-muenchen.de

Abstract. This paper describes a context modelling approach using *ontologies* as a formal fundament. We introduce our *Aspect-Scale-Context (ASC) model* and show how it is related to some other models. A *Context Ontology Language (CoOL)* is derived from the model, which may be used to enable context-awareness and contextual interoperability during service discovery and execution in a proposed distributed system architecture. A core component of this architecture is a reasoner which infers conclusions about the context based on an ontology built with CoOL.

1 Introduction

The trend towards pervasive computing [1] is driving a need for services and service architectures that are aware of the *context* of the different actors (any user, any service provider and even the environment or third parties) involved in a service interaction. For instance, context information (for definition of terminology see section 2) can be used to reduce the amount of required user interaction, as well as to improve the user interface of small mobile devices such as mobile phones [2], which are typical for pervasive computing scenarios. A key accessor to context information in any context-aware system is a well designed model to describe contextual facts and contextual interrelationships. Several approaches from the early days of modelling the context typically lack formality and are primarily concerned with requirements for the model from the customer perspective. More recent proposals such as [3] try to countersteer the lack of formality by introducing a graphical oriented approach to model contextual interrelationships. The context modelling approach introduced in this paper tries to close the formality gap by using *ontologies* [4] as a fundament to describe contextual facts and interrelationships. Particularly, this allows to determine service interoperability on the context level [5].

This paper is organized as follows: In section 2 we will introduce our ASC model after giving a motivation why we make use of ontologies as a fundament of our model. Section 3 shows how our ASC model can be used as transfer model for other proposed context models, considering a graphical context model as an example. In section 4 we propose a way how to plug in our ASC model

J.-B. Stefani, I. Demeure, and D. Hagimont (Eds.): DAIS 2003, LNCS 2893, pp. 236–247, 2003.
© IFIP International Federation for Information Processing 2003

into DAML-S. A context extension of a well established general purpose service model shown in section 5 motivates the design of our system architecture in section 6. Because relevance is more than just spatial and temporal proximity, we describe our approach of expressing relevance criteria in section 7, before we summarize our paper with a conclusion in section 8.

2 Model

Because of the fact that the terms *context* etc. in current publications are used in various ways it is necessary to define the terminology we use. The following is a short reflection of our terminlogy used throughout this paper, a more comprehensive introduction to this terminology can be found in [5]: A *context information* is any information which can be used to characterize the state of an entity concerning a specific aspect. An *entity* is a person, a place or in general an object. An *aspect* is a classification, symbol- or value-range, whose subsets are a superset of all reachable states, grouped in one or more related dimensions called *scales*. A *context* is the set of all context information characterizing the entities relevant for a specific task in their relevant aspects. An *entity is relevant* for a specific task, if its state is characterized at least concerning one relevant aspect. An *aspect is relevant*, if the state with respect to this aspect is accessed during a specific task or the state has any kind of influence on the task. A system is *context aware*, if it uses any kind of context information before or during service provisioning. The *situation* is the set of all known context information. These definitions are very similar to other definitions of context (e.g. [6,7,8]), but refine the expressiveness by introducing the terminology of an *aspect*, which is discussed in detail in section 2.2.

2.1 Ontologies and the Context Ontology Language

When dealing with context information it is always a challenge to describe contextual facts and interrelationships in a *precise* and *traceable* manner. For instance, to perform the task "print document on printer near to me", it is required to have a precise definition of terms used in the task, particularly what "near" means to "me". It is highly desirable, that each participating party in a service interaction shares the same interpretation of the data exchanged and the meaning "behind" it (so called *shared understanding*). This is done in our approach by the use of *ontologies* [4]. Ontologies seem to be well suited to store the knowledge concerning context.

An ontology is a specification of a conceptualization [9]. The term "ontology" itself is borrowed from philosophy, where it has a long history in refering to the subject of existence. In IT systems, ontologies are used to express the more or less complete knowledge about concepts (classes of subjects) and their attributes, as well as their interrelationships. Ontologies may be stored at different places and created by different authors, which offers the amount of flexibility and extensibility we need in distributed systems. The merging of different ontology fragments is one of the main tasks of a *reasoner*, which is called *inference engine* if it infers knowledge from symbolically coded axioms. A reasoner may be queried via some query language to deliver instances and their values, as well as concept and attribute names based on the ontologies known to the reasoner. A reasoner may also be used to validate consistency (within one ontology, but also with respect to related ones), and to assert inter-ontology relationships and "complete" the ontologies by computing implicit hierarchies and relationships based on given rules. One of the most advanced inference engines is the *OntoBroker* system [10], which we used to evaluate most of the inferencing issues during our research.

There have been proposed several languages designed for or being even able to describe ontologies in recent years. We analysed several ontology specification and query languages with a focus of the following two questions:

1. How well is the language capable to describe concepts, attributes and relations in a precise and traceable manner? (knowledge representation)
2. How well is the language capable to create effective queries towards the reasoner? (knowledge querying)

We found out, that any of the analysed languages which has advantages w.r.t. the first question has disadvantages w.r.t. the second one and vice versa. With this background we defined our *Context Ontology Language (CoOL)* not as a single, monolithic language. Instead, it is a collection of several fragments, grouped into two subsets.

The first subset, *CoOL Core*, is a projection of our model, which will be introduced in section 2.2, into two (three) different common ontology languages:

- OWL and DAML+OIL, which are both part of the Semantic Web's [11] ontology languages based on XML and RDF/S. See figure 2 on how *CoOL Core* is related to the Semantic Web stack. Because OWL is the successor of DAML+OIL covering nearly the same issues, we will use the term OWL as a representative for both languages in the reminder of this paper unless stated otherwise.
- F-Logic [12], which is a logic language combining object-oriented and predicate logic characteristics not based on XML.

The second subset, *CoOL Integration*, is a collection of schema and protocol extensions as well as common subconcepts of the model introduced in the next section, enabling the use of *CoOL Core* in several service frameworks, particulary Web Services. This paper deals mainly with *CoOL Core* and the model it is based on, whereas *CoOL Integration* is somewhat out of the focus of this paper.

Having a projection of the model in multiple ontology languages enables the following proposed procedure: For the knowledge representation issues, a developer may use any of the languages which seems to be adequate, e.g. using OWL because of the wide range of available tools helping to create and/or validate ontology fragments, or using F-Logic because of its object-oriented, compact syntax or its rule based extensibility. For knowledge querying issues, we preferred to use the *OntoBroker* inference engine, most notably because it supports F-Logic as knowledge representation *and* knowledge query language. This decision requires any knowledge not represented in F-Logic to be converted into F-Logic first, but this is no real disadvantage, because most other major reasoners have a similar requirement. This conversion is possible as long as the features of OWL in use do not exceed a certain subset (OWL-DL), as Borgida showed in [13]. F-Logic is more expressive than OWL, can be used as query language as well, and is much more appropriate for specifying *relevance conditions* (see section 7).

2.2 Our ASC Model

Our *Aspect-Scale-Context (ASC)* model is named after the core concepts of the model, which are *aspect, scale* and *context information*, see figure 1. Each *aspect* aggregates one or more *scales*, and each *scale* aggregates one or more *context information*. These core concepts are interrelated via *hasAspect, hasScale* and *constructedBy* relations.

Fig. 1. Aspect-Scale-Context (ASC) Model.

As anchored in the definitions at the beginning of the section, an aspect is a set of one or more related scales. Likewise, any aspect is a dimension of the situation space, being used as a collective term for information objects having the same semantic type.

A scale is an unordered set of objects defining the range of valid context information. In other words, a valid context information with respect to an aspect is one of the elements of the aspect's scales. For instance the aspect "GeographicCo-ordinateAspect" may have two scales, "WGS84Scale" and "GaussKruegerScale", and a valid context information may be an object instance created in an object oriented programming language such as Java with new `GaussKruegerCoordi-`nate("367032", "533074"). Scales based on primitive datatypes such as scalars instead of objects are captured by corresponding wrapper classes. Thus a valid context information of the aspect "SpatialDistanceAspect" with the given scales "MeterScale" and "KilometerScale" may be an object instance created with new `Integer(10)`.

On an abstract level, context information may be seen as content data complemented by some meta data characterizing the content data. Each context information has an associated scale defining the range of valid instances of that type of context information. Context information characterizing the content of another context information is a meta information and thus a context information of higher order and expresses the quality of the lower order context information, see figure 3. *CoOL Integration* includes already a set of standard quality aspects such as a *minimumError*, a *meanError* and or a *timestamp*, but any other kind of context information characterizing the quality of another context information may be assigned to the context information of interest using the *hasQuality* property of the ASC model.

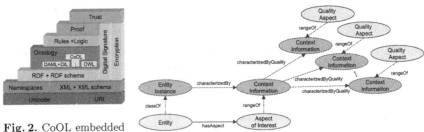

Fig. 2. CoOL embedded inside the Semantic Web stack.

Fig. 3. Context Information being an Entity itself.

As mentioned, scales are sets of context information. Each scale is constructed by one class of context information such as "WGS84Coordinate" and "Gauss-KruegerCoordinate" in the example of the last subsection. All scales within one aspect are constrained by the ASC model in a way, that there must exist a mapping function from one scale to at least one other of the already existing scales of the same aspect. This function is called *IntraOperation*, see figure 4.

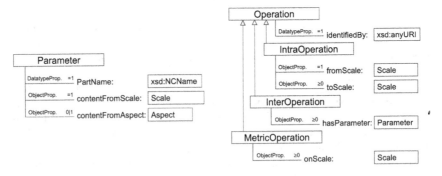

Fig. 4. Operations.

Like that, it is possible to access every scale from every other scale of the same aspect by a series of IntraOperations. In other words, a new scale of an aspect may be constructed by providing an IntraOperation from an existing scale. This allows to build multiple related scales by providing different Intra-Operations representing different scaling factors ("nautical miles", "km" or "m" for a "SpatialDistanceAspect" aspect). Depending on where the IntraOperation is specified (at the source scale or at the destination scale), the corresponding property *toScale* or *fromScale* has to be set.

Scales which require access to scales of one or more other aspects can be defined using *InterOperations*, see also figure 4. An example for such a scale would be "KilometerPerHourScale" of a "SpeedAspect" aspect. This scale can be defined using an InterOperation with two *Parameter*, delta_s and delta_t, where the parameter delta_s is from an aspect "SpatialDistanceAspect" and delta_t is from an aspect "DurationAspect".

Due to the fact that each scale is an *unordered set* of context information instance objects, there may be no relative sort order between the context information inherently given. Therefore we introduced the *MetricOperation* which may be used to compare two context information instance objects of the same scale in an implementation-defined manner to see if they match or what their relative sort order is by returning either the first or the second parameter. Thus the return value indicates the ordering of the two objects.

Information about the signature of any InterOperation, IntraOperation or MetricOperation is available in the signature specification pointed to with the property *identifiedBy*, e.g. an operation within a WSDL file or an AtomicProcess within a DAML-S grounding [14].

3   Transfer Model

The ASC model may be used as transfer model to employ the knowledge expressed in other context models. A good example is the nicely designed graphics oriented context model introduced in [3] by Henricksen et al., which is a context extension to the Object-Role Modelling (ORM) approach. In ORM, the basic modelling concept is the *fact*, and the modelling of a domain using ORM involves identifying appropriate fact types and the roles that entity types play in these.

Henricksen extended ORM to allow fact types to be categorised, according to their persistence and source, either as *static* (facts that remain unchanged as long as the entities they describe persist) or as *dynamic*. The latter ones are further distinguished depending on the source of the facts as either *profiled*, *sensed* or *derived* types. Using our ASC model, facts can be modelled as context information. In doing so, Henricksen's classification can be mapped by introducing a quality aspect consisting of the scale with the elements {static, dynamic profiled, dynamic sensed and dynamic derived}, which may be used to characterize any context information in a quality sense. Henricksen's quality indicators may be directly mapped to some quality aspect, similar to her history fact types, which may be addressed with a timestamp and/or time period quality aspect, which are both already basic aspects in CoOL. The last extension to ORM made by Henricksen for context modelling purposes are fact dependencies, which represent a special type of relationship between facts, where a change in one fact leads automatically to a change in another fact: the *dependsOn* relation. This behaviour is expressed in the ASC model by the existence of one or more corresponding Intra/InterOperations between the scales a pair of context information is based on each. Here our model is even more expressive, because it allows to specify exactly the kind of dependency. This example shows the potential of the ASC model to be used as transfer model for other context model approaches.

4   Relation to DAML-S

In the framework of the Semantic Web there has been done some serious effort in designing technologies that allow to discover, invoke, compose and monitor web resources. Among them there has been created an *ontology of services* called *DAML-S* [14], which can be used to create computer-interpretable descriptions of services from multiple perspectives. Within DAML-S three essential types of knowledge about a service have been identified: *ServiceProfile*, *ServiceModel* and *ServiceGrounding*.

Some selected elements of the current version of DAML-S find a corresponding counterpart in our Context Ontology Language. For instance, the non-functional attribute *geographicRadius* of a DAML-S ServiceProfile may be expressed as a context information based on an aspect *scope*, which is one of the default aspects within CoOL, whereas the non-functional attribute *qualityRating* may be mapped to some quality aspect. DAML-S covers only a few contextual aspects, and their specification is not very formal. To have a much more formal and thus computer-interpretable approach to describe the contextual requirements and impact of a service, we suppose to extend DAML-S with a fourth type of knowledge about a service, dealing with the contextual issues.

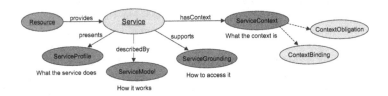

Fig. 5. DAML-S with Context Extension.

This new perspective (we call it *ServiceContext*, see figure 5) may serve as a more formal description of a service's contextual interoperability by providing a comprehensive but extensible model based on the ASC model. The obligations of a service w.r.t. the context of its usage (e.g. the geographic scope "delivery area" covered by the service with respect to a well defined aspect "region") can be expressed in a *ContextObligation* submodel. Another submodel *ContextBinding* may be used to establish a virtual link from some input or output parameter of an *AtomicProcess* of a *ServiceGrounding* to a specific aspect, enabling automatic determination of valid or even optimal parameters.

5   MNM Service Model and the Context Extension

The Munich Network Management (MNM) team introduced in [15] a generic model of commonly needed service-related terms, concepts and structuring rules to describe a service from different perspectives (e.g. service view vs. implementation view). Their model is intended to analyze, identify and structure the necessary actors and the corresponding inter- and intra-organizational associations between these actors. In this model the actors are grouped in either the *customer domain*, or the *service provider domain*. Structural elements which cannot be associated to any of these two domains are called *side independent*. In the model's *service view* these elements "build" the service in an abstract manner, thus prefer to call this set of elements the *abstract service*.

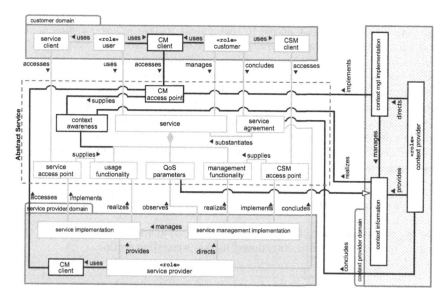

Fig. 6. Service Model with emphazised Context Extension (MNMplusCE).

The MNM service model has been designed primarily with network management tasks and carrier services in mind. But due to the level of abstraction this model can be applied to highlevel (non-carrier) services perfectly. Moreover, the model fits direct service usage approaches (client ↔ server) as well as intermediate service usage approaches (client ↔ middleware ↔ server). In the latter one a middleware component "fulfills" an abstract service, i.e. it behaves like a client towards the service provider domain, and behaves like a service provider towards the service customer domain by providing at least a service access point.

To be able to describe contextual dependencies and issues of context provisioning with the model in a similiar and consistent way, we extended the MNM service model with a *context provider domain* (see figure 6 on the right). This domain groups the actors responsible to manage the context observation, context processing and delivery as context information.

The context provider is not yet another service provider. Its extraordinary position is caused by, among others, the fact of being involved as a third party service provider in an interaction between the customer domain and a set of service provider domains simultaneously. The context management implementation offers a context management access point (CMAP) to give access to the context to both other domains in the model (customer domain and service provider domain) to enable context-aware services and context-aware service usage. A service client, a service provider or even a middleware component may determine the entities relevant for a specific task by an interface provided by the CMAP, which causes the associated context management implementation to deliver context information in an adequate manner.

The context management implementation offers a *context management access point (CMAP)* to give access to the context to both other domains in the model (customer domain and service provider domain) to enable context-aware services and context-aware service usage. A service client, a service provider or even a middleware component may determine the entities relevant for a specific task through an interface provided by the CMAP, which causes the associated context management implementation to deliver context information in an adequate manner. In the latter we refer to this contextual extended MNM service model as *MNMplusCE service model*. In this model, carrier services are a specialized derivative of highlevel services, and the Quality-of-Service (QoS) parameters describing a service instance are derived from context information in the model.

6   System Architecture

The overall architecture of our system is shown in figure 7, with a focus on the context provider domain as introduced in the preceeding section.

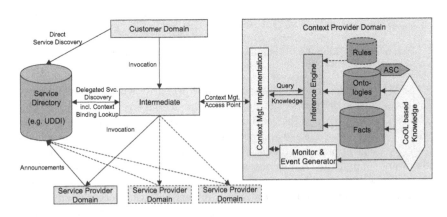

Fig. 7. System Architecture.

This architecture enables the Intermediate as a middleware component to "fulfill" an abstract service (see section 5), in particular it behaves like a client towards the service provider domain, and behaves like a service provider towards the service customer domain. By resolving the binding between the parameters of a service call and information from a context provider (*context binding*) at runtime, the intermediate is a central component in our architecture to enable context-awareness.

The context management implementation inside the context provider domain implements the context management access point (CMAP) interface and is responsible for the mapping to the query language (e.g. F-Logic) used to query the inference engine (e.g. OntoBroker). This engine is feeded with knowledge from different sources, specifying knowledge as conclusions from ontologies and facts based on those ontologies. Due to the fact that our ASC model is one of the base ontologies, the inference engine is able to determine knowledge about entities, aspects, scales and context information as desired for our purpose.

Any party interested in asynchronous notification about specific context conditions ("notify me when I am near the restrooms") may register with the context provider with a corresponding condition statement via the CMAP. The context provider is responsible for re-checking these conditions each time a part of the condition statement is affected by a change in the knowledge base.

7   Relevance

As mentioned we consider an entity as relevant for a specific task, if its state is characterized at least concerning one relevant aspect. Consequently we considered an aspect as relevant, if the state with respect to this aspect is accessed during a specific task or the state has any kind of influence on the task. The separation between customer domain, service provider domain and context provider domain in the MNMplusCE service model (see section 5) makes it necessary to declare the task-specific relevance towards the task-independent context provider domain through the CMAP. In other words, by specifying relevance conditions an abstract context-aware service becomes a concrete context-aware service.

We distinguish between external and internal relevance, depending on the domain of relevance determination. If the relevance of an entity is identified outside the context provider domain, e.g. at the customer domain, we call this an external relevance. In this case the other domain advises the context provider domain through the CMAP to a specific entity by an entity identifier, and the context provider delivers context information assigned to that entity. An example for an external relevance is a service client identifying an entity representing its own device. By sending this entity representative to the context provider domain, the context management implementation may be able to determine the current position of the client device by some sensor, and deliver an adequate context information to the service client, which uses this information while invoking the service implementation.

In contrast, if the relevance of an entity is identified in the context provider domain itself, we call this an internal relevance. It is essential to enable the context provider domain to determine internal relevance of one or more entities by providing some relevance condition.

A relevance condition is a filter, which can be used at several levels to identify one or more relevant entities out of the set of all known entities in the context provider domain. A first level filter specifies only an aspect of interest (e.g. "get all entities where you know something about the aspect *place*"). The corresponding F-Logic query would be similar to

```
FORALL E,C,S <-
    C:"urn:cool"#ContextInformation AND C["urn:cool"#characterizes->E] AND
    C["urn:cool"#hasScale->>S] AND S["urn:cool"#hasAspect->>"urn:aspects"#Place].
```

A second level filter specifies a condition about the context information based on the aspect of interest (e.g. "get all entities where you know that the current state with respect to the aspect *place* is *near*"). The corresponding F-Logic query would be similar to

```
FORALL E,C,S,V <-
    C:"urn:cool"#ContextInformation AND C["urn:cool"#characterizes->E] AND
    C["urn:cool"#hasScale->>S] AND S["urn:cool"#hasAspect->>"urn:aspects"#Place] AND
    C["urn:cool"#hasValue->V] AND equal(V,"urn:dist"#Near).
```

A third level filter specifies a condition about the quality based on the aspect of quality of a context information based on the aspect of interest (e.g. "get all entities where you know that the current state with respect to the aspect *place* is *near* and that information with respect to the quality aspect *age of information* is *less than or equal to 10 seconds*"). The corresponding F-Logic query would be similar to

```
FORALL E,C1,C2,S1,S2,V1,V2 <-
    C1:"urn:cool"#ContextInformation AND C1["urn:cool"#characterizes->E] AND
    C1["urn:cool"#hasScale->>S] AND S1["urn:cool"#hasAspect->>"urn:aspects"#Place] AND
    C1["urn:cool"#hasValue->V1] AND equal(V1,"urn:ci"#Near) AND
    C1["urn:cool"#hasQuality->>C2] AND C2["urn:cool"#hasScale->>S2] AND
    S2["urn:cool"#hasAspect->>"urn:aspects"#Age] AND C2["urn:cool"#hasValue->V2] AND
    lessorequal(V2,10).
```

Figure 3 on page 240 also illustrates the distinction between the levels visually. Note that the context information characterising an entity w.r.t. the aspect of interest is treated as an entity instance itself when characterized w.r.t. some quality aspect. The party specifying the relevance condition may be interested in the respective context information instead of the entities characterized by these context information. Thus the context provider may offer two separate functions to distinguish between them. The modification of the F-Logic query would be as easy as deleting the variable "E" in the FORALL part and any partial term containing the "E".

8   Conclusion and Outlook

In the previous sections we introduced the ASC model as a base model to express how some context information can be used to characterize the state of an entity concerning a specific aspect. A high degree of formality has been reached by using ontologies as a fundament for the model, which guarantees good automatic interpretation capabilities of an implementation of the model. We showed, how the ASC model fits into a general purpose service model where we made a context extension, making any service interaction based on that model context-aware. In our proposed system architecture the ontology reasoner is employed to determine interrelationship dependencies and relevance conditions, which may affect a service interaction at any stage. It became very clear that we consider relevance to be more than just spatial and temporal proximity. Finally we showed how our model can be used as transfer model by means of a specific example, and how it is related to DAML-S. Further work has to be done to complete the latter one when the DAML-S specification itself is officially released and stable.

References

1. Satyanarayanan, M.: Pervasive computing: Vision and challenges. IEEE Personal Communications (2001) 10–17
2. Strang, T.: Towards autonomous context-aware services for smart mobile devices. In Chen, M.S., Chrysanthis, P.K., Sloman, M., Zaslavsky, A., eds.: LNCS 2574: Proceedings of the 4th International Conference on Mobile Data Management (MDM2003). Lecture Notes in Computer Science (LNCS), Melbourne/Australia, Springer (2003) 279–293
3. Henricksen, K., Indulska, J., Rakotonirainy, A.: Generating context management infrastructure from high-level context models. In: Industrial Track Proceedings of the 4th International Conference on Mobile Data Management (MDM2003), Melbourne/Australia (2003) 1–6
4. Uschold, M., Grüninger, M.: Ontologies: Principles, methods, and applications. Knowledge Engineering Review **11** (1996) 93–155
5. Strang, T., Linnhoff-Popien, C.: Service interoperability on context level in ubiquitous computing environments. In: Proceedings of International Conference on Advances in Infrastructure for Electronic Business, Education, Science, Medicine, and Mobile Technologies on the Internet (SSGRR2003w), L'Aquila/Italy (2003)
6. Dey, A.K.: Understanding and using context. Personal and Ubiquitous Computing, Special issue on Situated Interaction and Ubiquitous Computing **5** (2001)
7. Schmidt, A., Laerhoven, K.V.: How to build smart appliances. IEEE Personal Communications (2001)
8. Schilit, W.N.: A System Architecture for Context-Aware Mobile Computing. PhD thesis, Columbia University (1995)
9. Gruber, T.G.: A translation approach to portable ontologies. Knowledge Acquisition **5** (1993) 199–220
10. Decker, S., Erdmann, M., Fensel, D., Studer, R.: Ontobroker: Ontology based access to distributed and semi-structured information. In et al., R.M., ed.: Semantic Issues in Multimedia Systems, Boston/USA, Kluwer Academic Publisher (1999) 351–369
11. Barners-Lee, T., Hendler, J., Lassila, O.: The semantic web. Scientific American **284** (2001) 34–43
12. Kifer, M., Lausen, G., Wu, J.: Logical foundations of object-oriented and frame-based languages. ACM **42** (1995) 741–834
13. Borgida, A.: On the relative expressiveness of description logics and predicate logics. Artificial Intelligence **82** (1996) 353–367
14. Ankolekar, A., Burstein, M., Hobbs, J.R., Lassila, O., Martin, D.L., McIlraith, S.A., Narayanan, S., Paolucci, M., Payne, T., Sycara, K., Zeng, H.: Daml-s: Semantic markup for web services. In: Proceedings of the International Semantic Web Workshop. (2001)
15. Garschhammer, M., Hauck, R., Kempter, B., Radisic, I., Roelle, H., Schmidt, H.: The MNM Service Model — Refined Views on Generic Service Management. Journal of Communications and Networks **3** (2001) 297–306

Discovering Web Services Using Behavioural Constraints and Ontology

Natenapa Sriharee and Twittie Senivongse

Department of Computer Engineering
Chulalongkorn University
Phyathai Road, Pathumwan, Bangkok 10330 Thailand
Tel. +66 2 2186991 Fax. +66 2 2186955
natenapa.s@student.chula.ac.th, twittie.s@chula.ac.th

Abstract. The ability to locate useful on-line Web Services is becoming critical for today's service-oriented business applications. A number of efforts have been put to enhance the service discovery process by using conceptualised knowledge, called ontology, of particular service domains to describe service characteristics. This paper presents an ontology-based approach to enhance descriptions of Web Services that are expressed in WSDL with ontology-based behavioural information, i.e. input, conditional/unconditional output, precondition, and conditional/unconditional effect of the services. Having a service ontology associated with each Web Service description, queries for services based on behavioural constraints can benefit from inferring semantics of the service from the service ontology. The service discovery process becomes closer to discovery by service semantics or behaviour, in contrast with discovery by matching of service attributes values – the mechanism that is supported currently by Web Services.

1 Introduction

Web Services are networked applications that are able to interact using standard application-to-application Web protocols over well-defined interfaces [1]. Standard Web Service architecture provides UDDI as a registry for service providers to advertise information about themselves and their services so that service consumers can search for the required providers and services [2]. The information model in UDDI roughly defines attributes that describe the service provider (i.e. business entity), the relationships with other providers (i.e. publisher assertion), the provided service (i.e. business service), and how to access the service instance (i.e. binding template). This set of information may refer to a tModel which is a specification of particular technical information (e.g. the interface and protocol used by the Web Service and expressed in WSDL [3]). Search can be done by name/key/category of business entities, services, or tModel. For example, a query could be "give me a list of providers who are in travel business" or "give me a flight booking service". UDDI will then match the attribute values as constrained in the query against those listed in the business or service descriptions.

J.-B. Stefani, I. Demeure, and D. Hagimont (Eds.): DAIS 2003, LNCS 2893, pp. 248–259, 2003.
© IFIP International Federation for Information Processing 2003

The fixed set of attributes in UDDI limits the way queries can be composed. There are times when service consumers may look for a particular service with some semantics or behaviour. For example, a service consumer may want to find a flight booking service that can deliver the ticket to the consumer's address after payment has been made. It may be difficult for a service provider to describe such behavioural information in terms of attributes. Also, as UDDI places no requirement on a business service to be exposed as a Web Service, many service providers may use UDDI only as a channel to advertise their homepages. For this reason, WSDL which can be seen as describing behavioural information, although in a low-level form of interface signature and communication protocol, is not applicable in such a case, and therefore it is not used by UDDI when searching for services.

This paper adopts the idea of *Semantic Web* [4], which uses *ontology* to describe semantics of information, by supporting discovery of Web Services based on their ontological semantics. We define an upper ontology that models the capability of a Web Service. The capability is behaviour-oriented and represented by the service operation, input, conditional/unconditional output, precondition, and conditional/ unconditional effect. Based on this upper ontology, a shared ontology of a particular service domain can be defined. Service providers can adhere to a shared service ontology to advertise the behaviour of their services. In the case that the shared ontology does not realise all detailed concepts of the service, the providers are allowed to extend it with a local ontology. We enhance the behavioural information of a Web Service expressed in WSDL by adding to it the ontology-based behaviour and present a framework for advertising and querying Web Services by behavioural constraints. Rule-based reasoning is also supported by the framework for determining the behaviour of the service when output or effect of the service are on some conditions. With this framework, behaviour-related query can be issued and service matching can take advantage of ontological inference.

Section 2 gives an overview of the ontology concept and Section 3 discusses related work on discovering Web Services using ontologies. Section 4 presents our upper ontology and service ontology and we show how ontology-based behavioural information can be added to a Web Service description in WSDL in Section 5. The framework for semantic service discovery is in Section 6 and we conclude the paper in Section 7.

2   Why Ontology?

An ontology is a formal explicit specification of a shared conceptualisation [5]. It was developed in Artificial Intelligence area to facilitate knowledge sharing and reuse. Fig. 1 shows an example of a NaturallyOccurringWaterSource ontology [6]. It shows common concepts or vocabularies (i.e. Class and Property) in such a knowledge domain and also the relationships between those concepts. A particular information instance or resource (i.e. Yangtze) can refer to its domain ontology and describe its own semantics. An inference engine can then infer more facts about the information instance (i.e. Yangtze is a Stream and a NaturallyOccuringWaterSource and EastChinaSea is a BodyOfWater).

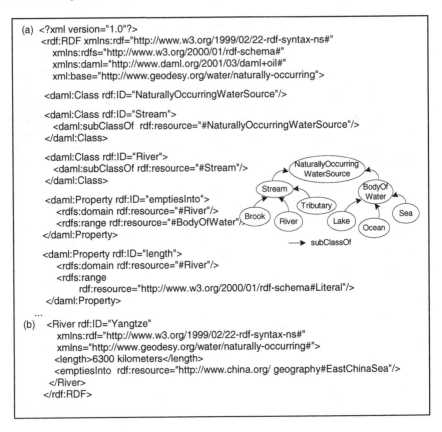

(a) `<?xml version="1.0"?>`
`    <rdf:RDF xmlns:rdf="http://www.w3.org/1999/02/22-rdf-syntax-ns#"`
`        xmlns:rdfs="http://www.w3.org/2000/01/rdf-schema#"`
`        xmlns:daml="http://www.daml.org/2001/03/daml+oil#"`
`        xml:base="http://www.geodesy.org/water/naturally-occurring">`

`    <daml:Class rdf:ID="NaturallyOccurringWaterSource"/>`

`    <daml:Class rdf:ID="Stream">`
`        <daml:subClassOf rdf:resource="#NaturallyOccurringWaterSource"/>`
`    </daml:Class>`

`    <daml:Class rdf:ID="River">`
`        <daml:subClassOf rdf:resource="#Stream"/>`
`    </daml:Class>`

`    <daml:Property rdf:ID="emptiesInto">`
`        <rdfs:domain rdf:resource="#River"/>`
`        <rdfs:range rdf:resource="#BodyOfWater"/>`
`    </daml:Property>`

`    <daml:Property rdf:ID="length">`
`        <rdfs:domain rdf:resource="#River"/>`
`        <rdfs:range`
`            rdf:resource="http://www.w3.org/2000/01/rdf-schema#Literal"/>`
`    </daml:Property>`
`    ...`
(b) `    <River rdf:ID="Yangtze"`
`        xmlns:rdf="http://www.w3.org/1999/02/22-rdf-syntax-ns#"`
`        xmlns="http://www.geodesy.org/water/naturally-occurring#">`
`        <length>6300 kilometers</length>`
`        <emptiesInto rdf:resource="http://www.china.org/ geography#EastChinaSea"/>`
`    </River>`
`    </rdf:RDF>`

Fig. 1. NaturallyOccurringWaterSource in DAML+OIL (a) Ontology (b) Resource instance

Several XML-based markup languages are available for describing ontologies including RDF, RDFS, DAML+OIL, and OWL [4]. W3C has developed RDF with the
goal to define a simple model for describing relationships between Web resources in
terms of their properties and values. RDFS adds on to RDF the concept of classes of
resources, class and property inheritance or subsumption, and domain and range of
property. Based on top of these two languages, DAML+OIL [7] can additionally
describe constraints on relationships of resources and their properties. These include
cardinality, restrictions, and axioms describing, for example, disjunction, inverse, and
transitivity rules. OWL is built upon DAML+OIL and will be a W3C recommendation for Web ontology language. To date, most of the available tools support
DAML+OIL such as OilED and Protégé for ontology editing; Jess, JTP, BOR, and
RACER for ontological reasoning; DQL and RDQL for querying. For the time being,
we hence choose DAML+OIL for our knowledge representation.

3 Related Work

Using the ontology concept to enhance service discovery has now become a hot research topic. The work in [8] presents how a service registry can use an RDF-based ontology as a basis for advertising and querying for services. In [9], DAML project proposes a DAML+OIL-based language called DAML-S as a new service description language. DAML-S consists of the Service Profile ontology which describes functionalities that a Web Service provides, the Process ontology which describes services by a process model, and the Grounding ontology which describes transport details for access to services. The Service Profile ontology specifies the descriptions of the service and service provider, functional attributes such as service category and quality rating, and functional behaviour described in terms of the operation provided, input, output, precondition, and effect of the operation. Their consequent paper [10] shows a query to find a service with a required operation, input, and output, and a matching algorithm is devised based on ontological inference. The work in [11] annotates the operation, input, and output description of a Web Service, described in WSDL format, with DAML+OIL-based ontological concepts. Precondition and effect of the service are also added to WSDL as additional information, but they are not used for queries as only the matching of the operation, input, and output is considered.

Our work is very close to the work in [10] and [11]. Both consider behavioural aspects in their service models but those aspects are not fully considered or used as query constraints for service matching. In our work, we enhance WSDL with DAML+OIL-based ontological information and consider a Web Service by its behavioural aspects all round. We allow the operation, input, output, precondition, and effect to be used as query constraints, and additionally consider the case when output or effect of the service has some conditions placed on them - the case when we provide a rule-based reasoning to determine the output and effect for query matching.

4 Ontologies for Service Descriptions

Semantics of services can be described by *upper ontology* and *service ontology*. Upper ontology models general capability and behaviour of services while service ontology represents semantic concepts that are specific to application domains of services. Service ontology is further classified into *shared ontology* and *local ontology*. Shared ontology is common for service providers in a particular service domain whereas local ontology can be derived from shared ontology in order to represent further concepts of the service.

4.1 Upper Ontology

This upper ontology focuses on capability and behavioural aspects of a Web Service (Fig. 2). It refers to the classes of concepts that are related to a service including its service community, operations that it supports, data for input and output, effects of the operations, and conditions before invoking the operation and for producing outputs or effects.

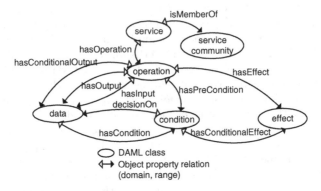

Fig. 2. Upper ontology for services

Properties of the concepts in the upper ontology consist of:

- *isMemberOf* specifies the service community to which the service belongs.
- *hasOperation* specifies an operation of the service.
- *hasInput* specifies an input data of an operation.
- *hasOutput* specifies an unconditional output data of an operation.
- *hasConditionalOutput* specifies a conditional output of an operation, i.e. the output that will be produced based on a certain condition.
- *hasPrecondition* specifies a condition that must be true before the execution of the operation.
- *hasEffect* specifies an effect or a change in the world after the execution of the operation.
- *HasConditionalEffect* specifies a conditional effect of an operation, i.e. the effect that will be produced based on a certain condition.
- *hasCondition* specifies a condition that must be true for producing a particular output or effect.
- *DecisionOn* specifies a resource or data whose value will determine the logical value of the condition for a particular output or effect.

4.2 Service Ontology

Semantic information specific to a particular service and common for service providers can be defined as a shared ontology. Service providers of the same service can refer to the shared ontology when creating their own WSDL descriptions. A shared ontology may be proposed by a group of service providers and built upon the upper ontology, some concepts that are shared with other ontologies, and the conceptual knowledge that is specific to this particular service domain. Fig. 3 (a) is an example of a shared ontology for a flight booking service.

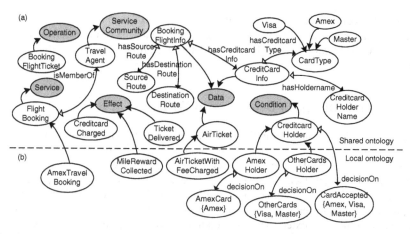

Fig. 3. Service contology. (a) Shared ontology for flight booking service (b) Local ontology for AmexTravel

Some of the semantic information in the shared flight booking ontology includes:

- *TravelAgent* that is a subclass of service community.
- *FlightBooking* that is a subclass of service and a member of *TravelAgent*.
- *AmexTravelBooking* that is a subclass of *FlightBooking* service.
- *BookingFlightTicket* that is a subclass of operation.
- *BookingFlightInfo* that is an input and a subclass of data, consisting of *CreditcardInfo*, *SourceRoute*, *DestinationRoute* etc.
- *CreditcardInfo* which is a subclass of data, consisting of *CardType* (such as amex, visa), name of holder etc.
- *AirTicket* that is an output and a subclass of data.
- *TicketDelivered* and *CreditcardCharged* that are subclasses of effect.
- *CreditcardHolder* that is a precondition and a subclass of condition, saying that the service consumer holds a credit card.
- *hasCreditcardType, hasHolderName, hasSourceRoute, hasCreditcardInfo* etc. which are properties of some classes.

Generally the basic idea is for all service providers to directly map their behaviour to one shared ontology of the service. However, it is possible that the semantics in the shared ontology may not contain all detailed aspects of the service behaviour and may not be mapped well for a particular service provider. In this case, the service provider may define a separate local ontology by deriving from the shared ontology of the service, and can use the concepts in both ontologies to declare links to the service behaviour. In Fig. 3 (b), a service provider called AmexTravel derives a local ontology from the shared flight booking ontology to refine some concepts. For example, *AirTicketWithFeeCharged* is derived from *AirTicket* to represent a special case of the output that the air ticket may come with extra fee. *MileRewardCollected* is another refinement, saying that by buying a ticket with AmexTravel, an additional effect is that the service consumer can collect mileage rewards. The condition *CreditcardHolder* is refined by specifying the types of credit cards that AmexTravel can accept, i.e. *Amex*, *Visa*, or *Master*. *CreditcardHolder* is further derived into the conditions *AmexHolder* and *OtherCardsHolder* that will be used to determine different outputs of flight booking.

5   Adding Ontological Behaviour to WSDL

Concepts within the shared ontology and local ontology will be used to annotate WSDL descriptions of Web Services. We borrow the idea from [12] to add behavioural semantics to WSDL file and specify a mapping to link the service's own behaviour to the shared and local ontology. In this way, WSDL elements that represent the service capability (i.e. wsdl:message, wsdl:part, wsdl:operation, wsdl:input, wsdl: output) can be associated with semantic extensions that specify the ontological behaviour. Other semantics extensions (i.e. condition and effect) are added as extra elements. In Fig. 4, a shared ontology called flightbooking.daml is provided. A service provider named AmexTravel derives a local ontology called amextravel.daml. Its service provides an operation to book a flight ticket, the input is the required flight information, and the precondition is that the service requires a credit card for booking. The output is however conditional; if the consumer holds an Amex card, the output will be the air ticket; otherwise the output will be the air ticket and a service charge. The effects of the operation are that the ticket will be delivered to the consumer's address and the credit card will be charged. In the case that the consumer is an Amex cardholder, rewarding mileage points will be an additional effect.

6   Ontology-Based Service Discovery

The annotated WSDL descriptions will be used in a framework to discover Web Services. This section describes the discovery framework, how it integrates with UDDI, and an example of query with behavioural constraints.

6.1   Service Discovery Framework

The framework consists of several components that cooperate in semantic Web Service discovery. The prototype is Java Web-centric using Servlet technology and integrating existing ontology-supporting tools (Fig. 5). In step (a), an ontology engineer can use the *Ontology Builder* to build a shared ontology for a service. A service manager, in the same manner, can build a local ontology, based on the shared ontology, by using the Ontology Builder. OilEd [13] is adopted for Ontology Builder in our prototype although other ontology editors will do also. When ontologies are available, the service manager will, in step (b), add ontological information into an existing WSDL description by using *Semantic Mapper*. As a result, the Semantic Mapper will generate an annotated WSDL and an RDF service description which corresponds to the annotated WSDL. The service manager can also, in step (c), use the *Condition Builder* to translate preconditions and conditions for outputs and effects in the shared ontology and local ontology into the rules for Jess engine [14]. Jess rules are stored in the *Rule DB* and will be used later to determine service behaviour at service matching time.

```xml
<?xml version="1.0" encoding="UTF-8"?>
<!DOCTYPE uridef [
<!ENTITY sh "http://www.wssemantic.com/flightbooking.daml#">
<!ENTITY lo "http://www.AmexTravel.com/amextravel.daml#"> ]>
<definitions
   name="AmexTravel"
   targetNamespace="http://www.AmexTravel.com/amextravel.wsdl"
   xmlns:tns="http://www.AmexTravel.com/amextravel.wsdl"
   xmlns:WSDLext="http://www.wssemantic.com/WSDLext.dtd"
   xmlns:sh="&sh;"
   xmlns:lo="&lo;"  ...>
...
  <portType name="AmexTravelPortType">
   <operation name="BookingTicket"
    WSDLext:semantic-operation="&sh;BookingFlightTicket">
    <documentation>Provide service for booking air ticket
         </documentation>
    <input message="tns:BookingTicketRequest"
        WSDLext:semantic-data="&sh;BookingFlightInfo">
    </input>
    <WSDLext:precondition
         WSDLext:semantic-condition="&sh;CreditcardHolder"/>
    <output message="tns:BookingTicketResponse" />
    <WSDLext:conditionalOutput
         WSDLext:semantic-data="&sh;AirTicket">
     <WSDLext:condition
        WSDLext:semantic-condition="&lo;AmexHolder">
      <WSDLext:conditionalEffect
        WSDLext:semantic-effect="&lo;MileRewardCollected"/>
      </WSDLext:condition>
    </WSDLext:conditionalOutput>
    <WSDLext:conditionalOutput
         WSDLext:data="&lo;AirTicketWithFeeCharged">
     <WSDLext:condition
        WSDLext:semantic-condition="&lo;OtherCardsHolder"/>
    </WSDLext:conditionalOutput>
    <WSDLext:effect WSDLext:semantic-effect="&sh;TicketDelivered"/>
    <WSDLext:effect WSDLext:semantic-effect="&sh;CreditcardCharged"/>
    </operation>
   </portType>
    <binding name="AmexTravelBinding" type="tns:AmexTravelPortType">
     ...
   <service name="AmexTravel"
        WSDLext:semantic-service="&lo;AmexTravelBooking "/>
     <WSDLext:servicecommunity
        WSDLext:semantic-community="&sh;TravelAgent"/>
     <port binding="tns:AmexTravelBinding" name="AmexTravelPort">
      <soap:address
        location="http://www.AmexHolder.com/BookingAmexTicket"/>
     </port>
   </service>
</definitions>
```

Fig. 4. Extending WSDL of AmexTravel with ontological information

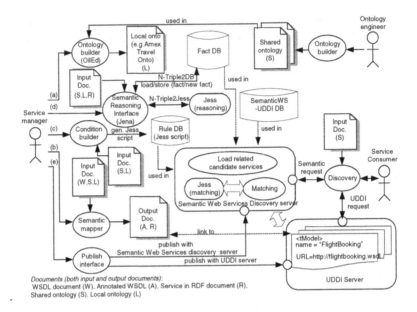

Fig. 5. Semantic Web Services discovery framework

In step (d), the RDF service description from step (b), the shared ontology, and the local ontology will be parsed by Jena module [15] within the *Semantic Reasoning Interface* in order to extract facts about the service. The facts are stored in the *Fact DB* in Jena's N-triple tuple format (i.e. <subject, predicate, object>). To reason for more facts, the Semantic Reasoning Interface is integrated with Jess which also provides a reasoning engine. The Semantic Reasoning Interface transforms existing N-triple tuple facts into Jess facts by using our predefined fact template, and then Jess engine can infer more facts especially those about the relations between the shared ontology and local ontology. Resulting facts from Jess will be transformed back to N-triple tuples and stored in the Fact DB. Facts in this DB will be consulted when matching a query against service descriptions.

In step (e), the service manager will publish service descriptions via the *Publish Interface*. A traditional Web Service description for a particular service provider (i.e. business entity, publisher assertion, business service, and binding template) will be registered with a UDDI server in a usual manner, with the annotated WSDL defined as a tModel for the binding template. To also provide for semantic discovery, an additional semantic entry will be registered with the *Semantic Web Services Discovery Server (SemanticWS-DS)*. The semantic entry consists of the annotated WSDL and the reference keys to a particular business service and business entity in UDDI server. With these keys, after we query by service behaviour and a service provider is found a match, we can retrieve the complete information about this provider from the UDDI server. This semantic entry is stored in the *SemanticWS-UDDI DB*.

The SemanticWS-DS performs semantic service matching. A service consumer can compose an RDF query based on the upper ontology and shared ontology of the service. The SemanticWS-DS extracts information from the query and loads the facts about the services from the Fact DB to compare with the query. The resulting candidate services will be further checked by Jess rule engine to determine their exact behaviour against the constraints in the query. For those matched services, their complete description will then be retrieved from the UDDI server by using the reference keys stored in the SemanticWS-UDDI DB. The steps taken by the SemanticWS-DS are exemplified in Section 6.2.

6.2 Query by Behavioural Constraints

Suppose that a service consumer wants to query for a flight booking service that accepts a visa card, returns an air ticket as the output, and delivers the ticket to the consumer's address. The consumer will issue an RDF query based on the concepts in the upper ontology and the shared ontology of the flight booking service to the SemanticWS-DS. The information extracted from the query is in Fig. 6 (a). The consumer requests for a *FlightBooking* service in the *TravelAgent* community and the service has the operation *BookingFlightTicket*. The precondition *CreditcardHolder* and the *CardType* says that the operation must allow booking with credit card and visa card is accepted. The operation must return an *AirTicket* with an effect *TicketDelivered* for the consumer. This extracted information is queried against the facts about the available services that are stored in the Fact DB in N-triple tuple format. Consider some facts that are obtained by inferring from the shared flight booking ontology and the local ontology of AmexTravel in Fig. 6 (b). The service community, service, and operation concepts in the query match with those in the service description of Amex-Travel. The output *AirTicketWithFeeCharged* of AmexTravel is defined as a subclass of the output *AirTicket* of the query so it is considered a match according to subsumption. Since *AmexHolder* and *OtherCardsHolder* defined in AmexTravel description are subclasses of the precondition *CreditcardHolder* of the query, AmexTravel is still a candidate service but further evaluation is required to check whether it accepts a visa card. The Fact DB returns all candidate services with exact or partial match with the query to the SemanticWS-DS.

The matching process continues by loading Jess rule scripts of the candidate services from the Rule DB in order to determine their behaviour that is based on some conditions. Fig. 6 (c) shows three Jess rules of AmexTravel. The information extracted from the RDF query is translated to Jess facts that are asserted into Jess rule engine. In this example, the assertion that specifies the precondition *Creditcard-Holder* with the card type visa fires the *precondition-CardAccepted* rule, and therefore the precondition of AmexTravel satisfies the precondition of the query. Since this assertion also fires the *conditionalOutput-OtherCards* rule, all of its output and effects are compared with the output and effect specified in the query. The result is that the output *AirTicketWithFeeCharged* of AmexTravel matches the output *Air-Ticket* of the query by subsumption, and the effect *TicketDelivered* matches exactly. By satisfying all constraints, AmexTravel is returned as a search result to the consumer.

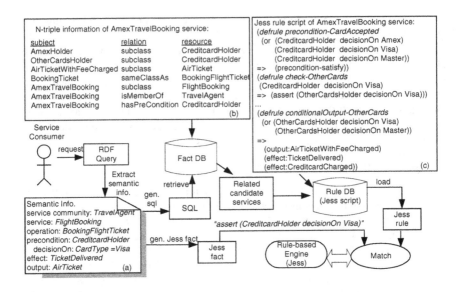

Fig. 6. Query by behavioural constraint (a) Semantics of query. (b) N-triple facts of Amex-Travel (c) Jess rule script of AmexTravel

7   Conclusion

This paper has proposed an approach to extend WSDL descriptions for Web Services with ontological information, based on an upper ontology, a shared service ontology, and a local ontology, in order to benefit from ontological reasoning. The approach allows queries for services based on capability and behavioural information such as the operation provided, input, output, and effect. Logical conditions can be placed on output and effect, and determined by a rule engine at query time.

Ranking query results by the degree of matching is an important issue that we will study further. Ranking may be based on the precedence assigned to those behavioural aspects in the upper ontology, relations between concepts, or the number of matched concepts and conditions. We also have a plan to explore the behavioural model that can enable automatic discovery of a group of services that altogether can satisfy a particular behaviour-related query. Such behavioural model is also expected to be useful for proving some behavioural properties of the service.

Acknowledgements

This work is supported by Thailand-Japan Technology Transfer Project and Chulalongkorn University-Industry Linkage Research Grant Year 2002.

References

1. W3C. Web Services (online). http://www.w3.org/2002/ws/
2. uddi.org. Universal Description, Discovery and Integration of Web Services (online). http://www.uddi.org
3. W3C. Web Services Description Language (WSDL) 1.1 (2001) (online). http://www.w3.org/TR/wsdl
4. semanticweb.org. Semantic Web (online). http://www.semanticweb.org
5. Gruber, T. R.: A Translation Approach to Portable Ontologies. Knowledge Acquisition Vol. 5 No. 2 (1993) 199-220
6. Costello, R., Jacobs, D.: RDF Schema Tutorial (online). http://www.xfront.com/rdf-schema/
7. daml.org. DAML+OIL (online). http://www.daml.org
8. Trastour, D., Bartolini, C., Gonzalez-Castillo, J.: A Semantic Web Approach to Service Description for Matchmaking of Services. Proceedings of the International Semantic Web Working Symposium (SWWS'01) (2001)
9. The DAML Services Coalition: DAML-S: Web Service Description for the Semantic Web. Proceedings of the 1st International Semantic Web Conference (ISWC 2002), Sardinia (Italy), Lecture Notes in Computer Science, Vol. 2342. Springer-Verlag (2002)
10. Paolucci, M. et al.: Semantic Matching of Web Services Capabilities. Proceedings of the 1st International Semantic Web Conference (ISWC 2002), Sardinia (Italy), Lecture Notes in Computer Science, Vol. 2342. Springer Verlag (2002)
11. Sivashanmugan, K. et al.: Adding Semantics to Web Services Standards. Proceedings of the International Conference on Web Services (2003)
12. Peer, J.: Bringing Together Semantic Web and Web Services. Proceedings of the 1st International Semantic Web Conference (ISWC 2002), Sardinia (Italy), Lecture Notes in Computer Science Vol. 2342. Springer Verlag (2002) 279-291
13. OilED, Version 3.5 (online). http://oiled.man.ac.uk/index.shtml
14. Jess the Rule Engine for the Java™ Platform, Version 6.1, 9 April 2003 (online). http://herzberg.ca.sandia.gov/jess/
15. Jena A Semantic Web Toolkit, Version 1.6.1 (online). http://www.hpl.hp.com/semweb/rdql.html

Requirements for Personal Information Agents in the Semantic Web

Wolfgang Woerndl

Technische Universität München, Munich, Germany
woerndl@in.tum.de
http://www11.in.tum.de/persons/woerndl/

Abstract. In this paper we first present some requirements for personal information agents in the Semantic Web. Then we outline our PINA project which tries to combine elements of identity management and information agents in the Semantic Web. The fundamental idea is to store references to Semantic Web annotations in identity servers as part of user profiles.

1 Introduction

Personalization of information offerings appears to be a promising concept to help people finding relevant information in the world wide network of information sources. Thus, a variety of systems have already been developed using user data they have collected or information users have explicitly made available. These systems offer personalized Web pages or make recommendations based on user profiles. User profiles thereby contain information such as demographic data (e.g. age, gender, Email addresses), specified interests or past transactions (e.g. bought books).

In addition, work on building the *Semantic Web* is recently gaining more and more attention (see [1] for a recent overview). The goal of the Semantic Web activities is to make available the meaning of information to computers. Thereby, software agents or other programs analyze and evaluate semantic meta data of information items to improve services. An important building block in this regard are ontologies that are shared between information providers.

A combination of personalization and Semantic Web could be beneficial because additional semantic information[1] to data sources could be used to improve customization of search results or other filtering services.

However, personalization also raises issues of privacy and trust. Firstly, any personalization application potentially poses privacy problems, because users have to provide information about themselves and want to know how their information is being used. Secondly, there is also the problem of trust. In the existing Web, it is more or less up to the user to (manually) decide whether

---

[1] For example, meta data to information sources, (semantic) annotations to Web pages or ontological classification of information items. In the following, the term "annotations" is used to describe all kinds of meta data or semantic information.

J.-B. Stefani, I. Demeure, and D. Hagimont (Eds.): DAIS 2003, LNCS 2893, pp. 260–265, 2003.
© IFIP International Federation for Information Processing 2003

information, e.g. search engine results, might be trustworthy or not. In the Semantic Web, this will not be the case, because agents have to determine the trustworthiness of information.

In this paper, we present requirements for personal information agents in the Semantic Web. We will also briefy introduce the Personal Information Agents (PINA) project which tries to combine elements of identity management and Semantic Web agents.

2 Requirements for Personal Information Agents

In this chapter, we outline some requirements for personal information agents in the Semantic Web in various research areas.

2.1 Agents in the Semantic Web

According to James Hendler, the ideal internet agent is as follows: "A good internet agent needs these same capabilities. It must be communicative: able to understand your goals, preferences and constraints. It must be capable: able to take options rather than simply provide advice. It must be autonomous; able to act without the user being in control the whole time. And it should be adaptive; able to learn from experience about both its tasks and about its users preferences." ([2])

Apart from the agent requirements such as autonomy, personal information agents have to take into account the semantic character of information. More precisely, the following aspects have to be considered:

- Segmentation of search and customization to take advantage of the agent paradigm
- Interoperability: handle multiple ontologies, for example different user profile models, and integrate mapping mechanisms between ontologies
- Heterogeneity: possibility to query different information sources
- Balance the trade-off between expressibility and (computational) complexity

2.2 Identity Management and User Profile Modelling

The basic idea of *identity management* is to separate user profiles and identities from the services that are using them. An identity management system would allow people to define different identities, roles, associate personal data to it, and decide whom to give the data to and when to act anonymously [3].

A generic user model and storage in an integrated repository is needed. User profiles should be stored in a non-redundant manner [4]. Information about users should be reusable for different applications and domains so that users do not have to enter their information such as Email addresses or interests again and again. Thereby, an ontology-based approach might be useful [5]. So far there is no widely accepted "user profile ontology" and a mapping of different personalization ontologies is required in real world scenarios. Another important aspect with regard to user modelling and identity management is to consider different roles and identities of users, for example "work" or "private" identites.

When combining Semantic Web and personalization technologies, one of the most important questions is: what is the relationship between Semantic Web annotations and user profiles? Are annotations part of a user's profile? Or maybe references to annotations? If annotations are not part of a user's profile at all, it is very difficult for agents to make any inferences about the trustworthiness of information sources.

2.3   Privacy and Trust

Privacy is "the claim of individuals, groups or institutions to determine for themselves, when, how and to what extent information about them is communicated to others." ([6]). The aspect of control for the user is essential. User need to know how, why and what part of their profile is being accessed. It is not reasonable to build user-adaptive systems without considering privacy. In addition, we can identify two aspects of privacy in our scenario. Firstly, privacy of users who provide semantic annotations to information sources. Secondly, privacy of users who access information sources or search for relevant pieces of data. Current systems often adress only one aspect and neglect the other.

The two most important features of privacy preserving identity management are authentification and authorization. *Authentification* provide means for users to securely assert their identity without necessarily revealing their true identity. An important feature is to define and control different pseudonyms which is the scope of the Liberty Alliance project (see www.projectliberty.org). The goal of this project is to define an open standard for federated identity management that allows users to link elements of their identity between accounts without centrally storing all their personal information. However, their focus is the management of identities and authentification in the WWW to provide a so called "single sign-on" (SSO) service and the Liberty Alliance cannot easily applied to agent-based information services.

Authorization is about controlling the access of services to user profile attributes. More precisely, requirements in our scenario are [3]:

- Flexible access right control system, e.g. through rules and negotiation
- Possibility to use a pseudonym instead of real identity
- Purpose binding of data accesses
- Possibility for the user to monitor access rights and accesses and revoke granted access rights if necessary
- Control whether user data may be distributed to other services (and users)
- Integration of cryptographic techniques for anonymous data transfers

Possible solutions to *trust* in the Semantic Web include the signing of information items by persons or institutions. Agents can then evaluate the digital signatures to proof the trustworthiness of annotations before presenting personalization results to users. But trust has to be adressed in combination with privacy. Therefore, the top layer in the Semantic Web layer cake by Tim Berners Lee (available at http://www.w3.org/2002/Talks/01-sweb/slide12-0.html, for example) should be named "Trust & Privacy" not just "Trust" because all efforts to improve trust and build a "Web of Trust" potentially decrease the privacy of users. In other words, there is a trade-off between trust and privacy in any personalization system that has to be taken into account when designing the application.

3   The Personal Information Agent (PINA) Project

The goal of the Personal Information Agent (PINA) project is to bring together identity and user profile management on the one hand, and Semantic Web technologies and agent technologies on the other hand. The purpose is to support semantic personalization of information sources and improve adaption of information to user profiles. This is especially done with respect to user privacy. A fundamental idea is to store references to Semantic Web annotations as part of user profiles.

The components of our architecture are depicted in Fig. 1.

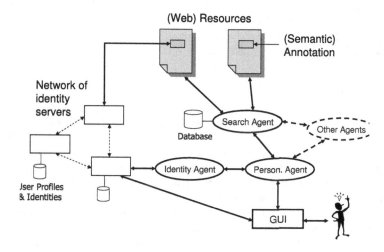

Fig. 1. PINA components.

The basic building blocks are as follows:

- (Semantic) Web resources with additional annotations[2]
- A network of identity management servers to store references to semantic annotation and handle the user profile management
- Information agents to provide personalization and other services
- Appropriate user interfaces and/or client-side tools

---

[2] The annotations could be stored in designated annotation servers separate form the information items.

In [3] we describe an identity management infrastructure which separates the identity management from the service applications. This is done in the domain of community support systems but can be used for other services that use personal information. Agents can access user profiles via an agent-based interface (FIPA). Different user identities are also part of the framework and can be used by personalization agents. We thereby cover the identity network part in Fig. 1. We are currently implementing the link to Semantic Web annotations.

Mechanisms to derive trust in the Semantic Web can then be designed using the binding of Semantic Web annotations to user identitites. A user can define and control different pseudonyms to mark Semantic Web annotations. The real identity of the user does not have to be disclosed. For example, a user can provide annotations under a pseudonym "wolfgangw" or "foo23". Agents then derive the trustworthiness of annotations by using these pseudonyms instead of real identities of users. The authenticity of pseudonyms is proven by the identity management network.

In [7,3] we also explain a concept for authorization in distributed management of user profiles. Thereby authorization is done by combining privacy enhancing technologies with access control. User profile agents negotiate access right to user information with service agents using privacy policies of services and preferences and access rules of users. Our approach is well suited for the agent scenario because the solution adheres to the agent paradigm of autonomy of components and also uses a message based protocol for the negotiation.

4   Conclusion

In this paper we have presented some requirements for personal identity management in the Semantic Web. We also outlined the architecture of the PINA project. The main idea is to combine identity management and (personal) information agents in the Semantic Web. The briefly presented solution stores a reference to a Semantic Web annotation in a distributed user profile management network. This approach allows for personalization services that exploit different identities of users and other identity management features. PINA also allows the realization of privacy mechanisms as summarized in [7] and [3].

Next steps in PINA include implementation of more components to test the effectiveness of the system in delivering customized information to users. In addition to identity agents and ontology agents or servers, we envision filter and personalization agents and a component that provides an appropriate user interface. Another point is whether the Liberty Alliance specification can be used (or adopted) to handle the authentification using different user identities between (personal) agents. For far, we use an easier authentification schema that is provided by our identity management infrastructure.

References

1. Fensel, D.; Hendler, J.; Lieberman, H., Wahlster, W. (Eds.): Spinning the Semantic Web: Bringing the World Wide Web to Its Full Potential. MIT Press (2003)
2. Hendler, J.: Is There an Intelligent Agent in Your Future? Nature (1999)
3. Koch, M., Woerndl, W.: Community Support and Identity Management. Proc. Europ. Conference on Computer-Supported Cooperative Work (ECSCW2001), Bonn, Germany (2001) 319–338
4. Kobsa, A.: Generic User Modeling Systems. User Modeling and User-Adapted Interaction 11, Kluwer (2001) 49–63
5. Razmerita, L., Angehrn, A., Maedche, A.: Ontology-Based User Modeling for Knowledge Management Systems. Proc. User Modeling 2003, Lecture Notes in Artificial Intelligence (LNAI) 2702, Springer (2003) 213–217
6. Westin, A.: Privacy and Freedom. New York (1967)
7. Woerndl, W., Koch, M.: Privacy in Distributed User Profile Management. The Twelfth International World Wide Web Conference (WWW2003), Budapest, Hungary (2003)

Towards an Intuitive Interface
for Tailored Service Compositions

Steffen Higel, Tony O'Donnell, Dave Lewis, and Vincent Wade

Knowledge and Data Engineering Group
Department of Computer Science
Trinity College Dublin, Ireland
{Steffen.Higel,Tony.ODonnell,Dave.Lewis,Vincent.Wade}@cs.tcd.ie

Abstract. Novel modes of interaction and tailored application delivery are a key challenge in ubiquitous computing. This paper proposes a method of adaptively delivering lightweight, disposable service compositions to a user in a smart space. The user intuitively requests these services through a single, environment interface, which infers goals through observing behaviour and context, and manages the configuration and interaction of the devices within the space. The composition is driven by generating tasks from these inferences, which can be resolved down to candidate services. We will discuss the proposed interaction between these components and highlight what direction our research will take.

1 Introduction

The human-computer relationship has moved from single machines with multiple users, through the PC age and on to spaces where many users are surrounded by a myriad of computing devices [Vertegaal, 2003]. In such an environment, the user cannot possibly interact with every distinct device, let alone every piece of software on these devices, and so instead we propose an interface to the environment which monitors a users actions and then communicates their needs to web-service representations of the functionality on those devices in the space. For developers, this emerging scenario introduces many challenges from efficiently building this interface, to delivering useful support. Our work proposes a system which will address this challenge. This paper outlines our research and highlights how natural interfaces can be used to enable users to interact with a ubiquitous computing environment, and also how support can be delivered through the dynamic composition of tailored, lightweight, disposable services.

2 Background

The research discussed in this paper divides into two areas, namely developing the environment interface and then providing support to users accessing it. Presented below is a brief background to these.

J.-B. Stefani, I. Demeure, and D. Hagimont (Eds.): DAIS 2003, LNCS 2893, pp. 266–273, 2003.

2.1 Adaptive Techniques

Software in its traditional form has been driven predominantly by a fixed set of design decisions, defined before development begins, which place finite limits on the capabilities of the end product. Although research into software which can learn and adapt to the preferences, behaviour and context of the user[Langley, 1997] has existed for quite some time, it was only during the 1990s that software applying these techniques to commercial software like AVANTI and indeed it is only in recent years that we have seen any definite move in the direction of products being used by end-users which feature adaptive components[Horvitz, 1999]. These agents can monitor a user's interaction with software and take actions on behalf of the user based on these assumptions.

Although in adaptive hypermedia systems, an area in which we have conducted a large amount of research, metadata (the data which describes the data) driven techniques made some headway in describing the scope of a piece of content, it did not operate on a sufficiently high level to give any meaningful hints to the system itself as to what goals this piece of content was trying to fulfill[Dagger et al, 2003]. The navigation through a collection of hypermedia documents is abstracted such that it can be viewed as a navigation through a series of concepts represented as nodes. These concepts will have one or more pieces of appropriate candidate pieces of content associated with them. This idea of candidacy can effectively be applied to another area of adaptive software, as will be demonstrated in this paper. The idea remains sound if you use it to abstract the functionality of an email program (the tasks like "view list of emails", "read specific email" and "write email" can be abstracted from the software libraries that provide them) or in service composition (where the functionality provided by a service can be viewed as being distinct from an instance of this service).

2.2 Ubiquitous Interfaces

With the ever-decreasing size and increasing power of computers embedded processors are appearing in devices all around us. As a result the notion of a computer as a distinct device is being replaced with a ubiquitous ambient computing presence[Dey et al, 2001], e.g. wearable computers. This proliferation of devices will present user interface designers with a challenge. While an average user might cope with having a different interface for their PDA, desktop PC and mobile phone, they will certainly have difficulty if the range of devices is greatly increased. In the past, designers have suggested creating a single interface appearing on all devices, however research has thus far not proved this to be the optimum solution[1]. We instead propose an ambient environment interface within the computing environment which observes the users activities and then acts on what the user wants. The environment then handles the individual interaction

---

[1] For example, developers of the Symbian OS found it was not feasible to offer the same user interface on Symbian-powered PDA's as on desktop computers.

with the devices, customising and configuring them, thus sparing the user. Later in this paper we will more fully describe such an environmental interface technology.

2.3 Service Composition

The field of service composition covers the techniques used to bind together two or more software components capable of intercommunication. Recent interest in the topic has surged due to the emergence of web-services - applications running on the World Wide Web, which use standardised methods for communication and self description[Edgar, 2001]. By dynamically chaining a number of these services together at run-time[Kcman et al, 2001], functionality and convenience can be added to the services to which an end user might traditionally be accustomed - those offered by a single vendor accessed with a web browser[Wu et al, 2003].

3   Proposed Architecture

Presented are the designs of two systems, an environment interface architecture and an automated and tailored service composition architecture, providing sufficient background to understand how an interaction between the two might take place.

3.1 TSUNAMI

TSUNAMI, Tailored Support of Users' Natural Activities with Mixed Initiative, is an interface technology that we are currently researching. The system monitors users for implicit inputs, such as vague gestures or conversation, and explicit inputs, such as verbal or typed commands, and uses these to predict what assistance the user requires to fulfill their perceived goal. Predictions are also guided by context information such as calendars, location and biographical information. Support is delivered with mixed initiative[Horvitz, 1999], that is, the system adjusts the pre-emptive support it gives on a per-user and per-task basis and is aimed at reducing the cognitive load placed on the user.

   Once a confident prediction is made, a task request is formed and dispatched to the Adaptive Service Composition Engine, ASCE, so that a solution can be prepared. However, at all times the user maintains overall control and can disregard the assistance being offered.

Inputs. TSUNAMI accepts inputs from a range of sources. Some of these allow natural actions to be used by means of sensors in the space. These will supply data on physical behaviour such as manipulation of objects, gestures or speech. Calendars can add temporal context. A user's biographical information helps inform predictions by indicating prior behaviour and preferences. The business\work context can ensure that predictions do not contradict corporate policies or assist with anti-social activities. Finally, the space can be equipped with declarative tools such as whiteboards or traditional PC-like interfaces. These allow unambiguous input.

In order to make these inputs intelligible to the system, they are first parsed to extract meaning. This parsing will use pattern matching based on existing cached knowledge. Where no pattern exists, or when parsing proves unsuccessful, some other remedial action will have to be taken. The nature of this action has yet to be investigated.

Prediction Selection. Each of the inputs above has a certain level of ambiguity ranging from the relatively clear declarative inputs to the much less precise sensor data. In order to reflect this, different types of inputs come with varying levels of confidence as to what they are trying to communicate. For example, if user Kate enters the space and says 'print myfile.doc' the system can be confident that it should do just that. On the other hand, if she makes a comment about the weather it may not mean that the air-conditioning should adjust itself.

TSUNAMI will address this problem in two ways. Inputs will have associated confidence levels, and combinations of inputs will produce aggregate confidence[2]. Given tasks will have minimum levels of confidence associated with them. This task confidence will be similar to that expressed in [Horvitz et al, 1998], where a measure of the utility of offering assistance successfully or otherwise, rather than not offering help, can be measured and used to arrive a point where the system can pre-emptively offer support.

In addition, TSUNAMI will provide a mechanism for evidence to degrade appropriately over time, so that a comment made an hour ago does not overly inform a prediction being considered now. It will also allow predictions to similarly decay, and introduce a lower threshold after which they will no longer be considered.

TSUNAMI will maintain a number of competing prediction hypotheses and once the aggregate confidence for a given prediction has been exceeded a meaningful request can be sent to the ASCE for a solution. In certain cases, where either the user is unhappy for the system to be pre-emptive or where the task is mission critical, TSUNAMI may interrupt the user for confirmation before sending this request.

3.2   Adaptive Service Composition

People have varying preferences regarding the behaviour and presentation of software. We have no reason to believe that composite services should be any different. A potential key advantage of dynamically composed software over monolithic ones is the ability for a given end user to at least express their preferences in these areas, if not to modify a service composition themselves. If web-service

---

[2] It is expected that input aggregation will make use of complex event processing [Luckham, 2002] techniques to allow simple events to be combined to form more meaningful higher-level composite events - e.g. making a phone call rather than lifting a receiver, finding a number, dialling and then speaking.

wrappers for existing software are developed, it is possible to very quickly create composite services with functionality that would take a considerable amount of time to develop using a monolithic model.

System Overview. ASCE, the Adaptive Service Composition Engine is a proposed system to facilitate the semi-automated creation of service compositions tailored to a user's needs[Conlan et al, 2003]. This approach to service composition has the potential to provide a series of benefits to software developers and end users alike. From the developer's and advanced user's perspective, the speedy and semi-automated selection and linking of distributed components saves time and effort. From the end user's perspective, this approach could result in applications which are coupled more closely with the their needs and preferences, along with providing a piece of software which offers levels of functionality greater than that of a monolithic service.

Details of Operation. The engine abstracts the subtasks that are needed to complete a given goal from the actual services that can fulfil them; as previously discussed, the functionality provided by a service is considered distinct from an actual instance of a service which provides that functionality. The Service Composition Toolkit is tasked with the former while the Service Integration Engine handles the latter. The process of adaptive service composition begins with the system receiving a description of a task (the format of which will be discussed later), which is passed to the Service Composition Toolkit. A cache of previously decomposed tasks is searched for similar initial requirements.

Assuming none are found, the toolkit will attempt to decompose the task itself, using service classifications (descriptions of what kinds of service exist, i.e. pay for something using a credit card, recommend a book, provide content on a specific topic to a student) down to a set of rules defining the required services and the order in which they should react. The service composition toolkit should be able to fall back on the input of a domain expert, a human with sufficient skill to break the task down using information provided by the service classifications, should the semantic gap between service descriptions prove to be too wide.

The Service Integration Engine takes the list of service classifications and maps them onto available services. It is assumed that there may be many services available which provide similar functionality. Each of these candidate services should be compared with the user profile, the user context and quality of service requirements, resulting in the most appropriate candidate being selected.

4   Integration and Inter-operation

The concept of service composition can ultimately facilitate the dynamic generation of useful composed services by an end-user who has received only a small amount of training. When this is combined with an intuitive interface there is a significant potential for user empowerment. However, to be truly effective, there must be efficient and well-structured communication between the two systems. Despite being discrete areas of research, which in the future will function independently but are still capable of inter-operation, it is still worthwhile for the systems to be examined from the outside-in. This will help to define the responsibilities and to define what data should be accepted and returned by of each system.

At the core of any interaction between TSUNAMI and the ASCE is the information passed them. This data will describe the tasks that TSUNAMI has interpreted from the actions of a user. The challenge is finding a useful balance between preparing a heavily detailed description of a task (which would expect too much of the TSUNAMI and too little of the ASCE) or sending a vague, light task description. It would seem reasonable to assume from this that the ASCE must be presented with some structured description of the task, with much of the contextual interpretation already performed by TSUNAMI.

It is therefore proposed that the task description passed from TSUNAMI to ASCE be expressed unambiguously in terms of inputs, pre-conditions, effects and outputs, rather than a vague, verbose specification. The generation and interpretation of these conditions, effects and outputs are still complex, but they place reasonable, structured, intelligible and logical requirements on each component.

Figure 1. Shows the inter-operation of the two systems, though its workings are best illustrated with a practical example:

Dave is on his way from his own company's office building to another regional headquarters. He is making this trip by car, and has just realised that he has forgotten the location of the meeting room and the exact time of the meeting. He also wants to check over the minutes of their previous meeting. His PDA hears him say "I need the email from Jim which details the meeting, the meeting location r and also has the minutes of the previous one." His PDA, acting as a sensor for TSUNAMI interprets this and passes its description of Dave's task (get the email from Jim about the meeting). TSUNAMI uses contextual information to resolve this down to a set of inputs, outputs, preconditions and effects:

Inputs: `Dave, need email from Jim with meeting details.`
Outputs: `Email and minutes displayed on appropriate device.`
Effects: `Meeting time and location are placed in Dave's diary.`
Preconditions: `None.`

The ASCE has access to services which provide information on Dave, including the URI to his email Inbox, a service which can access such a mailbox and search through it and another which can connect to some centralised diary system like Microsoft Exchange or Lotus Notes and add entries to it. It will compose these services together, searching a path through it's available services to get from the required inputs to the outputs and effects. Finally, the task of displaying the results must be handled. The ASCE has access to the contextual information which places Dave in his car on the way to the regional headquarters. It creates a new service composition which will convert and filter the document and then send it to the printer in the lobby of the headquarters. These composi-

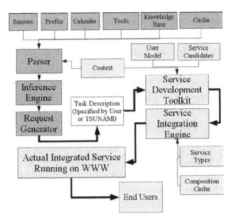

Fig. 1. The architectures of both the TSUNAMI and ASCE systems, with the common link between them.

tions are executed, the web services performing the tasks required of them and all of the information Dave requires is waiting for him when he arrives.

5   Conclusion and Further Research

It is the belief of the authors that a novel approach to user support in a ubiquitous computing environment has been proposed. The methods used to enable co-operation between existing techniques in adaptive composition and human computer interaction have been highlighted, along with future research directions of these areas. In addition, the research presented has a clearly defined focus, with the potential for experimental tests in the near future.

To assist with the design of TSUNAMI, a review of relevant research was conducted, including human-computer interaction, event processing, mixed- initiative support\attentive user interfaces and natural interfaces[3]. At present, a TSUNAMI testbed is under development which will simulate simple user interaction with the system. This simulation will allow a user to interact with a 2-dimensional model of an office, and will monitor point of view and speech. This experiment will test the basic system assertions, namely that our chosen inputs can be recorded, parsed, used to build complex event patterns and that these can be used to trigger task requests. Once the basic assertions have been proven, a more comprehensive test programme will begin. This will see an increased range of input axes, devices and deliverable tasks. Ultimately, it is envisaged that a full real world test will be carried out.

Research in the area of service composition has focused on two areas; developing services which can be used in a composition and the design of the Adaptive

---

[3] See assorted documents at
http://www.cs.tcd.ie/Tony.ODonnell/publications/index.html.

Service Composition Engine. As a testbed, a series of file conversion services will be built atop the traditional tools found on UNIX operating systems. Because the path used to convert one file format to another may not be trivial, it will provide an interesting challenge for the ASCE to see if it can automatically resolve the high level tasks down to actual services. At present, a basic tree search of DAML-S documents is being developed along with an investigation into existing automatic service composition techniques. Once this initial series of tests has been completed, work will begin on defining methods used for describing service compositions to aid storage and re-use along with integration with parallel research into quality of service and access control.

This work is funded in part by the Higher Education Authority (HEA) of Ireland under the auspices of the M-Zones project[4].

References

Edgar, 2001. Web Services: A Position Paper, Edgar, G., W3C workshop on Web services, 2001

Dey et al, 2001. References Distributed and Disappearing User Interfaces in Ubiquitous Computing, Dey, A., Ljungstrand, P., Schmidt, A., 2001

Langley, 1997. Machine learning for adaptive user interfaces, Langley, P., German Annual Conference on Artificial Intelligence, 1997

Kcman et al, 2001. Towards Zero-Code Service Composition, Kcman E., Melloul L., Fox A., Hot Topics in Operating Systems, 2001

Wu et al, 2003. Automatic Web Services Composition Using SHOP2, Wu D., Sirin E., Hendler J., Nau D.,Twelfth World Wide Web Conference, 2003

Conlan et al, 2003. Applying Adaptive Hypermedia Techniques to Semantic Web-Service Composition, Conlan O., Lewis D., Higel S., O'Sullivan D., Wade V., Adaptive Hypermedia 2003

Horvitz, 1999. Principles of Mixed-Initiative User Interfaces, Horvitz, Eric, Proceedings of the SIGCHI conference on Human factors in computing systems, pages 159-166, 1999

Dagger et al, 2003. An Architecture for Candidacy in Adaptive eLearning Systems to Facilitate the Reuse of Learning Resources, Dagger D., Conlan O., Wade V., eLearn 2003

Horvitz et al, 1998. The Lumiere Project: Bayesian User Modeling for Inferring the Goals and Needs of Software Users, Horvitz E., Breese J., Heckerman D., Hovel D. & Rommelse K., Fourteenth Conference on Uncertainty in Artificial Intelligence Intelligence, 1998

Vertegaal, 2003. Attentive User Interfaces, Vertegaal R., Communications of the ACM, Vol. 46, N0. 3, pages 31 - 33, March 2003

Luckham, 2002. The Power of Events: An Introduction to Complex Event Processing, Luckham, David, Pearson Education Inc, 2002

---

[4] [M-Zones] M-Zones (Managed Zones) http://www.m-zones.org.

Context-Based Addressing: The Concept and an Implementation for Large-Scale Mobile Agent Systems Using Publish-Subscribe Event Notification

Seng Wai Loke, Amir Padovitz, and Arkady Zaslavsky

School of Computer Science and Software Engineering
Monash University, Caulfield East, VIC 3145, Australia
swloke@csse.monash.edu.au,
ar_padovitz@hotmail.com,
a.zaslavsky@monash.edu.au

Abstract. We introduce the notion of context-based addressing, i.e. the ability to refer to and send messages to a collection of agents based on their current context, without knowing the precise identities of the agents. We describe a simple implementation of context-based addressing for mobile agents using Elvin, a publish-subscribe event notification system, as a proof-of-concept, and to investigate the feasibility of the event-based paradigm for implementing context-based addressing for mobile agents.

1 Introduction

Human-beings can be identified and referred to in numerous ways, ranging from our names, our nick-names, our titles, our roles, to where we live. The ability to address or refer to software agents using a variety of methods can provide flexibility and abstraction for system developers, particularly when the system being built is dynamic and large, involving a huge number of agents.

A dimension of dynamic behaviour is the property of agents being able to move from one host to another to perform computations. While not all agents require such a property, agent mobility has been recognized as beneficial in a number of large scale distributed applications, including information-centric applications [5] and a sizable number of mobile agent toolkits[1] have been developed for mobile multiagent applications. Proposals for the use of mobile agents in network management are also numerous (e.g., [1]). More recent applications of mobile agents include large networks of embedded systems such as wireless ad hoc sensor networks [4].

Large systems of mobile agents over large distributed environments are generally difficult to program and various techniques have been introduced. In this paper, we consider one aspect of programming mobile agents, i.e. the ability to refer to and send

---

[1] See http://mole.informatik.uni-stuttgart.de/mal/preview/preview.html

J.-B. Stefani, I. Demeure, and D. Hagimont (Eds.): DAIS 2003, LNCS 2893, pp. 274–284, 2003.

messages to a collection of agents based on their current context, without knowing the precise identities of the agents. By agent's context, we refer to the situation of an agent as is made known by the agent. For example, suppose we have a large number of mobile agents roaming over hosts distributed throughout an intelligent building performing various functions (e.g., as in the Hive project http://hive.sourceforge.net/ hive-asama.html), and, without explicitly addressing each agent, we want to send a message to all agents which are currently on hosts situated on the third floor, or we want to send a message to all agents launched by (and belonging to) John Smith, or we want to send a message to all agent's currently running on hosts with less than one gigabyte of available storage, or we want to send a message to all agents currently on hosts which provide a directory service, or we want to send a message to all agents which have not yet completed their tasks and are currently running on hosts with connections whose network traffic is increasing, or we want to send a message to all agents currently running on a host which will be disconnected from other hosts in the next three minutes. All these messages target agents according to the context which the agents are in, and the way we refer to these agents is via the current context rather than their names (though it is possible to find their names with such a context-based query as "send me your name if you are on a host on the third floor"). We think that such *context-based messaging* will be useful for distributed monitoring, management and control applications.

We propose a mechanism for supporting such context-based addressing, and demonstrate our ideas assuming that agents have access to context-information that will be used in addressing the agents, and that the agents proactively report their current context to a central server. What exactly the context information will be depends on the application semantics.

Our approach leverages on a publish-subscribe event-based communication system called Elvin. The publish-subscribe event paradigm has been useful for asynchronous communication between loosely coupled components of distributed systems. While implementations of publish-subscribe models may differ, the fundamental principles remain the same, and in this paper we use the name Elvin both as the name of a specific implementation and a generic representative of the class of event notification systems.

Elvin provides implicit invocation [2]: a component A can invoke another component B without A being required to know B's *name* or B's *location*. Components such as B 'register' interest in particular 'events' that components such as A 'announce'. When A announces such an event, the event system notifies (or invokes) B, even though A doesn't know that B or any other components are registered. This suits a dynamic environment, where A need not know B's location since B might be continually moving, and A can interact with other components in the environment without knowing their details (e.g., their name, or how many agents there are, thereby providing scalability). Elvin's mechanism to achieve implicit invocation is *content-based addressing* (or *undirected addressing*) where a notification is not explicitly directed by the producer to specific consumers, but is simply multicast to consumers whose subscriptions match the notification description. As we describe later, we can use content-based addressing as a means of selecting agents to send messages to.

The rest of this paper is organized as follows. Section 2 discusses relevant background concepts. Section 3 discusses our initial implementation, integrating Elvin's publish-subscribe communication mechanism with mobile agents, as first suggested in [6]. Section 4 discusses the notion of context-based addressing for collections and subcollections of agents that is based on content-based addressing. Section 5 concludes with future work.

2   Background

2.1   Publish-Subscribe Model

Generally, entities that wish to send messages "publish" them as events, while entities that wish to receive certain types of messages (or events) "subscribe" (or register) to those events. A publisher of a message is not aware of the recipients requesting that message and might not even be aware of their existence. Similarly, components that receive messages may not be aware of other components that may also listen to the same event and can only receive messages they are registered for. Often, an entity may become both a publisher and subscriber, sending and receiving messages within the system. To accomplish the event-based model, a separate entity is deployed between the producer and consumer of a message, which decouples the connection between those entities and provides the necessary mechanism for distributing a message to registered subscribers.

2.2. The Elvin Event Notification System

Elvin is built and used in a client-server architecture, in which an Elvin server is responsible for managing client connections and transferring messages between publishers and subscribers. Client Applications use the Elvin's client code and API in order to produce and consume information in a publish-subscribe fashion [8].

Consumers of notifications register their interest in specific events with the server. Upon receiving a notification (message) from a producer, the Elvin server forwards the notification to the relevant client subscribers by comparing the message content with the list of subscriptions it holds.

As the routing of a message is based on its content and not on intended recipients, it provides the flexibility to operate in a dynamic environment and is independent of the need to configure information relating to the recipients of a notification. The notification itself is encapsulated within an object and contains a list of key-value pairs. The notification element supports several data types, such as integers, floating points, strings etc. A consumer expresses its interest with a subscription element, which is built with a special subscription language containing simple logical expressions [3].

Consider the following subscription expression taken from [3]:

```
(TICKERTAPE == "elvin" || TICKERTAPE == "Chat") && ! re-
gex(USER, "[Ss]egall")
```

This subscription expression will match any notification whose TICKERTAPE field has the string value "elvin" or "Chat" except those whose USER field also matches the regular expression "[Ss]egall". This subscription would match the following notification example:

```
TICKERTAPE: "Chat"
USER:       "alice"
TICKERTEXT: "hello sailor"
TIMEOUT:    10
Message-Id: "07cf0b15003409-5i3N7XDKbPVaQ-28cf-22"
```

3 Integrating Mobile Agents with Elvin

Prior to this research, Elvin was successfully used in several applications, such as CSCW environments to achieve mutual awareness between different parties. However, application objects that were utilizing the Elvin mechanism in those applications were static, in the sense that they were located at the same host for their entire lifetime.

In contrast, mobile agents may be active and migrate between different hosts. During the lifetime of a mobile agent, it can execute on several agent places in different times and may need to communicate with other mobile agents as well as with static objects.

As Elvin's original focus is to provide an event-notification based communication for traditional distributed applications and architectures, in which objects that are using Elvin remain in the same location, it was initially unfit to be used as part of mobile code. Hence, new functionality had to be added to facilitate such integration. Furthermore, the newly developed capabilities were targeted to be used by any mobile agent toolkit and not be restricted to a specific one.

The new functionality that supports the use of Elvin in mobile code was developed to integrate easily with the regular mobile agent's code, requiring only minimal changes in the agent's program. As mobile agent toolkits mostly operate on a Java Virtual Machine, development of new functionality was done in the Java Environment.

3.1 Basic Elvin Client Constructs and Mobility Hurdles

Two fundamental constructs for performing Elvin communication are the *consumer* and *producer* objects. These objects are part of the Elvin Client library, which enables *consumer* objects to register callback methods that are activated for specific notifications, and allow *producer* objects to publish new notifications intended for listeners (that use the *consumer* object).

Another important Elvin Client construct is the *subscription* object, which describes the notification, and is sent to the Elvin Server.

The Elvin Client Library is used by applications to produce and receive notifications from other applications, whereas the Elvin Server process is controlling, coordinating and managing all communication between the clients. The Elvin Server behavior dictates that an application that consumes notifications (by using the *consumer* object) must exist in the same location in which it originally subscribed for the particular notification/s at the time the notification is sent by the server. An Elvin *connection* object describes the communication details and exists for each *consumer* object. Upon receiving an event, the server will broadcast a notification for that event to subscribing objects, in the location in which the original subscription took place (and as maintained by the Elvin *connection* object).

Mobile agents cannot use these Elvin constructs since they often change their location and still require receiving notifications. In such a scenario, the Elvin server is not aware of their new location and continues to send messages to the old location. It is also infeasible for them to return to their original subscribing location, and even if they do so, they will lose much of the notifications sent to them, while in transit or executing in other nodes. We will discuss solutions to this problem later.

In Figure 1, which illustrates this problem, a mobile agent first subscribes for events (stage 1), and then migrates to another location (stage 2). An Elvin Server contains a subscription registration from the agent, and a connection that is identified with the old location, thus sending new notifications to the wrong host.

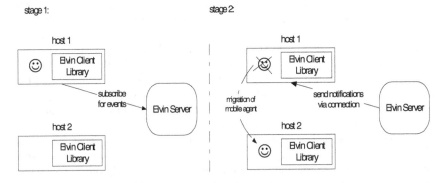

Fig. 1. The connection problem between the Elvin Server and a mobile agent

A second important mobility problem is concerned with the nature of migration of mobile agents. While in transit, a mobile agent has no concrete existence on a particular host and is therefore unable to receive Elvin messages. We consider this problem in more detail later.

A third hurdle in implementing a solution for mobile agents is the fact that all Elvin Client objects are implemented as non-serialisable objects. As such, they cannot migrate as part of the mobile agent code to new locations. This imposes obvious restrictions on the way mobile agents can use existing Elvin objects.

3.2 MobileConsumer

To solve the mentioned mobility problems, new functionality, represented by a *MobileConsumer* class was developed and added to the Elvin Client Library. The *MobileConsumer* class supports Java Serialization, and thus, can be transported to different hosts as part of the mobile agent. The functionality implemented in this class follows the approach suggested in [6], in which an agent removes all existing subscriptions before migrating to a new location and re-subscribes to the same notifications after arriving at the new location.

*The class embeds this kind of behavior and performs the required operations on behalf of its client (the mobile agent). A *MobileConsumer* object keeps information such as a serializable representation of Elvin subscriptions and Connections, and is implemented as a single object per client. Consequently, a mobile agent client needs only to use the *MobileConsumer* object in two predefined states: before the migration, and right after the migration.

Two public methods are provided for this purpose:

```
NotifyPreMigration( )
NotifyNewLocation(...)
```

The client uses the first function just before migrating to a new location, and the second is activated immediately after arriving at the new location. Ideally, these functions are implemented in callback functions that are activated just before and after migration (by the agent's toolkit execution environment). Such a feature is common in most mobile agent toolkits.

The following code snippet demonstrates the use of *MobileConsumer* and other Elvin classes in a basic scenario, in which a mobile agent subscribes for notifications:

```
MobileConsumer mc =
    new MobileConsumer(ElsvinServerURL);

public void onCreation(Object itin) / init(Object[] creationArgs)
{
     Subscription sub =
        new Subscription(strSubscription);
// NotificationHandler → class to handle
//   notification events
     NotificationHandler nh =
           new    NotificationHandler( );
     sub.addNotificationListener(nh);
     mc.addSubscription(sub);
}

public void onDispatching(MobilityEvent m) / beforeMove( )
{
     mc.notifyPreMigration();
}

public void onArrival(MobilityEvent e) / afterMove( )
{
     NotificationHandler nh =
         new NotificationHandler();
     mc.notifyNewLocation(nh, strSubscription);
}
```

The '/' separates the different names in the Aglet and Grasshopper toolkits for callback methods of similar purpose.

Using the event-based mechanism of Elvin is lightweight and efficient even for large volumes of messages, but has one drawback, which is the loss of messages during agent migration. We conducted experiments on the effect of agent transit on message lost in [7], and saw that the percentage of messages lost or not received by an agent while in transit is on average relatively low. In one sense, this is not an issue as we are not intending the event-based mechanism primarily as a guaranteed point-to-point communication device (we already have other means of doing so) but for large-scale event dissemination. Whether a small percentage lost of messages is significant depends on the semantics of the application, but results in the rest of this paper will work for other event systems comparable with Elvin. We also note that if message lost cannot be tolerated in an application, the problem can be easily solved by using a stateful, but more heavyweight event notification system.

4   Context-Based Addressing for Collections
4   and Subcollections of Agents

Given that mobile agents can now subscribe to Elvin and receive messages (i.e. notifications) matching the subscriptions, we can employ this mechanism for context-based addressing of agents in the following way. Each agent subscribes to Elvin for messages that relate to its context. An agent does this by using particular keywords in its subscription expression that relates to its context, effectively reporting its context to Elvin (i.e., the Elvin server). For example, an agent uses the following expression to "listen for" messages intended for agents who are low in credits and are currently on hosts which have less than 5GB of free disk space:

```
(CREDITS == "low" && DISKSPACE == "< 5GB")
```

Such a subscription expression will match the following notification, which in this example carries a command to agents in such a situation to come home:

```
CREDITS: "low"
DISKSPACE: "< 5GB"
COMMAND: "come_home"
Message-Id: "07cf0b15003409-5i3N7XDKbPVaQ-28cf-22"
```

Note that the attribute names, the possible values for each attribute, and their semantics must have been pre-defined, for example, based on an ontology of context attributes (perhaps pre-defined for given applications). We also note that the sending of the command notifications need not know the identifiers of those agents in the situation described above – such is the power and advantage of implicit invocation (or content-based addressing). Moreover, a "name" for the collection of agents in the above described situation has been effectively created. Such a "name" can be used to send a message to these agents, asking them to report their names, i.e. we can query to find out the which agents are currently in a particular context.

One can also refer to subcollections in that collection of agents by adding additional constraints and leaving it to the agent to check if the message received applies to itself. For example, suppose the notification was the following:

```
CREDITS: "low"
DISKSPACE: "< 5GB"
GROUP: "Tom"
COMMAND: "come_home"
```
Message-Id: "07cf0b15003409-5i3N7XDKbPVaQ-28cf-23"

The agent will still receive such a message as it matches with the above subscription, but in checking that it does not belong to Tom's group, it might decide to ignore such a message. Alternatively, the agent can shift such filtering to the Elvin server (reducing some network traffic) by using a more elaborate subscription expression that specifies it belongs to Jane's group (and so Elvin will not forward to the agent messages intended for Tom's group), such as the following:

```
(CREDITS == "low" && DISKSPACE == "< 5GB" && GROUP ==
"Jane")
```

Hence, an agent can inform Elvin of its current context and in this way receive messages suited to its context. An agent can effectively modify its subscription (by unsubscribing and resubscribing) updating the context information it provides to Elvin. Subscriptions carry information about agents' current context, and notifications, via particular attributes and values, can target agents in specified context – it is in this way that the content-based addressing of Elvin is, when context attributes are utilized (and when agents truthfully report their context to Elvin), viewed as context-based addressing. Other examples of context attributes that might be used include the location of the agent, the status of the agent's task execution, a fragment of the agent's state, a description of the agent's current execution environment (e.g., services available), and bandwidth for relevant connections (assuming discrete values for these context attributes).

4.1 Ad Hoc Namespaces

The above suggests that it is possible to define namespaces ad hoc over collections of agents. For example, one can create a namespace that relates to the geographical location of hosts. For example, suppose we consider the division of a building into logical areas such as the following. A building (call this Building1) has five floors, i.e. Floor1, Floor2, Floor3, Floor4 and Floor5. In each floor, we have five rooms numbered Room1, Room2, etc up to Room5. Suppose that there are one or more computers in each room, and that agents residing on a computer can find out the logical area (i.e., there is a means to map IP addresses to logical areas) they are currently in, and send a subscription to Elvin, with an attribute identifying the logical area they are currently in. We can then send a message to all agents in Room3 via notifications such as

```
LOGICAL-AREA: "Building1/Floor3/Room3"
COMMAND: "come_home"
...
```

Agents in Floor3 can subscribe to all messages for Floor3 agents via a subscription of the form:

```
(begins-with(LOGICAL-AREA, "Building1/Floor3/") || ...)
```

As agents move and update their context information with Elvin via subscriptions, the collection of agents referred to with the phrase "Agents in Floor3" might change.

Several namespaces can be used jointly. For example, apart from partitioning agents according to their geographical location, we might partition agents according to who their owners are. We can then refer to "Agents currently in Floor3 AND who belong to Seng", and send messages to such agents. With large numbers of agents in large numbers of hosts and ubiquitous embedded devices, such "names" provide a convenient means to refer to whole collections of agents. Such "names" as "Agents currently in Floor3 AND who belong to Seng" can be used within programs in applications involving agents or by users who want to control the agents directly (for example, a user's command such as "Agents currently in Floor3, move to John's machine" can be issued).

Our approach of context-based addressing relies on the agents proactively reporting to Elvin their current context via a subscription. However, this is not mere reporting as a subsciption carries with it the semantics of inviting messages (or notifications) that are relevant to the context specified, i.e. the agent via such a subscription is effectively saying to Elvin "This is my current context. Please forward messages (if any) that relate to this context" and any subsequent messages matching the subscription will be forwarded. Note that the agents are sending subscriptions to report their contexts rather than sending notifications. If the agents send notifications, than we have a monitoring model where agents notify subscribers about their contexts. However, we are implementing a messaging model, where agents are receiving messages according to their contexts, and hence, agents send subscriptions and not notifications. While a mix of such models can be employed in an application, our focus has been on a messaging model. We leave it up to the designer of the agents to ensure such behaviour in the agents he/she creates. The required efficiency of agents, network capacity, and application semantics will determine how often the agent should (re)issue such subscriptions[2].

4.2 A Programming Construct

There are two ways such context-based messaging can be used. One way is when the user needs to send commands to a collection of agent, referring to them by context. In such a case, a user interface can be built which will allow a user to specify such commands. The other way is when a software agent needs to send a context-based message to other agents. We describe here a programming construct for this purpose, as follows:

```
agents_in_context(<context expression>)#<message>
```

---

[2] Elvin is made to handle large numbers of such small messages efficiently.

whose semantics is to send `<message>` (e.g. a string) to the agents referred to by the `<context expression>`, which is a set of attribute-values as shown in the previous subsection. Using Elvin, executing this construct generates an Elvin notification to be forwarded to the Elvin server. Given a context expression, the set of agents referred to depends on the time the construct is evaluated since agents' contexts are expected to vary over time.

Such a construct can be implemented as a Java class for use in building applications.

5 Conclusions and Future Work

We have introduced the notion of addressing and messaging agents by the context or situation which they are currently in, which we called *context-based addressing*. We have also illustrated this concept via a simple implementation using Elvin. There are drawbacks in using Elvin, it being a stateless system so that messages might be lost when agents are in transit. However, this has not been the focus of this paper and other stateful event systems can be used. What we have shown is that the publish-subscribe event model can be employed to implement context-based addressing, provided the agents are built to proactively report their context to the event system via subscriptions (in effect expressing their desire to receive messages intended for their present context). In terms of context management, this means that the agents have to be programmed to know what context to report, and how often to report. A principled methodology is required in which the internal architecture of the agent is structured into a context-reporting module and application-specific modules. An alternative is to have other components report about the agents, but these components need to be build in some principled manner, and it would mean agents lose autonomy in deciding what and when to report. Applications of such context-based addressing have been suggested in the introduction, and our future work involves utilising such addressing in smart environment systems. Further experimentation will be required to test the scalability of our approach. The ability to network Elvin servers provide a means to support highly distributed scenarios. New versions of Elvin supports security in that only certain consumers (with the right key) can decipher the messages of certain producers.

References

1. Bieszczad, B. Pagurek, and T. White, *"Mobile Agents for Network Management"*, IEEE Communications Surveys, Vol. 1, No. 1, Fourth Quarter 1998.
2. J. Dingel, D. Garlan, S. Jha, and D. Notkin. Towards a Formal Treatment of Implicit Invocation. *Proceedings of the 1997 Formal Methods Europe Conference*, 1997. Available at http://www-2.cs.cmu.edu/afs/cs/project/able/ www/paper_abstracts/implicit-invoc-fme97.html
3. DSTC. The Elvin Subscription Language. http://elvin.dstc.edu.au/doc/esl4.html

4. H. Qi, F. Wang, "Optimal itinerary analysis for mobile agents in ad hoc wireless sensor networks," *The 13th International Conference on Wireless Communications*, vol. 1, pp.147-153. Calgary, Canada, July, 2001.

5. M. Klusch, F. Zambonelli (ed): Cooperative Information Agents – Best Papers pf CIA 2001. Intl. Journal of Cooperative Information Systems. 2002 Vol. 11, No. 3 and 4.

6. Loke. S.W., Rakotonirainy, A., and Zaslavsky, A.   Enabling Awareness in Dynamic Mobile Agent Environments (short paper). *Proceedings of the 15th Symposium on Applied Computing (SAC 2000)*, Como, Italy, March 2000, ACM Press.

7. Padovitz, A., Loke, S.W., and Zaslavsky, A. Using Publish-Subscribe Event Based Systems for Mobile Agents Communication. Submitted.

8. Segall, B., Arnold, D., Boot, J., Henderson, M., and Phelps, T. Content Based Routing with Elvin4, *Proceedings AUUG2K*, Canberra, Australia, June 2000 URL: http://elvin. dstc.edu.au/doc/papers/auug2k/auug2k.pdf

Exploiting Proximity in Event-Based Middleware for Collaborative Mobile Applications

René Meier and Vinny Cahill

Distributed Systems Group, Department of Computer Science
Trinity College Dublin, Ireland
{rene.meier,vinny.cahill}@cs.tcd.ie

Abstract. Middleware supporting event-based communication is widely recognized as being well suited to mobile applications since it naturally accommodates a dynamically changing population of interacting entities and the dynamic reconfiguration of the connections between them.
STEAM is an event-based middleware designed for use in ad hoc networks. STEAM differs from other event-based middleware in that its architecture does not rely on the presence of any separate infrastructure, event notification filters are distributed, and filtering may be applied to functional and non-functional attributes. In particular, filters may be applied to either the subject or the content of an event notification, or to non-functional attributes, such as location and time. Filters may be used to define geographical areas within which event notifications are valid, thereby bounding the propagation of these notifications. Such proximity-based filtering represents a natural way to filter events of interest in mobile applications.
This paper describes the architecture and implementation of STEAM and its use of proximity-based filtering. In particular, we show how proximity-based filtering can be used to reduce the number of events delivered to collaborative mobile applications.

1 Introduction

Middleware supporting event-based communication [1] is widely recognized as being well suited to addressing the requirements of mobile applications [2, 3]. Event-based middleware naturally accommodates a dynamically changing population of components and is particularly useful in wireless networks, where communication relationships among application components are typically dynamically reconfigured during the lifetimes of the components.

Existing research on event-based middleware for wireless networks has mainly focused on what may be termed *nomadic applications*. These applications are characterized by fact that mobile nodes make use of the wireless network primarily to connect to a fixed network infrastructure, such as the Internet, but may suffer periods of disconnection while moving between points of connectivity. Such applications typically employ *infrastructure networks* [4]. As a result, most of this work has concentrated on handling disconnection while entities move from one access point to another. In contrast, we focus on *collaborative applications* characterized by the fact that mobile nodes use the wireless network to interact with other mobile nodes that have come together at some common location. Although these applications may use infrastructure networks, they will often use *ad hoc networks* [4] to support communication

J.-B. Stefani, I. Demeure, and D. Hagimont (Eds.): DAIS 2003, LNCS 2893, pp. 285–296, 2003.
© IFIP International Federation for Information Processing 2003

without the need for a separate infrastructure. Consequently, this collaborative style of application allows loosely coupled components to communicate and collaborate in a spontaneous manner.

In this paper, we present the architecture and implementation of STEAM (Scalable Timed Events And Mobility), an event-based middleware for mobile computing, and outline how its features address the functional and non-functional requirements of such collaborative applications with a special emphasis on support for the use of ad hoc networks.

STEAM has been designed for IEEE 802.11b-based, wireless local area networks and is intended for applications that include a large number of highly mobile application components typically distributed over a large geographical area. Unanticipated interaction between nearby components is supported, enabling a component to dynamically establish connections to other components within its current vicinity. This allows components representing real world objects currently located within the same geographical area to deliver events at the location where they are relevant.

We envisage STEAM being utilized by collaborative applications in various domains including indoor and outdoor smart environments, augmented reality, and traffic management. In a traffic management application scenario, application components may represent mobile objects including cars, buses, fire engines, and ambulances as well as objects with a fixed location, such as traffic signals and lights. When within close proximity, such components may interact using STEAM in order to exchange information on the current traffic situation. As a simple example, an ambulance might disseminate its location to the vehicles traveling in front of it in order to have them yield the right of way. In general, inter-vehicle communication may contribute to better driver awareness of nearby hazards and is likely to lead to safer driving.

The STEAM event-based middleware has a number of important differences from other event services that support mobility [1, 2, 5, 6]:

- STEAM assumes an ad hoc network model supporting very dynamic coupling between application components.
- The architecture of STEAM is inherently distributed. The middleware is exclusively collocated with the application components and does not rely on the presence of any infrastructure.
- Application components are location aware. Geographical location information is provided by a location service and used to deliver events at the specific location where they are relevant.
- Distributed event notification filtering. Event notifications may be filtered at both the producer and the consumer side or may be filtered implicitly. Filters may be applied to functional and non-functional attributes associated with an event notification including subject, content, and geographical location.
- The STEAM middleware is fully distributed over the same physical machines as the components that comprise a collaborative application. This implies that the middleware located on every machine has identical capabilities allowing its components either to initiate or respond to communication. STEAM's architecture contains neither centralized components, such as lookup and naming services, nor the kind of intermediate components that are used by other event services to propagate event notifications from event producers to event consumers [1, 2, 6-8]. Generally, dedicated machines that are part of the event service infrastructure are used to host

such components in order to ensure that they are accessible to all application components in a system at any time. However, this approach is impractical in ad hoc environments due to lack of infrastructure and the possibility of network partition.

STEAM supports distributed event notification filters that may be applied to the functional and non-functional attributes of an event notification. Functional attributes include the subject and content of an event notification, whereas non-functional attributes may include context, such as the geographical location of a component, time, and the Quality of Service (QoS) available from the network. Combining distributed event notification filters, which may be applied on both the producer and the consumer side, enables a subscriber to describe the exact subset of event notifications in which it is interested, exploiting multiple criteria, such as meaning, geographic location, and time. For example, filters that are applied to location information allow application components to interact based on their current location; an event producer may define a geographical area within which certain event notifications are valid thereby bounding the area within which these event notifications are propagated. STEAM provides location filters, called proximity filters, that differ from traditional filters in that they are not inherently located on either the producer or the consumer side. Producers and consumers may both apply location filters to determine whether their current location is within the geographical scope of certain event notifications. STEAM exploits group communication, which has been recognized as a natural means to support event-based communication [9], as the underlying mechanism for components to interact. However, STEAM's approach differs from the traditional approach in that it utilizes a group communication mechanism based on proximity [10] enabling the mapping of location filters describing geographical scope to proximity groups.

We argue that the STEAM architecture and our approach to distributed event notification filtering helps to improve system scalability by omitting centralized components and by bounding the propagation of subscription information and event notifications. This reduces the use of communication and computation resources, which are typically scarce in mobile environments. In general, distributed event filtering limits the number of filters being applied at a particular location and balances the computational load of filter matching between the physical machines in a system. The number of producer side filters is independent of the potentially large number of subscribers and the number of consumer side filters depends solely on the number of local subscribers. As a result, filter evaluation time can be bounded for the events disseminated in a particular scope.

The reminder of this paper is structured as follows: Section 2 surveys related work. Section 3 focuses on the programming model supported by STEAM. Section 4 presents the STEAM architecture including the main middleware components and the employed communications model. Section 5 presents our initial evaluation of STEAM, which demonstrates how distributed event filtering reduces the number of events delivered to an application. Section 6 concludes this paper by summarizing our work and outlining the issues that remain open for future work.

2 Related Work

Middleware supporting event-based communication has been developed by both industry [7, 11] and academia [1, 2, 8, 12]. Most such middleware assumes that the components comprising an application are stationary and that a fixed network infrastructure is available. Existing research on event-based middleware for mobile computing has mainly focused on supporting nomadic applications using wireless data communication based on the infrastructure network model [1, 2, 5, 6]. Relatively little work has been done to address the distinct requirements, due to the lack of infrastructure, associated with supporting event-based communication in ad hoc networks. Application components using the ad hoc network cannot rely on the aid of access points when discovering peers in order to establish connections to them. Event messages can neither be routed through access points nor rely on the presence of intermediate components that may apply event filters or enforce non-functional attributes such as ordering policies and delivery deadlines.

In the remainder of this section, we introduce various event models that offer mobility support and briefly outline their respective architectures. JEDI [2] allows nomadic application components to produce or consume events by connecting to a logically centralized event dispatcher that comprises the event service infrastructure and has global knowledge of all subscription requests and events. JEDI provides a distributed implementation of the event dispatcher consisting of a set of dispatching servers that are interconnected through a fixed network. Nomadic entities may move using the moveOut and moveIn operations. The moveOut operation disconnects the entity from its current dispatching server, allowing it move to another location and then to use the moveIn operator to reconnect to another dispatching server at a later time. The dispatching server buffers all relevant information while an entity is disconnected and forwards it upon reconnection. Mobile Push [5] proposes a similar approach to supporting nomadic application components in which entities do not use the event service while moving. In addition, it supports mobile application components accessing the event service infrastructure through wireless connections while moving. However, both approaches rely on the presence of a separate event service infrastructure. Elvin [6] implements support for mobility through the use of a proxy server that maintains a permanent connection to the event server on behalf of nomadic client components. The proxy server stores events while a client is temporarily disconnected until the client reconnects. The proxy server allows clients to specify a time to live for each subscription to prevent large numbers of events being stored indefinitely. Clients must explicitly connect to a proxy server using a URL and must reconnect to the same proxy server each time.

Although these middleware services support mobility, their main goal is to handle disconnection while an entity moves from one access point to another. In contrast, STEAM accommodates a changing set of collaborative entities coming together at a location and supports communication between these entities without relying on a separate event service infrastructure.

3   Steam Architecture

The design of the STEAM architecture is motivated by the hypothesis that there are applications in which mobile components are more likely to interact once they are in close proximity. This means that the closer event consumers are located to a producer the more likely they are to be interested in the events that it produces. Significantly, this implies that events are relevant within a certain geographical area surrounding a producer. For example, in augmented reality games players are interested in the status of game objects or indeed other players, only when they are within close proximity. An example from the traffic management domain might be a crashed car disseminating an accident notification. Approaching vehicles are interested in receiving these events only when located within a certain range of the car.

3.1 Using Event Types and Proximities

STEAM implements an implicit event model [13] that allows event producers to publish events of a specific *event type* and consumers to subscribe to events of particular event types. Producers may publish events of several event types and consumers may subscribe to one or more event types.

To facilitate the kind of location-aware application described above, STEAM supports a programming model that allows producers to bound the range within which their events are relevant. Producers *announce* the type of event they intend to *raise* together with the geographical area, called the *proximity*, within which events of this type are to be disseminated. Such an announcement associates a specific event type with a certain proximity and implicitly bounds event propagation. Consumers receive events only if they reside inside a proximity in which events of this type are raised.

Producers may define proximities independently of their physical transmission range with the underlying group communication system routing event messages from producer to consumer using a multi-hop protocol. Proximities may be of arbitrary shape and may be defined as nested and overlapping areas. Nesting allows a large proximity to contain a smaller proximity subdividing the large area. Fig. 1 depicts two overlapping proximities of different shape and illustrates that multiple consuming and producing entities may reside inside a proximity. These proximities have been associated with events of *type A* and *type B* respectively. Consequently, consumers handling these event types receive events if they reside inside the appropriate proximity. Note that entities located inside these areas handling other event types will not affect the propagation of these events. An example of overlapping proximities might include a car disseminating an accident notification within the vicinity of a traffic light propagating its status to approaching vehicles.

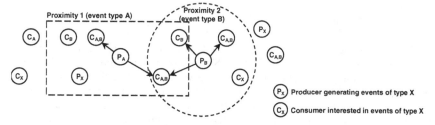

Fig. 1. Disseminating events using event types and proximities

3.2 Supporting Mobility

STEAM has been designed to support applications in which application components can be either stationary or mobile and interact based on their geographical location. This implies that the STEAM middleware as well as the entities hosted by a particular machine are aware of their geographical location at any given time. STEAM includes a location service that uses sensor data to compute the current geographical location of its host machine and entities. To suit outdoor applications, for example in the traffic management domain, STEAM exploits a version of the location service that uses a GPS satellite receiver to provide latitude and longitude coordinates.

In addition to supporting stationary and mobile entities STEAM allows proximities to be either stationary or mobile. A stationary proximity is attached to a fixed point in space whereas a mobile proximity is mapped to a moving position represented by the location of a specific mobile producer. Hence, a mobile proximity moves with the location of the producer to which it has been attached. This implies that mobile consumers and producers may be moving with a mobile proximity. For example, a group of vehicles heading in the same direction may cooperate to form a platoon in order to reduce their consumption of fuel. These vehicles might interact using a proximity that has been defined by the leading vehicle. Such a proximity might be attached to the position of the leader moving with its location.

3.3 Subscribing to Event Types

Consumers must subscribe to event types in order to have the middleware deliver subsequent events to them if they are located inside any proximity where events of this type are raised until they unsubscribe. A consumer may move from one proximity to another without re-issuing a subscription when entering the new proximity. Thus, subscriptions are persistent and will be applied transparently by the middleware every time a subscriber enters a new proximity. This implies that a subscription to a specific event type applies to all proximities handling these events even though the subscriber may only receive a subset of these events at any time. A single subscription may result in events of a particular event type raised by different producers in multiple proximities being delivered. Hence, the set of events received by a subscriber at a certain time depends on its movements as well as on the movements of producers and proximities.

3.4 Defining Event Types

Applications define event types to specify the functional and non-functional attributes of the events they intend to disseminate. A STEAM event type consists of *subject* and *content* representing its functional attributes, as well as of a self-describing *attribute list* representing its non-functional attributes. The subject defines the name of a specific event type and the content defines the names and types of a set of associated parameters. STEAM event instances are defined in a similar manner by specifying a subject, content parameter values, and attribute list. Producers and consumers must use a common vocabulary defined by the application to agree on the name of an event type. An event type and an event instance that have the same subject must have an identical content structure, i.e., the set of parameter names and types must be consistent. This approach allows an application to associate non-functional attributes to events of the same type as well as to individual event instances. An event type may include attributes such as proximity and ordering semantics, whereas event instance attributes may include event priority, temporal validity, and delivery deadline. As described in more detail below, distributed event filters may be applied to the subject, content, and attribute list defined by either an event type or an event instance.

3.5 Applying Event Notification Filters

STEAM supports three different event filters, namely *subject filters*, *content filters*, and *proximity filters*. These filters may be combined and a particular event is only delivered to a consumer if all filters match. Subject filters match the subject of events allowing a consumer to specify the event type in which it is interested. Content filters contain a filter expression that can be matched against the values of the parameters of an event. Content filters are specified using filter expressions describing the constraints of a specific consumer. These filter expressions may contain equality, magnitude and range operators as well as ordering relations. They may include variable, consumer local information such as the consumer's location. Proximity filters are location filters that define the geographic scope within which events are relevant and correspond to the proximity attribute associated with an event type.

4   Communications Architecture

The design of the STEAM communications architecture is motivated by our approach of bounding the scope within which certain information is valid and by the characteristics of the underlying wireless network. We employ a transport mechanism based on group communication and use a multicast protocol to route messages between the participants.

4.1 Using Proximity Groups

Group communication [14] has been recognized as a natural means to support event-based communication models [9]. Groups provide a one to many communication pattern that can be used by producers to propagate events to a group of subscribed consumers. STEAM exploits a *Proximity-based Group Communication Service* (PGCS) [10] as the underlying means for entities to interact. Proximity groups have been designed to support mobile applications using wireless local area networks [10]. To apply for group membership, an application component must firstly be located in the geographical area corresponding to the group and secondly be interested in the group in order to join, i.e., a group is identified by both geographical and functional aspects. In contrast, classical group communication defines groups solely by their functional aspect. STEAM defines both the functional and the geographical aspect that specifies a proximity group. The functional aspect represents the common interest of producers and consumers based on the type of information that is propagated among them, whereas the geographical aspect outlines the bounded scope within which the information is valid. Hence, STEAM maps subject and proximity to the functional and geographical aspect of proximity groups respectively. Furthermore, proximity groups can be either absolute or relative. An absolute proximity group is geographically fixed; it is attached to a fixed point in space. In contrast, a relative proximity group is attached to a moving point represented by a specific mobile node.

4.2 Locating Proximity Groups

Instead of requiring a naming service to locate entities that wish to interact, STEAM provides a discovery service that uses beacons to discover proximities. Once a proximity has been discovered, the associated events will be delivered to subscribers that are located inside the proximity. This service is also responsible for mapping discovered proximities to subscriptions and to the underlying proximity-based communication groups. Hence, it causes the middleware to join a proximity group of interest, i.e., for which it has either a subscription or an announcement, once the host machine is within the associated geographical scope and to leave the proximity group upon departure from the scope.

4.3 Mapping to Proximity Groups

Mapping announcements and subscriptions to groups requires a means to uniquely identify a group as well as for consuming and producing entities to retrieve the identifier of the specific group that disseminates certain events. Unique group identifiers are traditionally generated either statically or using global knowledge by means of a centralized lookup service. STEAM implements an addressing scheme in which identifiers representing groups can be computed from subject and proximity pairs. Each combination of subject and proximity (shape, dimension, and location) is unique throughout a system. The description of such a pair is used as stimulus for a hashing algorithm to dynamically generate identifiers using node local rather than global knowledge. Upon discovery of a proximity and the associated subject, producing and consuming entities compute the corresponding group identifier if the subject is of interest. This scheme allows entities to subsequently use these identifiers to join groups in which relevant events are disseminated. Moreover, it prevents entities that are not interested in certain events from joining irrelevant groups and as a result, from receiving unwanted events even though they might reside within the proximity of the group.

4.4 Mapping to Ad Hoc Networks

STEAM allows entities to define geographical scopes independently of the physical transmission range of these wireless transmitters. Consequently, STEAM supports multi-hop event dissemination in which nodes residing within the boundaries of a proximity forward event messages. Members of the corresponding multicast group recognize the identifiers of these event messages and subsequently deliver them. Nodes residing outside a proximity will discard event messages that they cannot associate with any proximity known to them.

Fig. 2 (A) outlines a single-hop event propagation scenario where the transmission range of the sender covers the entire scope of the proximity. Event messages are propagated within the transmission range and member nodes will deliver them. Fig. 2 (B) shows a multi-hop event propagation scenario in which the proximity exceeds the transmission range of the sender. The maximum number of hops a message may travel to reach any member of the group is bounded by the proximity.

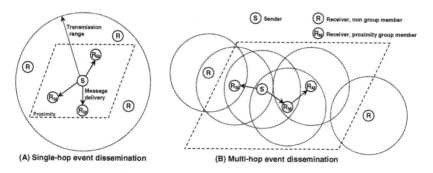

Fig. 2. Event dissemination scenarios

5 Experimental Results

This section presents our initial evaluation of STEAM, which demonstrates how bounding the propagation range of event notifications using proximity-based filtering can be used to reduce the number of events delivered to an application. A prototypical application scenario from the traffic management domain has been implemented for this experiment. The scenario simulates the interaction between vehicles passing through an intersection and the intersection's traffic light disseminating its light status. The scenario is modeled according to the intersection of North Circular Road (NCR) and Prussia Street (PST) located in Dublin's inner city. It is based on real data, which has been provided by Dublin City Council, describing vehicle movements and light status at the intersection over a period of 24 hours.

Fig. 3 (A) illustrates the intersection and outlines how the traffic flow can be broken up into two distinct phases. The intersection comprises two *approaches*; approach one describes the traffic flows arriving from east and west whereas approach two describes the traffic flows arriving from north and south. Approach one comprises three lanes and approach two comprises of four lanes. The traffic light for both approaches is considered to be located in the center of the intersection at the stated latitude and longitude. The *cycle* time defines the duration for the two approaches to complete their respective sequences of light changes. The proportion of the cycle length that is assigned to one particular approach is called the *split*. The split between the phase of approach one and two is 45% to 55%. The intersection data was acquired over a period of 24 hours starting on the 3rd of December 2002 at 6 pm. It consists of a sequence of records, each describing a cycle duration and the number of vehicles passing through the intersection on each individual lane during the cycle.

The experiment includes three notebook computers placed 5 meters apart communicating through wireless ad hoc connections, each equipped with a Lucent Orinoco Gold WiFi PCMCIA card. One machine hosts the traffic light and the other two the vehicles arriving on approach one and two respectively. The traffic light raises an event every second for each approach to disseminate the light status, approach name, and light location. Vehicles approach the intersection in their respective lanes at an average speed of 25 miles per hour (the intersection is located in a 30 miles per hour zone). Each vehicle follows a pre-defined route according to its approach lane simulated by its location service. Fig. 3 (B) depicts an example route of a vehicle in lane two of approach one. The available intersection data does not describe the behavior of an approaching vehicle in terms of queuing; it only indicates the number of vehicles passing the intersection during a green light sequence. Hence, vehicles are modeled to reflect this behavior arriving at the intersection in time to pass the light during a green light sequence.

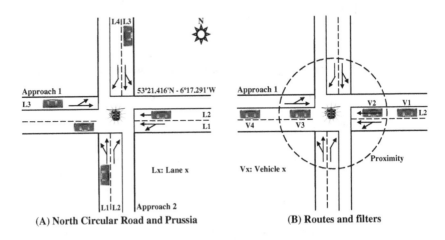

(A) North Circular Road and Prussia   (B) Routes and filters

Fig. 3. Modeling the intersection

Fig. 3 (B) also illustrates the use of distributed filters in the simulation. The traffic light announces events of type "Traffic Light" and the associated proximity, which defines the radius of the area of interest surrounding the traffic light. The radius has been set to 40 meters to allow for vehicle breaking distance (16 meters) and update rate (once per second) of the location service. This radius guarantees that an approaching vehicle receives at least two events before having to decide whether or not to stop at the light. Vehicles subscribe to "Traffic Light" events and define a content filter that matches events on their approach when they are moving towards the traffic light. This combination of filters causes vehicles one and four to discard "Traffic Light" events as they reside outside the scope of the proximity. Even though vehicles two and three are inside the proximity, only vehicle two will deliver "Traffic Light" events to its application. The content filter of vehicle three prevents event delivery since the vehicle is moving away from the traffic light.

This experiment comprises two runs using the same stimuli. The first run applies distributed events filters as described above whereas the second run lacks any filters assuming the communication range of the traffic light's wireless transmitter to limit event dissemination. We assume the radio transmission range in the modeled urban environment to be 200 meters.

Table 1 summarizes the number of vehicles passing through the intersection on each lane as well as the total number of events delivered to these vehicles in each experiment. It also includes the relative decrease of delivered events between the two experiments. The data in Table 1 shows a substantial reduction, averaging at around 95%, in the number of events delivered to the vehicles when applying distributed event filters. This is hardly surprising considering the bounding of the propagation range and the content filter discarding events once a vehicle has passed the traffic light. Applying distributed event filters in experiment one causes additional overhead due to proximity discovery. The traffic light announces its proximity by propagating beacons within the proximity area. Vehicles discover the proximity upon entering the area delivering a single beacon message to the middleware. Assuming this being equivalent to delivering an additional event per vehicle would reduce the relative decrease by approximately 1.4%. However, the overall number of events delivered would still substantially decrease, on average by over 93%.

Table 1. Results of the experiment

	Approach 1			Approach 2			
	Lane 1	Lane 2	Lane 3	Lane 1	Lane 2	Lane 3	Lane 4
Number of Vehicles	6652	3320	3728	3038	1383	2802	1135
No Event Filter	469945	235093	264557	210114	95743	193931	78730
Distributed Event Filter	24139	11905	13553	9436	4488	8805	3543
Relative Decrease	94.9%	94.9%	94.9%	95.5%	95.3%	95.5%	95.5%

6 Conclusions

We have described the architecture and implementation of STEAM, an event-based middleware for collaborative, location aware applications using wireless local area networks. STEAM differs from other event-based middleware in that its architecture does not rely on the presence of any infrastructure, event notification filtering may be distributed and may be applied to functional and non-functional attributes of an event notification. Our initial evaluation of STEAM shows that using proximity-based filtering to bound the propagation range of event notifications reduces the number of events delivered to an application. We plan to further evaluate our work using a variety of prototypical application scenario implementations.

Acknowledgements

The work described in this paper was partly supported by the Irish Higher Education Authority's Programme for Research in Third Level Institutions cycle 0 (1998-2001) and by the FET programme of the Commission of the European Union under research contract IST-2000-26031 (CORTEX).

The authors would like to thank Dublin City Council for providing the traffic data that made our evaluation of STEAM possible.

References

1. J. Bacon, K. Moody, J. Bates, R. Hayton, C. Ma, A. McNeil, O. Seidel, and M. Spiteri, "Generic Support for Distributed Applications," IEEE Computer, vol. 33, pp. 68-76, 2000.
2. G. Cugola, E. D. Nitto, and A. Fuggetta, "The JEDI Event-Based Infrastructure and its Application to the Development of the OPSS WFMS," IEEE Transactions on Software Engineering (TSE), vol. 27, pp. 827-850, 2001.

3. R. Meier, "Communication Paradigms for Mobile Computing," ACM SIGMOBILE Mobile Computing and Communications Review (MC2R), vol. 6, pp. 56-58, 2002.
4. B. P. Crow, I. Widjaja, J. G. Kim, and P. T. Sakai, "IEEE 802.11 Wireless Local Area Networks," IEEE Communications Magazine, pp. 116-126, 1997.
5. I. Podnar, M. Hauswirth, and M. Jazayeri, "Mobile Push:Delivering Content to Mobile Users," in Proceedings of the International Workshop on Distributed Event-Based Systems (ICDCS/DEBS'02). Vienna, Austria, 2002, pp. 563-570.
6. P. Sutton, R. Arkins, and B. Segall, "Supporting Disconnectedness – Transparent Information Delivery for Mobile and Invisible Computing," in Proceedings of IEEE CCGrid 2001. Brisbane, Australia: 2001, pp. 277-285.
7. Object Management Group, CORBAservices: Common Object Services Specification - Notification Service Specification, Version 1.0: Object Management Group, 2000.
8. A. Carzaniga, D. Rosenblum, and A. Wolf, "Design and Evaluation of a Wide-Area Event Notification Service," ACM Trans. on Computer Systems, vol. 19, pp. 283 - 331, 2001.
9. G. Banavar, T. Chandra, R. Strom, and D. Sturman, "A Case for Message Oriented Middleware," presented at Proceedings of the 13th International Symposium on DIStributed Computing (DISC'99), Bratislava, Slovak Republic, 1999.
10. M. O. Killijian, R. Cunningham, R. Meier, L. Mazare, and V. Cahill, "Towards Group Communication for Mobile Participants," in Proceedings of Principles of Mobile Computing (POMC'2001). Newport, Rhode Island, USA, 2001, pp. 75-82.
11. Sun Microsystems Inc., Java Distributed Event Specification. 1998.
12. M. Haahr, R. Meier, P. Nixon, V. Cahill, and E. Jul, "Filtering and Scalability in the ECO Distributed Event Model," in Proc. of the 5th Int. Symposium on Software Engineering for Parallel and Distributed Systems (ICSE/PDSE2000). Limerick, Ireland. 2000, pp. 83-95.
13. R. Meier and V. Cahill, "Taxonomy of Distributed Event-Based Programming Systems," in Proceedings of ICDCS/DEBS'02. Vienna, Austria, 2002, pp. 585-588.
14. F. Cristian, "Synchronous and Asynchronous Group Communication," Communications of the ACM, vol. 39, pp. 88-97, 1996.

A Flexible Middleware Layer
for User-to-User Messaging

Jan-Mark S. Wams and Maarten van Steen

Vrije Universiteit Amsterdam
Department of Computer Science
{jms,steen}@cs.vu.nl
http://www.cs.vu.nl/~{jms,steen}

Abstract. There is growing trend to unify user-to-user messaging systems to allow message exchange, independent of time, place, protocol, and end-user device. Building gateways to interconnect existing messaging systems seems an obvious approach to unification. In this paper we argue that unification should take place at the level of the underlying messaging models. Such a unification results in one messaging model that has maximum adaptability, allowing one system to deliver the same messaging services that all currently existing messaging systems deliver, as well as hitherto impossible mixes of those services.

We present a novel unified messaging model that supports maximum adaptability. Our approach supports the same services that all current messaging models support, including those of e-mail, fax, SMS, ICQ, i-mail, USENET News, AIM, blog, MMS, and voicemail.

To substantiate the claim that such a unified model can be implemented efficiently on a worldwide scale, we present the design of an accompanying highly adaptable and scalable messaging middleware system.

1 Introduction

User-to-user messaging services continue to increase in popularity. Billions of messages are daily relayed through messaging systems like e-mail, fax, SMS, ICQ, i-mail, USENET News, AIM, blog, MMS, voicemail and so on. For many people it is hard to imagine life without these services.

Technological change as well as change in expected service cause new features to be added to existing messaging systems and totally new systems to emerge. However, the unstructured way in which messaging systems have been constructed and changed so far has caused much unnecessary overhead, reinventing of wheels, and running into dead-ends that should have come as no surprise. Besides these development problems, there is an ever-growing incompatibility between all these systems that seemingly offer a very similar service. It would already be a huge step forward if the choice for the sending system would be independent from the choice of the receiving system. Users would then, for example, be able to use a cell-phone to send a photo to a bulletin board, and another user would be able to use a laptop in a café to look at it, while yet another user would receive the photo using a fax machine.

J.-B. Stefani, I. Demeure, and D. Hagimont (Eds.): DAIS 2003, LNCS 2893, pp. 297–309, 2003.
© IFIP International Federation for Information Processing 2003

Most existing messaging systems are built directly on top of one communication platform like the Internet, GPRS, or POTS. In this paper we introduce a middleware layer for user-to-user messaging systems that provides maximum adaptability. Maximum adaptability is needed to deal with the multitude of communication technologies and messaging services.

Adapting a messaging service to changes is usually realized by adapting (often extending) its **underlying system**. For example, user demand for off-line and multi-point access to Internet e-mail has lead to extensions known as POP and IMAP. Likewise, user demand for an electronic bulletin board system prompted the development of mailing-list servers on top of Internet e-mail. However, due to fundamental difficulties with addressing an ever-changing population [7], it turned out to be impractical to build a full-fledged bulletin board system like USENET News on top of Internet e-mail. Researching messaging systems has lead us to conclude that the associated messaging **model** sometimes lacks enough adaptability to make adapting the system practical. To assess the adaptability of a messaging service both the model as well as the system that implements it, need to be analyzed. In Section 3 we present a taxonomy, that allows analysis of messaging models.

Princeton University's WordNet defines "adaptability" as "the ability to change or be changed to fit changed circumstances." In the context of a taxonomy, "change" can be interpreted as a change of position. Hence we define:

A system has "maximum adaptability" within a given taxonomy, if the system can easily move or be moved to any position within that taxonomy.

Using our taxonomy to categorize (the models of) messaging systems, we show that non of the popular large-scale messaging systems has maximum adaptability; most such messaging systems lack an adaptable model . In Section 4 we introduce a unified messaging model that does have maximum adaptability and, therefore, could be used as a basis to unify all major existing messaging systems, including e-mail, fax, SMS, ICQ, i-mail, USENET News, AIM, blog, MMS, and voicemail. In Section 5, we focus on the main contribution of this paper, the design of a middleware layer for messaging with maximum adaptability. We dubbed this system **Unified Messaging System** or UMS for short. Our design demonstrates the feasibility of a large-scale UMS that supports maximum adaptability, and which is capable of providing the same services as existing messaging systems. To the best of our knowledge such a UMS does not yet exist. In Section 6 we give some example scenarios of the use of the UMS middleware layer. We conclude in Section 7.

2   Related Work

Work on "Unified Messaging" shows that some define unified messaging as "the ability to allow a user to receive faxes, voice-mails and e-mails in one personal mailbox." [8]. Since most user-to-user messaging is either Internet based or telephony based, unified messaging is sometimes defined as; "Internet-based integration of telephony and data services spanning diverse access networks" [6]. Neither of these approaches to unification comes close to ours.

There are also commercial offerings of unified messaging, basically these are centralized places where users can collect all there messages, usually limited to e-mail, voicemail, faxes, and phone-text messages. These kind of unifications are designed and/or implemented with gateways, interconnecting various systems, leading to complex addressing and a common-denominator service. Also these forms of unification are usually asymmetric in how they handle the sending and receiving of messages. Receiving messages from different messaging systems is straightforward: have one gateway/forwarder per connected messaging system. However, sending is not always (if at all) possible in a uniform way: differences between the way that messages can be delivered have to be dealt with by the user, often even if the recipient uses the same integrated messaging service. Our unified messaging is different in that we strive for one middleware layer, connecting many communication networks to user interfaces on many platforms.

Though the user-interfaces will, most likely, have to be redesigned and replaced, this approach has some enormous benefits. The number of interfaces reduces, combinations of messaging services become possible, it is much easier to add a new user interface or new communication network, and, most importantly, there is symmetry between sending and receiving.

3   A Taxonomy for Messaging Models

In this section we introduce a taxonomy for messaging models. Issues like throughput, latency, and portability are implementation dependent, and, although important, are ignored in our taxonomy. The taxonomy does also not take into account presence, secrecy, authentication, non repudiation, and integrity, because these can (and should) be done on an end-to-end basis [2]. We introduced our taxonomy in a previous paper [5], so we will just list the four dimensions and their values in Fig. 1.

dimension	values (from min to max)
time	immediate, impermanent, permanent
direction	simplex, duplex
audience	group, world
address	single, list, all

Fig. 1. The messaging system taxonomy.

Given this taxonomy, models of existing messaging systems can be classified and researched for adaptability. Fig. 2 shows the classification of eight messaging systems. Many interesting observations can been made when using the taxonomy to

system	time	direction	audience	address
e-mail	permanent	simplex	world	list
voicemail	permanent	simplex	world	single
news	impermanent	duplex	group	all
mailing-list	permanent	duplex	group	all
fax	immediate	simplex	world	single
IM	immediate	duplex	group	all
SMS	permanent	simplex	world	single
blog	permanent	duplex	world	all

Fig. 2. Classification of some existing messaging systems.

compare messaging models. For example, the fax messaging system and the SMS messaging system both are (immediate, simplex, world, single) systems, revealing that they share an underlying model. Due to the different output devices and infrastructure, their systems are, however, very different and incompatible. Interestingly but not surprisingly the SMS system is meeting exactly the same user demands for service extension that the fax system (invented over 100 years earlier) has met. Users will want support for sending a single message to multiple recipients, automatic forwarding to other recipients or locations, non-repudiation, authentication, and so on. Note that voice-mail systems are also (immediate, simplex, world, single) and was also confronted with similar user demands. As a side effect of our research, we have come to conjecture that messaging systems that have coinciding positions in the taxonomy, usually have coinciding development paths. Another interesting observation is that when a system is built on top of another system, its classification clearly reveals what property (if any) has been downgraded in favor of the upgrading of some other property. For example, the mailing-list messaging system is built on top of the e-mail system, downgrading audience in favor of upgrading its addressing capabilities.

Most messaging systems do not have the maximum value in all dimensions, in other words, they do not possess maximum adaptability. There is one messaging system in Fig. 2 that does have the maximum value in all dimensions: the blog system. The blog system (also known as weblog or what's-new-page) is a messaging system in which one person (or a small number of persons) collects noteworthy messages. Potentially every person on the Internet can read these messages and can append addenda (a message and its addenda are often called a "thread"). This type of messaging is more subtle than the other messaging systems with respect to controlling who can post what message. More precisely, most implementations of the blog-type messaging system put some restrictions on its duplex character (i.e., not every participant can start a thread). Some blogs have many readers (like slashdot.org), many blogs have a few dedicated readers. Since a blog system is (permanent, duplex, world, all), it might possess maximum adaptability. Unfortunately, it is stuck at the extreme of the taxonomy. Bloging is relaying a message to anyone who wants to hear it, therefor, it has to be adapted to enable more private forms of communication. We have come to the conclusion that non of the messaging systems we know of can be easily forged into a system with maximum adaptability.

4   The Unified Messaging Model

In this section we introduce a Unified Messaging Model (UMM) as underlying model for the messaging system we will define in Section 5. The UMM has to support four major objectives. First, the UMM has to support large-scale messaging: billions of users jointly exchanging billions of messages per day. Second, the UMM should not be dependent on trust and should allow for a distributed peer-to-peer implementation. Third, the UMM has to hinder SPAM by putting the recipient in control. Fourth, the UMM has to posses maximum adaptability: it should offer everything any existing messaging system has to offer. Moreover, it should allow users (or user agent software) to dynamically create new types of messaging systems on demand, mixing and matching messaging service properties at will.

We have kept our model as simple as possible. It has two main entities. The first entity is called **target**, and stands for a collection of user-to-user messages. A target is a generic in-box, news-group, channel, paper-role, tape and so on. The second entity is called **TISM**, short for **targeted immutable short message**. A TISM is a generic e-mail, news article, remark, fax, voice-mail-message and so on. The acronym TISM is used to reflect the choices we have made for our UMM. TISMs are targeted because they are directed towards targets—not users. They are immutable by design: that which has been sent, can no longer be modified. TISMs are said to be short, thereby focusing the UMM on real-life user-to-user messaging. The focus is thus not on large messages of, say, millions of bytes. To give the UMM maximum adaptability, four (dimensional) constraints are put upon targets. First, targets should allow for immediate, impermanent, and permanent storage. Second, targets should support an access control mechanism for posting TISMs into targets to allow simplex and duplex messaging on demand. Third, targets should support an access control mechanism for reading TISMs from targets, and to allow both group and world access to targets. Fourth, access to targets should allow individual (single), selected (list), and total (all) access to TISMs. If these objectives can be (orthogonally) materialized into an implementation, the result would be a messaging system with maximum adaptability. We will introduce such a messaging system in the next section.

5   Design of the Unified Messaging System

In this section we introduce the **Unified Messaging System (UMS)**. We start with a description of the implementation of targets and TISMs. The conceptual target and TISM from the UMM is implemented as a distributed shared object. Such an object not only encapsulates state and the implementation of operations on that state, but also encapsulates a distribution policy that prescribes how the state is distributed, replicated, and migrated across different locations. Distributed shared objects were first introduced in Globe [3]. For our UMS, we adopt the concept of distributed shared objects but provide a specific, more efficient, implementation for targets and TISMs.

In the following, we distinguish between referring to a target by its name, say T, and referring explicitly to its realization as a distributed shared object. In the latter case, we will talk about T's **instance**. A distributed shared object can be thought of as a collection of local objects, where each local object is hosted by a single site. Correspondingly, we will refer to a **local instance** of a target T. Likewise, we make a distinction between a TISM m, its instance, and a local instance of m.

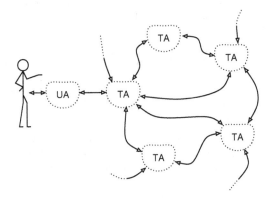

Fig. 3. Conceptual view.

5.1   Target Agents and User Agents

As with the design of our unified messaging model, we keep the design of the UMS as simple as possible. Apart from the actual user, there are only two types of communicating parties, as shown in Fig. 3. The first type is a **target agent** (**TA**). Its primary function is to store and forward (the state of) targets and TISMs, in addition to carrying out the associated distribution policies. As such, a TA is designed to be continuously operating, that is, on line. The second type is a **user agent** (**UA**), which is responsible for generating and managing keys that are need for security, as well providing the user access to facilities for sending and receiving TISMs. The UA is (part of) an application, and is thus not part of the middleware layer. Therefore, we only describe its lower-level part that is responsible for communication with the TAs. We do not go into the specifics of the higher-level parts like the GUI, or the representation of targets or collections.

Whenever a UA wants to create a target or TISM, it needs to contact a TA that is willing to operate as the **home** of that target or TISM. The home TA will store a local instance of every target or TISM created by such a UA, thereby providing minimal access guarantees to those objects. Access is provided until a specified expiration time, after which the local instance of the target or TISM can be permanently removed.

5.2   Key Management

The UA associates every target T with a (private,public) key pair (K_T^-, K_T^+), where K_T^- denotes a private key and K_T^+ a public key. Any information on target T that leaves a UA, is encrypted with K_T^-. This specifically includes TISMs and information on TISMs that are contained in target T. Every TISM has an associated target that contains it. A TISM has no associated key pair, but instead is encrypted with the private key of its associated target. End-to-end secure communication between UAs proceeds as follows. Whenever a UA encrypts a TISM for storage or transport by a TA, the TISM m is first encrypted with it own unique (random) symmetric key (SK), which, in turn, is encrypted with the key K_T^- that is associated with the target that is containing this TISM. This type of two-staged encryption is referred to as a hybrid protocol [1].

Not only does this scheme save time, because symmetric encryption and decryption is usually much faster than its asymmetric counterpart, but also cross posting will be (computationally) much cheaper. Cross posting is done by reading a TISM, m, from a target, T_1, and than posting it into an other target, T_2. The two targets will have different private keys, but that is of no consequence to the encrypted version of m, which is encrypted with the symmetric key SK. Only SK has to be decrypted and re-encrypted. In general SK will be much smaller than m, therefor decrypting/encrypting this way, takes less time. Cross posting this way will deliver similar gains in communication and storage.

5.3   The Content List

In the UMM a target is an unordered collection of TISMs. In the UMS a target is represented as a list of TISMs ordered by creation date, as shown in Fig. 4-a. We decided on the ordering, because it will make the "old" part of the list more static and thus easier to compress. Imagine a real-time messaging system sending a list of 1 million TISMs over the network every second for comparison to a replica list. Performance wise, a better alternative would be to sent the hash of a list of 1 million TISMs every second for comparison to the hash of the replica list. For efficient comparison and updating of lists, we introduce an elaboration on this simple hashing scheme, dubbed a **contentList**. A contentList is a list of descending dates with between each two dates either a list of TISMs or a hash of a list of TISMs and the number of TISMs in the hash, see Fig. 4. A contentList of a particular TISM list can range in size from a few bytes (see Fig. 4-b) to just over the size of that TISM list (see Fig. 4-e).

5.4   Information Flow

As mentioned, the UAs and TAs exchange information. The principal operation is simple. Each target and TISM is uniquely identified by the combination of a

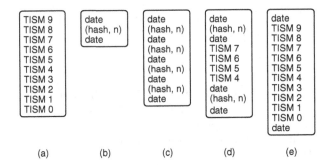

Fig. 4. An ordered list of TISMs in five different formats, (a) plain TISM list, (b) minimal contentList, (c) hash only contentList, (d) mixed contentList (e) TISM only contentList.

home TA and an ID unique relatively to that TA. If a UA needs (information on) a target or TISM it simply contacts the respective home TA. Requests and replies are transmitted in an asynchronous and connection less fashion (notably UDP). As shown in Fig. 5-a, incoming information is processed by the TA using a simple scheme of **decode** and **execute** functions. The decode function is responsible for analyzing the type of input information. For example, we make a distinction between requests for information on a target, and requests concerning a specific TISM. Depending on this type, the decode function passes the request to a specific execute function. The execute function processes the request, possibly storing data in, or fetching data from a local store. A reply is subsequently put in an output queue for transmission to the requester.

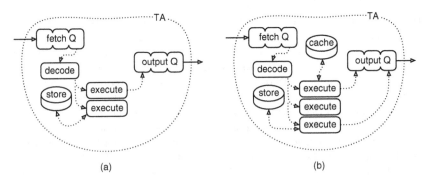

Fig. 5. Information flow within a TA, (a) basic scheme, (b) TA with replication.

With this simplistic scheme, UAs will have to pull any information directly from a home TA. With just this pull-on-demand scheme our messaging system would be fully functional. Obvious drawbacks are its lack of scalability and performance, and also its lack of robustness. These drawbacks are all caused by the fact that we are relying on a single home TA (per target or TISM). For example, every time a UA would want to know whether a target contained new TISMs, it would have to access the home TA of that target.

This basic scheme can be easily improved. For example, a pushing scheme could automatically deliver the information to a **close TA**: a TA on the same LAN as the UA, or a TA at the ISP. Other adaptations that improve the overall performance of the system can easily be thought of. In the context of developing distributed Web services, we have observed that differentiating distribution schemes is important for achieving performance [4]. For our messaging system, we believe such a differentiation is also important. What we are therefore seeking is an organization by which we can easily associate a specific **distribution** or **replication policy** separately with each target or TISM. Our basic scheme is already capable of supporting this flexibility as the decode function can distinguish different types of input information from which it can derive the appropriate execute function that should be executed.

We considered three ways of differentiating policies. The first option was to allow each target or TISM to run arbitrary (e.g., Java) code. The second option was to invent some replication scripting language and have a target or TISM carry a replication script. The third option was simply to assign identifiers to a fixed number of policies and let each target and TISM specify its prefered policy through this identifier. We chose the third option for both targets and TISMs because it has a low overhead per message. It is, however, reasonable flexible because policies can be added as updates to our messaging system in a backwards compatible fashion.

These adaptations lead to a slightly modified version of the internals of a TA, as shown in Fig. 5-b. First, we make a distinction between the storage and a cache. The storage is used for targets and TISMs for which the TA acts as the home. These objects can be removed only after the specified expiration time. Moreover, requests to store information on a target, or to store a TISM are executed only when they come from an authenticated and authorized UA.

The cache is used to **voluntarily** store information. The TA stays in full control of the cache: it can decide any time what to store or remove. The responsibility for having information on a target or TISM available lies completely with the home TA, which uses its storage for that purpose. There are two ways information finds its way into the cache of a TA. First, a request that has been forwarded by a TA might result in a reply from a peer. This information will then be relayed to the requesting UA and might be stored in the cache. Second, a replication of a target or TISM might be pushed to a TA because a peer executes a replication strategy. The TA could, for example, decide to cache the replica because it is associated with a popular target.

With this in mind, it makes sense for a UA to try to get a target or TISM from a close TA. This close TA will do a cache lookup, and if the lookup fails, it can forward the request to one of its peers. However, to protect against malicious and erroneous requests, only a **signed** request from a **known** UA can result in the forwarding of the request. Basically this means that a TA will only look in its own cache and storage to satisfy a request. If the request is signed by a known UA, the TA will forward it (unsigned) to a peer, notably the home TA for the referenced target or TISM, but the peer, in turn, will not forward the request any further (for the peer received the request from a TA, not an authenticated UA). Consequently, requests will not be forwarded ad infinitum in search for a non existing target or TISM. It may seem at first that this forwarding restriction can render some information unaccessible. However, targets and TISMs can never become unreachable because replication only improves performance and robustness: targets and TISMs remain available at their respective home TA.

The information flow for Fig. 5-b is similar to that of Fig. 5-a, however, the input flow for Fig. 5-b contains replicas of targets and TISMs that have to be dealt with. Information is fetched and decoded. In the case of a replica the identified replication policy is executed and will, if appropriate, result in the insertion of one or more replicas to the output queue. The replication policy does any of three things; update the cache, queue a reply to a UA, and queue one or more replicas to peer TAs. No general limit on forwarding of replicas is enforced. Due to the fact that replication policies need to be explicitly referenced by an identifier, limitations on replication are safely enforcible. In fact there are no rules for what replication strategy code can do. Typical behavior would include, checking the cache for related objects, storing (local instances of) objects in the cache, forwarding many objects to many peers, updating objects in the store, and so on.

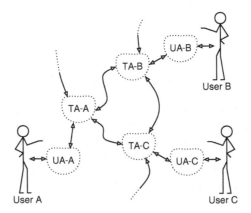

Fig. 6. Three UMS users A, B, and C.

6   Examples

In this section we will demonstrate the behavior of the middleware layer for some archetypical user-to-user communication patterns between three users A, B, and C. Let us assume each of the three users has their own UA and home TA, as seen in Fig. 6. For simplicity reasons, let us assume each UA contacts the middleware layer only through its home TA.

day	TA-A store	TA-A cache	TA-B store	TA-B cache	TA-C store	TA-C cache	comments
1	T						target T is created
2	T		m_1				user B posts TISM m_1
3	T	m_1	m_1				user A reads m_1
4	T	m_1	m_1		m_2		user C posts TISM m_2
5	T	m_1 m_2	m_1		m_2		user A reads m_2
6	T	m_2	m_1		m_2		TA-A de-caches m_1
7	T		m_1		m_2		TA-A de-caches m_2

Fig. 7. Cache and store utilization with e-mail like behavior.

day	TA-A store	TA-A cache	TA-B store	TA-B cache	TA-C store	TA-C cache	comments
1			T_1				target T_1 is created
2	m		T_1				user A posts TISM m
3	m		T_1	m			user B reads m
4	m		T_2 T_1	m			user B creates target T_2
5	m		T_2 T_1	m			user B forwards m
6	m		T_2 T_1	m		m	user C reads m
7	m		T_2 T_1	m	T_2	m	user C lists T_2

Fig. 8. Cache and store utilization with forwarding.

In Fig. 7 the storage and cache are depicted of the three TAs in a typical e-mail-like exchange. On day 1, user A instructs UA-A to create a new target T. TA-A stores the target and returns a unique ID to UA-A. User A sends users B and C the (address of TA-A, unique ID, public key) tuple in an other TISM (not shown). On day 2, user B has UA-B post a TISM m_1 to user A. TISM m_1 is put in the storage of TA-B, the changes to T are forwarded to TA-A due to the (e-mail mimicking) replication strategy of T. On day 3, user A requests the TISM m_1 from TA-A, and TA-A fetches it from TA-B. TA-A stores TISM m_1 in the cache (due to the replication strategy) and also forwards it to UA-A. On day 4, user C decides to post a TISM m_2 and user A reads m_2 on day 5. At days 6 and 7, m_1 and m_2 are discarded from TA-A's cache. At the end of day seven, T, m_1 and m_2 are not cached in any TA. This will be the typical situation with low-usage targets and TISMs. Note that the UA-A probably has a cache too and that this cache will hold on to T, m_1, and m_2 much longer.

In Fig. 8 we consider some other common behavior: forwarding a TISM to another user. For this, UA-B will create a new target, in which TISM m is cross posted. User A sends a TISM m to user B, and user B forwards TISM m to user C. On day 1, user B creates a target T_1 and forwards the relevant information to user A (not shown). On day 2, user A posts a TISM m into target T. On day 3, user B reads TISM m and decides that user C might be interested in TISM m. User B requests its UA-B to privately forward m to user C. UA-B creates a new target T_2, cross posts TISM m in target, and then forwards the (home TA of m, unique ID of m) and (home TA of T_2, unique ID or T_2, private key of T_2) tuples to UA-C in another TISM (not shown). On day 6, user C reads m. On day 7, user C decides to list the content of T_2, and finds only m is in T_2. Note that if user A were to post a new TISM into target T_1, this new TISM would not automatically show up in target T_2, as would be the case if user B had shared T_1 with user C. More sophisticated examples can be given, and practical usage of the UMS middleware layer probably is much more elaborated than these examples. It is the task of the UA to transform simple wishes from the user into the usage and creation of targets and TISMs. Typically a user would ask the UA to give some other user access to a set of coherent messages, analogous to the "newsgroup thread" or chain of "e-mail followups."

7   Conclusions

In the paper, we have introduced the design of a truly unified user-to-user messaging system in the form of a generic middleware layer for messaging. Our paper illustrates the feasibility of developing a such a middleware layer to allow efficient integration of existing messaging services. Compared to a messaging service offered by a collection of existing messaging systems and connecting gateways, our approach does not suffer from common denominator restrictions and frees the users from having to deal with differences between the individual underlying messaging systems. Our approach and its accompanying design should be able to support very large communities of users. It is flexible enough to simultaneously support a variety of replication schemes, a feature which has shown to be important when performance is an issue. In fact, we allow differentiation not only on a per-target basis, but can even support different schemes at the level of TISMs. To validate our approach, we are currently developing a prototype implementation.

References

1. A.J. Menezes, P.C. van Oorschot, and S.A. Vanstone. *Handbook of Applied Cryptography*. CRC Press, Fifth Printing, August 2001.
2. J.H. Saltzer, D.P. Reed, and D.D. Clark. End-to-End Arguments in System Design. *ACM Transactions on Computer Systems*, 2(4):277–288, November 1984.
3. M. van Steen, P. Homburg, and A.S. Tanenbaum. Globe: A Wide-Area Distributed System. *IEEE Concurrency*, 7(1):70–78, January 1999.
4. G. Pierre, M. van Steen and A.S. Tanenbaum. Dynamically Selecting Optimal Distribution Strategies for Web Documents", *IEEE Transactions on Computers*, pages 637–651, June 2002.
5. J.M.S. Wams and M. van Steen. Pervasive Messaging. *In IEEE Conference on Pervasive Computing*, pages 499–504, March 2003.

6. H.J. Wang, B. Raman, C. Chuah, R. Biswas, R. Gummadi, B. Hohlt, X. Hong, E. Kiciman, Z. Mao, J.S. Shih, L. Subramanian, B.Y. Zhao, A.D. Joseph, and R.H. Katz. ICEBERG: An Internet-core Network Architecture for Integrated Communications. *IEEE Personal Communications*, pages 10–19, August 2000.
7. A. Westine and J. Postel. Problems with the Maintenance of Large Mailing Lists. *RFC 1211*, March 1991.
8. C.K. Yeo, S.C. Hui, I.Y. Soon, and G. Manik. Unified Messaging : A System for the Internet. *International Journal on Computers, Internet, and Management*, September 2000.

.

Author Index

Lecture Notes in Computer Science

For information about Vols. 1–2806
please contact your bookseller or Springer-Verlag

Vol. 2844: J.A. Jorge, N.J. Nunes, J.F. e Cunha (Eds.), Interactive Systems. Proceedings, 2003. XIII, 429 pages. 2003.

Vol. 2846: J. Zhou, M. Yung, Y. Han (Eds.), Applied Cryptography and Network Security. Proceedings, 2003. XI, 436 pages. 2003.

Vol. 2847: R. de Lemos, T.S. Weber, J.B. Camargo Jr. (Eds.), Dependable Computing. Proceedings, 2003. XIV, 371 pages. 2003.

Vol. 2848: F.E. Fich (Ed.), Distributed Computing. Proceedings, 2003. X, 367 pages. 2003.

Vol. 2849: N. García, J.M. Martínez, L. Salgado (Eds.), Visual Content Processing and Representation. Proceedings, 2003. XII, 352 pages. 2003.

Vol. 2850: M.Y. Vardi, A. Voronkov (Eds.), Logic for Programming, Artificial Intelligence, and Reasoning. Proceedings, 2003. XIII, 437 pages. 2003. (Subseries LNAI)

Vol. 2851: C. Boyd, W. Mao (Eds.), Information Security. Proceedings, 2003. XI, 443 pages. 2003.

Vol. 2852: F.S. de Boer, M.M. Bonsangue, S. Graf, W.-P. de Roever (Eds.), Formal Methods for Components and Objects. Proceedings, 2003. VIII, 509 pages. 2003.

Vol. 2853: M. Jeckle, L.-J. Zhang (Eds.), Web Services – ICWS-Europe 2003. Proceedings, 2003. VIII, 227 pages. 2003.

Vol. 2854: J. Hoffmann, Utilizing Problem Structure in Planning. XIII, 251 pages. 2003. (Subseries LNAI)

Vol. 2855: R. Alur, I. Lee (Eds.), Embedded Software. Proceedings, 2003. X, 373 pages. 2003.

Vol. 2856: M. Smirnov, E. Biersack, C. Blondia, O. Bonaventure, O. Casals, G. Karlsson, George Pavlou, B. Quoitin, J. Roberts, I. Stavrakakis, B. Stiller, P. Trimintzios, P. Van Mieghem (Eds.), Quality of Future Internet Services. IX, 293 pages. 2003.

Vol. 2857: M.A. Nascimento, E.S. de Moura, A.L. Oliveira (Eds.), String Processing and Information Retrieval. Proceedings, 2003. XI, 379 pages. 2003.

Vol. 2858: A. Veidenbaum, K. Joe, H. Amano, H. Aiso (Eds.), High Performance Computing. Proceedings, 2003. XV, 566 pages. 2003.

Vol. 2859: B. Apolloni, M. Marinaro, R. Tagliaferri (Eds.), Neural Nets. Proceedings, 2003. X, 376 pages. 2003.

Vol. 2860: D. Geist, E. Tronci (Eds.), Correct Hardware Design and Verification Methods. Proceedings, 2003. XII, 426 pages. 2003.

Vol. 2861: C. Bliek, C. Jermann, A. Neumaier (Eds.), Global Optimization and Constraint Satisfaction. Proceedings, 2002. XII, 239 pages. 2003.

Vol. 2862: D. Feitelson, L. Rudolph, U. Schwiegelshohn (Eds.), Job Scheduling Strategies for Parallel Processing. Proceedings, 2003. VII, 269 pages. 2003.

Vol. 2863: P. Stevens, J. Whittle, G. Booch (Eds.), «UML» 2003 – The Unified Modeling Language. Proceedings, 2003. XIV, 415 pages. 2003.

Vol. 2864: A.K. Dey, A. Schmidt, J.F. McCarthy (Eds.), UbiComp 2003: Ubiquitous Computing. Proceedings, 2003. XVII, 368 pages. 2003.

Vol. 2865: S. Pierre, M. Barbeau, E. Kranakis (Eds.), Ad-Hoc, Mobile, and Wireless Networks. Proceedings, 2003. X, 293 pages. 2003.

Vol. 2867: M. Brunner, A. Keller (Eds.), Self-Managing Distributed Systems. Proceedings, 2003. XIII, 274 pages. 2003.

Vol. 2868: P. Perner, R. Brause, H.-G. Holzhütter (Eds.), Medical Data Analysis. Proceedings, 2003. VIII, 127 pages. 2003.

Vol. 2869: A. Yazici, C. Sener (Eds.), Computer and Information Sciences – ISCIS 2003. Proceedings, 2003. XIX, 1110 pages. 2003.

Vol. 2870: D. Fensel, K. Sycara, J. Mylopoulos (Eds.), The Semantic Web - ISWC 2003. Proceedings, 2003. XV, 931 pages. 2003.

Vol. 2871: N. Zhong, Z.W. Raś, S. Tsumoto, E. Suzuki (Eds.), Foundations of Intelligent Systems. Proceedings, 2003. XV, 697 pages. 2003. (Subseries LNAI)

Vol. 2875: E. Aarts, R. Collier, E. van Loenen, B. de Ruyter (Eds.), Ambient Intelligence. Proceedings, 2003. XI, 432 pages. 2003.

Vol. 2876: M. Schroeder, G. Wagner (Eds.), Rules and Rule Markup Languages for the Semantic Web. Proceedings, 2003. VII, 173 pages. 2003.

Vol. 2877: T. Böhme, G. Heyer, H. Unger (Eds.), Innovative Internet Community Systems. Proceedings, 2003. VIII, 263 pages. 2003.

Vol. 2878: R.E. Ellis, T.M. Peters (Eds.), Medical Image Computing and Computer-Assisted Intervention - MICCAI 2003. Part I. Proceedings, 2003. XXXIII, 819 pages. 2003.

Vol. 2879: R.E. Ellis, T.M. Peters (Eds.), Medical Image Computing and Computer-Assisted Intervention - MICCAI 2003. Part II. Proceedings, 2003. XXXIV, 1003 pages. 2003.

Vol. 2880: H.L. Bodlaender (Ed.), Graph-Theoretic Concepts in Computer Science. Proceedings, 2003. XI, 386 pages. 2003.

Vol. 2881: E. Horlait, T. Magedanz, R.H. Glitho (Eds.), Mobile Agents for Telecommunication Applications. Proceedings, 2003. IX, 297 pages. 2003.

Vol. 2884: E. Najm, U. Nestmann, P. Stevens (Eds.), Formal Methods for Open Object-Based Distributed Systems. Proceedings, 2003. X, 293 pages. 2003.

Vol. 2885: J.S. Dong, J. Woodcock (Eds.), Formal Methods and Software Engineering. Proceedings, 2003. XI, 683 pages. 2003.

Vol. 2886: I. Nyström, G. Sanniti di Baja, S. Svensson (Eds.), Discrete Geometry for Computer Imagery. Proceedings, 2003. XII, 556 pages. 2003.

Vol. 2887: T. Johansson (Ed.), Fast Software Encryption. Proceedings, 2003. IX, 397 pages. 2003.

Vol. 2888: R. Meersman, Zahir Tari, D.C. Schmidt et al. (Eds.), On The Move to Meaningful Internet Systems 2003: CoopIS, DOA, and ODBASE. Proceedings, 2003. XXI, 1546 pages. 2003.

Vol. 2889: Robert Meersman, Zahir Tari et al. (Eds.), On The Move to Meaningful Internet Systems 2003: OTM 2003 Workshops. Proceedings, 2003. XXI, 1096 pages. 2003.

Vol. 2891: J. Lee, M. Barley (Eds.), Intelligent Agents and Multi-Agent Systems. Proceedings, 2003. X, 215 pages. 2003. (Subseries LNAI)